50
STATES
500
CAMPGROUNDS

50
STATES
500
CAMPGROUNDS

WHERE TO GO • WHEN TO GO • WHAT TO SEE • WHAT TO DO

JOE YOGERST

NATIONAL GEOGRAPHIC

WASHINGTON, D.C.

Contents

Opposite: Tunnel Mountain in Banff National Park (p. 318) offers an abundance of camping opportunities as well as epic mountain views.

Pages 2-3: Lake Ouachita State Park (p. 31) in Arkansas offers water sports right outside your tent.

INTRODUCTION

Only over the past two centuries has camping evolved from a wilderness necessity into a recreational form and lifestyle choice. According to the data portal Statista, more than 40 million Americans camp each year, and they spend about $3 billion per annum buying camping equipment. And that's just tent campers. Millions more experience the great outdoors staying in cabins and glamping, and more than eight million American households own RVs.

The reasons that so many camp today aren't that much different from the early 1800s: a longing to connect with Mother Nature, a yearning to escape the confines of big-city life, and a desire to do these things with family, friends, and even solo.

Nowadays, camping means different things to different people. This book takes that into consideration by featuring a wide variety of overnight options in the great outdoors, from urban RV resorts and rustic national forest campgrounds, to traditional log cabins and Southwest-style casitas, to glamping safari tents and tree houses. Some of our campsites are family oriented, while some were created for those seeking a romantic weekend in the wilderness.

A lot of us have grown up with camping as an integral part of our lives. That's certainly true of myself. Some of my earliest memories are camping in Yosemite Valley with my parents in an army-green World War II surplus tent and watching a mountain lion out the window of a Southern California mountain cabin (still the only time I've seen a cougar in the wild).

It was on camping trips with the Boy Scouts that I learned how to paddle a canoe, trekked the mountains of Baja California, and first listened to Top 40 radio. I spent two college summers car camping in the national parks of the Southwest during my days off from working at the Las Vegas airport.

Later in life, I backpacked the Sierras, Grand Canyon, and Pyrenees; I canoe-camped along the Rio Grande and the Tara River in the Balkans; and I tent-camped my way across Asia and Africa. When my wife and kids came onto the scene, we spent eight straight years cabin-camping near Sedona in northern Arizona.

All told, I figure I've spent at least a year of my life sleeping under canvas or beneath the stars. And I've raised a couple of kids who are now as fixated with experiencing nature as their father (although one of them definitely prefers glamping to ordinary tents).

We had some pretty good early role models. Like Henry David Thoreau, who described his year of living alone in a cabin on the edge of a Massachusetts pond in a still-essential read, *Walden,* published in 1854. John Muir spent half a century extolling the virtues of nature after tramping through landscapes that would become national parks. Victorian-era travelers like Lady Florence Dixie and Isabella Bird proved that women could also camp, even at the places where a lot of their male counterparts feared to tread, like Patagonia and Kurdistan.

As ordinary citizens flocked to the wild, entrepreneurs jumped on the bandwagon. The portable camp stove was invented in 1849, a forerunner to the sleeping bag in 1876. Pierce-Arrow rolled out the first recreational vehicle in 1910, a seven-passenger motorcar dubbed the Special Touring Landau. By the 1920s, RV parks were popping up across America.

But before we dive into the 530 campgrounds, glamping places, and cabin clusters across the country that are featured in this book, a little housekeeping (pun intended). Because of contraction, expansion, renovations, and other factors that came about during the COVID-19 pandemic, some of the figures and rates in the info boxes may vary from what was correct at the time of publication.

Best of luck on your travels across the United States, Canada, and U.S. Caribbean, and may camping be as memorable and life changing for you as it has been for three generations of my family.

Find a quiet retreat in the cozy lakefront cabins at Breezy Point in Minnesota (p. 145).

RESPONSIBLE CAMPING

It may seem that camping is an ecofriendly way to travel, and in many ways it is. You're not relying on concrete and glass city structures, overindulgent restaurants, or overcrowded (you hope) destinations. But plenty of damage can still be done on a camping trip if you're not practicing responsible habits. Make your next excursion to the great outdoors a greener one by following these rules of thumb:

1. REMEMBER: PLANET OR PLASTIC?

In May 2018, National Geographic launched its Planet or Plastic? campaign, a multiyear effort to raise awareness about the global plastic crisis. A few fast plastic facts for you:

More than 40 percent of plastic is used once and then discarded, and 6.3 billion tons of plastic fill our landfills, landscapes, and oceans.

Nearly one million plastic bottles are sold every minute around the world.

Plastic takes nearly 400 years to degrade; a 2018 study found that only 9 percent of plastics are recycled.

Be mindful of the amount of plastic you use in your everyday life, but particularly what you bring to your campgrounds. Skip disposable plates and cutlery for multiuse utensils and durable dinnerware that can be washed and reused. Don't bring plastic straws, please. And always have a reusable water bottle rather than be dependent on plastic ones.

2. CONSIDER YOUR WASTE

It's not enough to just pack out your trash; you should also sort it. Bring along at least two trash bags for waste: one for trash, one for recycling—and a third for compost if you can. Separate your waste into each bag; then dispose of it properly. If your campground or trailhead doesn't have compost or recycling, bring it home, where you can get rid of it the right way.

3. GO BIODEGRADABLE

Soaps, toothpastes, even sunscreen can have nasty impacts on the environment and the surroundings you're enjoying on your adventure. Look for toothpastes, soaps, shampoos, and other hygiene products that are considered biodegradable. When it comes to sunscreen, look for reef-friendly varieties. Avoid permethrin in bug repellent. If there are on-site bathroom facilities, use them rather than natural water sources for bathing and otherwise.

4. LEAVE NO TRACE BEHIND

The golden rule of nature excursions: Only leave footprints behind. Clean up your trash, including food waste. Be mindful of what you're burning on the campfire. When you leave, your campsite should look exactly as it did when you arrived.

5. FOLLOW THE RULES

It shouldn't have to be said, but rules are there for a reason. Follow your campground's rules, including where and when you can have a fire, where you can pitch your tent, swimming regulations, and others. This helps ensure you have a campground to enjoy for years to come and leave as little impact on the space as you can.

HOW TO USE THIS BOOK

Icon Key

Throughout this guide, you'll see icons representing the type of shelter each campground offers, from RVs and tents to yurts and tree houses. You'll also see key amenities like hiking trails. The icons below symbolize each:

RVs		Glamping Tents	
RVs & Tents		Yurts	
Cabins		Equestrian Facility	
Trailers		Hiking Trails	
Tents		Geo Domes	
Tree Houses		Houses	

If you're lucky, you might spot a grizzly bear (from a distance) at the Riley Creek Campground (p. 18) in Denali National Park, Alaska.

Alabama

Campgrounds across the Heart of Dixie include Gulf Coast spots for anglers and boaters, sweet home Alabama log cabins, and wilderness glamping mountain chalets.

DESOTO STATE PARK

🏠 25, 🚐/⛺ 94 full hookup, ⛺ 18

7104 DeSoto Parkway NE, Fort Payne, AL 35967

Open: Year-round ▪ Rates: RV/tent full hookup $38, cabins from $107, tent only $15 ▪ Amenities: Restaurant, camp store, nature center, dump station, showers, laundry, picnic tables, grills, swimming pool, playground, volleyball, sports field, cable TV, internet ▪ ADA sites: Partial

Named for Spanish explorer Hernando DeSoto, who passed through the region in 1540, the state park lies at the extreme southern end of the Appalachian range. From full hookups and primitive tent camping to historic log cabins and modern mountain chalets, the park offers a variety of ways to spend a night in the Alabama wilderness. The park's country store, nature center, and Olympic-size swimming pool are all within a short walk of the campground, as is the DeSoto Lodge and the Mountain Inn Restaurant, which serves southern classics like catfish, fried chicken, seafood gumbo, and pecan pie. Thirty miles (48 km) of hiking trails lead to waterfalls and rock formations in canyons along the western edge of Lookout Mountain. DeSoto boasts

From a scenic lookout on Pulpit Rock Trail, take in your surroundings at Cheaha State Park.

Civil War history, and the Cherokee artisan and scholar Sequoyah lived in a village on the park's south side.

BEAR CREEK LOG CABINS

🏠 7

923 County Road 252, Fort Payne, AL 35967

Open: Year-round ▪ Rates: From $100 ▪ Amenities: Kitchens, private bathrooms, hot tubs, fireplaces, air-conditioning, cable TV, grills, fire pits, washers and dryers, towels and bedding, VCR and DVD players ▪ ADA sites: No

For those who envision sweet home Alabama as a log cabin in the woods, Bear Creek is the place for you. Located on 201 acres (81 ha) of forest and farmland in the state's northeast corner, the cabins were built with timber salvaged from original 1850s' pioneer homes. The units range from one and two bedrooms to a four-bedroom lodge that can sleep as many as 10 people. Bear Creek lies on the edge of Little River Canyon National Preserve, a federal wilderness area with panoramic overlooks along State Highway 176 and hiking trails that plunge down to waterfalls, pools, and swimming holes.

NOCCALULA FALLS PARK CAMPGROUND

🏠 2, 🚐/⛺ 76 full hookup, 7 partial hookup, ⛺ 43

1500 Noccalula Road, Gadsden, AL 35904

Open: Year-round ▪ Rates: RV/tent full hookup $25, partial hookup/tent only $19, cabins from $121 ▪ Amenities: Dump station, showers, laundry, picnic tables, fire rings, gift shop, swimming pool, playground, volleyball, firewood, ice, cable TV, internet ▪ ADA sites: Partial

Named for a Cherokee legend, this city park and campground in northern Alabama perches on the edge of Black Creek Gorge. Noccalula caters to both RV and tent campers, with several cabins for those who don't bring their own shelter. The campground lies near the hub of a trail network with 15 different hiking and biking paths into the gorge and along its rim. This action-packed park also features a petting zoo, miniature golf, botanical garden, and narrow-gauge train, as well as its namesake waterfall, a 90-foot (27 m) cascade that plunges into a pool with a large cave behind.

CHEAHA STATE PARK

🏠 16, 🚐/⛺ 72 full hookup, ⛺ 42

19644 State Highway 281, Delta, AL 36258

Open: Year-round ▪ Rates: RV/tent full hookup from $31, tent only from $15, cabins from $138 ▪ Amenities: Restaurant, camp store, showers, laundry, picnic tables, grills or fire rings, firewood, ice, potable water, swimming pool, playground, dog park, amphitheater ▪ ADA sites: Yes

Alabama's highest point—2,407-foot (734 m) Cheaha Mountain—is the focus of a state park within Talladega National Forest that offers abundant outdoor recreation and several overnight options. The park's four campgrounds (two developed and two primitive)

huddle around a stone lookout, the Bunker Tower and the Bald Rock Lodge, both erected by the Civilian Conservation Corps (CCC) in the 1930s. The stone cabins and chalets cluster along the edge of Cheaha Lake. Also created by the CCC, the small lake offers campers a chance to fish, boat, or take a refreshing dip in the middle of the muggy Alabama summer. The rugged, highland terrain also attracts rock climbers, hikers, and mountain bikers. A segment of the Pinhoti Trail traverses the park on its 335-mile (540 km) journey from south Alabama to northern Georgia. In addition to jaw-dropping views, Bunker Tower has exhibits

about the Depression-era workers who developed the park. The campground area also harbors the Walter Farr Native American Relic Museum.

UNIVERSITY STATION RV RESORT

🏚 4, 🚐/🏕 450, 4 RV rentals

3076 State Highway 14 West, Auburn, AL 36832

Open: Year-round ▪ Rates: RV/tent full hookup from $65, partial hookup from $30, no hookup from $25, cabins/RV rentals from $40 ▪ Amenities: Convenience store, gas station, dump station, laundry, showers, propane, firewood, potable water, playground, picnic area,

Historic log cabins and modern chalets are just some of the camping options at DeSoto State Park.

RV wash and maintenance, golf cart rental, internet ▪ ADA sites: No

Auburn University football fans flock to this RV park in the fall to tailgate before and after Tigers games. Campers can catch live tunes on the resort stage and shout out cheers around a bonfire on Friday nights before games. On game days, they can watch the telecast on the resort's big screen TV or hop a shuttle to and from Jordan–Hare Stadium. The rest of the year, University Station is a mild-mannered, family-oriented campground for visiting Auburn staff or students or anyone passing through on their way between Atlanta and Montgomery. The 400-plus sites are fairly tightly packed, but the loops are flanked by trees and lawn areas, giving the resort a countrified feel even though it's just 10 minutes from the university campus.

EAGLE COTTAGES AT GULF STATE PARK

🏠 11

1 Bald Eagle Circle, Gulf State Park, Gulf Shores, AL 36542
Open: Year-round ▪ Rates: From $600 (two- to three-night minimum stay) ▪ Amenities: Kitchens, private bathrooms, heating and air-conditioning, daily housekeeping, towels and bedding, guidebook and DVD library, outdoor seating, fire pit, flat-screen TVs, internet ▪ ADA sites: Yes

One of more intriguing overnight options offered at any of the nation's parks, Eagle Cottages at Gulf State Park offers an eco-immersion adventure that includes guided tours with a veteran naturalist, bikes to explore the rest of the sprawling Gulf Coast

Head to Bankhead National Forest for trails that lead to Turkey Foot Falls.

sanctuary, and breakfast each morning in your deluxe waterfront cabin. Elevated on stilts to protect them from storm surges, the cottages feature three bedrooms and baths, full kitchen, a large living room, and outdoor spaces with stylish furnishings and artwork that easily matches the level of a four- or five-star hotel. In addition to the bikes and hikes, Eagle guests can paddle or fish Lake Shelby, bask on Gulf of Mexico beaches, attend seminars at the park's Learning Center, or browse exhibits at the Interpretive Center, one of only two dozen structures worldwide certified as a sustainably designed Living Building.

DAUPHIN ISLAND PARK CAMPGROUND

🚐 75 full hookup, 🚐/🏕 75 partial hookup

109 Bienville Boulevard, Dauphin Island, AL 36528
Open: Year-round ▪ Rates: RV/tent full hookup from $48, partial hookup from $38 ▪ Amenities: Camp store, dump station, showers, laundry, picnic tables, fire rings, ice, firewood, playground, sports courts, bike rentals, dog park, boat ramp, fish cleaning station, internet ▪ ADA sites: Partial

This awesome municipal campground on a barrier island off the Alabama coast is no one-trick pony. Sure, there are sun, sea, and sand, but Dauphin Island also offers a level of natural and historical attractions normally not found at Gulf of Mexico beach towns. Trees shade most of the pads and offer protection from any wind that blows in off the Gulf. And there's on-site bicycle rental for campers who want to explore more of the 16-mile-long (27.5 km) island via the Bienville Boulevard Bike Path or the town's quiet backstreets.

The park is bookended by a white-sand strand on its south side and a harbor area on the north.

Take advantage of all Gulf State has to offer: beaches, beautiful Gulf of Mexico waters, and wildlife, including pelicans.

The latter features public boat ramps, the Billy Goat snack and ice cream stand, and the ferry terminal for Fort Morgan on the other side of the entrance to Mobile Bay. Bird watchers flock to the Dauphin Island Audubon Sanctuary beside the campground, history buffs head for nearby Fort Gaines, and campers with kids tend to gravitate toward the hands-on Estuarium aquarium.

WALES WEST RV PARK & LIGHT RAILWAY

🚐 / 🏕 77 full hookup

13670 Smiley Street, Silverhill, AL 36576

Open: Year-round ▪ Rate: $50 ▪ Amenities: Camp store, snack bar, showers, laundry, picnic tables, potable water, ice, propane, swimming pool, hot tub, beach, playground, library, exercise room, nature trail, cable TV, internet ▪ ADA sites: Partial

It's all about trains at Wales West, where two miniature trains loop around campsites at an RV park inspired by the narrow-gauge railway lines of Wales. Located near Alabama's Gulf Coast and artsy Fairhope, the park continues the British Isles theme with its other major attraction: Lake Victoria—named after the queen, of course, and blessed with features her majesty would no doubt cherish (catch-and-release fishing) and probably not so much (a twisty waterslide). For their erudite campers, Wales West offers a library. And for the wee ones there's an indoor heated swimming pool, playground, and those tiny choo-choos. From the Cottontail Express at Easter to the Arctic Express in winter, the theme changes with the seasons. But Wales West is *always* fun.

MILLERS FERRY CAMPGROUND

🚐 / 🏕 65 partial hookup

111 East Bank Park Road, Camden, AL 36726

Open: Year-round ▪ Rate: RV/tent $26 ▪ Amenities: Dump station, showers, laundry, picnic tables, fire rings, grills, lantern posts, potable water, playground, fish cleaning station, boat ramps, fishing pier, basketball court ▪ ADA sites: Yes

Created by the U.S. Army Corps of Engineers, Millers Ferry lies along Lake Dannelly, a dammed portion of the Alabama River. It's a favorite hangout of anglers and boaters, and the adjacent East Bank Public Use Area offers a small beach with a no-boating swimming area. Campsites have power and water hookups but no sewer. Many of the pads are shaded, and a good number are situated right on the water. For campers who bring a boat along for the trip, there's a lot of water to cover: Millers Ferry lies at the downstream end of an Alabama River Trail that stretches 105 miles (169 km) upriver to Old Cahawba Archaeological Park (once Alabama's capital), Selma, and Steeles Landing.

CLEAR CREEK RECREATION AREA

🚐 / 🏕 81 partial hookup, 🏕 21

8079 Fall City Road, Jasper, AL 35503

Open: March to October ▪ Rates: RV/tent partial hookup from $30, tent only from $20 ▪ Amenities: Dump station, showers, picnic tables, grills, lantern posts, potable water, boat ramps, beach, playground, horseshoes ▪ ADA sites: Yes

Although Bankhead National Forest is dubbed the Land of 1,000 Waterfalls, this campground focuses on another water body—Lake Lewis Smith—a large, three-fingered reservoir that's deeper (264 feet/80 m) than any other lake in Alabama. Compared to many Forest Service campsites that lean toward the primitive side, Clear Creek is well equipped. Its assortment of water/power and tent-only campsites is complemented by showers, sports courts, and summertime interpretive programs. There's a dedicated bike path, as well as the 2.5-mile (4 km) Raven Cliffs Interpretive Trail, which circumnavigates the campground. ▪

SOMETHING SPECIAL

Bankhead National Forest

Bankhead National Forest, just a 90-minute drive from Birmingham, feels worlds away. The serene, wooded landscape covers more than 180,000 acres (72,843.4 ha) and offers 90 miles (144.8 km) of recreational trails. Along those trails you'll find plenty of wonders: moss-covered bluffs, Alabama's only National Wild and Scenic River (the Sipsey Fork), streams, and a sandstone canyon. But the real draw to the forest, called the Land of 1,000 Waterfalls, is to see the plethora of tumbling cascades. Spot a few, including Turkey Foot Falls, a short, easy walk from the Sipsey River Picnic Grounds and Recreation Area; the Caney Creek Falls, which are wet year round; and the Sougahoagdee Falls, a great springtime destination for hikers.

Alaska

Find lakefront retreats, glacial sites, and vast expanses of wilderness throughout camping sites—from rustic to posh—across Alaska.

BETWEEN BEACHES ALASKA

 4

64605 MacDonald Spit, Seldovia, AK 99663

Open: Year-round ▪ Rates: From $175 (winter), $300 (summer); 2-night minimum ▪ Amenities: Kitchenettes, heating, gas barbecue, art gallery, NOAA tide charts, paddling ▪ ADA sites: No

A restored 1950s homestead cabin and newer units fashioned from reclaimed wood, doors, and windows salvaged from a 1914 salmon cannery highlight this cozy cottage collection on the Kenai Peninsula. Located on MacDonald Spit between two deep-blue bays, the lodge is owned and managed by a former commercial fishing boat captain turned artist, who maintains a workshop and gallery on the property. All cabins feature electric heater, indoor bathroom, kitchenette, heated mattress pads, hot and cold running water, private outdoor shower, and outdoor seating area with barbecue, hammock, and Adirondack chairs. Between Beaches offers complimentary kayaks and rowboats for guests who wish to explore the shore. Among other activities in the area are berry picking, clamming, wildlife watching, hiking, and fishing.

Breathtaking Alaska backcountry views are on offer from your cabin at Ultima Thule Lodge.

ALASKA ADVENTURE CABINS

 7

2525 Sterling Highway, Homer, AK 99603

Open: Year-round ▪ Rates: From $175 ▪ Amenities: Kitchens, internet, satellite TV, viewing decks, gas grills ▪ ADA sites: Partial

The town of Homer provides an iconic Alaskan setting for a cluster of rustic overnight digs overlooking Kachemak Bay. The eclectic rentals range from a modern log cabin with panoramic windows and roomy, three-story stone-and-timber house, to a restored 1940s Pullman sleeper and the *Double Eagle* (a restored fishing boat that helped with the *Exxon Valdez* cleanup). Each cabin—as well as the railcar and fishing boat—is outfitted with a full kitchen, bathrooms, and lounge area, as well as internet service and satellite TV. Depending on size, they accommodate one to 12 guests, and two of the cabins boast washer-dryers. The units are arrayed across 17 acres (6 ha) of heavily wooded shoreline that includes a bald eagle nest. Downtown Homer is just five minutes down the road. Founded by coal and gold miners in the 1890s, it's one of Alaska's most picturesque towns, as well as a hub for marine ecotours, sea kayaking, wildlife photography, and hiking on the Kenai Peninsula.

ORCA ISLAND CABINS

8

Humpy Cove & Resurrection Bay, Seward, AK 99664

Open: May to September ▪ Rates: From $345 (including round-trip water taxi from Seward) ▪ Amenities: Kitchens, coolers, private bathrooms, potable water, propane stove and barbecues, solar heating, fire rings, firewood, water sports equipment ▪ ADA sites: No

It would be difficult to find a more magical campsite anywhere on Earth—a wilderness island floating along the eastern edge of Resurrection Bay with unencumbered views of the glaciers, ocean, and peaks that make the Kenai Fjords a national treasure. It's all about yurts on Orca Island, glamping tent-cabins that sleep two to four guests on queen beds and futons. All of the yurts are elevated on lofty decks, and two of them are situated on their own little rocky islet and accessed via a wooden pedestrian bridge. You need a boat to get there, of course—the water taxi from the small-boat harbor in Seward farther up the fjord. Given the remote locale, everything is solar powered, including the hot-water showers. There's no food service, so guests need to carry all food and beverages on the water taxi and cook their meals on the indoor propane stove or outdoor barbecue with each yurt. However, there's no shortage of aquatic gear, including fishing poles and tackle, kayaks, paddleboards, and rowboats, for exploring adjacent Humpy Cove or reaching hiking trails on the nearby mainland. The resort offers two-hour scenic cruises on Resurrection Bay, but longer maritime day trips to Kenai Fjords National Park are available only from Seward. There's also an art gallery featuring Alaska landscapes and seascapes rendered by one of the long-time resort hosts.

Try your hand at steelhead fishing during a stay at Alaska Adventure Cabins.

EKLUTNA LAKE CAMPGROUND

🚐 / 🏕 50 no hookup
Mile 10, 39370 Eklutna Lake Rd, Chugiak, AK 99567
Open: Year-round ▪ Rate: Tent sites $20 ▪ Amenities: Restroom, food storage lockers, potable water (hand pump), fire rings with grills, picnic tables, bike and kayak rental ▪ ADA sites: Partial

This wilderness campsite on the edge of Anchorage takes full advantage of the summer and winter activities on tap in enormous Chugach State Park. Perched at the western end of its namesake lake in a valley carved by glaciers eons ago, the campsite offers easy access to water activities and several hiking routes including the 38-mile (61 km) Eklutna Traverse across four glaciers to Girdwood. The valley's ATV trail is open four days a week from April to November. Campsites are arrayed along a loop in woods near the rocky shore. Stocked with salmon and trout, Eklutna Lake offers excellent

fishing from boat or shore. Cross-country skiing, snowmobiling, and dog mushing count among the winter activities. And the valley shelters plenty of wildlife: grizzly and black bear, moose and muskrat, Dall sheep and mountain goats on the upper slopes.

RILEY CREEK CAMPGROUND

🚐 / 🏕 122 no hookup,
🏕 20 walk-in tent only
Denali Park Road, Denali National Park and Preserve, AK 99755
Open: Year-round ▪ Rates: RVs $27-$34, tents $17; all sites free in winter (mid-September through mid-May) ▪ Amenities: Dump station, laundry, camp store, showers, fire pits with grills, picnic tables, food storage lockers, potable water, firewood, ice, internet ▪ ADA sites: Partial

With more than 140 total sites, Riley is far and away Denali National Park's biggest campground. It's also the easiest to access—just minutes off Parks Highway (State Route 3) from Anchorage and Fairbanks. Short trails lead to the visitors center, post office, general store, and terminal for narrated bus tours into the heart of the park. It's not uncommon to see moose and other critters wandering through the campground; rangers strongly advise against feeding or approaching any wildlife. And be forewarned: This is bear country, so store food appropriately. If Riley isn't wilderness enough for your liking—and you're not quite up to the challenge of back-country Denali—consider one of the five campgrounds arrayed along Park Road deeper in the park. The most remote of these is Wonder Lake and its 28 tent-only sites. Located 85 miles (136 km) from

Riley Creek Campground is Denali National Park's biggest, with more than 140 sites to set up camp.

Riley, it's the closest organized campground to Denali peak, North America's highest mountain.

ALPENGLOW LUXURY CAMPING

 7

31090 West Glenn Highway, Chickaloon, AK 99674

Open: May to September ▪ Rates: From $109 ▪ Amenities: Showers, hot tub, breakfast, coffee hut with Wi-Fi ▪ DA sites: No

It's almost as if you can reach out and touch Matanuska Glacier while sitting on the porch of your safari-style tent at Alpenglow. About a two-hour drive northeast of Anchorage in the gorgeous Matanuska Valley, the rustic resort immediately raised the bar on Alaskan glamping when it opened in 2015. Alpenglow offers two types of canvas: Deluxe Tents that sleep up to three people in queen and twin beds and two-person Forest Tents tucked into the woods. Located on permanent wooden platforms, the tents come with plenty of warm bedding and covered front porches with Adirondack chairs or rocking chairs. Restrooms, showers, and cedar hot tub are just a short walk away. The tents are totally unplugged: no electricity or heating. The resort "base camp" features a fire pit, lounge areas, board games, and a place to charge electronics. Complimentary light breakfast is served each morning. Alpenglow shares the site with MICA Guides, which offers glacier trekking, heli-tours, zip line adventures, and more.

ULTIMA THULE LODGE

🏠 5

Wrangell–St. Elias National Park, AK

Open: Early May to late September ▪ Rate: $8,550 (all inclusive) for four-night minimum stay ▪ Amenities: Dining room, bar, library, sauna, hot tub, fire pits, yoga yurt ▪ ADA sites: No

To the ancient Greeks, Ultima Thule was a mythical place beyond the northern borders of their known world. That's exactly how the modern Alaskan version feels: a lodge located in the wilds of Wrangell–St. Elias National Park, more than 100 miles (160 km) from the nearest road, and reachable only by aircraft. Perched along the Chitina River, the lodge evolved from a rustic family homestead into a unique Alaska backcountry experience featuring plush cabins,

Take advantage of paddleboarding on Bear Lake in Kenai Fjords National Park, where you can see icebergs along your ride.

largely home-grown gourmet meals, an exceptional wine list, and unique outdoor activities. Foremost among the activities are SuperCub flights with legendary bush pilot Paul Claus, who can pull off a corkscrew landing on glaciers or glider-like touchdowns on steep mountainsides. Scattered through a garden flush with lupines and other summer blooms, the red-roofed log cabins feature king-size beds, hot-water showers, sitting areas, and front porches with views across the Chitina Valley.

BROOKS LODGE

🏠 16

Brooks River, King Salmon, AK 99613
Open: June to September ▪ Rates: Cabins from $50/$130 ▪ Amenities: Dining hall, bar, fishing equipment, fly-fishing, fishing guides and instructors ▪ ADA sites: Partial

Brooks has been a bastion of creature comforts in the Katmai National Park wilderness since it was founded as a remote fishing camp in 1950. A location near fabled Brooks Falls and its bear-watching platforms makes the lodge a prime location for grizzly spotting. Cabins are rustic but comfy with two bunk beds, private bath, and a small front porch with seating. The only way to reach Brooks is by airplane. Bear watching is complemented by flightseeing tours, fishing on Naknek Lake, and guided road tours to the volcanic Valley of 10,000 Smokes.

SILVER SALMON CREEK LODGE

 9, 3

Lake Clark National Park, Soldotna, AK 99669
Open: June to September ▪ Rates: Cabins from $783, tents from $775 (all inclusive) ▪ Amenities: Dining hall,

internet, laundry, gift shop, sport-fishing, coastal boat tours ▪ ADA sites: No

Even if you're not into wildlife photography or world-class fly-fishing, Silver Salmon Creek is an awesome place to experience the Alaska wilderness. Located on Cook Inlet along the outer edge of Lake Clark National Park, the lodge renders dreamy views of the Kenai Peninsula and a chance to see grizzlies frolicking on the beach. Guests have a choice of rustic cabins at the main lodge or a tented camp on a salmon-fishing creek 10 miles (16 km) into the wilderness.

BARTLETT COVE CAMPGROUND

⛺ 33

Park Road, Gustavus, AK 99826
Open: Year-round ▪ Rate: Free ▪ Amenities: Food storage caches, toilets, fire pit, warming shelter, fire ring, firewood, potable water ▪ ADA sites: No

Although most people explore Glacier Bay National Park by water—

via kayak or cruise ship—you can also camp in the celebrated national park in the Alaska panhandle. But it does require some planning. Reaching the walk-in campground at Bartlett Cove entails chartering a small aircraft or hopping the Alaska Marine Highway ferry to Gustavus, a hamlet on the edge of the park. If you're not inclined to walk or bike, Gustavus Taxi will then whisk you the eight miles (12 km) to the Glacier Bay visitors center and a trailhead for the short walk to the campground. Campers can transport gear to their campsites with wheelbarrows stationed at the parking lot. Located in the lush Pacific Northwest rainforest, Bartlett Cove offers an awesome setting that *Country Living* magazine ranked among the 21 most beautiful campgrounds in America. But camping is primitive, with few amenities other than designated storage areas for bikes and kayaks. All campers must attend a 30-minute orientation at the visitor information station in order to obtain a camping permit and bear-proof food container. ▪

SOMETHING SPECIAL

Lake Clark National Park & Preserve

This is the land of true Alaskan wilderness: volcanic peaks and craggy mountains, salmon runs and bears foraging, all set around a majestic turquoise lake. Lake Clark National Park (established 1978) preserves the ancestral homelands of the Denai'ina people, the original inhabitants of the south-central Alaska region. The park itself pays homage to the land's cultural heritage, and Indigenous people depend on its land and water.

There are loads of ways to experience the park: Watch the salmon run from monitoring platforms along the Newhlen River. Take an aerial tour of the park over the Cook Inlet and Mount Iliamna Volcano, then land on a beach where you can spot bears foraging and playing. Catch the Mulchatna caribou herd migrating across the tundra, traveling in groups of two to 20,000. Or kayak the Turquoise Lake, a glacial body of water reflecting the 6,000-foot-high (1,828.8 m) rock walls and ice that surround it.

Arizona

Plan a stay in a vintage travel trailer, a casita on a ranch with 130 resident horses, or a tent in Oak Creek Canyon in this Southwest ideal.

BONITA CANYON CAMPGROUND

🚐/🏕 25 no hookup
Bonita Canyon Drive, Chiricahua National Monument, AZ 85643
Open: Year-round ▪ Rate: $20 ▪ Amenities: Dump station, restrooms, picnic tables, grills, potable water, food storage containers ▪ ADA sites: Yes

The rocky pinnacles of Chiricahua National Monument provide a dramatic backdrop for a secluded campground tucked into a wooded canyon in Arizona's southeast corner. The Chiricahua highlands are remote even by Arizona standards, sparsely populated by humans but home to black bears and mountain lions, as well as more exotic species like coatimundis, ringtail cats, and even the occasional jaguar or ocelot. Located close to the mouth of Bonita Canyon, the campground lies near trails to the Faraway Historic District and Rhyolite Canyon, as well as a scenic drive that reaches Massai Point (and even more trailheads). All of the national monument beyond the road corridors is designated federal wilderness.

Camp beneath the rim at the coveted Havasupai Campground in the Grand Canyon.

THE SHADY DELL

🚐 13 vintage trailers
1 Old Douglas Road, Bisbee, AZ 85603
Open: Year-round ▪ Rates: From $85 ▪ Amenities: Restaurant, kitchenettes and dishes, towels and bedding, heating and air-conditioning, bathhouse, outdoor seating, communal barbecues ▪ ADA sites: No

One of America's original vintage travel trailer resorts, Shady Dell was founded in 1927 to serve early auto travelers along Highway 80. In more recent years, this Bisbee glamping spot has inspired Kate Pierson of the B-52s and others to collect old-timey trailers. With models from the 1940s and 1950s, Shady Dell could easily double as a museum of American movement during that era. There are a classic 1955 Airstream and a birchwood-paneled 1950 Park Model Spartanette, rarities like a 1959 Boles Aero and 1957 El Rey, and pure oddities like a 1947 Chris Craft yacht converted into dryland use and an equally ancient Airporter bus decked out South Pacific tiki style. The resort's Dot's Diner serves the kind of food (pancakes, burgers, BLTs, and shakes) that hungry road warriors would have devoured back in the day and still do today.

TANQUE VERDE RANCH

🏠 69 casitas, salas (smaller rooms), and haciendas

14301 East Speedway Boulevard, Tucson, AZ 85748
Open: Year-round ▪ Rates: From $190 B&B and $470 all-inclusive ▪ Amenities: Restaurant, bar, gift shop, spa, fitness room, nature center, swimming pool, sports courts, bike shop, laundry, ice, playground, kids' camp, internet ▪ ADA sites: Yes

Secluded in the saguaro forest on the eastern edge of Tucson, Tanque Verde is one of Arizona's oldest ranches of any kind, let alone duding. Founded by Emilio Carrillo in 1858—little more than a decade after the region came into the United States via the Gadsden Purchase—TVR has seen quite a bit of Arizona history. The salmon-pink adobe casitas, salas, and haciendas crawl up a cactus-studded hillside behind the old wooden ranch house, all of them spacious and decorated with Southwest-style pottery, paintings, and blankets. More succulents frame the casita patios with their views of Mount Lemmon or the Rincon Mountains of neighboring Saguaro National Park. Evenings revolve around the ranch's Carrillo Dining Room, Dog House Saloon, and outdoor Cowboy Cookout with live music.

With more than 130 resident horses, Tanque Verde runs heavy on equestrian activities, from morning breakfast rides to an old vaquero way station in the hills behind the ranch to horsemanship lessons and cattle penning (git along little dogies). There are numerous hiking routes around the ranch and a trailhead for the national park's popular Douglas Springs Trail. TVR also offers tennis, archery, yoga, and meditation, as well as a falconry experience, guided Jeep tours into the Rincons, and an ATV experience.

ANTLER RIDGE CABINS
🏠 8

103 Main Street, Greer, AZ 85927
Open: Year-round ▪ Rates: From $125 ▪ Amenities: Kitchens, private bathrooms, fireplaces, heating and air-conditioning, towels and bedding, picnic table, grill, playground, fishing pond, firewood, satellite TV, internet ▪ ADA sites: No

Hovering at around 8,300 feet (2,529 m) in the White Mountains, Antler Ridge offers a completely different take on the Arizona getaway. It's all about trees up here—the spruce, pine, aspen, oak, and Douglas fir that shade the traditional homeland of the White Mountains Apache people, who still inhabit much of these highlands. The cabins are large, modern, and well placed for views of Greer village and Apache National Forest. Each features a full kitchen, at least one bathroom with shower/tub, an open-plan living and dining area, and an outdoor deck for grilling, napping, or contemplating nature. Open all year, Antler Ridge offers a cozy base for cross-country skiing in the national forest or downhill at Sunrise Park.

CANYON DE CHELLY NATIONAL MONUMENT
🚐 / 🏕 90 no hookup

South Rim Drive (Highway 7), Chinle, AZ 86503
Open: Year-round ▪ Rate: $14 ▪ Amenities: Restaurant, camp store, dump station, restrooms, picnic tables, grills, potable water, amphitheater ▪ ADA sites: Partial

Hundreds of ancient Puebloan sites are scattered across the Southwest, but no others approach the astonishing blend of natural beauty and human heritage found at Canyon de Chelly. Managed jointly by the National Park Service and Navajo Parks, the national monument is also a place of living culture where the Navajo people live, ranch, and farm. Located near the park's western entrance, Cottonwood Campground lies between the visitors center and historic Thunderbird Lodge near the start of the North Rim and South Rim scenic drives. It's dry camping (no hookups), but most of the sites are shaded by mature cottonwoods. Campers can tour the park on their own along the scenic drives and hiking trails or join a ranger walk, guided horseback ride, or Jeep tour.

SHASH DINÉ ECORETREAT
🏠 2, 🏕 3, 2 wagons, 2 hogans

U.S. Highway 89, Navajo Route 6211, Page, AZ 86040
Open: Year-round ▪ Rates: Glamping tents from $210, cabins from $150, wagons $150, hogans from $190 ▪ Amenities: Bedding, drinks and snacks, books and games, wood-burning stoves, breakfast, communal restroom/shower ▪ ADA sites: Partial

Located in the Navajo Nation between the Grand Canyon and Lake Powell, this high desert

Under Canvas makes camping glamorous just a few miles from the Grand Canyon's South Rim.

From your campsite at Bonita Canyon, explore numerous trails throughout the Chiricahua National Monument.

glamping retreat offers traditional safari tents and seldom-found digs like traditional Navajo hogan dwellings, restored sheepherder covered wagons, and an ultramodern cube house that looks as if it fell from outer space. Tracing her Navajo lineage back 18 generations, co-owner Baya Meehan has suffused the camp with many local traditions from *ch'il ahwééh* (Navajo tea) and other culinary treats, to a two-day Navajo Experience that includes hogan accommodation, dinnertime storytelling, and a personalized tour of the Grand Canyon's East Rim.

MANZANITA CAMPGROUND
🚐/🏕 18 no hookup
5900 North State Route 89A,
Sedona, AZ 86336

Open: Year-round ▪ Rate: $22 ▪ Amenities: Restroom, picnic tables, fire rings with grills, firewood, potable water ▪ ADA sites: No

Oak Creek Canyon provides a lush, green setting for this small but popular national forest campground just north of Sedona— so small in fact that RVs and trailers are verboten. However, it's perfect for tents and camper vans. Arizona ash and box elders provide plenty of shade to take the edge off the region's notorious summer heat. A gravel beach borders the rock-strewn creek. Noise restrictions make Manzanita even more sublime. If Manzanita is fully booked, Coconino National Forest also offers campsites at

nearby Cave Springs and Pine Flat in Oak Creek.

ARIZONA NORDIC VILLAGE
🏠 4, 🚐/🏕 9 no hookup, 🏕 8
16848 U.S. Highway 180, Flagstaff, AZ 86001
Open: Year-round ▪ Rates: Cabins from $50, yurts from $40, RV/tent no hookup $20 ▪ Amenities: Camp store, restroom, showers, woodburning stoves, lanterns, picnic tables, fire rings, grills, firewood, library, games, outdoor movies, winter sports lessons, trail passes ▪ ADA sites: No

Hunkered beneath huge old-growth trees on the western flank of the San Francisco Peaks, the Nordic Village is one of the few Arizona resorts that

Experience ranch life, including guided horseback rides through the saguaro forest, at Tanque Verde Ranch.

caters equally to warm weather and snow season campers. In winter, you can start snowshoeing, skate skiing, or cross-country skiing from right beside your cabin, yurt, or campsite. Coconino National Forest also maintains snowmobile and fat-bike trails in the winter. And Arizona Snowbowl is just down the road for those who prefer downhill or snowboarding. During hotter times, the trails literally melt into hiking, horseback, and mountain biking routes. While the lodge does offer a store with drinks and snacks, there's no on-site restaurant. Five of the yurts are found in the backcountry more than a mile (1.6 km) from the lodge and cannot be accessed by private vehicle.

UNDER CANVAS GRAND CANYON
🏕 91

979 Airpark Lane, Valle, AZ 86046
Open: April to October ▪ Rates: From $249 ▪ Amenities: Restaurant, gift shop, bathhouses, communal fire pits and grills, organic bath products, guest experience coordinator, yoga, USB chargers, internet ▪ ADA sites: Yes

Camping rises to an incredibly comfortable peak at Under Canvas Grand Canyon. Located in the mixed pinyon-juniper and sagebrush country about 40 minutes from the canyon's South Rim, the upscale resort offers five tent styles—Suites, Deluxe, Safari, Hive, and Stargazers—with windows above the bed for contemplating the night sky.

Larger tents are outfitted with king beds, cowskin rugs, and comfy leather camp chairs or sofas, as well as private bathrooms with hot-water showers separated from the rest of the living/sleeping area by a sturdy barn door. Water misters and mini-fans diminish the summer heat, while wood-burning stoves take the edge off chilly nights in the cooler months. Smaller tents offer king or twin beds and no private bath.

The resort revolves around a canvas-covered lodge that shelters the lobby, gift shop, food-ordering area, and indoor dining. Out back is a much larger alfresco dining area with communal fire pits, heat lamps, and a small stage for evening live entertainment. A separate tent expedites complimentary activities like painting and ornament making.

HAVASUPAI CAMPGROUND
🏕 varies

Havasu Creek, Havasupai Indian Reservation, Supai, AZ 86435
Open: Year-round ▪ Rate: $100 per person (three-night minimum stay) ▪ Amenities: Restrooms, picnic tables, potable water ▪ ADA sites: No

One of the planet's most spectacular campgrounds sits amid waterfalls and aquamarine pools in a red-rock side branch of the Grand Canyon on the Havasupai Reservation. Campers need to undertake a 10-mile (16 km) hike from the parking lot at Hualapai Hilltop to the campsites in Havasu Canyon. You can backpack equipment and provisions or use a pack mule gear transport service ($100 one way; $200 round trip). Located beside Havasu Creek, the campground doesn't offer many frills beyond pit toilets, drinking water, and picnic tables. But you're there for otherworldly landscapes, not creature comforts. Havasupai means "people of the blue-green waters" and you won't question why this tribe has taken that moniker when you look out from your tent at the base of the cascade. Groceries and hot meals are available at a café, stores, and frybread (a traditional Native American flat dough bread) stalls in Supai village, around a 2-mile (3.2 km) walk from the campground. Advance reservations via the Havasupai Reservations website are required before entering the canyon and often must be booked months in advance to secure your campsite and admission onto the reservation's protected lands. ▪

SOMETHING SPECIAL

The Havasupai Tribe

For more than 1,000 years, the Havasu Baaja ("people of the blue-green waters") have lived in a remote village below the rim of the Grand Canyon, thriving off the harsh desert landscape for centuries.

The hike to the Havasupai campgrounds and reservation is an 8-mile (12.9 km) trek into the remote landscape, but campers with a reservation make the in-and-out effort to perch beside the beloved Havasupai Falls.

The culture of the Havasupai tribe has changed with modern times, but their remote location hasn't. Mail is carried in and out of the canyon by mule train, and residents travel by foot or horseback. The reservation itself was established in 1880 and enlarged in 1975. It covers 188,077 acres (76,112.1 ha) inside the canyon, and residents continue to practice cultural life, including traditional arts and crafts.

Arkansas

Enjoy all that Arkansas has to offer. Discover the beauty of Cove Lake, spend the night in a tree house, or dock your RV near historic Hot Springs National Park.

HIGHLIGHTS

Capital: Little Rock

Total National Parks: 1 (Hot Springs National Park)

Total State Parks: 52 (Largest is Hobbs State Park)

State Bird: Mockingbird

State Flower: Apple blossom

State Land Mammal: White-tailed deer

Wildlife Spotting: Elk; badgers; spotted skunks; red-tailed hawks; ivory-billed woodpeckers; indigo buntings; cricket frogs; Ouachita dusky salamanders; Western pygmy rattlesnakes; collared lizards

MISSISSIPPI RIVER STATE PARK

🚐 / 🏕 14 full hookup, 26 no hookup, 🏕 3

2955 State Highway 44, Marianna, AR 72360

Open: Year-round ▪ Rates: RV/tent full hookup $36, no hookup $13, tent only $12 ▪ Amenities: Bathhouse, picnic tables, grills, lantern hanger, boat ramps/docks ▪ ADA sites: Yes

A unique blend of state and federal assets preserves a wild stretch of the Mississippi watershed in northeast Arkansas. The state park shares Beech Point, Lone Pine, and Storm Creek Lake with St. Francis National Forest. Located on a peninsula that curls into Bear Creek Lake, Beech Point is the largest and best equipped of the three, as well as the only one with full-hookup RV sites. Fishing, boating, swimming, and wildlife watching on the park's seven water bodies are the main events. But there's plenty of scope for hiking too, including the Bear Creek Loop nature trail near the campground. The St. Francis River empties into the mighty Mississippi along the park's eastern edge. In October 1815, surveyor Joseph Brown ventured up the St. Francis and trekked west through woods

Mount Magazine is the highest peak in Arkansas, standing at 2,753 feet (839.1 m).

that are now included in the park to establish the baseline for the first official survey of the Louisiana Purchase. For campers who crave a dose of city life, Memphis is little more than an hour's drive.

THE CABINS AT DRY CREEK AT THE OZARK FOLK CENTER

🏮 53

1030 Park Avenue, Mountain View, AR 72560

Open: Year-round ▪ Rates: $90-$130 ▪ Amenities: TV, mini-fridge, microwave, kitchen utensils, iron and ironing board, hair dryer, coffee pot, swimming pool, game room, general store, restaurants, internet ▪ ADA sites: Yes

There's almost always music in the air around these cabins in the highlands of northern Arkansas. That's because they're beside the Ozark Folk Center, which strives to preserve and propagate the region's traditional music and dance through festivals, concerts, workshops, and Ozark Highlands Radio. Comfortable and modern, the Ozark-style cabins offer a variety of layouts with king or queen beds (and pullout sofas for extra guests), as well as private bathrooms, kitchenettes, picture windows, and porches or decks. Canines are welcome, but sorry, cats, you gotta stay home. A short footpath leads to the folk center entrance and attractions like the

Crafts Village, Homespun Gift Shop, Skillet Restaurant, and a 1,000-seat auditorium that hosts the annual folk and blues festivals.

BUFFALO OUTDOOR CENTER

🏮 28, 🚐 14 full hookup

4699 State Highway 43, Ponca, AR 72670

Open: Year-round ▪ Rates: Cabins from $129, RV full hookup $49 ▪ Amenities: Dump station, camp store, showers, laundry, picnic tables, grills, internet ▪ ADA sites: Yes

The nation's first national river (established in 1972) provides a bucolic backdrop to a wilderness resort that offers cabins and RV camping, as well as hiking, mountain biking, and float trips down the wild and scenic Buffalo River. Cabins throughout the campground vary greatly in size, style, and location. Some are tucked into the riverside woods, others perched on mountaintops; some are ideal for couples, others large enough for families. Buffalo Outdoor Center (BOC) also offers multiday canoe/kayak rental for self-guided float trips down the national river, adventures that can last anywhere from two days to an entire week for those who want to explore its full length (132 miles/212 km). BOC also offers a small but stunning RV park, a mountaintop location with concrete pads, and awesome views across the Ozarks.

TREEHOUSE COTTAGES
 8

165 West Van Buren (U.S. Highway 62), Eureka Springs, AR 72632
Open: Year-round ▪ Rates: From $179 ▪ Amenities: Fireplaces, private bathrooms, Jacuzzi tubs, kitchenette and dining area, cable TV, Blu-ray player and library, outdoor electric grills, heating and air-conditioning, luggage assistance, iPod dock, internet ▪ ADA sites: No

"Luxury in the trees" is the motto of this upscale resort in historic Eureka Springs. Spread across two wooded locations, the lofty lodges feature four-poster beds, roomy private bathrooms, a comfy lounge area with fireplace, wraparound porch, and heart-shaped Jacuzzi tubs with forest views. Half a dozen restaurants are within walking distance, and the Victorian treasures of downtown Eureka Springs are just down the road. The cottages are also a great base for exploring this corner of the Ozarks. You will find the restaurants, shopping, and music halls of Branson, the Civil War battlefield at Pea Ridge, and boating on Beaver Lake are less than an hour's drive away.

STONEWIND RETREAT
🏔 8

15840 Wilson Branch Drive, Chester, AR 72934
Open: Year-round ▪ Rates: From $169 ▪ Amenities: Kitchen, private

baths, hot tubs, massage, wellness classes ▪ ADA sites: Yes

It's entirely possible that guests at StoneWind might feel as if they've woken up somewhere in the Himalayan foothills rather than the hill country of northern Arkansas because this tranquil retreat does have an exotic air. That feeling is due in large part to the romantic yurts, all of them outfitted with king or queen beds, full kitchen, private bath with walk-in shower, and alfresco hot tub on the wooden deck. But in keeping with that Asian vibe, StoneWind also offers qigong ("vital life force") self-healing and deep breathing workshops, meditation classes, and in-yurt Reiki and massage treatments. And just in case you're running away to get married, the retreat can arrange an elopement ceremony with the in-house minister presiding in the stone garden.

COVE LAKE RECREATION AREA
🚐 / 🏕 36 no hookup

19 Cove Lake Loop, Paris, AR 72855
Open: Year-round ▪ Rates: RV/tent $15, cabins $35 ▪ Amenities: Dump station, showers, picnic tables, fire rings, grills, boat ramps, potable water, boat rentals, miniature golf, playground, snack bar ▪ ADA sites: Partial

This laid-back Forest Service campground lies in the shadow of Mount Magazine, the highest point in Arkansas at 2,753 feet (839 m) above sea level. Many of the campsites are right on the water, making it easy to boat, swim, or angle for catfish, bass, bluegill, perch, and other species that inhabit Cove Lake. A 9.5-mile (15 km) trail leads uphill to the summit of Mount

Bird-watching—including spotting a Cooper's hawk—is one of the draws to Ouachita National Forest.

Park your RV for the weekend, then rent kayaks to paddle your way through Mississippi River State Park.

Magazine and its unobstructed view across the Arkansas River Valley and the often mist-shrouded Ouachita Range. Schluterman's at Cove Creek Supply Company offers guided ATV tours of the surrounding Ozark–St. Francis National Forest. Campers equipped with a hang-glider can launch themselves from a pad on the south side of the summit.

LAKE OUACHITA STATE PARK
12, / 58 full hookup, 23 no hookup, 12
5451 Mountain Pine Road, Mountain Pine, AR 71956
Open: Year-round ▪ Rates: RV/tent full hookup $36, RV/tent no hookup $14, tent only $14, cabins from $68

▪ Amenities: Dump station, bathhouse, picnic tables, fire rings, playground, boat rental, boat ramp, beach, fishing supplies ▪ ADA sites: Yes

The Ouachita Mountains reach fever pitch at a lakeside campground with a wide array of ways to get wet. Campsites and cabins are scattered across a heavily wooded peninsula that juts into arguably the state's most scenic lake. All sites are within walking distance of a marina that offers speedboat, pontoon, canoe, kayak, and pedal boat rentals, as well as bait and fishing supplies. Boat slips and mooring buoys are also available to rent, and the park offers bald eagle watching cruises

and guided kayak tours. Right offshore is the Lake Ouachita Geo Float Trail, a water-based interpretive route (the first of its kind in the country) that guides boaters to 12 markers that describe the lake's unique geological features including Whirlpool Rock, Submarine Slide, a geologic fish shelter, and miniature caves created by waves wearing away the soft limestone. Among the park's land-based activities are the Caddo Bend Trail, a four-mile (6.4-km) loop trail that takes you to the end of the peninsula, and a visitors center with interpretive programs.

GULPHA GORGE CAMPGROUND
/ 40 full hookup

Bring the whole family for a weekend at Crater of Diamonds State Park, where you can scour the dirt for precious diamonds.

305 Gorge Road, Hot Springs National Park, AR 71901

Open: Year-round ▪ Rate: $30 ▪ Amenities: Dump station, picnic tables, grills, potable water, amphitheater ▪ ADA sites: Partial

If ever a place had a split personality, it's Hot Springs National Park in central Arkansas. The park is world renowned for Bathhouse Row, a cluster of eight historic geothermal spas constructed between 1892 and 1923 when Hot Springs was one of the nation's most fashionable places to "take the waters." The more posh history is offset by the other features of Hot Springs National Park. The park also boasts a rugged backcountry, a mountainous spine cloaked in pristine pine-oak-hickory forest. Here is where you will find a fantastic spot to set up for a weekend escape. Gulpha Gorge Campground is tucked into a wooded valley on the south side of Hot Springs Mountain. The full-hookup sites are arrayed along Gulpha Creek, which is too shallow for swimming but just right for cooling your feet on typically sweltering summer days. The short but steep Gulpha Gorge Trail connects the campground with a network of hiking routes that ramble across the mountain and down to Bathhouse Row.

CATHERINE'S LANDING

📞 19, 🚐/🏕 181 full hookup, 🏕 4, 🏚 7

1700 Shady Grove Road, Hot Springs, AR 71901

Open: Year-round ▪ Rates: RV from $54.45, cabins from $211, yurts from $140, tent only from $48.40 ▪ Amenities: Dump station, camp store, showers, picnic tables, fire pits, grills, swimming pool, playground, fitness center, boat rental,

disc golf course, bike and golf cart rental, dog park and dog wash, propane, internet ▪ ADA sites: Yes

For those who take their camping with creature comforts, Catherine's Landing offers all the trappings of a full-service resort plus extras like a zip line through the forest canopy, disc golf course, nature trail, and boats for exploring Lake Catherine. In addition to nearly 200 full-hookup RV pads and a handful of tent-only sites, campers can also crash in yurts and cute little cottages. The resort rents bikes, boats, and golf carts. There's a dog-washing station for dirty pooches and a concierge to help campers plan activities in the Hot Springs area and beyond. In case you're wondering why all of the resort streets are named after cows and dairy products (Guernsey, Holstein, Cheese Curd, Two Percent), it's because the site was once a dairy farm.

CRATER OF DIAMONDS STATE PARK

🚐/🏕 47 full hookup, 🏕 5

209 State Park Road, Murfreesboro, AR 71958

Open: Year-round ▪ Rates: RV/tent $36, tent only $14 ▪ Amenities: Restaurant, dump station, showers, laundry, picnic tables, fire rings, grills, playground, amphitheater, internet, water park, gift shop, mining equipment rental ▪ ADA sites: Partial

This southwest Arkansas state park is the only place on planet Earth where ordinary people can camp beside a diamond field and search for gems they are free to take home. Visitors uncover around 600 diamonds each year amid the remains of an ancient volcano. Some of them are truly enormous—like the 40.23-carat Uncle Sam diamond found in 1924. Most are fairly small and insignificant, but that doesn't make them any less valuable in the minds of those (especially kids) who unearth them. And its not uncommon for the hopeless romantic to visit the park for a stone to use on an engagement ring. For campers who tire of digging and sifting, the park also offers the Diamond Discovery Center museum, Diamond Springs Water Park (Memorial Day to Labor Day), and a short trail to the Little Missouri River. ▪

SOMETHING SPECIAL

Crater of Diamonds State Park

A stay at Crater of Diamonds State Park means the opportunity to dig for the beloved gem across a 37.5-acre (15.2 ha) plowed field. But diamonds have a long history in Arkansas beyond visits to the park:

The first diamond was discovered in what is now the park by a farmer, John Huddleston, in 1906. Huddleston owned a portion of the diamond-bearing crater, which went

on to change hands over the years. From 1952 to 1972, the area was privately owned, until Arkansas purchased it to make a state park.

You can find all colors—white, brown, and yellow—of diamonds in a variety of sizes on your dig in the park. Most are the size of a match head. In 2020, more than 353 diamonds were found at the park, 17 of them more than 1 carat in size. The largest diamond found by a visitor to the park was the Amarillo Starlight Diamond, which was 16.37 carats.

California

The vast state of California offers a variety of experiences, from coastal retreats to desert oases to redwood-shaded grounds.

ELK PRAIRIE CAMPGROUND

🏕 4, 🚐/🏔 75 no hookup
127011 Newton B. Drury Scenic Parkway, Orick, CA 95555
Open: Year-round ▪ Rates: RV/tent $35, cabins from $80 ▪ Amenities: Showers, picnic tables, fire pits with grills, firewood, potable water, food storage containers, amphitheater ▪ ADA sites: Yes

The drive to save the world's tallest trees started in 1917 when a group of San Francisco nature lovers cruised up the coast in their newfangled cars to see the redwoods. Seeing the coastal giants were under threat from mining and logging, they began raising money to purchase land that would soon become Prairie Creek State Park and its redwood-shaded campground. The camp takes its name from the Roosevelt elk that graze the adjacent meadow. Trails lead to various redwood groves and other park landmarks like Gold Bluffs Beach and incredible Fern Canyon, a ravine strewn with boulders, fallen redwoods, and slender waterfalls where Steven Spielberg shot scenes from one of the Jurassic Park movies. Yet the park's biggest thrill remains sleeping beneath the ruddy titans that line Prairie Creek.

At Grant Grove Campground, you'll be sleeping among California's legendary redwoods, some as tall as 350 feet (106.7 m).

WILDHAVEN SONOMA

🏕 40
2411 Alexander Valley Road, Healdsburg, CA 95448
Open: Year-round ▪ Rate: From $129 ▪ Amenities: Camp store, bathhouse, bedding, space heaters, fans, private deck, fire pits, communal barbecue and outdoor eating area, firewood, ice, kayak and stand-up paddleboard (SUP) rental, bike rental, river access, yoga sessions, hammocks, live music, internet ▪ ADA sites: Yes

Wine, water, and song are just a few of the lures of a new glamping resort in gorgeous Sonoma County about 90 minutes north of San Francisco. Wildhaven is a hip reincarnation of an old RV resort along the Russian River in the Alexander Valley. Campers can access the river for swimming, tubing, or kayaking on three semi-private beaches, one of them equipped with a rope swing. Yoga sessions are held on a grassy bluff above the river, and live music and wine tastings are staged in the middle of camp. A dozen wineries lie within a short drive, and the spectacular slice of the Northern California coast is an hour away.

LAGO LOMITA VINEYARDS TREEHOUSE

🏕 1, 🏠 1
25200 Loma Prieta Avenue, Los Gatos, CA 95033
Open: Year-round ▪ Rate: From $250

▪ Amenities: Bathroom, breakfast, private deck, dedicated workspace, kitchen, laundry, bedding and towels, heating, vineyard, internet ▪ ADA sites: No

Perched in the Santa Cruz Mountains high above Silicon Valley, Lago Lomita offers one of Bay Area's most romantic getaways: a luxury tree house perched in two giant Douglas firs surrounded by ridge-top vineyards. Larger than some San Francisco apartments, the 400-square foot (37-sq m) tree house includes a queen bed and a private deck with a view of the distant Pacific—a panorama that's even more spectacular when the fog rolls along the coast and your lofty retreat is still bathed

MORE TO CONSIDER

- **The Trailer Pond:** Five restored vintage travel trailers—still equipped with their original iceboxes—beside a lake on Alta Colina Vineyard near Paso Robles. *thetrailerpond.com*

- **Evergreen Lodge Cabins:** Historic cabin resort (with a restaurant, swimming pool, and spa) near Hetch Hetchy on the west side of Yosemite National Park. *evergreenlodge.com*

- **AutoCamp Russian River:** Tricked-out Airstreams, a swanky clubhouse, and river adventures lure glampers to this upscale resort in the Russian River wine region. *autocamp.com/russian-river*

- **Scorpion Canyon Campground:** The ferry from Ventura Harbor is the only way to reach this super-remote national park camping spot on Santa Cruz Island. *nps.gov/chis/planyourvisit/camping.htm*

- **Mendocino Grove:** Glamping along Highway One in a coastal forest 150 miles (250 km) north of San Francisco. *mendocinogrove.com*

- **Furnace Creek Campground:** With summer temperatures hitting 120°F (49°C), campers might want to consider a winter sojourn at this Death Valley National Park campground. *nps.gov/deva/planyourvisit/camping.htm*

in sunshine. Down at ground level, a full bathroom and kitchen are available to tree house guests.

VENTANA BIG SUR GLAMPING

🏕 15, ⛺ 63 tent only

48123 Highway 1, Big Sur, CA 93920

Open: Year-round ▪ Rates: Glamping tents from $240, tent only from $80 ▪ Amenities: Restaurant, snack bar, showers, housekeeping, bedding and towels, picnic tables, fire pits with grills, firewood, ice, potable water, drinks coolers, USB ports, lanterns ▪ ADA sites: Partial

The "rustic" portion of the posh Ven-

Comfort and the wild come together on a wilderness weekend at Ventana Big Sur.

tana Big Sur resort features tent-only campsites and upscale glamping tents spread along Post Creek in a canyon shaded by towering coastal redwoods. Campsites are tent only and primitive, with hot showers the only creature comfort that you don't have to bring yourself. Glamping tents are outfitted with double beds, hot and cold water sinks, electric lighting, and Adirondack chairs on private decks. Campers and glampers do not have access to the neighboring resort with its luxury spa, infinity pool, and private jet service. However, the yummy Smokehouse eatery is just beyond the campground entrance, and the legendary Nepenthe cliff-top restaurant only a five-minute drive down Highway One.

ORANGELAND RV PARK

🚐 195 full hookup

1600 West Struck Avenue, Orange, CA 92867

Open: Year-round ▪ Rates: From $75 ▪ Amenities: Camp store, dump station, showers, laundry, picnic tables, swimming pool, playground, miniature golf, shuffleboard, gym, dog run, dog washing station, cable TV, internet ▪ ADA sites: Partial

It would be hard to find a more conveniently located RV park anywhere in the vast Los Angeles metro area. It's a 10- to 15-minute drive from both Disneyland and Knotts Berry Farm. Angel Stadium (Major League Baseball) and the Honda Center (NHL hockey and "A" list concerts) are within walking distance, and a 25-theater cineplex is right across the street. At the nearby ARTIC (Anaheim Regional Transportation Intermodal Center) station, campers can hop a train to downtown L.A. or San Diego. On-site, campers have miniature golf and a

Find plenty of recreational activities, from nature trails to table tennis, at the Evergreen Lodge Cabins.

swimming pool to amuse themselves. Orangeland doesn't accommodate tent, car, or van camping.

CRYSTAL COVE BEACH COTTAGES

🏯 24

35 Crystal Cove (off Pacific Coast Highway), Newport Beach, CA 92657
Open: Year-round ▪ Rates: Cottages from $197, private rooms from $39 ▪ Amenities: Restaurants, bar, park store and gallery, kitchens, private bathrooms, bedding and towels, private decks, picnic tables, beach, beach rentals, tide pools ▪ ADA sites: Yes

A throwback to the Southern California beach scene of long ago, the cottages were built between 1920

and 1940 as private homes and later restored by the state park authority and Crystal Cove Conservancy into charming seaside digs. The colony includes 14 individual cottages ideal for families or small groups of friends and 10 dorm-style units with shared bathrooms, kitchens, and decks. Poised at the bottom of sandstone cliffs, the cottages are right on the sand. Another 22 cottages along the north end of the beach are being restored and will be available for rental in the future. Two of the cottages have been converted into restaurants: seaside Beachcomber and a clifftop Shake Shack.

KATE'S LAZY DESERT

🚐 6

58380 Botkin Road, Landers, CA 92285

Open: Year-round ▪ Rate: $200 ▪ Amenities: Kitchens or cooktops, private bathrooms, picnic tables, grills, air-conditioning, space heaters ▪ ADA sites: No

One of the many offbeat overnight spots in the Mojave Desert around Joshua Tree National Park, Lazy Desert revolves around six revamped Airstream traveler trailers. Created by former B-52s singer Kate Pierson and artist Monica Coleman, many of the design themes were inspired by classic B-52 songs or the area's UFO appeal. All of the units boast a double bed, private bathroom with shower, a proper kitchen or cooktop, indoor dining table, and outdoor sitting area with barbecue. The resort is around a 30-minute

A stay in a Lago Lomita tree house offers a taste of California, including rolling vineyards (and accompanying wine tastings).

drive from the national park's west entrance station.

GRANT GROVE VILLAGE

☎ 49, 🚐/🏕 301 no hookup
Generals Highway (State Route 180), Grant Grove Village, CA 93628
Open: Year-round ▪ Rates: RV/tent no hookup from $18, cabins from $109 ▪ Amenities: Restaurant, camp store, gift shop, showers (for cabins), picnic tables, fire pits with grills, potable water, firewood, ice, food storage containers, amphitheater ▪ ADA sites: Yes

With three campsites, cabins, and a commercial cluster, Grant Grove Village is the hub of Sequoia-Kings Canyon National Parks. Just over 300 campsites are divided among three campgrounds around the village. Sunset is the largest (156 individual sites), Crystal Springs the smallest (35 sites), but Azalea (110 sites) is the only campground open through the winter when the nearby giant sequoias often carry a dusting of fresh snow. The historic cabins—the oldest dating from 1910—range from deluxe units with private bathrooms and heating for those chilly High Sierra nights to canvas-roofed tent cabins with no heating or bathrooms. No matter where you crash in the village, the famous General Grant Tree is roughly a 20- to 30-minute walk. Often called the "Nation's Christmas Tree," the 274-foot-tall (83.5 m) behemoth is the world's third largest tree of any kind.

YOSEMITE HIGH SIERRA CAMPS

🏕 5
Tioga Road (State Highway 120), Tuolumne Meadows, CA 95389
Open: July to August/September ▪ Rates: From $152 per person, per night ▪ Amenities: Meals, bathrooms or bathhouse, potable water, laundry wash basins, blankets, comforters, sheets, and pillows (but no sleeping bags or towels) ▪ ADA sites: No

A pioneer of American glamping, Yosemite's High Sierra Camps trace their roots to 1916 when Stephen Mather—first director of the recently created National Park Service—authorized the development of tented camps in the park's backcountry. Starting from Tuolumne Meadows, campers hike or ride mules along a 49-mile (79 km) loop trail that connects five tented camps scattered through the high country between the Sierra Crest peaks and Half Dome. Luggage is transported between the camps on pack mules. Tents are dormitory style, so you may be sharing with someone you don't know. Meals are prepared by the camp staff. The hike between overnight spots is anywhere from four and a half to six hours. All mule trips are guided, but hikers have the option of trekking between the camps on their own or with a guide.

EMERALD BAY STATE PARK

🚐/🏕 66 no hookup, 🏕 31 tent only, 22 boat-in tent only
89 South Shore Lake Tahoe, Tahoma, CA 96142
Open: May/June to September ▪ Rates: RV/tent no hookup from $35, tent only from $25, boat-in $35 ▪ Amenities: Showers, picnic tables, fire rings with grills, potable water, food storage containers, amphitheater ▪ ADA sites: Yes

Set along Lake Tahoe's south shore, Emerald Bay could easily be a national park with its incredible blend of scenery, culture, activities, and even extraordinary architecture. The park's iconic feature is Vikingsholm, an over-the-top waterfront mansion erected in the 1920s by an heiress who thought the bay resembled a Scandinavian fjord. The park also offers two very different overnight choices: a traditional campground with around 100 sites that sprawls across forested Eagle Point, and a boat-in area with a dock and mooring buoys on the other side of the bay for campers who arrive by boat. ▪

SOMETHING SPECIAL

Joshua Tree National Park

Three geological features define Joshua Tree National Park: the eponymous trees that are twisted and bristled throughout the park, rugged rock formations, and stark desert landscapes.

Hiking trails are scattered throughout the park, particularly around the boulders of Hidden Valley. One of the newer additions to Joshua Tree, the Discovery Trail, is an easy loop that quickly covers the park's geological highlights. For a longer trek, consider the Black Rock Canyon Panorama Loop, for epic views from a higher elevation gain.

For a popular camping destination within the park, Jumbo Rocks is a family-friendly spot named after the rock formations throughout. The best time to visit is from October through May, when temperatures are milder (though cold at night). It's best to avoid the summer months and scorching heat. Reservations at the campground are required year-round.

Colorado

"Rocky Mountain high" takes on a whole other meaning at these mountain retreats perched on canyon rims, nestled in forests, and in close proximity to hot springs.

STATE FOREST STATE PARK

🏠 15, 🚐/🏕 32 partial hookup, 🏕 154, ⛺ 11 (primitive 40+)
56750 State Highway 14, Walden, CO 80480
Open: Year-round ▪ Rates: RV/tent partial hookup $36, no hookup/tent only $28, primitive $18, cabins from $90, yurts from $120 ▪ Amenities: Dump station, restrooms, showers, laundry, picnic tables, fire rings, grills, potable water, fishing piers, boat ramps, horse corrals, amphitheater ▪ ADA sites: Yes

Despite its drab, generic name, this rugged state park is incredibly colorful—a mosaic of forest, meadow, and wetlands beside the mighty Medicine Bow Range in north-central Colorado. It offers three distinct overnight options: camping, cabins, and yurts. Campers can choose from five developed and 14 primitive campgrounds, some of the latter deep in the backcountry. The cabins are divided between North Park Campground and North Michigan Lake. Never Summer Nordic operates yurts at dispersed locations around the park, including the wilderness routes to Montgomery Pass and Ruby Jewel. State Forest is renowned for summer hiking and biking, winter sports, and wildlife viewing. With more than 600

Morefield Campground offers access to cliff dwellings like the Balcony House, in Mesa Verde National Park.

resident moose, it's probably the best place in the Rockies to spot the largest member of the deer family in its natural habitat.

MORAINE PARK CAMPGROUND

🚐/🏕 143 no hookup, 🏕 101
Morane Park Road, Rocky Mountain National Park, Estes Park, CO 80517
Open: Year-round ▪ Rates: $20 (winter), $30 (summer) ▪ Amenities: Dump station, restrooms, picnic tables, fire rings with grills, potable water, food storage containers, firewood, ice, amphitheater, park shuttle ▪ ADA sites: Yes

The snowcapped peaks (and colossal elk) often seem close enough to reach out and touch at the largest campground in Rocky Mountain National Park. This high-altitude hangout (8,160 feet/2,487 m) is located along the edge of a large "park," or meadow, about a 10-minute drive from Beaver Meadows Visitor Center and the town of Estes Park. Wildflowers are abundant in the spring and wildlife throughout the year. Nearby trails lead to Cub Lake, Fern Falls, and into the ultra-high country via the 7-mile (11.2 km) Ute Trail.

REVEREND'S RIDGE CAMPGROUND

🏠 5, 🚐/🏕 59 partial hookup, 🏕 38, ⛺ 2
313 Reverend's Ridge Road, Golden

Gate State Park, Black Hawk, CO 80422
Open: Year-round ▪ Rates: RV/tent partial hookup $36, tent only $28, cabins and yurts $90 (two-night minimum stay) ▪ Amenities: Dump station, showers, laundry, picnic tables, fire pits, grills, potable water, amphitheater ▪ ADA sites: Yes

One of Colorado's most storied state parks, Golden Gate Canyon was once a gateway to the gold fields. When the ore ran out, locals turned to ranching and then Prohibition moonshining. Reverend's Ridge is the larger of the park's two campgrounds and the only one open in winter. Besides RV/tent sites, it also

A thrill for campers of all ages: sandboarding at the Great Sand Dunes near Piñon Flats Campground

offers a handful of cabins and yurts. Although it's located far from the park's visitors center, Reverend's Ridge is convenient for several great hiking/biking/horseback routes, including the 3.5-mile (5.6 km) Raccoon Trail and 9.1-mile (14.6 km) Mule Deer Loop. The campground is named for Donald Tippet, a local Methodist minister who famously sparred with the moonshiners but lived to tell the tale and eventually became bishop of San Francisco.

MOUNTAINDALE CABINS & RV RESORT

🏠 4, 🚐 / ⛺ 91 full hookup

2000 Barrett Road, Colorado Springs, CO 80926

Open: Year-round ▪ Rates: Cabins from $80, RV $59 ▪ Amenities: Dump station, showers, laundry, picnic tables, fire rings, playground, fitness room, volleyball court, game room, hot tub, dog park, internet ▪ ADA sites: Partial

Red Creek Canyon on the southern outskirts of Colorado Springs provides an arboreous setting for a motor home campground within striking distance of Pikes Peak, Royal Gorge, and historic Cripple Creek. Catering only to RVs, all sites are full hookup, and even the longest units are easily accommodated. The park sprawls across 45 wooded acres (18 ha) with trails through the ponderosa pines to Red Creek and up a small mountain. For those who don't have their own RV, Mountaindale is an authorized Cruise America dealership offering rental motor homes. It's about a half-hour drive into downtown Colorado Springs, but Hunt Brothers Pizza will deliver right to your campsite.

ROYAL GORGE CABINS

🏠 9, ⛺ 8

45054 West U.S. Highway 50, Cañon City, CO 81212

Open: Year-round ▪ Rates: Cabins from $399, glamping tents from $209 ▪ Amenities: Restaurant, bar, shower house, bedding and towels, picnic tables, fire rings, grills, evaporative coolers, internet ▪ ADA sites: No

Cañon City's poshest accommodation lies near the North Rim of the famous canyon within easy reach of the stupendous Royal Gorge Bridge, as well as Arkansas River float trip outfitters, zip line adventures, and the interactive Dinosaur Experience museum. The designer digs include one- and two-bedroom modern luxury cabins or single- and double-canvas glamping tents. All cabins are equipped with full kitchens, private bathrooms, flat-screen TVs, and fireplaces, while the canvas offerings feature queen beds, hardwood floors covered in carpets, indoor seating area, private patio, air-conditioning, and fire ring. The resort's 8 Mile Bar & Grill serves burgers, chicken, tacos, and other favorites for dining on-site or taking back to your tent or cabin.

PIÑON FLATS CAMPGROUND

🚐 / ⛺ 88 no hookup

State Highway 150, Great Sand Dunes National Park & Preserve, Mosca, CO 81146

Open: April to October ▪ Rate: $20 ▪ Amenities: Camp store, dump station, restrooms, picnic tables, fire rings with grills, potable water, firewood, food storage containers, amphitheater ▪ ADA sites: Yes

Upgraded to national park status in 2004 after 70 years as a national monument, Great Sand Dunes showcases the largest dunes in North America (750 feet/229 m) against a backdrop of the majestic Rockies. The park's only campground, Piñon

Flats lies at the end of the paved road along the eastern edge of the highest dunes. Deer, elk, and pronghorn antelope often graze the grasslands and piney woodlands around the camp, and black bears sometimes descend from the highlands in search of easy meals. Dunes Overlook Trail (2.3 mile/3.7 km round trip) heads due north from the campground, while another short trail runs west to the base of the dunes and Medano Creek, which runs with water between April and June when "beach play" is possible. Night skies are incredible above the often-cloudless San Luis Valley, and free ranger programs are offered summer and fall at the campground amphitheater.

MOREFIELD CAMPGROUND
15 full hookup, / 167 no hookup, 85

Mile Marker 4, Mesa Top Ruins Road, Mesa Verde National Park, CO 81330
Open: April to October ▪ Rates: RV full hookup $50, RV/tent no hookup and tent only $36 ▪ Amenities: Restaurant, camp store, gas station, dump station, showers, laundry, picnic tables, grills, potable water, firewood, ice, food storage containers, amphitheater, internet ▪ ADA sites: Yes

Mesa Verde's only campground appeals to those who dig panoramic views or the notion they're sleeping on the same mountain where Native Americans lived thousands of years ago. Located near the park entrance on the zigzag road up from Cortez and Mancos, Morefield nestles in a high valley near vertiginous lookouts like the Knife Edge and Point

Lookout. Not only is it supersized (267 total sites), but for a national park campground, it's refreshingly well equipped with a restaurant, camp store, coin-operated laundry, and gas station. Evening programs at the Morefield amphitheater are the stuff of national park legend, started in 1907 by park archaeologist Jesse Fewkes. Campers should take advantage of the ranger-led Cliff Palace Twilight Tour offered between May and September, which highlights sunset on the face of Mesa Verde's most celebrated ruin.

DUNTON HOT SPRINGS
13

52068 Road 38, Dolores, CO 81323
Open: Year-round ▪ Rates: From $730 ▪ Amenities: Restaurant, bar, spa, swimming pools, fitness center, library, turndown service, daily

From your woodsy yurt in State Forest State Park, keep an eye out for roaming moose. More than 600 live near the grounds.

At Dunton Hot Springs, taking a warm dip with majestic views is the highlight of this Wild West resort.

housekeeping, laundry and dry cleaning, concierge, Tesla charger, internet ▪ ADA sites: No

Built around the historic saloon and dance hall from a Wild West–era mining camp and frontier hot springs resort, Dunton features fully restored log cabins that in many cases were constructed by their original 19th-century inhabitants. All of them are architecturally distinct and the decor even more eclectic, with everything from vintage bearskin rugs and antique snowshoes to a Rajasthani wedding bed and artfully framed Native American coat. The Well House cabin boasts a private hot spring and cold plunge pool. Dunton offers other ways to soak in the calcium bicarbonate–infused waters including a restored bathhouse, several outdoor pools, and the natural source of the hot springs. Naturally there's a spa with yoga, meditation, and various treatments. The reincarnated saloon now offers modern dining rather than pioneer grub, and the resort offers a wide range of outdoor adventures, both summer and winter.

SOUTH RIM CAMPGROUND

🚐 / 🏕 23 partial hookup, 65 no hookup
South Rim Road, Black Canyon of the Gunnison National Park, Montrose, CO 81401
Open: Year-round ▪ Rates: RV/tent partial hookup $22, no hookup $16 ▪ Amenities: Restrooms, picnic tables, fire rings with grills, potable water, food storage containers, amphitheater ▪ ADA sites: Yes

It's not quite as famous as another famous South Rim in the American Southwest, but this western Colorado cliffhanger is a lot less

crowded—a campground that hovers on the edge of the spectacular Black Canyon of the Gunnison River. From the northern edge of the campground it's only about a five-minute walk to the first canyon overlook along a Rim Rock Trail that runs half a mile (1.6 km) to Tomichi Point and its view right down to the Gunnison River. South Rim Road links the campground with other stupendous vistas. Black Canyon offers two other overnight spots. North Rim Campground is accessed via an unpaved road from Crawford. East Portal Campground in neighboring Curecanti National Recreation Area—the only developed riverside camping place—is around 5 miles (8 km) from the south entrance station. Open between May and October, East Portal is popular with river-running paddlers.

COLLECTIVE VAIL

🏕 6
4098 State Highway 131, Wolcott, CO 81655
Open: May to September ▪ Rates: From $299 ▪ Amenities: Restaurant, room service, signature bath

products, concierge, turndown service, housekeeping, device charging outlets, laptop-compatible safes, barbecue grills, blackout curtains, in-room massage, internet ▪ ADA sites: Partial

Glamping doesn't get more extravagant anywhere else in Colorado and maybe the whole Rockies than at Collective Vail. Located on 4 Eagle Ranch, the posh resort sports just six tents, which makes it easy to craft a bespoke experience that includes horseback riding, fly-fishing, wine tasting at a local vineyard, and farm-to-table treats at the ranch's Three Peaks Lodge. Tents come with a king, queen, or twin beds with down duvets, sturdy wooden floors covered in rugs, and outdoor seating areas to watch the evening alpenglow on the Rockies. The larger Summit Tents offer rain showers in an adjacent private bathroom tent, while the smaller Journey Tents share a bathhouse. Get to know your fellow glampers at the daily Sage Social Hour or savoring artisanal s'mores around the evening campfire. ▪

Black Canyon of the Gunnison National Park

First founded as a national monument in 1933, Black Canyon of the Gunnison was named a national park in 1999. The Tabaguache Ute tribe was long familiar with the canyon and its natural barriers (no evidence exists of humans living in the gorge, only on the rims) before the first explorers from Europe made their way to it in 1765.

The small park—the canyon runs a 53-mile (85.3 km) stretch—offers

the rare opportunity to see some of the steepest cliffs in North America, as well as the peregrine falcon diving for prey among them. Its biggest cliff is the Painted Wall, which stands at 2,250 feet (685.8 m) tall.

The Gunnison River runs through the canyon, dropping an average 43 feet per mile (13 m)—more than six times the descent of the Colorado River through the Grand Canyon. There is a 14-mile (22.5 km) stretch of white-water adventure to be had via expedition guides, featuring class II to IV rapids.

Connecticut

Northeast charm surrounds you at campgrounds from the Berkshires and farm stays to the Natchaug State Forest and Hawk's Nest Beach.

HIGHLIGHTS

Capital: Hartford

Total National Parks: 0

Total State Parks: 139 (Largest is Pachaug State Forest)

State Bird: American robin

State Flower: Mountain laurel

State Animal: Sperm whale

Wildlife Spotting: Black bears; bobcats; fishers; muskrats; white-tailed deer; bald eagles; eastern bluebirds; redheaded woodpeckers; Connecticut warblers; eastern painted turtles; garter snakes; redback salamanders; mudpuppies

HOUSATONIC MEADOWS STATE PARK

🏕 4, 🚐/⛰ 57 no hookup

90 U.S. Highway 7, Sharon, CT 06069

Open: May to September ▪ Rates: RV/tent sites $17/$27 (state resident/nonresident); cabins $50/$60 (resident/nonresident) ▪ Amenities: Dump station, showers, fire pits, picnic tables, potable water ▪ ADA sites: Yes

Whether you're into woods or water, Housatonic Meadows makes a great getaway in the Berkshires that ramble across the state's western edge. This superbly situated campground spreads along the west bank of the Housatonic River, giving campers quick and easy access to paddling, catch-and-release fly-fishing (for trout or bass), or simply dangling their toes in the chilly mountain water. Trails lead through the state park and adjoining Housatonic State Forest to the summit of Pine Knob (1,120 feet/341 m) and a stretch of the Appalachian Trail that wanders through the woods just west of the campground. Called the "covered bridge section" because of its historic wooden spans, the stretch of river upstream from the park features class II and III rapids. Landlubbers can visit the same

Cozy up with a good book by the fire in the Library Cottage at the Winvian Farm cottages and tree houses.

bridges by driving U.S. Highway 7 to West Cornwall.

CLUB GETAWAY

☎ 90

59 South Kent Road, Kent, CT 06757

Open: May to October ▪ Rates: From $429 per person (all inclusive) ▪ Amenities: Restaurant, air-conditioning, water sports, adventure sports, fitness classes, tennis courts, live music, dance parties, beach, internet ▪ ADA sites: Yes

True to its name, this eclectic camp in the Housatonic Valley of western Connecticut offers country getaways. But they're anything but rustic; theme-wise, they're all over the map, ranging from multiday family camps and party-hearty adults-only dates to special one-off events like a Gilmore Girls Fan Fest and Camp John Waters. Guests sleep in rustic cabins with private bathrooms, heating and air-conditioning, daily housekeeping, and memory foam beds. But the great outdoors beckons: a lake that's fully equipped for swimming, sailing, paddleboarding, and other aquatic pursuits, as well as throwback summer camp activities like archery, arts and crafts, dodgeball, volleyball, and kickball. Although meals include summer camp classics like pancakes and hot dogs, the dining room also offers seafood selections, carving stations, kosher, vegetarian, and gluten-free choices. Adult Getaways have an

updated Club Med vibe, while Family Camps are structured for both parents and kids to run amok in the surrounding woods (300 acres/121 ha).

WINVIAN FARM

☎ 18

155 Alain White Road, Morris, CT 06763

Open: Year-round ▪ Rates: From $699 ▪ Amenities: Restaurant, wine cellar, spa, swimming pool, organic gardens, Tesla charging station, internet, hot tubs, fireplaces, sound systems, bicycles ▪ ADA sites: Yes

Founded in the 1770s and still owned by the family that purchased the property in the 1940s, Winvian Farm brings plush accommodations, gourmet grub, and luxury body treatments to a secluded part of the Litchfield Hills in western Connecticut. Guests overnight in spacious bungalows, each decked out by a different interior designer. There's also a two-story tree house suspended 35 feet (10.6 m) above the forest floor. The Restaurant at

Tiny "cub" huts sleep a family of four at Bear Creek Campground, part of the Lake Compounce–Crocodile Cove amusement park complex.

Winvian Farm offers a Relais & Chateaux dining experience and a wine cellar with vintages from more than a dozen countries. Between meals there are health and beauty treatments at the farm spa, yoga and sauna sessions, biking and hiking on the 113-acre (45 ha) property, canoeing and kayaking, cooking classes, bocce and croquet, and even hot-air ballooning.

BEAR CREEK CAMPGROUND

🏠26, 🚐56 partial hookup, ⛺ 40, 5 tipis
Bear Creek Highway, Bristol, CT 06010
Open: April to October ▪ Rates: Cabins from $71, tipis from $52, RV sites from $32, tent sites from $32 ▪ Amenities: Dump station, showers, picnic tables, fire pits, camp store, laundry, playground, basketball/ volleyball courts, theme park shuttle, internet ▪ ADA sites: Partial

The nation's oldest theme park also boasts one of New England's top family-oriented camping options. Located on the outskirts of Hartford, Bear Creek is part of a Lake Compounce–Crocodile Cove amusement complex that traces its roots to 1846—more than a century before the first Disney park. Created in 2014, the campground offers one- and two-bedroom cabins and tiny "cub huts" that can sleep a family or four, as well as tipis, RV pads, and tent-only campsites. Bear Creek offers a modicum of recreational options, but most campers hop the shuttle to the two theme parks. Lake Compounce revolves around roller coasters and other thrill rides, while Crocodile Creek water park is all about getting wet.

CHARLIE BROWN CAMPGROUND

🏠2, 🚐/⛺ 128 partial hookup
98 Chaplin Road, Eastford, CT 06242
Open: April to October ▪ Rates: RV/ tent partial hookup from $56.75, cabins from $100 ▪ Amenities: Dump stations, showers, camp store, laundry, internet, game room, sports fields, horseshoes, play- ground, beach, fire rings, picnic tables, propane ▪ ADA sites: Partial

Set along the edge of Natchaug State Forest about halfway between Hartford and Providence, this coun- trified campground is ready-made for families with kids or groups of RV enthusiasts who want to hang out in proximity. Overnight spots include grassy sites along the Natchaug River and Ribbet Pond, rustic cabins away from the water, and a "safari field" with eight RV/ tent sites arrayed around large octagonal shelters with picnic tables and fire pit. The concept behind the octagons is providing groups with multiple tents or recreational vehi- cles a common place to share meals and activities right beside their campsites. A swimming beach, paddling, and fishing are the main attractions, but Charlie Brown also offers a game arcade and outdoor play areas. Good grief, there's even a big TV in the rec room for live sports and movie nights.

GREEN FALLS CAMPGROUND

🚐/⛺ 18 no hookup
Green Fall Pond Road, Voluntown, CT 06384
Open: April to October ▪ Rates: RV/ tent sites $17/$27 (state resident/ nonresident) ▪ Amenities: Restrooms, picnic tables, potable water, beach, boat ramp ▪ ADA sites: Partial

Connecticut's largest nature reserve, Pachaug State Forest, sprawls across 27,000 acres (110 sq km) of wetlands and woodland near the Rhode Island border. Green Falls Campground— which takes its name from an adja- cent lake and cascade—lies near its southern end, around 30 minutes from Norwich or Mystic. With no hookups or other amenities, the camping is pretty basic. But the location is ideal for water activities on Green Falls Pond or hiking the park's spiderweb of wilderness trails, some of them leading into nearby Rhode Island. Among the state forest's specialty routes are the Rhododendron Sanctuary Trail, a wooden boardwalk path that's best during the June and July bloom, and the Pachaug Enduro Route for motorbikes and ATVs. Hikers should keep an eye out for old stone fences, cellars, and mill ruins constructed when the area was heavily populated prior to the 20th century.

STRAWBERRY PARK CAMPGROUND

☎4, 🚐 262 full hookup, 🚙45 travel trailers

42 Pierce Road, Preston, CT 06365

Open: May to October ▪ Rates: RV full hookup from $47, RV partial hookup from $40, travel trailers from $95, cabins from $125 ▪ Amenities: Restaurant, dump stations, showers, camp store, laundry, swimming pools, hot tub, pickleball, sports fields, basketball/volleyball courts, horseshoes, bocce, disc golf, game room, massage, propane, firewood, internet, cable TV, golf cart rental, dog runs, amphitheater, picnic tables, fire pits ▪ ADA sites: Yes

Special events are the hallmark of this large, private camping resort in southeast Connecticut. Strawberry Park stages more than a dozen themed events each year, including the Bluegrass Festival that kicks off the summer season in May, the Blast from the Bayou Cajun Zydeco Festival in June, and haunted Halloween weekends in the fall. Between festivals, the resort offers plenty of ways to keep campers busy: three swimming pools, bocce ball and disc golf, afternoon and evening bingo, and even a summer vacation YouTube video contest with pretty good prizes. Through the summer, Strawberry Park offers more than a dozen group activities and competitions every day, from magic shows, Simon says, and toddler story time, to giant Jenga, water-gun bowling, and a hopscotch obstacle course.

ODETAH CAMPING RESORT

🏠14, 🚐 43 full hookup, 163 partial hookup, ⛰ 25, 🏠 3

Along with camping, Housatonic Meadow State Park offers fly-fishing and kayaking on its scenic river.

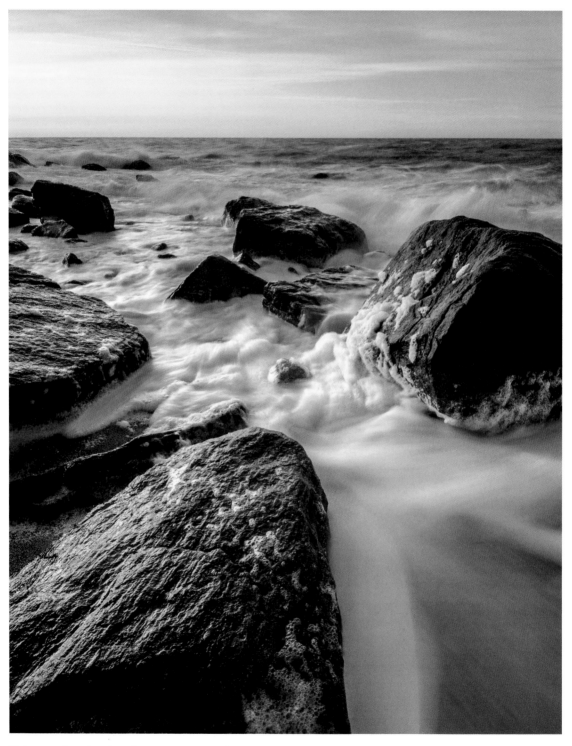

Wake up early and peek out from your tent to watch the sun rise over frothing water at Hammonasset Beach State Park.

38 Bozrah Street Extension #1300, Bozrah, CT 06334

Open: May to November ▪ Rates: RV hookup from $55.50, cabins from $83, yurts from $97, tent sites from $42 ▪ Amenities: Restaurant, ice cream stand, camp store, spa services, dump station, showers, laundry, fire rings, picnic tables, dog runs, miniature golf, beach, boat rental, tennis/basketball/volleyball courts, playgrounds, horseshoes, movies, dog runs, internet ▪ ADA sites: Partial

Founded in 1905, this full-service resort on the western edge of Norwich offers a variety of overnight options: cabins, yurts, and more than 300 RV and tent sites. However, it doesn't feel crowded thanks to a lakeside location surrounded by almost 500 acres (200 ha) of woods. From swimming, boating, and volleyball to evening bonfires and live music, campground life largely revolves around the lake. There's pretty good fishing for trout, bass, bluegill, and other species. During the busy summer season, Odetah screens nightly movies (with popcorn, drinks, and ice cream) in the social hall. Meanwhile, parents can pamper themselves with massage, facials, and mani-pedis at the Wellness in the Woods day spa.

HAWK'S NEST BEACH COTTAGES

🏠 45

West End Drive, Old Lyme, CT 06371

Open: May to October ▪ Rates: From $425 per week ▪ Amenities: Kitchens, screened-in porches, picnic tables, heating and ceiling fans, flat-screen TVs, internet, laundry, fireplaces, convenience store, tennis courts, horseshoes ▪ ADA sites: Partial

Offering good old-fashioned Connecticut Yankee vacations since 1895, Hawk's Nest is still owned and operated by the Garvin family that founded the seaside retreat all those years ago. The 45 one- and two-story clapboard cottages are just up from the beach, clustered around a Garvin Store (opened in 1910) with ice cream, doughnuts, hot coffee, and beach necessities. All the cottages boast screened-in porches with picnic tables and heating, and many also have ceiling fans and washer/dryers. Hawk's Nest offers daily activities for all ages during the summer, including a small-town Fourth of July celebration.

HAMMONASSET BEACH STATE PARK

🏠 8, 🚐 40 partial hookup, 383 no hookup, ⛺ 56

1288 Boston Post Road (Highway 1), Madison, CT 06443

Open: May to October ▪ Rates: RV/tent partial hookup $35/$45 (state resident/nonresident), RV/tent no hookup $20/$30 (resident/nonresident), cabins $70/$80 (resident/nonresident) ▪ Amenities: Dump station, showers, camp store, fire rings, picnic tables, potable water, beach, playground, volleyball, amphitheater, firewood, ice ▪ ADA sites: Yes

Connecticut's largest public beach also boasts one of its largest public campgrounds—more than 400 total sites plus eight cabins beside the sea. Located on a sandy, marshy peninsula along Long Island Sound between New Haven and New London, the park features 2 miles (3.2 km) of sandy shore for swimming and paddle sports, plus a boardwalk, snack bars, and picnic pavilions. Campers with a keen interest in bird watching or who just want to stretch their legs can hike short trails through the wetlands of adjacent Hammonasset Natural Area Preserve. The park's Meigs Point Nature Center offers a year-round slate of ranger/docent programs and guided outdoor activities. The center nurtures 10 themed gardens, including plots that reflect Native American and European colonial agricultural traditions. ▪

SOMETHING SPECIAL

Natchaug State Forest

Along with being a beautiful spot to camp, the Natchaug State Forest is a popular Connecticut destination for horseback riding, fishing, and riverfront picnics. Its name means "land between rivers," for its spot between the Bigelow and Still Rivers, which join at the Natchaug.

Established in 1917 as a state forest, this beloved spot also features historic artifacts, including a stone fireplace and chimney from the birth home of General Nathaniel Lyon, the first Union general killed in the Civil War.

Summer brings about a world of options for the forest, including equestrian trails (and even horse camping), fishing, hiking, mountain biking, and backpacking. In the winter, take advantage of Connecticut's snow with cross-country ski trails and snowmobiling tours throughout the forest.

To make a long weekend of a visit to Natchaug, tack on a stop at Mansfield Hollow State Park and Mashomoquet Brook State Park, just a short drive away.

Delaware

Lakefront tent camping, RV resorts in walking distance to the beach, and glamping around Rehoboth Bay are just a few of the options available in the Blue Hen State.

LUMS POND STATE PARK

🚐 / 🏕 64 full hookup, 🏕 5, ⛺ 2

1068 Howell School Road, Bear, DE 19701

Open: Year-round ▪ Rates: RV/tent full hookup and yurts from $40, tent only from $15 ▪ Amenities: Camp store, snack bar, dump station, showers, picnic tables, fire rings with grills, potable water, boat launch, boat rentals, fishing pier, playground, sports courts, ball fields, disc golf, dog park ▪ ADA sites: Yes

Delaware's largest freshwater lake is the focus of a park with a recently renovated waterfront campground and plenty of activities for campers both on land and in the water. Overnighters have a choice of full-hookup pads or comfy yurts beside a trail leading down to the waterfront. The park's Go Ape zip-lining circuit and Treetop Journey course offer an adrenaline-packed adventure via rope ladders, a Tarzan swing, and high-flying zip lines. Hikers, bikers, and horseback riders can explore the Little Jersey Trail, an 8.1-mile (13 km) loop through the Delmarva bays and trees that populate the park. Another multi-use trail runs alongside a portion of the historic Chesapeake & Delaware Canal. Lums Pond also offers an off-leash

Paddle your way through large groves that grow from the waters of Trap Pond.

dog walking area; equestrian center; radio-controlled model airplane field; and canoe, kayak, and pedal boat rental. Less than a half hour from Wilmington, Lums Pond offers the closest wilderness escape to Delaware's largest city.

BLACKBIRD STATE FOREST

🏕 8 no hookup

502 Blackbird Forest Road, Smyrna, DE 19977

Open: Year-round ▪ Rate: $25 ▪ Amenities: Restrooms, picnic tables, fire rings with grills, firewood, potable water, fishing pond, dumpster ▪ ADA sites: No

Blackbird lies about halfway between Wilmington and Dover. The reserve's Tybout Campground offers a handful of primitive sites and not much in the way of amenities. But the location is perfect for hiking or biking 40 miles (64 km) of trail through pine, oak, maple, poplar, and other trees. For campers who want to get way off the grid, the trail system connects five primitive campsites scattered across the woods. Blackbird Forest Education Center offers interactive exhibits on local nature, and the state forest is a stop on the Harriet Tubman Underground Railroad Historic Byway. Prior to the Civil War, free Blacks took refuge in Blackwood Forest, and fugitive slaves passed through during their journey to the North.

YOGI BEAR'S DELAWARE BEACHES—JELLYSTONE PARK CAMP RESORT

🏚 23, 🚐 / 🏕 229 full hookup, 🏕 3

8295 Brick Granary Road, Lincoln, DE 19960

Open: April to October ▪ Rates: RV/tent full hookup $49, tent only from $35, cabins from $109 ▪ Amenities: Camp store, snack bar, dump station, showers, laundry, picnic tables, fire rings, firewood, ice, swimming pool, playgrounds, sports courts, playing field, game room, movie theater, dog run, golf cart rental, cable TV, internet ▪ ADA sites: Yes

Hey, Boo Boo! There's a place in Delaware where campers can meet Yogi, Cindy, and other characters from the Yogi Bear cartoons. Part of a chain of Jellystone Park campgrounds across the United States and Canada, the Delaware version is also close to Atlantic beaches. Like the others, this one is jam-packed with amenities and offers a variety of overnight options from RV "Super Sites" with patios and barbecue grills to four different cabin styles. The resort's newest attraction is a splash pad with three waterslides and super-soaker bucket. Each weekend at Jellystone Park revolves around themes that range from Cindy Bear's Hawaiian Luau and 1970s Time Machine to Boo Boo's Abracadabra magic weekend and Yogi's Bear Bones Bash at Halloween.

TALL PINES CAMPGROUND RESORT

🏠 13, 🚐 / ⛺ 22 partial hookup, ⛺ 14

29551 Persimmon Road, Lewes, DE 19958

Open: Year-round ▪ Rates: RV/tent partial hookup from $40, tent only from $30, cabins from $70 ▪ Amenities: Camp store, snack bar, dump station, showers, laundry, picnic tables, fire rings with grills, potable water, firewood, ice, propane, swimming pool, splash pad, playground, volleyball, miniature golf, bike rental, internet ▪ ADA sites: Partial

This sprawling campground near the Delaware shore is primarily aimed at seasonal campers staying months or even the whole year. But it does offer a handful of RV pads, tent-only sites, and cabins for those who are just passing through. Outfitted with full kitchens, private bathrooms, flat-screen TVs, and air-conditioning, Deluxe Suite Cabins can easily sleep a family of six. From miniature golf and pickup volleyball games to a swimming pool and splash pad, there's plenty to keep the kids occupied around the resort. Campers can rent bikes to tool around the resort or cruise down the Georgetown-Lewes Rail Trail, a route that leads to Lewes Beach and Cape Henlopen State Park.

CAPE HENLOPEN STATE PARK

🏠 12, 🚐 / ⛺ 120 partial hookup, ⛺ 43

15099 Cape Henlopen Drive, Lewes, DE 19958

Open: Year-round ▪ Rates: RV/tent partial hookup from $30, tent only from $20, cabins $70 ▪ Amenities: Camp store, snack bar, dump station, showers, laundry, picnic tables, fire rings with grills, playground, beach, boat rental, basketball courts, bike repair station, amphitheater ▪ ADA sites: Yes

Where Delaware Bay meets the Atlantic Ocean, Cape Henlopen offers a heady mix of history, nature, recreation, and nearby shopping and entertainment. The park landscape ranges from wild beaches and pristine coastal dunes to bald cypress swamp and loblolly pine forest that visitors can explore on foot or cycle via the park's free Borrow-A-Bike Program. Seaside Nature Center harbors a two-story touch tank and aquariums swarming with local sea creatures, plus a live osprey nest camera and various family-friendly activities. Henlopen's rich history ranges from 16th-century Spanish explorers and 17th-century Dutch settlers to military observation towers and coastal gun batteries left over from World War II.

Cape Henlopen's campground and cabins are tucked between the Great Dune and Pinelands area in the heart of the park. Hiking trails fan out through the dunes and woods, beaches on both sides of the cape, the nature center, and Fort Miles Historic Area. Civilization is also close at hand: the Tanger Outlet stores and the carnival-like atmosphere of the popular Rehoboth Beach boardwalk are a short drive from the campground. Another off-park option is hopping the Lewes Ferry across Delaware Bay for a day at the beach in Cape May, New Jersey.

BIG OAKS CAMPING

🏠 20, 🚐 / ⛺ 45 full hookup, 45 partial hookup, ⛺ 30, 5 mobile homes

Along with RV and traditional tent camping, Massey's Landing offers upscale safari tents that sleep six.

In addition to RV and tent camping, Cape Henlopen offers a bayfront fishing pier and access to ocean waves.

35567 Big Oaks Lane, Rehoboth Beach, DE 19971

Open: May to October ▪ Rates: RV/tent full hookup from $67, partial hookup from $57, tent only $41, cabins $100, mobile homes $200 ▪ Amenities: Camp store, dump station, showers, laundry, picnic tables, fire rings, firewood, ice, swimming pool, playground, game room, sports courts, shuttle service, cable TV, internet ▪ ADA sites: Partial

The best thing about bedding down at Big Oaks is the location: just off super-busy Highway One that leads into Rehoboth Beach with its boardwalk, breweries, outlet shops, and vintage Funland amusement park yet far enough away to render a little peace and quiet in a woodsy location. The resort's RV pads, tent sites, cabins,

and rentable Park Model mobile homes are spaced fairly close together, so don't expect much privacy. There's no lack of recreation and entertainment, from the mock pirate ship and swimming pool to live bluegrass bands, karaoke, Skee-Ball, cornhole tournaments, and movie nights. Bring a bike, and you can ride the Junction & Breakwater Trail along the old Penn Central Railroad right-of-way.

DELAWARE SEASHORE STATE PARK

🚐/🏕 227 full, 4 partial, and 82 no hookup, 🏕 33
39415 Inlet Road, Rehoboth Beach, DE 19971

Open: Year-round ▪ Rates: RV/tent full hookup from $32, RV/tent partial hookup from $30, no hookup from $25, tent only from $20 ▪ Amenities:

Restaurants, camp store, dump station, showers, laundry, picnic tables, fire pits with grills, potable water, beach, volleyball, fishing pier, fish cleaning station, boat rental, boat ramps ▪ ADA sites: Yes

It's all about water at a park that straddles a sandy isthmus between the open Atlantic and Rehoboth Bay. Campsites are split between two campgrounds on either side of Indian River Inlet—more than 300 total, from full hookups to tent only. Both overnight spots are convenient for swimming, surfing, and shore fishing along the ocean beaches, as well as crabbing, clamming, and paddling on the bay side. The park's full-service Indian River Marina offers sport fishing charters, a boat supply store, fuel dock, slip rentals, and waterfront bar and

At Delaware Seashore State Park, you're surrounded by water: Indian River Bay to one side, the Atlantic to the other.

restaurant. Farther up the coast, Indian River Life-Saving Station (built in 1876) brings the past to life through historical exhibits and living history programs featuring old-time sea rescue techniques.

HOLLY LAKE CAMPSITES
☎ 30, 🚐 / 🏕 420 full hookup, 200 no hookup

32087 Holly Lake Road, Millsboro, DE 19966

Open: Year-round ▪ Rates: RV/tent full hookup from $60, no hookup from $45, cabins from $93 ▪ Amenities: Camp store, snack bar, dump station, showers, laundry, picnic tables, fire rings, firewood, ice, swimming pool, splash pad, playground, sports courts, miniature golf, disc golf, dog run, internet ▪ ADA sites: Partial

One of the largest camping resorts on the eastern seaboard rambles through woods on the inland side of Rehoboth Bay. More than half the pads are full-hookup RV pads, but Holly Lake also boasts a good number of tent-only sites and rustic cabins equipped with bunk beds, microwaves, mini-fridges, air-conditioning, and outdoor areas with picnic tables, charcoal barbecue grills, and water spigots. Reaching the ocean requires a 20-minute drive to Rehoboth Beach or Cape Henlopen in the north or a 45-minute jaunt to Bethany Beach in the south.

MASSEY'S LANDING
☎ 50, 🚐 / 🏕 286 full hookup, 45 partial hookup, 🏕 2, 🏕 7, 3 rental RVs

20628 Long Beach Drive, Millsboro, DE 19966

Open: April to October ▪ Rates: RV/tent full hookup from $49, glamping tents/cabins from $149, tent only

$39, rental RVs from $149 ▪ Amenities: Restaurant, snack bar, camp store, showers, laundry, picnic tables, fire rings, grills, firewood, ice, propane, swimming pool, beach, playground, game arcade, sports courts, boat ramp, boat slips, fishing pier, golf cart rental, shuttle service, dog run, ATM, cable TV, internet ▪ ADA sites: Yes

Set around three lagoons and a cove on the west side of Rehoboth Bay, Massey's is one of the few Delaware resorts with a genuine glamping experience. The safari-style tents feature queen beds, a lounge area, a dresser to stow your clothes and other gear, and an outdoor area with rocking chairs, picnic table, and fire ring. All bedding and towels are included, and glampers get a golf cart to navigate the landing. If the tents are fully booked, Massey's also offers waterfront camping and cabins.

TRAP POND STATE PARK
☎ 8, 🚐 / 🏕 137 partial hookup, 🏕 12, 🏠 2

33587 Baldcypress Lane, Laurel, DE 19956

Open: Year-round ▪ Rates: RV/tent partial hookup from $22, tent only from $15, cabins from $50, yurts from $40 ▪ Amenities: Camp store, dump station, showers, laundry, picnic tables, fire rings with grills, playground, boat launch, boat rental, boat docks, fishing pier, disc golf, sports courts ▪ ADA sites: Yes

Delaware's oldest state park (opened in 1951) sometimes feels more like the Deep South than the mid-Atlantic. That's because it shelters the nation's northernmost grove of bald cypress trees, a permanently flooded forest that campers can discover by paddling the Terrapin Branch Water Trail or hiking the Cypress Point Trail. The campground sprawls beneath towering loblolly pines at the opposite end of the pond from the bald cypress forest. Those who book waterfront sites can slip their canoe or kayak into the water right beside their RV or tent. The around-the-pond Bob Trail (4.6 miles/7.4 km) skirts the edge of the campground, and there's a short connector to the Cypress Point route. ▪

SOMETHING SPECIAL

Rehoboth Beach

Many of Delaware's coastal campgrounds are in easy distance to the state's most visited beach: Rehoboth. Established on the oceanfront area near the Rehoboth Bay, Rehoboth (as well as connecting Dewey Beach and nearby Bethany Beach) began as religious encampment grounds with one-room wooden structures surrounding a center structure called "the tabernacle."

In 1937, the quaint coastal town officially changed its name to the

"City of Rehoboth Beach," and the rest was history. Now Rehoboth boasts a lively downtown area, which has been named one of America's best as both an LGBTQ-friendly and family-friendly destination.

Things not to miss on your visit to the boardwalk: the famous Thrasher's French Fries; the Ice Cream Store (with more than 70 flavors, including unique options like Booger, a green-colored cake batter blend, and Devil's Breath Carolina Reaper Pepper Ice Cream); and Dogfish Head Brewings & Eats, an outlet of the Delaware-original brewery.

Florida

The Sunshine State has plenty of ways to soak up sand and fun, from Disney's family-friendly spot near the park to chickee camping in the Everglades.

COLDWATER GARDENS
🏠 4, ⛰ 3, ⛺ 1, 🏕 6, 🏠 1
7009 Creek Stone Road, Milton, FL 32570
Open: Year-round ▪ Rates: Glamping tents from $75, the tiny house from $130, cottages from $150, tent sites from $30, camping platforms from $40, the tree house from $170 ▪ Amenities: Cottages, the tiny house, and the tree house have kitchens, bathrooms, climate control, outdoor seating areas; most glamping/camping sites have potable water, grills, and fire pits ▪ ADA sites: Yes

Besides a wooded wilderness location in the Florida Panhandle, the cool thing about Coldwater is seven different ways to overnight near Pensacola and its fabulous beaches. Among the choices are glamping tents, a tiny house, ecodesigned cottages, hillside and creek-side tent camping, an elevated stargazer camping platform, and a roomy tree house. The sites are arrayed around aquaponic, hydroponic, and soil-based gardens where vegetables, herbs, flowers, and shiitake mushrooms are raised. Big Coldwater Creek is ripe for canoeing, kayaking, tubing, and fishing, while Blackwater River State Forest and Park offer multiple hiking and biking trails.

Visitors are welcomed by Fort Jefferson on arrival to Garden Key Campground in Dry Tortugas National Park.

FANCY CAMPS AT TOPSAIL HILL PRESERVE STATE PARK
🏕 2
7525 West County Highway 30A, Santa Rosa Beach, FL 32459
Open: Year-round ▪ Rates: From $130 ▪ Amenities: Showers, fire rings, picnic tables ▪ ADA sites: Partial

Glamping beside the Gulf is the forte at Fancy Camps, a private outfitter inside Topsail Hill Preserve State Park near Panama City. Their roomy bell tents come equipped with queen beds, end tables with lamps, heating/cooling units, electronic charging stations, area rugs, and outdoor seating areas. Glampers can request a camp stove to rustle up their own meals, order hot and cold beverages at Kith + Kin coffee shop on the edge of the campground, or drive into Santa Rose Beach for local culinary favorites like Elmo's Grill and Stinky's Fish Camp. A blend of pine forest, coastal dunes, wetlands, and three miles of beach, Topsail Hill offers 15 miles of hiking trails, water sports on the Gulf of Mexico, ranger programs, wildlife viewing, and bike rental. For those who aren't glamping, the state park features plenty of RV/tent sites and cabins.

PELLICER CREEK CAMPGROUND
🚐 30 full hookup
10255 U.S. Highway 1, St. Augustine, FL 32086

Open: Year-round ▪ Rate: $50 ▪ Amenities: Fire rings, picnic tables, fishing pier, canoe/kayak launch, cable/satellite TV, internet ▪ ADA sites: Partial

Small but strategic, this relaxed RV resort lies along the Pellicer Creek Canoe Trail and less than a half-hour drive from St. Augustine's historical attractions, several Atlantic coast beaches, and Fort Matanzas National Monument. The full-hookup sites include Wi-Fi and cable TV. A boat ramp gives campers easy access to paddling a creek inhabited by bald eagles, great blue herons, gators, and other creatures.

JETTY PARK CAMPGROUND, PORT CANAVERAL
🏠 8, 🚐/⛰ 101 full hookup, 64 partial hookup, ⛰ 20
9035 Campground Circle, Cape Canaveral, FL 32920
Open: Year-round ▪ Rates: RV full hookup from $39, RV partial hookup from $34, tents from $27, cabins $120 ▪ Amenities: Dump station, showers, camp store, laundry,

MORE TO CONSIDER

• **Biscayne National Park:** Boat-in tent camping on remote Elliott Key and Boca Chita Key with views of high-rise Miami in the distance. *nps.gov/bisc/planyourvisit/camping .htm*

• **Bahia Honda State Park:** Beach-front RV and tent camping with numerous water sports in the Florida Keys. *floridastateparks.org /bahiahonda/*

• **Flamingo Campground:** RV and tent sites, and glamping safari tents, on Florida Bay in the heart of Ever-glades National Park. *flamingo everglades.com/camping/*

• **Fort Pickens Campground:** RV and tent camping on a barrier island in Gulf Islands National Seashore near Pensacola. *nps.gov/guis/plan yourvisit/fortpickens-campground .htm*

• **Rainbow Springs State Park:** RV and tent camping with swimming and paddling around a sapphire-colored lake near Ocala. *visitrainbow springs.com*

• **Trails Lake Campground:** Chickee huts, cabins, RV and tent sites on the edge of the Everglades and Big Cypress National Preserve. *evergladescamping.net/*

internet, shuffleboard, horseshoes, playground, grills, picnic tables, dog runs • ADA sites: Yes

Watch SpaceX Falcons and other rockets take off from the comfort of your campsite at Jetty Park in Port Canaveral. Situated just south of NASA's Kennedy Space Center and its legendary launch pads, Jetty Park

has been a favorite with outer space aficionados since Gemini, Apollo, and space shuttle days. The camp-ground is also handy for splashing or surfing in the nearby Atlantic, fishing off the park pier, or watching giant cruise ships and Trident sub-marines cruise the Port Canaveral Channel. Popular seafood restau-rants flank the campground, there's

a nearby bait-and-tackle shop, and just down the shore is the dock for Victory Casino Cruises and its half-day gaming voyages into the open Atlantic. Wildlife watchers should keep a sharp eye for dolphins, sea turtles, and manatees in the channel and behind the surf line.

LAKE LOUISA STATE PARK

🏠20, 🚐/🏕11 full hookup, 49 partial hookup, 🏕2, 🐎6

7305 U.S. Highway 27, Clermont, FL 34714

Open: Year-round ▪ Rates: Glamping from $120, RV/tent sites $24, cabins $120; equestrian $5 per person ▪ Amenities: Dump station, showers, picnic tables, potable water, grills, firewood ▪ ADA sites: Yes

Located on the western outskirts of Orlando, Lake Louisa likes to bill itself as a "natural theme park" where guests get their thrills through horseback riding, hiking, and kayak-ing rather than roller coasters or fly-ing elephant rides. Sprawling along the edge of the Green Swamp and its namesake lake, the park's camp-ground and trails are shaded by old-growth cypress and oak trees. Campers can sack out in two-person and four-person glamping tents, lakeside cabins, and RV/tent sites arrayed across an isthmus between two lakes. The park's Wanderlust Club includes a year's worth of unlimited complimentary kayak and bike rental, as well as discounts on guided kayak and horseback tours. The equestrian camping area fea-tures five paddocks, hitching posts, water supply, and ample pasture.

DISNEY'S FORT WILDERNESS RETREAT

🏠409, 🚐/🏕700 full hookup, 100 partial hookup

Luxe tree houses are just one of the ways to glamp or camp at Coldwater Gardens.

Fort Wilderness Resorts offers frontier-style camping with easy access to the "Happiest Place on Earth."

4510 North Fort Wilderness Trail, Lake Buena Vista, Florida 32830
Open: Year-round ▪ Rates: RV from $129, tent from $93, cabins from $368 ▪ Amenities: Child care, shuttles and water taxis, laundry and dry cleaning, ATMs, mail service, safe deposit boxes, internet, cable TV, picnic tables, grills, firewood, potable water, showers ▪ ADA sites: Yes

Walt Disney's enduring vision of replicating the American frontier for modern travelers is the inspiration behind Fort Wilderness, a Wild West–themed camping area amid all the other attractions at Walt Disney World near Orlando. Set beneath pine and cypress trees along the south shore of Bay Lake, the sprawling camp offers RV and tent sites, as well as deluxe log cabins. Hiking trails and golf cart routes link the campsites to the fort's many activities: swimming pools, horseback riding, archery, canoeing, arcade games, and the ever popular Chip 'N' Dale's Campfire Sing-a-Long. A frontier-flavored musical revue takes the stage each night at the camp's Pioneer Hall. Four dining options and an old-timey saloon round out the dining and entertainment options. Water taxis flit across the lake to Disney's Grand Floridian and Contemporary Resort where guests can hop a monorail to the Magic Kingdom and Epcot theme park.

PERIWINKLE PARK & CAMPGROUND

🚐 45 full hookup, 🚐/⛺ 35 partial hookup, ⛺ 10
1119 Periwinkle Way, Sanibel, FL 33957
Open: Year-round ▪ Rates: RV/tent $45-$62 ▪ Amenities: Dump station, showers, laundry, picnic tables, ice, propane, aviaries, golf cart rental ▪ ADA sites: Yes

Sanibel Island's talcum-powder-fine beaches are the main allure of Periwinkle, but this RV resort on Florida's sunny west coast doubles as a rescue center for exotic birds abandoned by their owners. Yes, that really is a scarlet macaw over yonder. The campsite adjoins and shares

From John Pennekamp Coral Reef State Park, explore the colorful world beneath the waves.

facilities with a snowbird mobile-home park. The closest beach is around a 10-minute walk, and nearby are several restaurants, bait-and-tackle shops, and souvenir outlets.

TEN THOUSAND ISLANDS WILDERNESS WATERWAY

🏕 13 ground, 15 beach, 17 chickee

Everglades National Park, FL

Open: Year-round ▪ Rate: $15 wilderness permit + $2 per person, per day camping fee ▪ Amenities: Some campsites have toilets and picnic tables; only beach sites allow campfires; others require gas camp stoves ▪ ADA sites: No

Meandering across 99 miles (159 km) between Everglades City and Flamingo, this long-distance canoe and kayak route delivers the ultimate Everglades National Park camping adventure. Along the way are primitive ground campsites and wooden chickee platforms. Protected from the open Gulf by mangroves and barrier islands, the Ten Thousand Islands route follows an interconnecting web of bays, rivers, and channels protected within the confines of the Marjorie Stoneman Douglas Wilderness. Paddlers need to bring everything they need (food, water, equipment, tent) for what's normally a week-long passage. They can make their way back to their starting point via the Outside Trail, a 75-mile (120 km) route with beach campsites that curls around the outside of Ten Thousand Islands.

JOHN PENNEKAMP CORAL REEF STATE PARK

🚐/🏕 39, 🚐 3

Mile Marker 102.5 Overseas Highway, Key Largo FL 33037

Open: Year-round ▪ Rate: $36 ▪ Amenities: Visitors center, showers, laundry, playground, café, boat ramp, water sports rental, dump station, grills, picnic tables ▪ ADA sites: Yes

One of the best places to scuba dive or snorkel on the North American continent, Pennekamp is located about an hour south of Miami on the Atlantic side of Key Largo. Curling around a wooded area behind the marina, the campground is a short walk from the park visitors center, aquarium, beaches, and water sports facilities. Pennekamp features daily glass-bottom boat, snorkel, and scuba tours, while the dive shop offers a full range of PADI scuba instruction, including a resort course for beginners. Short trails meander through the park's mangroves and tropical hammocks. In addition to all of the tropical fish on the reef, waters around the park also harbor dolphins, manatees, sea turtles, the rare American crocodile, and copious bird life.

GARDEN KEY CAMPGROUND

🏕 8

Garden Key, Dry Tortugas National Park, FL

Open: Year-round ▪ Rates: $15 ($7.50 seniors) ▪ Amenities: Composting toilets, grills, picnic tables, nonpotable water ▪ ADA sites: No

Daily floatplanes and ferries whisk campers from Key West to Garden Key in the Dry Tortugas and a sandy campsite with a definite desert island vibe. Tucked into the subtropical shrubbery next to historic Fort Jefferson (built before the Civil War), the waterfront campsites are first come, first served. Given an almost total lack of amenities, campers need to bring along everything they need on the plane or boat, including all food, water, tent, and water sports gear. Surrounded by pristine coral reefs, Garden Key offers plenty of scope for scuba diving, snorkeling, kayaking, and wildlife watching, while the massive fort (the largest brick masonry structure in the Western Hemisphere) offers U.S. military and prison history. ▪

SOMETHING SPECIAL

Everglades National Park

More than 1.5 million acres (607,028.5 ha) of wetlands make up Everglades National Park, the third largest park in the lower 48 states. If you like wildlife spotting, this is the spot for you: Hundreds of animals make their way through the vast expanse of coastal mangroves, sawgrass marshes, and pine flatwoods.

Plan your visit for December through April, when humidity and rain are lower and insect bites are easier to avoid. While camping is always an option with reservations at designated spots, there's also plenty to do on a day trip to the park, including kayaking and canoeing through the waterways, hiking, fishing, boating, bird watching, and biking. Yes, biking. Despite its vast expanses of water, Everglades offers great trails for cyclists, including the Shark Valley tram road, a 15-mile (24.1 km) paved scenic loop, the Snake Bight Trail that leads to a great boardwalk for bird watching, and the Rowdy Bend Bike Trail through a buttonwood grove and coastal prairie.

Georgia

Islands, beaches, and lakes, oh my! With plenty of waterfront camping destinations (and inland options too), Georgia's got a peachy option for every type of camper.

SEA CAMP CAMPGROUND

⛺ 18

Cumberland Island National Seashore, Cumberland Island, GA 31558
Open: Year-round ▪ Rate: $22 ▪ Amenities: Restrooms, cold showers, picnic tables, fire rings with grills, potable water, food storage containers ▪ ADA sites: Partial

Fall asleep to the sound of waves crashing on a wild Atlantic shore at this beachside campground at Cumberland Island National Seashore. It's a bit of a schlep to get there. Campers must hop a ferry from a dock beside the National Park Service Visitor Center in St. Marys, and then carry all their gear half a mile (0.8 km) across Cumberland Island to Sea Camp. Ah, but what bliss when you finally arrive: tree-shaded sites beside the sea; the beach just beyond your tent flap; and trails leading to the island's historic sites, wildlife-rich salt marshes, and moss-hung maritime forest. You can also stroll one of the longest undeveloped beaches along the Atlantic seaboard, 18 miles (29 km) of sand inhabited by prehistoric horseshoe crabs, loggerhead turtles, wild horses, and other creatures. If Sea Camp is full, there's a campground at Stafford Beach and three wilderness campgrounds, one overlooking

Beachfront Sea Camp offers ocean access, as well as nature trails through tree-lined paths.

a salt marsh and the other two tucked inside the oak-palmetto forest.

STEPHEN C. FOSTER STATE PARK

🚐 18, 🚐/⛺ 66 partial hookup

17515 State Highway 177, Fargo, GA 31631
Open: Year-round ▪ Rates: RV/tent from $35, cabins from $145 ▪ Amenities: Dump station, showers, picnic tables, fire rings, potable water, boat rental, boat ramp, fish cleaning station ▪ ADA sites: Yes

Situated on an island in the middle of the Okefenokee wetlands—the largest blackwater swamp in North America—this secluded state park and its campground exude a true wilderness feel. Foster offers RV/tent sites with power and water, as well as two-bedroom cottages inside the park and "off-campus" eco-lodge cottages on the outer edge of the swamp. Declared one of Georgia's seven natural wonders, the Okefenokee is inhabited by a vast array of animals from black bears, river otters, and bobcats to sandhill cranes, cottonmouths, and plenty of alligators. In addition to wildlife watching, campers can peruse a night sky nearly devoid of ambient light or dive into boating, fishing, biking, and geocaching. The swamp also harbors the headwaters of the Suwannee River, which composer Stephen Foster (the campground's

namesake) immortalized with his 1851 song "Old Folks at Home."

KOLOMOKI MOUNDS STATE PARK

🚐/⛺ 25 partial hookup

205 Indian Mounds Road, Blakely, GA 39823
Open: Year-round ▪ Rate: $30 ▪ Amenities: Dump station, showers, picnic tables, fire rings with grills, playground, miniature golf, boat ramp, amphitheater ▪ ADA sites: Yes

The sophisticated Native American culture that suffused the American South before European conquest and settlement is the main focus of Kolomoki. And along with a celebration of its rich cultural heritage and history, this southwest Georgia state park also offers plenty of outdoor fun. The eight ceremonial and burial mounds protected within the park's boundaries were constructed between A.D. 200 and 900 by the Swift Creek and Weeden Island peoples; the largest rises 56 feet (17 m). A museum beside the mounds illuminates the life and times of these ancient inhabitants. The campground is located deeper in the park, a loop that borders Lake Kolomoki.

Besides water activities, campers can stretch their legs on three short nature trails through the park's four ecosystems.

HISTORIC BANNING MILLS
🏚16, ⚲ 7

205 Horseshoe Dam Road, Whitesburg, GA 30185

Open: Year-round ▪ Rates: Tree houses from $209, cabins from $119 ▪ Amenities: Restaurants, spa treatment, adventure sports, swimming pool, miniature golf, billiards room, paddleboats ▪ ADA sites: No

Tree houses, cottages, and log cabins are three ways to spend the night on the grounds of a historic 1840s textile mill converted into a modern outdoor adventure resort. Reached via rope bridges with wooden slats, the tree houses are without doubt the most audacious way to sleep at Banning Mills. But don't think they're not comfy. The one- and two-story units come with a king

bed, private bathroom with shower, kitchenette, fireplace, and a covered back deck for contemplating the surrounding woods. Get ready to pump up your heart rate and adrenaline elsewhere on the property. Break your own record-setting speeds with the fun amenities on offer throughout the campground—according to the Guinness Book of Records, Banning Mills boasts the world's longest zip line and tallest artificial climbing wall. There are also horseback riding, birds of prey nature programs, and kayaking on the Chattahoochee River. There's even room service: Meals prepared at the lodge restaurant can be served at your tree house, cottage, or cabin.

CLOUDLAND CANYON STATE PARK
🏚16, 🚐/⛰ 72 partial hookup, ⛰ 30, 🏕 10, 🥾13

122 Cloudland Canyon Park Road, Rising Fawn, GA 30738

Open: Year-round ▪ Rates: RV/tent

partial hookup $36, tent only $20, backcountry $8, cabins $160, yurts $100 ▪ Amenities: Camp store, dump station, showers, laundry, picnic tables, fire rings with grills, disc golf, playgrounds, geocaching, bike rental, fishing pond, firewood, ice ▪ ADA sites: Yes

Tucked up in Georgia's rugged northwest corner, Lookout Mountain has seen more than its fair share of history: Civil War battles, Cherokee heritage, and 16th-century Spanish conquistadors have all left their mark on this area. But the massive, elongated mountain also has its wild side—and none more so than Cloudland Canyon, an 800- to 1,800-foot (250-550 m) gap filled with caverns, creeks, and waterfalls ripe for exploring. The park's RV pads, walk-in campground, yurt village, and cottages are located on a lofty peninsula flanked by steep sandstone cliffs, the various overnight spots linked by road and the West Rim Loop Trail. Experienced cavers and climbers can explore the canyon's most radical geological features, while ordinary mortals can trek the gorge via the Sitton's Gulch Trail and aptly named Can't Hardly Trail. Meanwhile, the Cloudland Connector Trail provides a challenging mountain biking route across the park.

LAKE WINFIELD SCOTT CAMPGROUND
🚐/⛰ 31 partial hookup no

439 Lake Winfield Scott Road, Suches, GA 30572

Open: Year-round ▪ Rates: From $18 ▪ Amenities: Showers, picnic tables, grills, lantern posts, potable water, boat ramp ▪ ADA sites: Yes

Set up your RV with a waterfront view at Margaritaville at Lake Islands.

Retreats, like this one aimed at connecting kids with nature, are held at Lake Winfield Scott Campground in Chattahoochee-Oconee.

One of the earliest (or latest if you're headed southbound) spots to camp along the Appalachian Trail, Lake Winfield Scott lies deep in the Chattahoochee National Forest of northern Georgia. Don't expect power, water, or any other hookups; this is classic dry camping. But there are showers and a lake that's especially refreshing after trekking 2,200 miles (3,500 km) from Maine. Campers craving a restaurant meal can choose biscuits, burgers, brisket, and more at Bootlegger's Grill in nearby Panther's Gap.

BLACK ROCK MOUNTAIN STATE PARK

🏚10, 🚐/🏕 44 partial hookup,
🏕12, 🧍4

3085 Black Rock Mountain Parkway, Mountain City, GA 30562
Open: Year-round ▪ Rates: RV/tent partial hookup $34, tent only $22, backcountry $20, cabins $160 ▪ Amenities: Camp store, showers, laundry, picnic tables, fire rings with grills, playground, internet, cable TV, firewood, ice ▪ ADA sites: Yes

Georgia's highest state park (3,640 feet/1,109 m above sea level) floats in the Blue Ridge Mountains near the state's triple frontier with North and South Carolina. The mountain takes its name from the underlying dark metamorphic rock, obscured by thick forest in most places but obvious behind the waterfalls that plunge from the peak's heights.

Reached via a sinuous mountain road that some longer RVs might find hard to navigate, the campground and cabins are found along ridgelines with stunning views across the rugged terrain. The wooden cottages are especially nice: two- and three-bedroom units with private bathrooms, kitchens, living areas, and back porches with rocking chairs and killer views of sunrise or sunset. Naturally, hiking is the main activity: six trails are inside the state park and dozens more in surrounding Chattahoochee National Forest.

MARGARITAVILLE AT LANIER ISLANDS

🏚3, 🚐130 full hookup

If glamping is more your style, there are companies that will set up luxe tents along the shores of Lake Lanier.

7650 Lanier Islands Parkway, Buford, GA 30518

Open: Year-round ▪ Rates: RV full hookup from $55, cabins from $189 ▪ Amenities: Restaurant, bar, camp store, showers, laundry ▪ ADA sites: Partial

Georgia's most extravagant camping experience is located less than an hour north of Atlanta on an island in big Lake Lanier. It may not be Key West or the Caribbean, but that doesn't mean it's not party time 24/7 at a resort that boasts a beachside tiki bar, booze cruises, live outdoor entertainment, and tropical-flavored Jimmy Buffett tunes. The full-hookup RV sites and cabins occupy a peninsula all their own, with a shuttle bus that whisks campers to the resort's Chill Zone bars and restaurants, Port of Indecision Marina for boat rentals, tee times on the Legacy on Lanier golf course, and the family-friendly Water Park at Lanier Islands. Open year-round, as the temperatures begin to cool, Margaritaville transforms from island oasis into a winter wonderland with snow tubing and a lakeside holiday light show.

GLAMPING AT CLARKS HILL LAKE
🏕 4

Wildwood Park, 3780 Dogwood Lane, Appling, GA 30802

Open: Year-round ▪ Rates: From $149 ▪ Amenities: Showers, playgrounds, beach, boat ramp, boat rentals, s'mores packages, lawn games, fire pits ▪ ADA sites: No

Founded by a husband and wife longing for a more intriguing way to introduce their kids (and other families) to the great outdoors, the Georgia Glamping Company offers several locations around the state, including a waterfront site on Clarks Hill Lake. Around a 30-minute drive from Augusta and its legendary golf club, the location is intimate, private, and remote enough to leave the world behind. The family-style safari and bell tents feature king or queen beds—plus bunk beds for the kids—as well as heating and air-conditioning, mini-fridges, coffee-makers, and electric outlets. Out front are porches, barbecue grills, picnic tables, hammocks, and string lights. A beach area expedites swimming, boating, and angling on a lake renowned for bass fishing. The glampground is located in Wildwood Park, a Columbia County green space that's also home to the International Disc Golf Center and its three championship courses.

RIVER'S END CAMPGROUND & RV PARK
🏠 8, 🚐 72 full hookup, 14 partial hookup, ⛺ 9

5 Fort Avenue, Tybee Island, GA 31328

Open: Year-round ▪ Rates: RV full hookup from $57, RV partial hookup from $47, tent only from $32, cabins from $75 ▪ Amenities: Dump station, showers, laundry, picnic tables, fire rings, swimming pool, fitness room, TV room, firewood, ice, propane, dog parks, cable TV, internet ▪ ADA sites: Partial

True to its name, this Tybee Island resort lies near the spot where the Savannah River finally flows into the ocean. While locals flock to River's End for a beach vacation, out-of-staters can also use the campground as a base for visiting nearby Fort Pulaski National Monument and Savannah (20 minutes by car). A variety of overnight options includes full and partial hookup RV pads, a handful of tent-only sites, and fully furnished cabins with kitchens and private bathrooms. Tybee Island Light Station & Museum—Georgia's oldest and tallest lighthouse—is just a 10-minute walk. It's also a short stroll to beaches flanking Lighthouse Point, as well as restaurants, shops, and adventure outfitters along Highway 80. ▪

SOMETHING SPECIAL

Kolomoki Mounds State Park

Occupied by Indigenous peoples from A.D. 350 to 750, what is now Kolomoki Mounds State Park is the oldest and largest Native American site in the southeastern United States. The centerpiece of the park is the great temple mound, which stands at 57 feet (17.4 m) above two small burial mounds and several ceremonial sites.

The original village of Kolomoki contained nine mounds. Houses for the villagers were built around the sites, containing both a summer and winter structure (the permanent population fluctuated between 225 and 525 people, depending on the time of year). Around 750, the Native Americans who lived and worshipped around Kolomoki stopped using it as a ceremonial center.

Today, the park honors Kolomoki's history and preserves 1,293 acres (523.3 ha), including eight of the original mounds, two lakes, 5 miles (8 km) of hiking trails, and numerous campsites.

Hawaii

A tropical paradise awaits at campgrounds across the Hawaiian Islands, including tent camping in view of volcanic action, glamping on an old sugarcane plantation, and camper van destinations in a misty cloud forest.

HAWAII VOLCANOES NATIONAL PARK

🏠 10, ⛺ 25 no hookup

Hawaii Volcanoes National Park, HI 96718

Open: Year-round ▪ Rates: Nāmakanipaio $15, Kulanaokuaiki $10, cabins $80 ▪ Amenities: Restrooms or vault toilets, picnic tables, grills, potable water ▪ ADA sites: Yes

With lava-spewing Kilauea on one side and towering Mauna Loa on the other, the national park's two drive-in campgrounds are in the middle of the volcanic action. Located right off Highway 11 near the park entrance and the sinuous road to the Mauna Loa trailhead, Nāmakanipaio Campground is the larger of the two. Shaded by eucalyptus and 'ōhi'a trees, it features basic tent-only sites with asphalt pads and adjoining lawn areas, as well as a handful of rustic cabins.

Kulanaokuaiki Campground is much farther into the park, with nine tent-only campsites on the edge of the Ka'ū Desert. There's no running water; cooking and campfires are verboten. But unlike its larger cousin, it offers quick and easy access to several hiking routes, including the Maunaiki Trail

The Big Island of Hawaii, home to Kilauea, offers a one-of-a-kind camping experience: volcanic action.

through the Ka'ū Desert and the vehicle-free Hilina Pali Road to the coast.

For those who didn't bring their own tent to the islands, Volcano House Lodge provides two-person tents (which they put up and take down) with air mattresses, hotel linens, cooler, lantern, and camp chairs. No matter where or how you camp at Hawaii Volcanoes—and no matter what time of year—campers should pack warm, waterproof clothing for the park's notoriously chilly, damp nights.

PUNALU'U BLACK SAND BEACH PARK

⛺ 22 no hookup

Ninole Loop Road, Pahala, HI 96777

Open: Year-round ▪ Rates: $5/$20 (state resident/nonresident) ▪ Amenities: Restroom, showers, picnic tables, beach, potable water, boat ramp ▪ ADA sites: Yes

It doesn't get more classic Hawaii than this waterfront campground near the Big Island's southern extreme. The overnight conditions are basic at best: a tent-only area with a restroom and outdoor showers on a patchy lawn beside the sea. But the location is iconic: a black-sand beach, coconut palms, volcano-stone tide pools, colorful tropical fish, a water

lily–filled lagoon, and the possibility that a green turtle might scamper onto the sand or a nene goose might wander past your tent. The surfing isn't awesome so leave your board behind, but the offshore waters are suitable for swimming, snorkeling, and paddling. Granted, Punalu'u is a long drive from Hilo or the Kona Coast. But there is nearby sustenance: a mom-and-pop grocery store in Pahala, as well as food trucks and the legendary Punalu'u Bake Shop in Naalehu. It's also close to the extraordinary green-sand beach at Papakōlea, near the place where Polynesian migrants first came ashore in the Hawaiian Islands more than 1,500 years ago.

HALEAKALA NATIONAL PARK

🏠 3, ⛺ 26 no hookup

30000 Haleakala Highway, Kula, HI 96790

Open: Year-round ▪ Rates: Tents $15, cabins $75 ▪ Amenities: Restrooms, picnic tables, fire pits with grill, potable water ▪ ADA sites: Yes

HIGHLIGHTS

Capital: Honolulu

Total National Parks: 2 (Hawaii Volcanoes and Haleakalā National Parks)

Total State Parks: 50 (Largest is Waimea Canyon State Park)

State Bird: Nene (Hawaiian goose)

State Flower: Yellow hibiscus

State Animal: Monk seal

Wildlife Spotting: The Hawaiian hoary bat is the only native land mammal; native birds include the pueo (Hawaiian owl); noio (a tern); nene; plus monk seals, hawksbill turtles, and lizard fish

Set up camp on Kalalau Beach along the Kalalau Trail, at the foot of Kauai's colorful Nā Pali Coast.

Maui's diverse national park offers three ways to camp: above the clouds, beside the ocean, or deep inside an extinct volcanic crater. Located near the park's Summit Entrance and the main road from lowland Maui, Hosmer Grove Campground hovers at 7,000 feet (2,134 m) above sea level. It often dips below freezing after dark, but overnights at Hosmer make it easy to catch the peak's legendary sunrise rather than driving two hours from the beach hotels. The forest provides plenty of shade, and Hosmer even flaunts its own short nature trail through the native scrubland and an "alien forest."

Kīpahulu Campground lies on the park's ocean side, reachable only by driving the vertiginous Hana Highway around Maui's east end or the scenic (and often barely paved) Piilani Highway along the island's south shore. Down at sea level, the weather is decidedly tropical. The ocean is a bit rough for swimming, but campers can take a dip in the nearby Pools at 'Ohe'o. The third way to camp Haleakala is backpacking into the huge, main crater from trailheads along the summit. Two primitive campsites with pit toilets are limited to 25 persons per night. The crater also holds three rustic cabins built in the 1930s.

CAMP OLOWALU

🏠 6, 🚐 varies, 🚙 35, ⛺ 21
800 Olowalu Village Road, Lahaina, HI 96761
Open: Year-round ▪ Rates: Glamping tents from $140, cabins $1,500 per night for all six, car and tent camping $24 per person ▪ Amenities: Bathhouse, picnic tables, barbecue grills, fire pits, beach, dishwashing station, device charging stations, internet ▪ ADA sites: Yes

This is glamping Hawaiian style on an old sugarcane plantation near Lahaina on Maui's south shore. Set on raised wooden platforms beneath coconut palms, the resort's double and family "tentalows" feature twin beds, plus all towels and bedding. They also offer a dressing area with sink and mirror beside a private outdoor shower, food and beverage cooler, lockable wooden chest for storing valuables, and Adirondack chairs on the front deck. On the lawn outside are shared picnic tables, barbecue grill, and dishwashing station. Originally established in

1955 as an Episcopal church retreat, Olowalu also offers vintage beachside A-frame group cabins and no-hookup car and tent camping with access to a shared bathhouse and other amenities. The resort also provides 2.5-hour guided kayak tours of the offshore reef.

WAI'ANAPANAPA STATE PARK

🏠 12, 🚐 / 🏕 6 no hookup

Honokalani Road, Waianapanapa, Hana, HI 96713

Open: Year-round ▪ Rates: Camper van/tent sites $20/$30 (state resident/nonresident), cabins $70/$100 ▪ Amenities: Restrooms, outdoor showers, picnic tables, fire rings, potable water ▪ ADA sites: Yes

Lava rocks and water are the main attractions of a campground perched at the far eastern end of Maui. The park accommodates tents and camper vans but not large RVs. A dozen modest cabins are also available. Campers have numerous ways to while away the day at Wai'anapanapa: swimming at the small black sand strand, watching the seabird colonies nesting in the volcanic cliffs, pondering the anchialine pools that give the park its Hawaiian name ("glistening freshwater"), or venturing into the huge volcanic tubes (caves) near the park entrance.

KŌKE'E STATE PARK

🏠 2, 🚐 / 🏕 9 no hookup, 🏠 2

3600 Kokee Road, Hanapepe, HI 96716

Open: Year-round ▪ Rates: Cabins $150-$190, barracks $30-$60, camper vans and tents $20/$30 (state resident/nonresident) ▪ Amenities: Snack shop, gift shop, restroom, showers, picnic tables,

potable water, grills at some sites ▪ ADA sites: Yes

"Hawaii mountain high" is the theme of the campground and cabins in the misty cloud forest of Kauai. But bring a raincoat and waterproof flysheet, because these highlands are among the rainiest spots on Earth. A local nonprofit, Hui o Laka, manages the historic Civilian Conservation Corps cabins and barracks, as well as the Kōke'e Museum & Shop—all of the structures arrayed around a grassy quad. The barracks include shared accommodation in large bunk rooms and semiprivate rooms with two single beds.

A little farther up the road, Kōke'e Campground sits at the edge of Kanaloahuluhulu Meadow, a grassy space surrounded by thick cloud forest vegetation. From the state park hub, roads and hiking routes lead to viewpoints overlooking the fabled Nā Pali Coast along

the island's north shore and to the edge of equally famous Waimea Canyon. The multicolored "Grand Canyon of the Pacific"—around 3,000 feet (914 m) deep in places—stretches more than 10 miles (16 km) across the top of Kauai. With an overnight camping permit from the Hawaiian Division of State Parks, backpackers can overnight at four primitive campsites in the canyon bottom.

KALALAU TRAIL CAMPING

🏕 no hookup (number varies)

Kuhio Highway, Hanalei, HI 96714

Open: Year-round ▪ Rates: $20/$30 (state resident/nonresident) ▪ Amenities: Toilets, beach ▪ ADA sites: No

This spectacular route along the Nā Pali Coast is on the bucket list of every serious hiker. It's not for the timid or the inexperienced. The roller-coaster trail (11 miles/18 km) traverses five jungle valleys and a

Follow trails from the base to the summit of the crater at Haleakala National Park in Maui.

Among other natural treasures—and campsites—Waianapanapa State Park offers a rocky black sand beach.

super-harrowing segment, Crawler's Ledge, that hangs 300 feet (91 m) above the sea. Tent camping is allowed at two spots along the way: Hanakoa Valley, about halfway along the trail, and Kalalau Beach, at the very end. The campsites are situated on tree-shaded terraces built by long-ago Hawaiians for taro farming, but there are no amenities other than composting toilets. Campers must carry all food, water, and equipment on their backs. A state park permit is required for all overnight stays.

PĀLĀ'AU STATE PARK

▰▲ no hookup (number varies)
Kalae Highway, Kualapuu, HI 96757
Open: Year-round ▪ Rates: $20/$30 (state resident/nonresident) ▪ Amenities: Restrooms, picnic tables, grills ▪ ADA sites: Yes

A grove of native ironwood trees shades a quiet campground on Molokai's north shore in a park that rambles across cliffs that hover more than 1,000 feet (304 m) above the island's historic leper colony. Sacred to native Hawaiians, Pālā'au is known for both its vertigo-inducing views and Ka Ule O Nanahoa, a large phallic-shaped rock believed to boost the fertility of those who leave offerings. Campers can hike or take a mule down a steep, switchback-laden trail leading to Kalaupapa National Historical Park and the remains of two seaside settlements where islanders with Hansen's disease (better known as leprosy) were banished well into the 1960s. The park is still home to many of those who were exiled there. More tent sites are available at Waikolu Campground in Molokai State Forest Reserve, around a half-hour drive from Pālā'au.

MALAEKAHANA BEACH CAMPGROUND

☎ 13, ⛺ / ▰▲ 74 no hookup, ⛺ 4
56-335 Kamehameha Highway, Kahuku, HI 96731
Open: Year-round ▪ Rates: Camper vans/tents $9.41 per person, *hale* huts $58.82, plantation cottages $117.65 ▪ Amenities: Camp store, snack bar, restrooms, outdoor showers, sports equipment rentals ▪ ADA sites: Yes

Hawaii's most populated island is well endowed with beach resorts, but the only place to camp is at Malaekahana Beach on the North Shore. The private campground offers tent and camper van sites along the shore, as well as rustic *hale* huts and plantation-style cottages that sleep four people. Surf and stand-up paddleboard (SUP) lessons are available at the campground activities center, which also rents surfboards, paddleboards, bodyboards, kayaks, and bikes. Some of the North Shore's top sights are nearby, including the Polynesian Culture Center, the Kahuku food truck village, and the Banzai Pipeline of surfing fame.

HULOPOE BEACH PARK

▰▲ no hookup (number varies)
Manele Road, Lanai City, HI 96763
Open: Year-round ▪ Rates: $80 (non-residents of Lanai) ▪ Amenities: Restrooms, picnic tables, grills, outdoor showers ▪ ADA sites: Partial

Perched on a gorgeous crescent-shaped beach, Lanai's only campground lies within walking distance of the Maui ferry pier and the posh Four Seasons resort. Tent-only sites are on a grassy, coconut palm–shaded area behind the beach. Stays are limited to three nights, and only Lanai residents can camp at Hulopoe Beach over national holiday weekends. Everything offshore is a marine life conservation reserve; swimming and snorkeling are allowed, but not kayaking, spearfishing, or other activities that might disturb the underwater flora and fauna. Manele General Store is roughly an eight-minute walk from the beach, although campers who don't have to ask the price can also dine at the Four Seasons. Jeep and car rentals expedite exploring the rest of the isle. ▪

SOMETHING SPECIAL

Hawaiian Culture

Nearly 1,500 years ago, canoes came ashore what we now know as Hawaii. The paddlers—and the islands' first-known residents—had rowed about 2,000 miles (3,218.6 km) from the Marquesas Islands. Five hundred years later, people from Tahiti (more than 2,500 miles/4,023.4 km from Hawaii) made the journey as well.

The two cultures blended to become what is a uniquely Hawaiian culture. Over time, traditions from both blended to bring about new customs, including many things the Hawaiian Islands are well known for: surfing, hula dancing, and exchanging flower garlands called leis.

Native Hawaiians are working hard to preserve their unique culture and heritage, and more than half the population still engages in cultural activities, including speaking the Hawaiian language, as well as spiritual and religious practices.

Idaho

Park your camper on lake- and riverfronts, try your hand at ranch life, or anchor yourself close to nearby national parks in the Gem State.

HUCKLEBERRY TENT & BREAKFAST

🏕 3

180 Thunderbolt Drive, Clark Fork, ID 83811

Open: Year-round ▪ Rates: From $99 ▪ Amenities: Breakfast, restroom, showers, fire ring, s'mores, potable water, camp kitchen, citronella torches and candles ▪ ADA sites: No

Idaho's woodsy panhandle region provides the remote and rugged venue for a glampground on a backwoods homestead near the spot where the Clark Fork of the Columbia River pours into Lake Pend Oreille. Perched on raised wooden platforms, the safari-style (and luxurious) canvas tents are outfitted with queen-size beds, cozy patchwork quilts, wood-burning stoves, area rugs, and furnished front porches. Glampers wake up to a homegrown, farm-style breakfast each morning and are free to prepare other meals in the shared camp kitchen. The solar-heated shower is fed by natural spring water. In addition to serving breakfast, the husband-and-wife owners are happy to share their knowledge of local hiking, biking, and fishing, as well as homesteading, farming, and off-the-grid life.

There's nothing like camping with horses, which you can do at the Silver Spur Ranch.

CAMP COEUR D'ALENE

🏠 19, 🚐 57 full and partial hookup, 🏕 19

10588 East Wolf Lodge Bay Road, Coeur d'Alene, ID 83814

Open: May to October ▪ Rates: RVs from $40, tents $30, cabins from $99 ▪ Amenities: Dump station, camp kitchen, showers, swimming pool, playground, dog run, water sports, laundry, firewood, internet, horseshoes, picnic tables, fire rings ▪ ADA sites: Yes

This full-service RV and camping resort shares its gorgeous Idaho Panhandle location with the huge glacial lake and the outdoorsy city that bear the same name. Clustered around the pool and bathhouse, most of the campsites offer plenty of shade. There's a trailhead for a walk in the woods, and the camp boasts its own small lake for swimming, pedal boats, and canoes. Best of all, the resort is within easy reach of Coeur d'Alene, a town with dining, shopping, and outdoor adventures. Activities range from boating and fishing on the vast lake to hiking or biking the 73-mile (117 km) Trail of the Coeur d'Alenes, watching for bald eagles on the North Region Idaho Birding Trail, or taking the kids to Silverwood Theme Park with its roller coasters and other thrill rides.

MARYJANESFARM

🏠 2, 🚐 4, 🏕 5

1000 Wild Iris Lane, Moscow, ID 83843

Open: May to September ▪ Rates:

HIGHLIGHTS

Capital: Boise

Total National Parks: 1 (Yellowstone National Park)

Total State Parks: 27 (Largest is City of Rocks National Reserve)

State Bird: Mountain bluebird

State Flower: Syringa

State Tree: Western white pine

Wildlife Spotting: Black bears; moose; bighorn sheep; woodland caribou; Idaho pocket gophers; Idaho ground squirrels; yellow-billed cuckoos; great-horned owls; downy woodpeckers; Lincoln's sparrows; bobolinks; Idaho giant salamanders; tailed frogs; painted turtles; northern alligator lizards

From $239 (two-night minimum stay) ▪ Amenities: Breakfast, kitchen area, bathtubs, shower house, firewood ▪ ADA sites: No

Most folks know MaryJanesFarm as a food-and-lifestyle publisher and a purveyor of organic foods and farmhouse decor. But MaryJane Butters also offers overnight digs on the Idaho farm where her ever expanding empire started in the 1990s. Butters—who is credited with coining the term *glamping* around 20 years ago—calls her B&B a "bed and bath" because of the signature outdoor claw-foot tubs. The tents are outfitted with full-size beds, rustic furnishings, and kerosene lamps for guests who prefer to bathe at night beneath a sky full of stars. Gourmet organic breakfast is provided by the host; guests can rustle up lunch and dinner in an outdoor kitchen area with hotplate, sink, and campfire. Premade campfire foil meals, box lunches, and MaryJane's line of organic dehydrated meals are also available. Guests are welcome to lend a hand with farm chores or hike or bike the miles of trails around a spread located about a 20-minute drive from downtown Moscow and the University of Idaho campus.

RIVER DANCE LODGE
🏠8, ⛺3

7743 U.S. Highway 12, Kooskia, ID 83539

Open: Early spring to late fall ▪ Rates: Cabins from $170, glamping tents from $110, tents $10 per person ▪ Amenities: Restaurant, shower house, kitchens, fireplaces, barbecues, firewood, charcoal ▪ ADA sites: No

This outdoor adventure resort overlooks the Middle Fork of the Clearwater River between the Nez Perce Nation and the rugged Bitterroot range near the bottom of the Idaho Panhandle. Overnight digs include modern log cabins, glamping tents, and good old-fashioned tent camping

in the Idaho wilderness. Cabins are outfitted with a small fridge, microwave, and charcoal barbecue for those who want to cook their own meals. River Dance also offers an all-inclusive plan that includes all of your daily grub. The cabins sport queen beds, private bathrooms, gas fireplaces, and outdoor hot tubs. Glamping tents feature antique claw-foot tubs in a private bathing area behind the comfy canvas tents, while tent campers share a restroom and shower house. But don't expect to spend much time indoors (other than sleeping). River Dance offers a full range of outdoor activities: white-water rafting and kayaking, mountain biking, fly-fishing, hiking, and tracing the Lewis & Clark Trail through the Clearwater River Valley.

PONDEROSA STATE PARK
🏠10, 🚐/⛺ 44 full hookup, 111 partial hookup

1920 Davis Avenue, McCall, ID 83638

River Dance Lodge is meant for outdoor adventurers, with easy access to river kayaking and rafting.

Open: Year-round ▪ Rates: RV/tent sites $37, cabins from $115 ▪ Amenities: Dump station, showers, picnic tables, grills, fire rings, potable water, boat ramp, firewood, camp store, volleyball, horseshoes, internet ▪ ADA sites: Partial

Some of the tallest old-growth trees in the Pacific Northwest—150-foot (45 m) ponderosa pines that were saplings when the Pilgrims landed on Plymouth Rock—lend their name to this eclectic Idaho state park. RV and tent sites are scattered across four campsites on a wooded peninsula that cleaves Payette Lake, while the park's spiffy cabins cluster near the visitors center. Hiking and biking trails meander through the thick woods to sandy beaches, boat ramps, the lofty Osprey Cliff Overlook, and landlocked Lily Marsh. During the warmer months, rangers and naturalists offer guided walks and evening campfire programs. When the weather turns cold, the park maintains cross-country ski and snowshoe trails through the snowy woods. Flanked by the snowcapped peaks of Payette National Forest, the state park lies within easy walking and biking distance of McCall, an old logging town now renowned for its Winter Carnival, annual Sled Dog Challenge, and Central Idaho Historical Museum.

GLACIER VIEW CAMPGROUND
🚐/⛺ 64 no hookup

Redfish Lake Road, Stanley, ID 83278

Open: May to September ▪ Rates: $20-$40 ▪ Amenities: Dump station, restrooms, fire pit with grill, picnic tables, playgrounds, boat ramp,

There's a new way to glamp at Moose Creek Ranch: in a retro Airstream at the base of the Tetons.

potable water, firewood ▪ ADA sites: Partial

The largest of 11 campgrounds at Redfish Lake Recreation Area, Glacier View offers basic RV and tent sites and plenty of northern Rocky Mountain atmosphere. Sites are well spaced for privacy and generally boast lots of shade. Loop A features sites right on Redfish Lake Creek, and the entire campground is within short walking distance to boating, swimming, fishing, and sandy beaches along the north shore. Nearby Redfish Lake Lodge offers a restaurant, boat rentals, and rustic cabins. As part of Sawtooth

National Forest, the campground provides an ideal location for exploring the largely unfettered wilderness of central Idaho.

EAGLE COVE CAMPGROUND

🏠 2, 🚐/⛺ 47 partial hookup, 🏇 19

27608 Bruneau Sand Dunes Road, Bruneau, ID 83604
Open: Year-round ▪ Rates: RV/tent hookup from $24, cabins from $55 ▪ Amenities: Dump station, restrooms, fire rings with grills, picnic tables, camp store, boat ramp, equestrian campsites, internet ▪ ADA sites: Partial

It may look more like the Sahara than the typical vision of Idaho, but Bruneau Dunes State Park typifies the state's super-arid southwest corner. Highlighting the park's oasis-like ambience are small deep-blue lakes fronting sandy hills that rise as high as 470 feet (140 m). The RV/tent sites and rustic cabins at Eagle Cove are arrayed along two loops near the smaller of the two lakes. From the campground, a short spur connected with a 5.6-mile (7.4 km) hiking trail ascends to the highest dune and snakes its way through the lakes and wetlands. The park visitors center offers a Junior Ranger program, rental sandboards, and loaner

Find Redfish Lake, forest, and glacier views from the comfort of your tent in Sawtooth National Forest.

fishing equipment. Bruneau Observatory features weekend night sky programs from March to October. Off-road vehicles are verboten on the dunes. However, horses are welcome on two trails. The equestrian camping area features corrals and water spigots.

LAVA FLOW CAMPGROUND

🚐/🏕 42 no hookup

1266 Craters Loop Road, Arco, ID 83213

Open: May to November ▪ Rates: $8-$15 ($4-$7.50 seniors); free November and April ▪ Amenities: Restrooms, grills, picnic tables, potable water; no hookups, showers, or dump station ▪ ADA sites: Partial

True to its name, Lava Flow lies amid the twisted basaltic scenery of Craters of the Moon National Monument in eastern Idaho. Sagebrush, wildflowers, and stunted, gnarly trees complement a rock-strewn terrain formed by volcanic events over the past 15,000 years. Although it bears little resemblance to actual lunar landscapes, the park was used to train Apollo astronauts before their moon missions. The campground is close to the visitors center and a scenic drive that meanders through the hardened magma fields. Night sky and other ranger programs take the stage at Lava Flow's amphitheater during the warmer months.

SILVER SPUR RANCH

🏠 8, 🏕 7-8

2385 Medicine Lodge Road, Dubois, ID 83423

Open: May to September ▪ Rate: $3,000 per person, per week (all inclusive) ▪ Amenities: Horse and tack, tents or cabins, professional

guide, all meals and snacks ▪ ADA sites: No

This eastern Idaho spread offers a unique camping adventure: a five-day horse drive across a 100,000-acre (40,000 ha) ranch while sleeping in remote tented camps each night. Between dawn and dusk, guests saddle up their own mounts and help full-time cowpokes herd 40 or more horses up to 20 miles (32 km) per day. Campfire drinks and dinner—and either hot springs or a refreshingly cold creek—await at the end of each ride. The horse drive and its three nights on the open range in tents is book-ended by stays at rustic cabins beside the Silver Spur ranch house.

MOOSE CREEK RANCH

🏠10, 🚐 7, 🏕 6, 🚐1

2733 East 10800 South, Victor, ID 83455

Open: Year-round ▪ Rates: Cabins from $265, glamping tents from $80, travel trailer from $289, RV full hookup from $145 ▪ Amenities: Bathhouse, fire pits, picnic tables, laundry, recreation room, ice, horseshoes, volleyball, bocce, horse corral, internet ▪ ADA sites: Yes

A 40-minute drive west of the beloved Jackson Hole ski and recreation area, Moose Creek is perfectly poised for day trips into Grand Teton and Yellowstone National Parks. But even with America's most iconic national parks right next door, the wide-ranging resort offers plenty of excuses to linger around the ranch: hiking and biking trails in the surrounding Caribou–Targhee National Forest, fly-fishing on Moose Creek, and white-water rafting the Snake River in summer, with fresh powder at Grand Targhee ski resort in winter. The ranch offers a wide variety of sleeping options, including cabins, glamping tents, full-hookup RV sites, and a single Airstream trailer. Moose Creek cabins come with private bathrooms, a refrigerator, fireplace, and a cozy front porch; most have cooking facilities. Fashioned from wood and canvas, the creekside glamping tents feature queen beds and wood-burning stoves. The ranch also provides a daily linen service and a "campfire valet" who supplies your camping needs including wood and s'mores fixings. ▪

SOMETHING SPECIAL

Craters of the Moon National Monument and Preserve

Located in central Idaho, Craters of the Moon National Monument and Preserve may seem as if you've landed on the surface of the moon. In fact, you're walking on a massive, dried lava flow that formed more than a thousand years ago.

Eight eruptions, spewing about every 2,000 years, created the lava field that exists today—and it's not over. The volcano is dormant, not dead, and it's about time for another eruption. Don't panic: That eruption is likely to happen sometime within the next few centuries if the 2,000-year intervals are being maintained.

Camping is available at Craters of the Moon, as well as a fantastic interactive program for kids looking to become junior rangers at the park.

Illinois

Fishing, hiking, cooking demonstrations, wine tasting, kayaking, horseback riding, and cross-country skiing are just some of the numerous activities offered at campgrounds throughout Illinois.

MISSISSIPPI PALISADES STATE PARK

🚐/🏔 110 partial hookup, 131 no hookup

16327A State Route 84, Savanna, IL 61074

Open: Year-round ▪ Rates: RV/tent partial hookup $20, no hookup $10 ▪ Amenities: Dump stations, showers, laundry, picnic tables, fire rings, potable water, boat ramp ▪ ADA sites: Yes

Cast for catfish, watch American bald eagles dance in the updrafts, clamber up the Twin Sisters rock climbing route, or count river traffic on the Big Muddy at this popular western Illinois park. The towering limestone cliffs also offer a great view of Iowa on the other side of the wide water. Surrounded by deciduous forest, the Y-shaped campground is also a brilliant place to capture fall color with your eyes or camera. It's open in winter for cross-country skiing, snowshoeing, sledding, and even ice fishing when the river shallows freeze over. A warren of hiking trails along the campground's northern edge enables exploration of the riverside wilderness.

Don't miss a visit to the Garden of the Gods Wilderness Area within Shawnee National Forest.

CAMP SULLIVAN

☎4, 🚐/🏔 10 partial hookup, 🏔15

14630 Oak Park Avenue, Oak Forest, IL 60452

Open: Year-round ▪ Rates: RV/tent partial hookup from $27, tent only from $21, cabins from $42 ▪ Amenities: Camp store, showers, picnic tables, fire rings with grills, picnic shelters, climbing wall ▪ ADA sites: Partial

Camping in the Windy City? For sure. But only at Camp Sullivan in the leafy Cook County Forest Reserve. Located just a half-hour drive from the Loop and all of those skyscrapers, the camp, with its trademark red barn, dates to the early 20th century, when Chicago philanthropist Helen Sullivan transformed an old farm into a kids' summer camp. It wasn't opened to general public campers until 1915 as part of the county's effort to provide more outdoor opportunities in the metro area.

Sullivan offers RV and tent camping, as well as small cabins with bunk beds that can sleep as many as eight friends or family members. The cabins aren't heated but are equipped with ceiling fans for muggy Chicago summers. Out front are a seating area, picnic tables, and fire ring. Inside the red barn is a 25-foot (7.6 m) climbing wall, and the camp is surrounded by the Tinley Creek Trail System, which lures hikers and bikers in summer and cross-country skiers in winter. There are also a couple of fishing ponds. Not your typical Chicago.

STARVED ROCK STATE PARK

☎22, 🚐/🏔 129 partial hookup

State Highway 178, Oglesby, IL 61348

Open: Year-round ▪ Rates: RV/tent partial hookup $25, cabins from $120 ▪ Amenities: Restaurants, bar, gift shop, dump station, showers, picnic tables, fire pits with grills, potable water, firewood, playground, boat ramp, boat rentals, ATM ▪ ADA sites: Yes

The park derives its odd name from an 18th-century Native American siege in which a band of Illinois starved in their clifftop retreat rather than surrender to the surrounding enemy warriors. Starved Rock is now one of the state's most diverse recreation areas, popular for aquatic activities along a 7-mile (11.2 km) stretch of the Illinois River that

Lincoln's New Salem Historic Site re-creates the village where the president lived from 1831 to 1837.

borders the park, as well as hiking 18 sandstone canyons carved over the millennia by erosion and glaciation. The large campground and its power-enabled pads lie south of Highway 71 along the park's southern boundary.

Starved Rock Lodge and its iconic log cabins are situated in the heart of the park, near its namesake rock and other lofty viewpoints like Lover's Leap and Eagle Cliff. Erected in the 1930s by the Civilian Conservation Corps, the cabins are both cute and cozy. The lodge offers a variety of activities to campers, cabin guests, and the general public, including historic trolley tours, guided hikes, and river cruises. Massage and aromatherapy are offered in a log cabin spa, and the lodge offers live music and musical tribute shows.

CAMP ARAMONI
🏕 11
809 North 2199th Road, Tonica, IL 61370
Open: Year-round ▪ Rates: From

$450 (two-night minimum stay) ▪ Amenities: Restaurant, camp store, private bathrooms, mini-fridges, USB charging stations, luxury bath products, towels and bedding, bikes, lawn games, hiking trails, concierge ▪ ADA sites: Call ahead

Set amid the remains of an old brickworks 90 minutes south of Chicago, Aramoni was unveiled in summer 2021 as a romantic wedding venue and the latest, greatest glamping spot in the Midwest. Manufactured by a leading South Africa safari supplier, the tents are named after Illinois wildflowers and equipped with king or queen beds, bathrooms, luxury linens, private decks, and outdoor campfire area. The main 1870s brickyard building has been preserved and renovated into the Barn, home to the Aramoni restaurant and general store, as well as a venue for wine tasting, cooking demonstrations, and other glamping events. With Matthiessen and Starved Rock state

parks nearby, the camp also offers prime outlets for outdoor adventure and exploration.

LINCOLN'S NEW SALEM
🚐/🏕 100 partial hookup, 100 no hookup
15588 History Lane, Petersburg, IL 62675
Open: April to October ▪ Rates: RV/tent partial hookup $20, no hookup $10 ▪ Amenities: Snack bar, showers, picnic tables, fire rings, potable water, playground, horseshoes ▪ ADA sites: Partial

Overnight in the village where young Abe Lincoln famously split rails, served as postmaster, managed a general store, studied law, fell in love, and ran for office for the first time. The future president never owned his own home in New Salem, bunking down instead in the store or local tavern. Visitors today can choose from RV or tent sites beneath big shade trees with plenty of lawn all around. The campground sits near the visitors center and Kelso Hollow Amphitheater, where historical plays about Honest Abe, Broadway plays, Shakespeare productions, and music concerts are staged during the summer. A faithful reconstruction of the New Salem where Lincoln lived, the village contains 23 log buildings with 19th-century furnishings, staffed by historical interpreters clad in period dress who spin tales about the local boy who made good.

CABINS & COTTAGES AT SHALE LAKE
🏚 10
1499 Washington Avenue, Staunton, IL 62088
Open: Year-round ▪ Rates: From $99 ▪ Amenities: Restaurant, winery,

kitchens, private bathrooms, heating and air-conditioning ▪ ADA sites: Yes

One doesn't immediately think of Illinois when talking about wine. Yet that state's department of agriculture recognizes more than 170 winemakers in the Land of Lincoln. There's even what could be described as wine country in south-central Illinois not far from St. Louis, with a budding wine tourism vibe that includes overnight stays at places like the Winery at Shale Lake. Along with its reds, whites, and rosés, the vintner has created some mighty fine hilltop cottages that overlook the vineyards and lakeside cabins, all of them with screened-in decks or front porches for considering the scenery and sipping the local vintage.

ELDON HAZLET STATE RECREATION AREA

☎ 20, 🚐/🏕 328 partial hookup, 🏕 36

20100 Hazlet Park Road, Carlyle, IL 62231

Open: Year-round ▪ Rates: RV/tent partial hookup $20, tent only $8, cabins from $100 ▪ Amenities: Camp store, dump station, showers, laundry, picnic tables, fire rings, playground, potable water, firewood, amphitheater, marina, boat ramps, boat rental, swimming pool, beach, basketball court, archery range ▪ ADA sites: Yes

When the U.S. Army Corps of Engineers created Carlyle Lake in the 1960s, they included marinas, waterfront resorts, swimming beaches, hiking trails, and six developed campgrounds. With more than 300 RV and tent sites, Eldon Hazlet is the largest and best equipped of the six campgrounds. Set on a peninsula that juts into the lake's western shore, the camp offers plenty of ways to get into the water, including three boat ramps, a swimming beach, fishing piers, and sailing club with rental craft. The rec area also harbors the Hazlet Lakefront Cottages, outfitted with kitchens, living areas, private bathrooms, and covered porches overlooking the water.

Camping at Starved Rock State Park includes trail access to canyon waterfalls throughout the wilderness area.

Historic Giant City Lodge was built nearly a century ago and still offers comfort to campers looking to escape.

GIANT CITY LODGE
🏠 34

460 Giant City Lodge Road, Makanda, IL 62958
Open: Year-round ▪ Rates: From $85 ▪ Amenities: Restaurant, bar, gift shop, swimming pool, picnic areas, playground, satellite TV, internet ▪ ADA sites: Yes

Listed on the National Register of Historic Places, the lodge and vintage cabins at Giant City State Park were erected nearly a century ago. Since then, a couple dozen modern Bluff and Prairie cabins have been added to this woodsy resort in southern Illinois. Even the oldest cabins come with private bathrooms, heating and air-conditioning, and a TV for those who need something beyond the great outdoors for entertainment. Cabin dwellers also have full access to lodge amenities like the Bald Knob dining room (try the fried chicken), swimming pool, wraparound balcony, observation tower, and great room with its stone fireplace. Trails cut through the natural sandstone passages that lend the lodge its name.

TIMBER RIDGE OUTPOST & CABINS
🏠4, 🎣2, 🏡3

546 North Iron Furnace Road, Elizabethtown, IL 62931
Open: Year-round ▪ Rates: Cabins from $129, tree houses from $175, houses from $149 ▪ Amenities: Restaurant, gift shop, kitchens, private bathrooms, fire pits, grills, boat rental, fishing pond, spa treatments ▪ ADA sites: No

These upscale cabins and tree houses are secluded in the dense hickory-oak forest of Shawnee National Forest. Two of the cabins date from the 1850s when the area was pioneered by Euro American settlers, and the others are modern log cabins with all the amenities (queen beds, kitchens, private bathrooms, heating and air-conditioning). One of the tree houses hangs in the limbs of a mighty, 200-year-old white oak, while the other rises between adjacent red and white oaks. They also feature kitchen areas and private baths, as well as a ground-level campfire area with chairs and barbecue grill. The three houses feature two to four bedrooms plus kitchen and multiple bathrooms. Timber Ridge offers common wilderness pursuits like fishing, kayaking, and horseback riding, as well as offbeat endeavors like outdoor deep tissue massage and guided wild mushroom foraging. The bizarre rock formations of nearby Garden of the Gods Wilderness are featured on the Illinois state quarter.

FORT MASSAC STATE PARK
🚐/🏕 50 partial hookup

1308 East 5th Street, Metropolis, IL 62960
Open: Year-round ▪ Rate: RV/tent $20 ▪ Amenities: Dump station, showers, picnic tables, fire rings with grills, potable water, playground, boat ramp ▪ ADA sites: Partial

Located near the confluence of the Ohio and Mississippi Rivers in the deep south of Illinois, Fort Massac offers both history lessons and outdoor adventure in a gorgeous shoreline setting. The campground blends big shade trees and grassy areas near the Ohio River, a park visitors center, and a reproduction frontier timber fort beside the remains of the original French colonial fort. Outdoor activities range from river boating and fishing to disc golf or hiking/biking the 8.8-mile (14 km) George Rogers Clark Discovery Trail along the Ohio. A highlight of the state park year is the annual Fort Massac Encampment in October, which re-creates the ambience of the 18th-century frontier fort through historic uniforms, weapons, music, and more. In addition to its Superman Museum and Man of Steel statue, the adjoining town of Metropolis offers numerous restaurants for those who relish a break from camp food. ∎

SOMETHING SPECIAL

Shawnee National Forest

Set between the Mississippi and Ohio Rivers, the Shawnee National Forest covers 289,000 acres (116,954.2 ha) with oak-hickory forests, flourishing wetlands, lush canyons, razorback ridges, and unique geological features.

One of the forest's most notable features is a portion of the historic Trail of Tears (1830-1850). Cherokee forced to walk this route, considered one of the most difficult stretches, were trapped for weeks unable to cross the frozen Mississippi River. The Trail of Tears National Historic Trail remembers the injustices and hardships faced by those who walked it with historic placards outlining the journey along the route.

Other historic areas of the forest include sites used in the Underground Railroad, the Illinois Iron Furnace, and the Millstone Bluff archaeological site, an ancient Native American village perched on a bluff.

Indiana

The Hoosier State offers sandy dunes, glamping by the Indy 500, waterfront spots for tents, and much more.

HIGHLIGHTS

Capital: Indianapolis

Total National Parks: 1 (Indiana Dunes National Park)

Total State Parks: 25 (Largest is Brown County State Park)

State Bird: Cardinal

State Flower: Peony

State Tree: Tulip tree

Wildlife Spotting: Allegheny wood rats; bobcats; muskrats; meadow jumping mice; bald eagles; hairy woodpeckers; eastern bluebirds; ornate box turtles; ringneck snakes; little brown skinks; cave salamanders; American bullfrogs; plains leopard frogs

INDIANA DUNES STATE PARK

🚐/🏕 140 partial hookup
County Road 100 East, Chesterton, IN 46304
Open: Year-round ▪ Rates: From $23 ▪ Amenities: Camp store, dump station, showers, picnic tables, fire rings, firewood, ice, potable water, volleyball, beach, playground, snack bar ▪ ADA sites: Yes

The shifting sands of northern Indiana are preserved by both a state park created a century ago and one of the nation's newest national parks. But only one of them offers year-round camping at a location close to Lake Michigan: Indiana Dunes State Park. Shielded from the lake's blustery winds by tree-covered dunes, the campground makes it easy to reach the shore via the Beach Trail or a more challenging route across Mount Tom, a huge dune. Campers hankering for a slice of big city life (or Chicago-style pizza) can catch a train right outside the park's front gate to the Windy City. Dunewood Campground in adjoining Indiana Dunes National Park offers an additional 66 RV/tent campsites between April and October.

SHIPSHEWANA NORTH PARK CAMPGROUND

🏛18, 🚐/🏕 14 full hookup, 41 partial hookup

Take in the shifting dunes of Indiana Dunes State Park from a plethora of boardwalks.

5970 State Highway 5, Shipshewana, IN 46565
Open: April to October ▪ Rates: RV/tent full hookup from $40, RV/tent partial hookup from $30, cabins $59 to $129 ▪ Amenities: Snack shop, dump station, showers, picnic tables, fire rings, ice, dog run, sports field, internet ▪ ADA sites: Yes

Home to the nation's third largest Amish community, Shipshewana attracts a steady stream of visitors to its famous flea market, handicraft outlets, black buggy tours, and shows at Blue Gate Performing Arts Center. But the small town also flaunts a pretty cool campground—literally cool, because its star amenity is a frozen custard stand. In addition to full hookup and power/water RV sites, the campground also offers "Amish cabins" with the structure and furniture handcrafted by local artisans. All are equipped with heating and air-conditioning, as well as a front porch swing. The larger, more expensive units also come with towels, bed linens, private bathrooms, and, most surprising, given the community's Amish heritage, color TVs.

LOST BRIDGE WEST CAMPGROUND

🚐/🏕 239 partial hookup, 86 no hookup
9214 Lost Bridge Road West, Andrews, IN 46702

Open: Year-round ▪ Rates: RV/tent partial hookup from $16, partial hookup from $12 ▪ Amenities: Camp store, dump station, showers, picnic tables, fire rings with grills, boat rental, boat slips, boat ramps, playground, potable water, sports courts, amphitheater, fish cleaning station ▪ ADA sites: Yes

Lake Salamonie in northeast Indiana provides a blissful waterfront setting for a state recreation area campground with more than 300 sites scattered across a hitchhiking-thumb-shaped peninsula on the south shore. With a beach, marina, boat rental, five boat ramps, overnight mooring buoys, and a camp store that sells bait and tackle, Lost Bridge revolves around water activities. The park also sports woodsy hiking and biking trails that transform into cross-country ski, snowshoe, and snowmobile routes in winter.

More than half of White River's campsites are along the waterfront.

PROPHETSTOWN STATE PARK

🚐/⛺ 55 full hookup, 55 partial hookup
State Highway 225, West Lafayette, IN 47906
Open: Year-round ▪ Rates: RV/tent full hookup from $23, partial hookup from $16 ▪ Amenities: Dump station, showers, picnic tables, fire rings, swimming pools, sports courts, playground, potable water, firewood, ice ▪ ADA sites: Yes

First and foremost, Prophetstown honors the region's original Native American inhabitants. But Indiana's newest state park (established in 2004) also celebrates the indigenous tallgrass prairie and pioneer farmers. Located at the confluence of the Wabash and Tippecanoe Rivers, the park occupies the site of an early 19th-century village founded by the great Shawnee leader Tecumseh and

his brother Tenskwatawa ("The Prophet"). Located in the heart of the park, the campground is near the park's water park, a reproduction Native American village, and a 1920s farm museum with living history programs. The park is also a stop on the Indiana Birding Trail. Tippecanoe Battlefield, where future president William Henry Harrison clashed with The Prophet in 1811, lies across the road from the park entrance.

WHITE RIVER CAMPGROUND

🚐/⛺ 55 full hookup, 29 partial hookup, 6 no hookup, ⛺ 12
11299 East 234th Street, Cicero, IN 46034
Open: May to October ▪ Rates: RV/tent full hookup $25/$30 (county resident/nonresident), partial hookup $20/$25, no hookup/tent only $15/20 ▪ Amenities: Dump station,

camp store, showers, laundry, picnic tables, fire rings, boat ramp, fishing pier, horseshoes, volleyball, playground ▪ ADA sites: Yes

This standout Hamilton County campground flows along the banks of the White River on the northern outskirts of Indianapolis. There's no shortage of overnight options, around half of them right on the river. Fishing and paddle sports are the main activities. If you didn't bring your own watercraft, the county parks and recreation department partners with White River Canoe Company on two- to three-hour float trips downstream from Lafayette Trace to the campground. The bright blue Patterson Historic Bridges—three steel truss spans constructed between 1890 and 1904—link the campground to Strawtown Koteewi Park on the eastern side of the river.

GLAMPTOWN AT INDIANAPOLIS MOTOR SPEEDWAY

⛺ 70, 🏠 15
4790 West 16th Street, Indianapolis, IN 46222
Open: Race week in late May ▪ Rates: Glamping tents from $1,300, tiny homes $4,000 (four-night stay) ▪ Amenities: All bedding, private bathrooms and showers, power outlets, luggage service, parking, admission tickets ▪ ADA sites: No

The Speedway may have cribbed the title from the 19th-century Pennsylvania horse track and famous Stephen Foster song, but that's about the only resemblance to the camptown races of old. Located right beside the lake in the infield of the famous motor racing circuit, these luxury glamping tents and tiny houses add a whole new dimension to experiencing the Indy 500. The tents come with all bedding, camp chairs, and access to a private bathhouse with hot showers. Raising the bar even higher, the tiny houses are equipped with kitchens and private bathrooms. Both options also include 24-hour security, infield parking pass, luggage service, and admission to various Indy Race Week events at the Brickyard (Indianapolis Motor Speedway), including the main event. Glamptown exists only during the Indy 500, and guests must book a four-night stay from Thursday afternoon to Monday morning. Indy Motor Speedway also provides more than 1,000 RV/tent camping spaces in the asphalt, gravel, and grass parking lots that surround the world's largest sports venue.

ABE MARTIN LODGE & CABINS
☎ 83

1405 State Road 46 West, Nashville, IN 47448

Open: Year-round ▪ Rates: From $105 ▪ Amenities: Restaurant, gift shop, microwave, mini-fridge, coffeemaker, swimming pools, game arcade, internet, Tesla charging station ▪ ADA sites: Yes

Brown County State Park provides a sylvan setting for a wilderness resort named after a fictional cartoon character. From 1904 to 1947, Indianapolis-based artist and humorist Kin Hubbard produced a nationally syndicated comic strip with Abe Martin as the main protagonist. The bearded, wisecracking old-timer and

his sidekicks lived in Brown County, a fact that prompted the Indiana State Parks authority to dedicate the park to Hubbard and name its lodge after the crotchety but lovable Abe. The lodge offers three cabin types: rustic, family, and cabin suites. All feature beds, air-conditioning, heating, and private bathrooms with showers, as well as wristbands for admittance to the lodge's indoor Aquatic Center water park. Elsewhere, Indiana's largest state park offers more than a dozen hiking and equestrian trails, two lakes, the state's oldest covered wooden bridge, a nature center with interpretive programs, and some of the best mountain biking routes in the Midwest. Three campgrounds provide RV and tent sites.

Abe Martin Lodge & Cabins offers a welcome stay for families whether you want a rustic experience or a cozy cabin idyll.

Live as a president once did—at least for a weekend—along Little Pigeon Creek within Lincoln State Park.

HARDIN RIDGE RECREATION AREA

🏠2, 🚐/⛺ 85 partial hookup, 82 no hookup, ⛺ 36

6464 Hardin Ridge Road, Heltonville, IN 47436

Open: April to October ▪ Rates: RV/tent partial hookup from $27, RV/tent no hookup $20, tent only $20, cabins $50 ▪ Amenities: Dump station, showers, picnic tables, fire rings, boat ramps, playground, beach, amphitheater ▪ ADA sites: Yes

Indiana's largest reservoir is the centerpiece of a Hoosier National Forest campground just a half-hour south of Bloomington and the university campus, where the sporting Hoosiers play their games. More than 200 RV and tent sites, some of them with power and water hookups, are found along six loops on a wooded ridge above Lake Monroe. Campers can slide their motorized and nonmotorized craft into the lake on a three-lane boat ramp or take a dip at a roped-off, family-friendly swimming beach. Behind the shore, Hardin Ridge Trail is a 2-mile (3.2 km) dual hiking and mountain biking route. Those questing tougher hikes can explore the Charles C. Deam Wilderness, just a 10-minute drive to the east. Restaurant dining and power boat rental are available at Fairwinds Marina on the lake's west side.

LINCOLN STATE PARK

🏠10, 🚐/⛺ 150 partial hookup, 119 no hookup

15476 County Road 300 East, Lincoln City, IN 47552

Open: Year-round ▪ Rates: RV/tent partial hookup from $16, RV/tent no hookup from $12, cabins $80 ▪

Amenities: Dump station, camp store, showers, picnic tables, fire rings, potable water, playgrounds, boat ramp, boat rental ▪ ADA sites: Yes

Although the nation's 16th president is most associated with Illinois and Kentucky, Abe Lincoln spent his most formative years (ages seven to 21) in tiny, backwoods Little Pigeon Creek village in southern Indiana. He later called his boyhood home "the very spot where grew the bread that formed my bones." In the 1930s, the frontier settlement was transformed into a state park with a large campground and cabins along the shore of Lincoln Lake. The Lincoln family farm is long gone, but the park boasts plenty of other structures and sites that featured in young Abe's life. Yet the park offers far more than memories. Hiking, boating, fishing, and naturalist programs are complemented by summer concerts and a musical tribute to Lincoln at the park's modern amphitheater.

COLUCCI RIVER CABINS

🏠7

17735 Magnet Valley Road,

Cannelton, IN 47520

Open: Year-round ▪ Rates: From $205 ▪ Amenities: Kitchens, hot tubs, barbecues, picnic tables, heat and air-conditioning ▪ ADA sites: Yes

With their distinctive peaked roofs, these stylish waterfront cabins summon visions of Scandinavia rather than southern Indiana. But the location is truly all-American: along the banks of the Ohio River in Hoosier National Forest just downstream from Louisville. Boasting two to four bedrooms, the cabins are all equipped with full kitchens, private bathrooms, living areas with pullout couches, dining rooms, wraparound porches with rocking chairs, barbecue grill, picnic table, and hot tub with river views. With the Hoosier National Forest literally right outside the front door, there's plenty of scope for hiking, including the 12.3-mile (20 km) Mogan Ridge West Trail, the 7.2-mile (11 km) Oriole West Trail, and the short Buzzard Roost Trail along bluffs above the Ohio River. And just down the road is a small Civil War memorial and cemetery. ▪

SOMETHING SPECIAL

The Indy 500

The Indianapolis 500 stock car race has been held at the Indianapolis Motor Speedway in the state's capital nearly every year since 1911. Called "the greatest spectacle in racing," the Indy 500 is considered one of the best stock car races in the world.

The race field traditionally consists of 33 drivers who race 200 laps (2.5 miles/4 km per lap) at more than 200 miles per hour (321.9 km/h).

The winner takes home the Borg-Warner Trophy (along with a large cash prize), commissioned in 1935 and first won by driver Louis Meyer in the 1936 race. But a more famous tradition is the victory milk that the winner every year drinks in the victory lane. The tradition was started by Louis Meyer, who regularly drank buttermilk and happened to have some out of habit after winning his 1936 race.

Iowa

Lakes and rivers define some of Iowa's best campgrounds, but there's plenty inland too, including a farm stay, woodsy bluffs, and underground caverns.

SUGAR BOTTOM CAMPGROUND

🚐/🏕 13 full hookup, 195 partial hookup, 6 no hookup, 🏕 17

2192 Mehaffey Bridge Road Northeast, Solon, IA 52333

Open: May to September ▪ Rates: RV/tent full hookup $26, RV/tent partial hookup from $20, tent only $14 ▪ Amenities: Dump station, showers, picnic tables, fire pits with grills, potable water, beach, boat ramp, fish cleaning station, playgrounds, disc golf, volleyball, horseshoes, amphitheater ▪ ADA sites: Yes

The largest of the three U.S. Army Corps of Engineers campgrounds at Coralville Lake on the Iowa River, Sugar Bottom complements its many power and water pads with a handful of full-hookup and tent-only sites. Located about halfway down the lake's eastern shore and with several campsites right along the water, the campground is most conducive to aquatic sports. However, there's also an 18-hole disc golf course and the single-track, 12-mile (19.3 km) Sugar Bottom Mountain Bike Trail. The Colville Lake Recreation Area also harbors the University of Iowa Raptor Rescue Center and the Devonian Fossil Gorge, where the remains of ancient marine animals were exposed during floods in 1993 and 2008.

Don't skip a descent into the subterranean world of Maquoketa Caves State Park.

HONEY CREEK STATE PARK

📷4, 🚐/🏕 28 full hookup, 78 partial hookup, 45 no hookup

12194 Honey Creek Place, Moravia, IA 52571

Open: Year-round ▪ Rates: RV/tent full hookup from $18, RV/tent partial hookup from $12, RV/tent no hookup from $6, cabins $50 ▪ Amenities: Dump station, showers, picnic tables, fire pits with grills, potable water, boat ramp, boat dock, fish cleaning station ▪ ADA sites: Yes

Iowa's second largest lake provides a woodsy waterfront location for a park with two campgrounds and a handful of rustic camper cabins. Scattered across a peninsula that extends far into Rathbun Lake, most of the RV and tent sites are steps away from spots where campers can swim, fish, or boat. But just a few of them—three primitive, tent-only sites—are located right on the lakeshore. Watercraft rentals are available at nearby Honey Creek Resort, which also offers indoor and outdoor water parks, a restaurant, and an 18-hole golf course. Among the park's 5 miles (8 km) of hiking routes is the Woodland Interpretive Trail, where displays provide information on the park's ancient Native American mounds.

LEWIS & CLARK STATE PARK

🚐/🏕 12 full hookup, 65 partial hookup

21914 Park Loop, Onawa, IA 51046

Open: Year-round ▪ Rates: RV/tent full hookup from $18, RV/tent partial hookup from $12 ▪ Amenities: Dump station, showers, picnic tables, fire pits with grills, potable water, boat ramps, playground, beach ▪ ADA sites: Partial

An oxbow lake that was a giant bend in the Mississippi River when the Corps of Discovery camped here in August 1804, Lewis & Clark honors the famed explorers with a full-scale replica of the keelboat *Best Friend* and other watercraft used on their journey to the Pacific and back. Campsites are mostly with power and water, with about a third of them along the shore of Blue Lake. The nearest towns for food, gas, and other supplies are Onawa, Iowa, 5 miles (8 km) to the east and Decatur, Nebraska, 6.6 miles (10.6 km) to the west. A highlight of the state park year is the annual Lewis & Clark Festival in June, which includes a living history encampment, historic talks, live bluegrass music, and films about the groundbreaking journey across America.

FILLENWARTH BEACH COTTAGE COLONY

🏠 25

87 Lakeshore Drive, Arnolds Park, IA 51331

Open: May to October ▪ Rates: From $69 ▪ Amenities: Kitchens, private bathrooms, bedding and towels, air-conditioning, housekeeping, private decks or backyards, barbecue grills, swimming pools, lake swimming area, scenic cruises, water skiing, sailing, rowboats, canoes, sports courts, lawn games, rec room, playgrounds, internet ▪ ADA sites: Partial

Owned and operated by the Fillenwarth family since it was founded shortly after World War I, this sprawling waterfront resort beckons families from around the Upper Great Plains to summer fun on water and land. Equipped with queen beds and sofa sleepers, the redwood-colored Cottage Colony cabins come with kitchens, full baths, and some sort of outdoor seating and grilling area. The cottage cluster boasts its own swimming pool, but it's also mere steps from West Lake Okoboji, one of the gems of Iowa's glacier-shaped Lake District.

Fillenwarth offers plenty of opportunities to hang out on your own or mingle with other guests at daily arts and craft sessions; the weekly get-acquainted party; or wine, beer, and chocolate tastings. Among the resort's many complimentary activities are sailing, water-skiing, scenic lake cruises, swimming pools, and self-propelled boats. What makes Fillenwarth even more conducive to family vacations is its proximity to other lakeshore attractions like Arnold's Amusement Park, the Iowa Great Lakes Maritime Museum, and scenic cruises on the historic *Queen II* lake steamer (official "Flagship of the Iowa Navy").

RED CEDAR LODGE

🏠 3

1880 Gilbert Street, Charles City, IA 50616

Open: Year-round ▪ Rates: From $239 (two-night minimum stay) ▪ Amenities: Kitchens, private bathrooms, bedding and towels, fireplaces, heating and air-conditioning, decks, gas barbecue, fire ring, lawn furniture, community hot tub, cable TV, internet ▪ ADA sites: Yes

These large deluxe cabins overlook the Cedar River around a two-hour drive from Dubuque. All of the A-frame abodes feature full kitchens with all of the necessary dinnerware and cooking utensils, plus outdoor barbecue grills. Large windows illuminate living and dining areas and bedrooms outfitted with rocking chairs and other sturdy wooden furnishings. Out back, roomy decks overlook a lawn that tumbles down to a riverside where guests can cast for walleye. Open year-round, Red Cedar is located near three regional bike trails and more than 200 miles (321 km) of marked snowmobile routes. Outfitters in nearby Charles City rent kayaks, and tubes for running the town's Whitewater Riverfront course or more gentle thrills along the Cedar River.

HARVEST FARM CAMPGROUND RESORT

🏠 3, 🚐/🏕 56 partial hookup, 🏕 13

3690 318th Avenue, Cresco, IA, 52136

Open: April to October ▪ Rates: RV/tent partial hookup $38, tent only from $28, cabins from $120 ▪ Amenities: Camp store, beauty salon, dump station, showers, laundry, picnic tables, fire pits, firewood, potable water, playgrounds, boat rental and shuttle service, boat landing, sports courts ▪ ADA sites: Partial

Over the past quarter century, the Ferrie family has transformed their

Upscale cabins at Red Cedar Lodge offer river access and golfing nearby.

Pitch your tent at Pikes Peak State Park, where you have nearly 1,000 acres (404.7 ha) to explore.

dairy farm into a first-class campground along the Upper Iowa River, where the state's iconic pastures and cornfields give way to riverine forest and riverside cliffs. But it's almost like the cattle never left. The general store, laundry room, and office are tucked inside the old barn, a vintage grain silo rising beside it. The campsites are arrayed across rolling lawns where milk cows once grazed. And two of the cabins were designed and built by local Amish craftsmen. A location right on the river means that campers can hop the Harvest Farm shuttle upstream to start float trips on the Upper Iowa lasting anywhere from 1.5 to 4.5 hours.

PIKES PEAK STATE PARK

🚐/🏕 48 partial hookup, 17 no hookup

32264 Pikes Peak Road, McGregor, IA 52157
Open: Year-round ▪ Rates: RV/tent partial hookup from $18, RV/tent no hookup from $12 ▪ Amenities: Camp store, dump station, showers, picnic tables, fire pits with grills, potable water, playground ▪ ADA sites: Yes

Visitors cherish this eastern Iowa state park for expansive views from bluffs along the Mississippi River. The campground hides in thick woods just steps from Deer Ridge Overlook, one of the best spots to contemplate America's most storied waterway. Trails along the 500-foot (152 m) bluffs link the campground with other landmarks like Bridal Veil Falls and Point Ann. For campers who are into the past, there's a lot of history too. Much like the homonymous summit in Colorado,

the park takes its name from explorer Zebulon Pike, who surveyed the bluffs in 1805 during an expedition up the Mississippi. More than two centuries earlier, in 1673, Jesuit missionary Jacques Marquette and mapmaker Louis Jolliet became the first Europeans to reach Iowa when they stepped ashore here. Seven miles (11 km) north of the park, Effigy Mounds National Monument showcases more than 200 incredible animal-shaped mounds sculpted by Native Americans long before the arrival of Euro Americans.

MAQUOKETA CAVES STATE PARK

🚐/🏕 24 partial hookup, 🏕 6
9688 Caves Road, Maquoketa, IA 52060
Open: Year-round ▪ Rates: RV/tent

Lewis & Clark State Park offers more than 600 acres (242.8 ha) of camping in a stand of old-growth forest.

partial hookup from $18, tent only from $6 ▪ Amenities: Dump station, showers, picnic tables, fire pits with grills, potable water, playground ▪ ADA sites: Yes

Maquoketa has been attracting visitors since the 1860s to a geological wonderland that includes limestone surface formations and subterranean spaces. Although it would be cool to camp underground, the recently renovated campground is on the surface, the sites scattered among pine trees along the western edge of Raccoon Creek. Campers can hike rim trails or descend into the creek-carved gorge to investigate Hernando's Hideaway, Shinbone, Rainy Day, and massive Dancehall Cave, as well as the Natural Bridge and Balanced Rock. All told, the park offers 6 miles (9.6 km) of hiking routes through deep ravines and lush forest. Bucking the image of Iowa as pancake flat, Maquoketa's rough-and-tumble topography derives from a location in the state's Paleozoic Plateau (or Driftless Area), a slightly elevated region that avoided the most severe effects of glaciation during the ice ages. Learn more about the offbeat geology at the park's new interpretive center.

MOON RIVER CABINS
🏠5
905 South Riverview Drive (U.S. Highway 52), Bellevue, IA 52031
Open: Year-round ▪ Rates: From $150 (two-night minimum stay) ▪ Amenities: Restaurant, kitchens, private bathrooms, fireplaces, bedding and towels, heating and air-conditioning, fire pits, barbecue grills, flat-screen TVs and DVD players, housekeeping, internet ▪ ADA sites: No

Like the Henry Mancini song that shares its name, Moon River is a dream maker and a huckleberry friend along the Mississippi River between Dubuque and Davenport. Although the cabins are thoroughly modernized, they trace their roots to the 1930s and Army Corps of Engineers construction of Lock & Dam No. 12 at Bellevue, Iowa. Once the project was done and the workers moved on, the distinctive log cabins passed into private vacation accommodation. Like the dam builders of 90 years ago, today's cabin dwellers can nap in a hammock strung between riverside pines, relax around a fire pit, or barbecue in a grassy area overlooking the Mississippi. Although the cabins feature full kitchens, several eateries are within walking distance, including the Riverside Grille, Richman's Café, and Flatted Fifth Blues & BBQ. Moon River is also near Bellevue State Park with its Butterfly Garden and South Bluff Nature Center.

PINE GROVE CAMPGROUNDS & CABINS
🏠2, 🚐/⛺ 324 partial hookup
18850 270th Street, Eldridge, Iowa 52748

Open: April to October ▪ Rates: RV/tent partial hookup from $22, cabins from $125 ▪ Amenities: Dump station, showers, swimming pool, picnic tables, fire pits with grills, potable water, playgrounds, sports courts, golf course, equestrian area, boat rental ▪ ADA sites: Partial

Not your average county campground, Pine Grove offers campers access to a wide array of outdoor activities, from summertime biking, hiking, and 18 holes of golf to winter sledding, snowshoeing, and cross-country skiing. The park also harbors Walnut Grove Pioneer Village, which preserves nearly two dozen 19th-century structures on a site that was once a crossroads settlement and overland stagecoach stop. Managed by the county conservation board, it's the most centrally located of the park's five campgrounds at Scott County Park, as well as the only one with rental cabins. Outfitted with modern bathrooms and kitchens, queen and sofa beds, heating and air-conditioning, and wireless internet, the cabins easily sleep six. Cabins can be reserved, but campsites are first come, first served. ▪

SOMETHING SPECIAL

Bellevue State Park

Bellevue State Park boasts some of the best views of the Mississippi River from its spot in Iowa's Jackson County. The prime spot to see the famous waterway is from the park's 250-foot-tall (76.2 m) limestone bluff, which overlooks the Upper Mississippi River Wildlife Refuge and the town of Bellevue.

For a closer look at the local fauna, head to the park's South Bluff Nature Center, where you can learn about endemic species of animals and plants, as well as the historical cultures of the Indigenous people of this area. There's also a 1-acre (0.4 ha) butterfly garden with nearly 60 different species (open spring to fall).

For a taste of history, you can take an easy hike to Pulpit Rock or the ancient Native American mounds that date back to the Middle Woodland Culture, as late as 500 B.C.

Kansas

There's no place like Kansas, especially when it comes to the campgrounds, which offer a robust selection of camper parking, lakefront tent options, and even camping amid a prairie dog town.

DEER CREEK VALLEY RV PARK

🚐 59 full hookup

3140 Southeast 21st Street, Topeka, KS 66607

Open: Year-round ▪ Rate: $45 ▪ Amenities: Restaurant, dump station, showers, laundry, picnic tables, ice, propane, swimming pool, playground, horseshoes, dog run, tornado shelter, cable TV, internet ▪ ADA sites: Partial

Whether you're cruising Interstate 70 on a cross-country trip or staying over for sights in Topeka like the state capitol building and Evel Knievel Museum, Deer Creek Valley offers a great place to plant your motor home, trailer, or camper. Set on the city's semirural east side, this RV-only campground offers full hookups, the most cherished and family-friendly amenities (including laundry facilities, a swimming pool, dog run, and playground), and even a barbecue joint with pulled pork and beef brisket just beyond the front gate. More tasty treats await along South Kansas Avenue, the restaurant row in downtown Topeka, 3 miles (4.8 km) west of Deer Creek Valley. Or make your way to Lake Shawnee, just a short drive from the campground, for

Take time to watch the sunset over Milford Lake.

fishing, boating, Jet Skiing, paddle boating, and a beautiful walking trail that circumnavigates the water.

ACORNS RESORT

☎ 25, 🚐/🏕 59 full hookup, 2 partial hookup, 🏠 3

3710 Farnum Creek Road, Milford, KS 66514

Open: Year-round ▪ Rates: RV/tent from $25, cabins from $90, yurts $50 ▪ Amenities: Restaurant, bar, camp store, dump station, showers, laundry, picnic tables, fire rings with grills, playground, beaches, boat rental, boat ramp, fishing dock, amphitheater, internet ▪ ADA sites: Partial

Kansas may be as far from the ocean as you can get in North America, but that doesn't mean the Sunflower State doesn't offer beach vacations. Overlooking Milford Lake near Manhattan, Acorns Resort offers waterfront cabins, yurts, and campsites scattered across a parklike setting shaded by cedar and oak forest. Campers can take a dip on the sandy strand or rent a kayak, canoe, paddleboard, or pontoon boat to get on the lake. Those who tow their own watercraft can park their vessel at one of the resort's rentable boat slips. From live music and scavenger hunts to sunset cruises, naturalist programs, and yoga sessions, Acorns also hosts many special events and group activities during the summer.

HIGHLIGHTS

Capital: Topeka

Total National Parks: 0

Total State Parks: 28 (Largest is El Dorado State Park)

State Bird: Western meadowlark

State Flower: Sunflower

State Animal: Buffalo

Wildlife Spotting: Nine-banded armadillo; black-tailed jackrabbits; plains pocket gophers; least shrews; prairie king snakes; western worm snakes; prairie lizards; Great Plains skinks; black vultures; golden eagles; yellow-billed cuckoos; western meadowlarks; prairie chickens

SHADY GROVE CABINS

☎ 9

1319 Kansas Street, Downs, KS 67437

Open: Year-round ▪ Rates: From $55 ▪ Amenities: Kitchenettes, barbecues, private bathrooms, bedding and towels, heating and air-conditioning, cable TV, internet ▪ ADA sites: No

In 1926, Route 24 between Detroit and the Colorado Rockies was designated as one of the first official U.S. highways. Gas stations, diners, and motor hotels followed along its path, including a cluster of cute little roadside cabins, Shady Grove, in Downs, Kansas. An extreme makeover completed in 2016 added 21st-century amenities like Wi-Fi and cable TV, as well as kitchenettes with mini-fridges and microwaves. Each of them boasts unique decor and a distinct personality—for example, the Harley Cabin with its motorcycle motifs and gleaming diner-style table and stools, and the Cowboy Cabin with its wooden bunk beds, hanging horseshoes, and Wild West art. The cabins are popular with anglers hoping to snag bass, walleye, and catfish at nearby Waconda Lake; Shady Grove can hook you up with a local fishing guide. The Downs area also has a handful of worthy sights including Waconda Heritage Village and Hopewell Church and the world's largest ball of twine (43 feet/13.1 m circumference).

PRAIRIE DOG STATE PARK
🏠4, 🚐/🏕 10 full hookup, 89 partial hookup, 123 no hookup, 🏕 7

13037 State Highway 261, Norton, KS 67654

Open: Year-round ▪ Rates: RV/tent full hookup from $22, partial hookup from $21, no hookup $10, cabins from $45 ▪ Amenities: Dump stations, showers, picnic tables, fire rings, grills, beach, boat ramps, playground, archery range ▪ ADA sites: Yes

True to its name, this west Kansas park boasts a thriving prairie dog town that houses at least 300 of the furry little critters. Arrayed along the north shore of Sebelius Lake, six campgrounds offer a variety of sites and easy access to the lake via boat ramps, a fishing dock, and swimming beach. Away from the water, a 1.4-mile (2.2 km) nature trail links the lakeshore and prairie dog town. The park preserves two pioneer-era structures: a one-room schoolhouse and an adobe homestead constructed in the 1890s that's the oldest surviving example of its kind in Kansas.

HISTORIC LAKE SCOTT STATE PARK
🏠2, 🚐/🏕 4 full hookup, 55 partial hookup, 44 no hookup

101 West Scott Lake Drive, Scott City, KS 67871

Open: Year-round ▪ Rates: RV/tent full hookup from $22, partial hookup from $21, no hookup $10, cabins $75 ▪ Amenities: Camp store, dump station, showers, picnic tables, fire rings with grills, firewood, ice, potable water, playground, disc golf, marina, fishing pier, bait and tackle, boat rental, boat ramps, beach ▪ ADA sites: Partial

El Cuartelejo—the remains of the nation's northernmost known Native American pueblo dwelling—is the cornerstone of an eclectic state park on the Great Plains of western Kansas. Four of the six campgrounds are arrayed around the shore of Lake Scott, the park's outdoor recreation hub. The vast majority of sites are dry, but there's a camp store for groceries and other supplies, as well as a range of other amenities that take the edge off primitive camping. A hiking/biking/equestrian trail links four of the campgrounds, from Elm Grove in the south to Timber Canyon in the north.

But history is still the main focus. Constructed in the mid-17th century by Taos Indians fleeing the Spanish conquistadors in the Rio Grande Valley, El Cuartelejo is one of 26 archaeological sites in and around Lake Scott. On the other end of the park's history, Steele Homestead—built by a settler who donated the land that became the state park—is now a museum of pioneer life. And just south of the park is the spot where the Battle of Punished Woman's Fork played out in 1878 as the last clash between Native Americans and the U.S. Cavalry in Kansas.

CIMARRON CAMPGROUND
🚐/🏕 12 no hookup

Forest Route 700, Elkhart, KS 67950

Open: Year-round ▪ Rate: $7 ▪ Amenities: Restrooms, picnic tables, fire

Keep an eye out for prairie chickens around Cimarron National Grassland.

From the bluffs of Lake Scott State Park, take in sweeping grassland views as far as the eye can see.

rings with grills, firewood, potable water ▪ ADA sites: Partial

"The middle of nowhere" aptly describes this secluded overnight spot amid the short-grass prairie of Cimarron National Grassland in southeast Kansas. The Cimarron River and nearby fishponds provide enough moisture to sustain the cottonwood trees that shade many of the campsites. That same mixture of water and foliage attracts a variety of birds, as well as whitetail deer, pronghorn antelope, and smaller mammals to the area. Other than solitude, the main lure for campers is angling for trout catfish in the ponds. The closest spots for groceries and other supplies are Elkhart (13 miles/21 km) and Rolla (17 miles/27 km).

GUNSMOKE RV PARK

🏠 1, 🚐 / 🏕 94 full hookup
11070 108th Road @ Wyatt Earp Boulevard, Dodge City, KS 67801
Open: March to November ▪ Rates: TV/tent $49.50, cabin $50 ▪ Amenities: Camp store, dump station, showers, laundry, picnic tables, propane, ice, swimming pool, playground, game room, mail service, tornado shelter, dog run, internet ▪ ADA sites: No

Marshal Dillon, Miss Kitty, and Chester would no doubt appreciate that fact that their long-running TV show (1955-1975) inspired a modern campground on the western edge of Dodge City. The camp store, game room, and showers are located behind the faux Wild West facade near the entrance. And there's a cinder-block bunkhouse (with bunk beds) for anyone who didn't bring their own bedding. But the adjacent swimming pool betrays the fact that Gunsmoke is a thoroughly modern RV park rather than a genuine relic of Dodge City as the wildest town west of the Mississippi. The Boot Hill Museum, Trail of Fame, House of Stone and other historic attractions are just six minutes down Wyatt Earp Boulevard from the campground.

LIGHTHOUSE LANDING RV PARK & CABINS

🏠 4, 🚐 46 full hookup
9 Heartland Drive, South Hutchinson, KS 67505
Open: Year-round ▪ Rates: RV $38, cabins from $60 ▪ Amenities: Bathhouse with showers, laundry, picnic

Pittsburgh State University Outdoor Activities Club members squeeze their way through a crevice at Elk City State Park.

tables, fire rings, firewood, ice, propane, playground, tornado shelter, internet ▪ ADA sites: No

Lighthouse Landing is a place for those who have always fantasized about sleeping in a little house on the prairie. Channeling the spirit of author Laura Ingalls Wilder—who wrote about her Kansas childhood in best-selling books—the four cabins boast a rustic charm complemented by blue skies, wheat fields, and a pond flush with migratory birds. Unique in size and style, the cabins form a tiny prairie village near the campground entrance, with check-in at a reproduction schoolhouse that doubles as the manager's residence. All but one of the cabins boast a kitchen, private bathroom, dining/sitting area, and living room, plus a porch in front and a view of wide-open spaces out back. The rest of Lighthouse Landing is the realm of full-service RV sites. Right outside the park front gate is a truck stop gas station with groceries and fast food.

BLUESTEM POINT CAMPING AREA

🏚7, 🚐/🏕 70 full hookup, 197 partial hookup, 233 no hookup
618 Northeast Bluestem Road, El Dorado, KS 67042
Open: Year-round ▪ Rates: RV/tent full hookup $22, RV/tent partial hookup $19 to $21, RV/tent no hookup $10, cabins from $35 ▪ Amenities: Dump stations, showers, laundry, picnic tables, fire pits, grills, potable water, ice, playgrounds, beach, boat ramps, bait shop, fish cleaning station ▪ ADA sites: Yes

One of four campgrounds in El Dorado State Park, Bluestem takes its name from a native grass (*Andropogon gerardi*) that thrives in the

Flint Hills, an area of the Great Plains that boasts the most pristine tallgrass prairie left in North America. Located on a jagged peninsula that juts into El Dorado Lake, the campground blends cabins and campsites, as well as aquatic sports and terrestrial pursuits like hiking, biking, and horseback riding along seven trails. With around 500 sites plus cabins, it's a huge campground by any standard. But they're nicely spaced in nine areas along the point. A few sites are shaded, but most are open to the blue skies and intense sun of the Great Plains summer. Campground size is also mitigated by the 4,500 acres (1,821 ha) of lakeshore, woodland, and prairie protected by the largest state park in Kansas. Just across the water from Bluestem Point, Shady Creek Marina offers pontoon boat rental.

ELK CITY STATE PARK

🏚1, 🚐/🏕 11 full hookup, 85 partial hookup, 54 no hookup
4825 Squaw Creek Road, Independence, KS 67301
Open: April to October ▪ Rates: RV/tent full hookup $22, partial hookup $21, no hookup $10, cabin $95 ▪ Amenities: Dump stations, showers, picnic tables, fire rings, potable water, playgrounds, archery, disc golf, sports courts, beach, boat ramps, fishing dock, kids' fishing pond, amphitheater ▪ ADA sites: Yes

It's not the highest point in Kansas—that would be Mount Sunflower along the border with Colorado—but Elk City is far and away the state's most impressive elevation. Millions of years ago, the park's limestone and shale bluffs were the bed of an ancient inland sea. Now they provide panoramic views over southeast Kansas via the Table Mound Hiking Trail (2.75 miles/4.4 km). The park also offers a dedicated mountain bike trail and access to the long-distance Elk River Trail. Like so many other Kansas state parks, there's a man-made lake for swimming, boating, and phenomenal fishing: a world-record 126-pound (57 kg) flathead catfish was hooked here. Campsites are located on Sunset Point along the lakeshore and farther back among a mix of hickory-oak forest and open prairie. The campgrounds also offer loads of amenities beyond the restrooms and shower-houses, including an 18-hole par 3 golf course, kids fishing pond, horseshoe pits, and biking and hiking trails. ▪

SOMETHING SPECIAL

El Dorado State Park

There are more than 2,000 acres (809.4 ha) of park and 4,000 acres (1,618.7 ha) of wildlife area to explore at El Dorado State Park, and that's not to mention 98 miles (157.7 km) of shoreline and plenty of waterways too. All of this combines into a fantastic locale not only for camping but also for fishing, boating, hiking, and biking.

Throughout the park there is plenty to be discovered: old river channels, submerged railroad beds, and wildlife spotting for white-tailed deer, songbirds, and waterfowl. Anglers will be drawn to the sportfishing in the park's waters, and equestrians will appreciate the park's numerous horse trails and hitching posts.

Kentucky

Explore old-growth forests, ancient caves, and the state's famous bourbon and bluegrass from the Appalachians to the Mississippi River and Kentucky's lakefront retreats.

COLUMBUS-BELMONT STATE PARK

🏠 1, 🚐 / ⛰ 35 partial hookup, 🚐 2

350 Park Road, Columbus, KY 42032
Open: Year-round ▪ Rates: RVs/tents $22-$40, campers from $45, cabin from $30 ▪ Amenities: Dump station, bathhouse, playground, gazebo, showers, fire rings, grills, picnic tables, internet, snack bar, gift shop, laundry, potable water, firewood, ice ▪ ADA sites: Yes

RV and tent sites, campers, and a single log cabin are among the overnight options at a campground set on bluffs above the Mississippi River at the far western tip of Kentucky. The park's strategic location featured in two pivotal events in American history. In 1838, it served as a temporary camp on the infamous Trail of Tears, a place where more than 1,000 Cherokee were ferried across the river. Thirteen years later, Union forces overran the heavily fortified Confederate "Gibraltar of the West" in a battle that kicked off the western campaign of the Civil War. The campground lies within walking distance of park history museum details and war relics like a giant experimental cannon named "Lady Polk" and a massive iron chain that impeded

Union navigation on the Mississippi before the 1861 battle. But it's not all history. Columbus-Belmont also boasts a miniature golf course, hiking trails, and a boat ramp for sliding small watercraft into the Mighty Mississippi.

LAKE BARKLEY CANAL CAMPGROUND

🚐 16 full hookup, 75 partial hookup, 19 no hookup

1010 Canal Campground Road, Grand Rivers, KY 42045
Open: March to October ▪ Rates: RV/tent full hookup $34, partial hookup $26-$30, no hookup $18 ▪ Amenities: Dump station, showers, fire rings, grills, picnic tables, playground, laundry ▪ ADA sites: Yes

The bountiful waterways of Land Between the Lakes National Recreation Area are the main attraction of a U.S. Army Corps of Engineers campground where boating, fishing, and swimming are the main activities. Sites for RVs and tents are arrayed along seven loops, some of them overlooking the Barkley Canal, which connects the flooded Cumberland and Tennessee Rivers, and others near the boat ramp on Browns Point. The campground amphitheater hosts interpretive programs. Most RV sites are equipped with power and water, but only a few offer sewage. Campground beaches are for the exclusive use of campers.

HIGHLIGHTS

Capital: Frankfort

Total National Parks: 1 (Mammoth Cave National Park)

Total State Parks: 45 (Largest is Green River Lake State Park)

State Bird: Cardinal

State Flower: Goldenrod

State Animal: Gray squirrel

Wildlife Spotting: Black bears; bobcats; red foxes; minks; river otters; peregrine falcons; bald eagles; mountain bluebirds; Kentucky warblers; northern cardinals; six-lined racerunner; broadhead skink; eastern corn snake; Kentucky spring salamander; Jefferson salamander

JOHN JAMES AUDUBON STATE PARK

🏠 6, 🚐 / ⛰ 70 partial hookup, ⛰ 17

3100 U.S. Highway 41, Henderson, KY 42420
Open: Campsites March to November, cottages year-round ▪ Rates: RV/tent partial hookup $23-$30, tent only $17, cottages from $80 ▪ Amenities: Dump station, showers, fire rings, grills, picnic tables, playground, canoe/kayak rental, gift shop, camp store, potable water, tornado shelter ▪ ADA sites: Yes

Dedicated to the life and times of the celebrated American artist and naturalist, this tranquil park and its campground lie just across the Ohio River from Evansville, Indiana. Audubon and his family lived here between 1810 and 1819 in a house that's now filled with mementos, original paintings, and a complete set of his iconic Birds of America series. The park offers half a dozen lakeside cottages tucked into 700 acres (283 ha) of

You can't camp *in* Mammoth Cave, but you can explore the system on a guided tour.

The next best thing to camping inside Mammoth Cave—which would be awesome if the Park Service allowed it—is overnighting above the world's longest known cave system (more than 400 miles/640 km). The Kentucky national park offers three drive-up campgrounds and 13 backcountry sites. But the only one within walking distance of the visitors center and cavern entrance is the big Mammoth Cave Campground. Scattered through thick woodland, the sites have plenty of shade to take the edge off the area's hot, humid summers. The campground is also close to the Green River Ferry for those who want to explore the overground wonders of the park's west side. In addition to restaurants and gift shops, the nearby Lodge at Mammoth Cave offers historic cottages with private bathrooms that can sleep anywhere from one to 16 people depending on the number of bedrooms.

BLUE HERON CAMPGROUND

🚐 / 🏕 45 partial hookup
Camp Ground Road, Strunk, KY 42649
Open: April to November ▪ Rates: $20 (seniors $10) ▪ Amenities: Dump station, showers, fire rings with grills, picnic tables, playground, pond ▪ ADA sites: Yes

Woods and water are the lure of a National Park Service campground located in Big South Fork National Recreation Area on the rugged Cumberland Plateau in southeast Kentucky. The campground takes its name from an abandoned coal-mining town that has been preserved as a museum since closing in 1962. The heavily wooded area around the campground is rife with waterfalls,

old-growth forest that provides a habitat for bald eagles, great blue herons, belted kingfishers, and other feathered friends. The state park campground has been closed for several years due to dam repair; check the website to monitor reopening. Created in the 1930s when eclectic parks were all the rage, Audubon also has a nine-hole golf course (with pro shop), tennis courts, hiking trails, boating, and fishing. The nature center features exhibits, art classes, and interpretive programs on a variety of topics.

MAMMOTH CAVE CAMPGROUNDS & COTTAGES

☎ 30, 🚐 / 🏕 111
1 Mammoth Cave Parkway, Mammoth Cave, KY 42259
Open: Campground year-round, cottages mid-March to October ▪ Rates: RV full hookup $50, RV/tent partial hookup $20 (seniors $10), cottages from $7 ▪ Amenities: Dump station, showers, laundry, fire pits, picnic tables, camp store, gas station, post office, campfire circle, firewood, ice, potable water ▪ ADA sites: Yes

natural arches, and secluded hollows, while the nearby Big South Fork of the Cumberland River offers white-water rafting and paddling with rapids that range up to class IV. The national recreation area also offers hiking, horseback riding, and mountain biking trails, as well as rock climbing, night sky and astronomy programs, and annual events like the Spring Planting & Music Festival and the Haunting in the Hills Storytelling Festival before Halloween.

LEVI JACKSON WILDERNESS ROAD PARK

🚐/⛰ 23 full hookup, 105 partial hookup, ⛰ 10+

998 Levi Jackson Road, London, KY 40744

Open: Year-round ▪ Rates: RV full hookup $38, RV partial hookup $28-$34, tent $22 ▪ Amenities: Dump station, showers, camp store, laundry, grills, picnic tables, playground, basketball, volleyball, amphitheater ▪ ADA sites: Partial

Family fun combined with nature and history color this municipal campground astride the historic Wilderness Road in eastern Kentucky. A large swimming pool with water slide, miniature golf, and treetop adventure course with zip lines and rope bridges, as well as a reproduction working watermill (which produces fresh ground cornmeal) are a few of the many attractions of a park first developed by the Civilian Conservation Corps in 1935. Campers can hike portions of the original Wilderness Road and Boone Trace that 18th-century settlers followed across the Appalachians. The park's Mountain Life Museum preserves original pioneer-era buildings relocated from around Kentucky.

HOMEGROWN HIDEAWAYS

🏠 3, ⛰ 2, 🚐 1, ⛺ 2

500 Floyd Branch Road, Berea, KY 40403

Open: Year-round ▪ Rates: Cabins, tents, yurts, and trailer $25-$95, RV partial hookup $30, tents $10-$15 ▪ Amenities: Communal kitchen and dining area, bathroom with shower, laundry, playground, hiking trail, farm stand, fire pits, firewood ▪ ADA sites: Partial

The artsy-craftsy town of Berea in the Appalachians of eastern Kentucky provides an apropos setting for

HomeGrown HideAways offers a number of stay options on a family farm in the woodsy Appalachians.

Kentucky is famous for its Derby, so why not try camping with an equestrian twist at Kentucky Horse Park?

a bucolic cabin and camping retreat on a working family farm. Tucked up a hollow around 20 minutes east of Berea, the little resort offers a variety of overnight choices including cabins, yurts, permanent tents, and Airstream trailer, as well as partial hookup RV and primitive tent sites. Devoid of internet and cell service, HomeGrown is largely unplugged. There's no meal service, but a communal kitchen serves those who want to cook on their own. The husband-and-wife owners can organize a range of local activities including fishing, tubing, canoe/kayak or bike rental, guided nature hikes, and visits to craft workshops or the summer concert series in Berea.

ZILPO CAMPGROUND

🏠12, 🚐/🏕 30 partial hookup, 136 no hookup

Zilpo Road, Salt Lick, KY 40371
Open: April to October ▪ Rates: RV/tent partial hookup $30, no hookup $22, cabins $75 ▪ Amenities: Dump station, showers, camp store, fire rings with grills, picnic tables, potable water ▪ ADA sites: Partial

Daniel Boone National Forest provides a sylvan setting for a waterfront campground in Zilpo Recreation Area on a peninsula that juts into Cave Run Lake. Campsites and cabins are arrayed along 3 miles (4.8 km) of shoreline that bound this excellent Forest Service campground. A ramp and dock expedite watercraft activities while campers can swim boat free in a roped-off area. Cabins feature air-conditioning and electricity but not bathrooms or running water.

KENTUCKY HORSE PARK CAMPGROUND

🚐/🏕 260 partial hookup

Campground Road, Lexington, KY 40511
Open: Year-round ▪ Rates: RV/tent partial hookup from $30, primitive RV/tent from $24 ▪ Amenities: Dump stations, showers, fire pits with grills, picnic tables, camp store and gift shop, swimming pool, hiking trail, playgrounds ▪ ADA sites: Yes

Real and mechanical horsepower go head-to-head at this Clydesdale-size campground (260 sites) on the grounds of a working thoroughbred ranch, equestrian competition venue, and theme park on the outskirts of Lexington. Every site offers RV water and power hookups, and there's a grassy overflow area with primitive RV/tent camping if the regular campground fills up. From basketball, tennis, and volleyball courts to a large swimming pool, KHP Campground offers plenty of outdoor recreation. Also, campers are entitled to discount tickets to Horse Park attractions like the American Museum of the Horse and Stall Side Chats.

CAMP BESPOKE

🏠16, 🏡 8, 12 tipis

500 Mercedes Drive, Williamstown, KY 41097
Open: Year-round ▪ Rates: Cottages $175, cabins $225, tipis from $285 ▪ Amenities: Heating and cooling, internet, mobile check-in ▪ ADA sites: No

Located around an hour's drive from Cincinnati, Louisville, and Lexington, Camp Bespoke is Kentucky's hot new glamping location. Opened in 2020, the eco-friendly resort sprawls across 30 bucolic acres (12 ha) on the edge of the state's vaunted bourbon and bluegrass regions. The modish cabins and cottages are fashioned from repurposed shipping containers, while the dozen Nomadic tipis are made with 100 percent organic cotton. On-site movie nights, live entertainment, and gourmet food boxes are complemented by off-site Bespoke Experience Packages based around bourbon, Thoroughbred horses, Kentucky arts and crafts, and local culinary traditions. Camp Bespoke is the brainchild of four women, all of them local health care professionals, who turned their vision of a unique, sustainable, upscale camping experience into a $3 million reality. ▪

Mammoth Cave National Park

Under the hills of Kentucky, the world's longest known cave system twists and turns for more than 390 miles (627.6 km). Curious tourists have wandered Mammoth Cave's tunnels for about 200 years, but spelunkers continue discover and chart new limestone caverns and passageways.

The only way to descend the labyrinth is on a ranger-led tour, which typically follows electrically lit passageways. For a different perspective, grab a kerosene lamp as tourists did two centuries ago for the Violet City Lantern Tour. The soft light casts monster-size shadows, and without the usual illumination to see, your other senses heighten. Listen for water cascading through the caverns, feel the ancient cave walls, and smell the fresh cave air.

Louisiana

World Heritage sites, Cajun country, and sites along the Mississippi are just a few of the experiences camping in Louisiana affords.

POVERTY POINT

🏠 5, 🚐 / ⛰ 45 full hookup,
9 partial hookup, 4 bayou cabins
1500 Poverty Point Parkway, Delhi, LA 71232
Open: Year-round ▪ Rates: RV/tent sites from $20, cabins from $150 ▪ Amenities: Dump station, showers, fire pits with grill, picnic tables, food storage containers, fish cleaning station, children's water park, internet ▪ ADA sites: Yes

Campers get two bangs for their bucks at Poverty Point: a UNESCO World Heritage site that revolves around massive earthen mounds that were created around 3,000 years ago by Native Americans and a nearby state park with cabins and campground.

The two-bedroom overwater cabins are gorgeous. Perched on spacious wooden decks above Poverty Point Reservoir, they come with fully equipped kitchens, bathrooms, towels, linens, outdoor decks, and your own small boat dock. Dry-land cabins crouch beneath big trees along Bayou Macon. The RV/tents sites are arrayed around three loops near the lake's southernmost shore. Black bears inhabit the surrounding woods, and campers should take care to secure their food at night and whenever they're away from their campsite.

Paddle through cypresses and Spanish moss at Lake Fausse Pointe State Park.

The state park's North Marina Complex sits near the lake's north end, an extensive facility that includes boat slips, boat ramp, fishing pier, boardwalk, swimming beach, canoe and boat rental, and camp store. Poverty Point World Heritage site lies along Bayou Macon around a 20-minute drive from the campground. The archaeological park features a museum, guided tours, and educational programs. The earthen mounds, arranged in a semicircle, are North America's largest Late Archaic period ceremonial site. Erected between 1700 and 1100 B.C., they are accessible via a 2.6-mile (4.1 km) hiking trail.

DARBONNE POINTE

🏠 4, 🚐 / ⛰ 32 partial hookup
147 Old Highway 15, Farmerville, LA 71241
Open: Year-round ▪ Rates: RV/tent sites from $35, cabins from $175 ▪ Amenities: Dump station, showers, grills, picnic tables ▪ ADA sites: Yes

Pastel cabins color the waterfront at Darbonne Pointe campground in far northern Louisiana. Located on the opposite side of Lake D'Arbonne from Farmerville, the resort provides an excellent base for boating, fishing, and other aquatic activities. The chromatic two-bedroom cabins sleep as many as eight and come fully equipped with kitchen, bathroom, towels, linens, washer and dryer, flat-screen TVs, and front porches with

HIGHLIGHTS

Capital: Baton Rouge

Total National Parks: 0

Total State Parks: 21 (Largest is Chicot State Park)

State Bird: Brown pelican

State Flower: Magnolia

State Tree: Bald cypress

Wildlife Spotting: Coyotes; American beavers; muskrats; swamp rabbits; American alligators; snapping turtles; Louisiana pine snakes; harlequin coral snakes (venomous); roseate spoonbills; yellow-crowned night-herons; Louisiana water-thrushes; purple gallinules; southern toads; crawfish frogs; Louisiana slimy salamanders

lake views. Around half the RV/tent sites are on the water. A swimming pool and sandy beach beg campers to go for a dip, and there's a boat ramp for sliding watercraft into the lake.

CLOUD CROSSING CAMPGROUND

🚐 / ⛰ 13 no hookup
Cloud Crossing Road, Goldonna, LA 71031
Open: Year-round ▪ Rate: Free ▪ Amenities: Restrooms, fire rings with grills, picnic tables, lantern hooks, potable water, boat ramp ▪ ADA sites: Yes

Proof that good things come in small packages, Cloud Crossing harbors just 13 campsites but a wide range of outdoor adventure in Kisatchie National Forest. Hiking, biking, fishing, paddling, and boating (in small, motorized watercraft) count among the activities in and around the campground. Saline Bayou National

Anglers will love a stay at Poverty Point cabins, set right along a 2,700-acre (1,092 ha) lake.

Wild and Scenic River—and its 19 miles (30 km) of pristine Louisiana wilderness—meanders along the eastern edge of Cloud Crossing. One of the other attractions of this little Forest Service campground is that it's free of charge throughout the year.

SAM HOUSTON JONES STATE PARK

☎ 8, 🚐/🏕 35 partial hookup
107 Sutherland Road, Lake Charles, LA 70611
Open: Year-round ▪ Rates: RV/tent $20-$33, cabins from $85, back-country camping $9 ▪ Amenities: Dump station, showers, fire pits, picnic tables, disc golf, playground, boat launches ▪ ADA sites: Yes

Don't let the name fool you: this southwest Louisiana park and its woodsy campground may honor the memory of two historical figures, but they're very much about natural history rather than the human past. Set along the meandering West Fork of the Calcasieu River on the outskirts of Lake Charles, the park offers classic bayou terrain: towering bald cypress trees emerging from flooded areas and longleaf pines on dry land. Wedged between two lagoons, the campground offers plenty of shade and easy access to hiking trails and an old stagecoach road that leads along the river and through the park's thickly wooded backcountry. While you're walking, keep a sharp eye out for bobcats,

nutria, gators, waterfowl, and the other swamp creatures that inhabit the park. Sam Houston Jones also offers wooden cabins with bathrooms and kitchens, all of them outfitted with cooking and eating utensils, towels, linens, heating, and air-conditioning.

KINCAID LAKE RECREATION AREA

🚐/🏕 41 partial hookup
214 Kisatchie Lane, Boyce, LA 71409
Open: Year-round ▪ Rates: RV/tent $25-$30; primitive camping $10 ▪ Amenities: Dump station, showers, fire rings, grills, picnic tables, lantern hooks, potable water, fishing piers, boat ramps, playground ▪ ADA sites: Partial

Located just half an hour from Alexandria and off-ramps from Interstate 49, Kincaid Lake and its three campgrounds are convenient for long-distance travelers questing a quiet place to spend the night or those who want to savor the area's woods and water on a longer stay. While aquatic sports like boating, fishing, waterskiing, wakeboarding, and swimming at the park's small beach are undoubtedly the main attraction, Kincaid caters to land-lubbers via great hiking trails and wildlife watching. The 6-mile (9.6 km) Kincaid Loop Trail makes a good half-day hike; campers yearning for more of a challenge can hoof all or part of the nearby Wild Azalea Trail, a 23.9-mile (38 km) route through the Kisatchie National Forest wilderness.

CHICOT STATE PARK

☎ 20, 🚐 / 🏕 198 partial hookup, 🏕 8

3469 Chicot Park Road, Ville Platte, LA 70586

Open: Year-round ▪ Rates: RV/tent $20-$28, glamping tents from $85, cabins from $150, backcountry camping $9 ▪ Amenities: Dump station, showers, laundry, fire pits, picnic tables, fishing pier, fish cleaning station ▪ ADA sites: Partial

Hands down, Chicot boasts the coolest state park cabins in all of Louisiana (and maybe even the South). Eight of them are overwater bungalows that sit perched on stilts, connected to the shore by wooden walkways and bridges, with screened-in porches for afternoon naps or sunset drinks, and their own little fishing piers. But there are plenty of other places to lay your head for the night—more than 200 RV and tent sites are scattered through the trees along the western shore of Lake Chicot, plus you can also find primitive backcountry camping for those who like their wilderness with fewer folks. Located about equidistant from Baton Rouge and Alexandria, the park is also home to the Louisiana State Arboretum, where hiking trails that lead through 600 acres (242 ha) of natural woods and wetlands are complemented by indigenous plants native to the region.

LAKE FAUSSE POINTE STATE PARK

☎ 8, 🚐 / 🏕 14 full hookup, 32 partial hookup, 5 canoe campsites

5400 Levee Road, St. Martinville, LA 70582

Open: Year-round ▪ Rates: RV/tent full hookup from $25, RV/tent partial hookup from $20, canoe campsites $18, primitive backcountry camping $9, cabins from $150 ▪ Amenities: Dump station, showers, fire pits with grills, picnic tables, boat launch, water playground, amphitheater, laundry, internet, canoe/kayak/boat rental ▪ ADA sites: Partial

Deep in the heart of Cajun country, Lake Fausse Pointe lies amid a maze of bayous, swamps, and marshes in the Atchafalaya Basin, the nation's largest wetland. Many of the campsites and cabins back right onto the water and boast their own small boat docks. Hiking paths (there are three trails on offer), boardwalks, and a canoe trail provide gateways into the watery wilderness and a food chain dominated by the resident gators. Boat rentals are available within the campground, too. Cajun food and culture flourish in nearby towns like Lafayette, Breaux Bridge, and New Iberia (where visitors can also tour the Tabasco Sauce factory). If you're looking for a peek into the past, head to St. Martinville or the Longfellow-Ecangeline State Historic Site.

Miles of trees can be explored at the Kisatchie National Forest Wilderness Area.

Grand Isle State Park, the southernmost camping spot in Louisiana, offers easy access to beaches along the Gulf of Mexico.

GRAND ISLE STATE PARK

🚐/🏕 49 partial hookup, 🏕 14,
🏕 1

108 Admiral Craik Drive, Grand Isle,
LA 70358

Open: Year-round ▪ Rates: RVs $25-
$33, tents $18 ▪ Amenities: Dump
station, showers, fire pits, grills, picnic tables, fishing pier, fish cleaning
station ▪ ADA sites: Partial

If Grand Isle has that end-of-the-
earth feeling, that's because it prac-
tically is. Astride a barrier island
near the spot where the Mississippi
River flows into the Gulf of Mexico, this waterfront state park is the
southernmost place you can pitch a
tent or hook up your RV in Louisiana. Beyond the shore, there's nothing but open water until you reach
the Yucatán Peninsula roughly
600 miles (1,000 km) due south.
The shoreline campground, with
half the sites backing onto the
beach, offers a little something for
everyone with a fishing pier, boat
dock, and 2.5-mile (4 km) nature
trail. Grand Isle is a great place for
birding and other wildlife watching.
And between the gulf, Bayou Fifi,
and the park's own small lagoon,
there's plenty of scope for kayaking
or paddleboarding.

BAYOU LOG CABIN

🏠 4

200 West Kass Lane, Port Sulphur,
LA 70083

Open: Year-round ▪ Rate: $200
(two-night minimum stay on weekends) ▪ Amenities: Kitchens, showers, docks, boat slips, charters,
boat rental ▪ ADA sites: No

It's all about fishing at this remote
resort in the Mississippi Delta
downstream from New Orleans.
The traditional Cajun-style

cabins—raised on wooden stilts
above Hermitage Bayou—are fully
furnished and outfitted for an
angling expedition. Among their
many amenities are full kitchens
and bathrooms, heating and
air-conditioning, satellite TV,
queen beds, open-air decks with
swinging chairs, fish cleaning stations, and private docks with boat
slips. You can fish or shrimp right
off the dock, join the resort's daytime or nighttime fishing charters,
or try your luck in a small rental
boat. For a change of pace, Bayou
also offers airboat swamp tours.

PONTCHARTRAIN LANDING

🏠 12, 🚐/🏕 125 partial
hookup, 🚐 2, 3 houseboats

6001 France Road, New Orleans,
LA 70126

Open: Year-round ▪ Rates: RV/tent
from $62, villas/cabins from $140,
houseboats from $250, travel trail-
ers from $95 ▪ Amenities: Restau-
rant, bar, camp store, boat slips,
boat ramp, dump station, showers, swimming pool, hot tub, playground, laundry, picnic tables,
propane, dog run, internet, cable
TV ▪ ADA sites: Yes

The foremost RV resort in the Crescent City invites campers to hitch
up a boat behind their rig and take
advantage of a location on the canal
that links big Lake Pontchartrain
and the Mississippi River. The
resort's twin marinas provide shelter
for up to 40 small boats. For those
who can't bring their own watercraft, neighboring Sea Brook Harbor & Marine rents pontoon boats
by the hour or day. All RV sites feature water and electric hookups, but
the more expensive sites are right
on the water. Pontchartrain Landing also offers shoreline villas that
can sleep anywhere from one to 16
people, as well as "floating villa"
houseboats moored to the bank.

This full-service resort is home
to the waterfront Lighthouse Bar &
Restaurant, which can organize a
crawfish boil at your RV site or
villa and catered parties beside the
swimming pool. The menu includes
New Orleans favorites like shrimp
and grits, gumbo, jambalaya,
and po' boy sandwiches. Pontchartrain Landing also has shuttle
service to and from the French
Quarter in New Orleans and all
of its world-famous attractions and
distractions. ▪

SOMETHING SPECIAL

Lake Fausse Pointe

Home to bald eagles, alligators, and
otters, the Atchafalaya River easily
deserves a place among the country's finest natural areas. The Atchafalaya (a Native American word
meaning "long river") stretches
about 140 miles (225.3 km) north-
ward from the Gulf of Mexico with
a floodplain more than 20 miles
(32.2 km) wide in places. Few roads

cross this wilderness, and access to
the interior is hard for those without
a boat and a guide to point the way
amid trackless waterways.

Lying just outside Atchafalaya's
western levee, Lake Fausse Pointe
offers a sampling of this environment
but with the conveniences of a modern park. Visualize the scene by
imagining yourself enjoying a cool
drink on a cabin porch while an alligator glides across the bayou below.

Maine

New England's finest coast offers glamping in everything from tiny homes and tree houses to tent and RV sites perched right on the waterfront.

HUTTOPIA SOUTHERN MAINE

🏕 70, 🏠 17

149 Sand Pond Road, Sanford, ME 04073
Open: May to October ▪ Rates: Glamping tents from $135, tiny homes from $220 ▪ Amenities: Restaurant, bar, bathhouse, camp store, lounge/game room, swimming pool, beach, floating dock, playground, sports fields, laundry, firewood, canoe rental, internet ▪ ADA sites: Yes

Forget the fine wines. The coolest thing that France has exported to North America in recent years is Huttopia. This self-proclaimed "new art of camping" offers three different types of glamping tents—from smaller basic canvas to larger models with kitchenettes and private bathrooms—as well as two-bedroom tiny houses. The central "village" includes a bistro with bar, heated swimming pool, and lodge-like Living Center with comfy sofas, wood-burning stove, and board/table games. Daily activities can include anything from culinary classes to outdoor movies and evening storytelling or magic shows around a communal campfire. Located near the state's southern tip, Huttopia lies around a half-hour drive from

Suspended bridges connect glamping tree houses at Seguin Tree Dwellings.

Kennebunkport and the Maine coast. Très bon!

SEGUIN TREE DWELLINGS

🌳 3

5 Islands Road, Georgetown, ME 04548
Open: April to January ▪ Rates: From $189 ▪ Amenities: Private bathrooms, kitchens, linens and towels, screened-in porch, electric heaters, internet, canoe and kayak rental ▪ ADA sites: No

Maybe it's a bit pretentious calling them "dwellings" rather than houses, but these chic shacks really do stand head and shoulder above the tree house stereotype. Their overall design and minimalist decor are strikingly modern, and each comprises two elevated structures connected by a rope bridge or wooden deck. Perched on a heavily wooded hilltop overlooking the Back River, each of the dwellings boast king-size beds, fully equipped kitchens, and panoramic windows, and one of them even features a cedar hot tub. An ongoing artist-in-residence program has attracted poets, writers, and photographers to Seguin. Tree dwellers can hike the woods, paddle the river, or cruise down the road to local attractions like Josephine Newman Audubon Sanctuary, the beach at Reid State Park, or Five Islands Lobster Company in Georgetown.

HIGHLIGHTS

Capital: Augusta

Total National Parks: 1 (Acadia National Park)

Total State Parks: 32 (Largest is Baxter State Park)

State Bird: Black-capped chickadee

State Flower: White pine cone and tassel

State Animal: Moose

Wildlife Spotting: Moose; black bears; bobcats; white-tailed dear; Canada lynx; bald and golden eagles; ospreys; great gray owls; roseate terns; northern red belly snakes; smooth green snakes; eastern garter snakes; eastern painted turtles; eastern red-backed salamanders; bullfrogs

TOPS'L FARM

🏚 8, 🏕 5

365 Bremen Road, Waldoboro, ME 04572
Open: May to October ▪ Rates: From $125 ▪ Amenities: Meals, bathhouse, camp store, lockboxes, charging station, picnic area, book exchange, board and lawn games, potable water, ice, fire pits, outdoor movies ▪ ADA sites: No

River and woods converge on a vintage farm converted into a 21st-century glamping retreat where guests can slumber in modern safari tents and wooden camps or an antique farmhouse and cottage. The farm primarily caters to weddings and other groups. Solo travelers can book a stay during Tops'l Overnights between Memorial Day and Halloween, all-inclusive weekends that include dinner, lodging, activities, and entertainment. Founded by sailor and beekeeper M. S. Smith in 1936 (hence the name), the 83-acre (33 ha) spread is still a working farm with crops and livestock. The property lies near the confluence of the Medomak River and Muscongus Bay not far from Waldoboro village, where glampers can catch a show at the historic Waldo Theatre or sample local suds at Odd Alewives Farm Brewery.

UNDER CANVAS ACADIA

🏕 63

702 Surry Road, Surry, ME 04684
Open: May to October ▪ Rates: From $314 ▪ Amenities: Restaurant, camp store, activities concierge, evening entertainment, communal fire pits, organic bath products, daily housekeeping ▪ ADA sites: Call ahead

Under Canvas brings its Western-style glamping to the East Coast with a brand-new campus spread across a gorgeous waterfront plot near Mount Desert Island. The spacious, comfy safari tents are scattered through 100 acres (40 ha) of Maine woods about a 30-minute drive from the Acadia National Park Visitor Center near Bar Harbor. The camp includes the popular Stargazer tents with a viewing window above the beds that Under Canvas made famous out West, as well as a new huge Cadillac Mountain model with two private bathrooms that can easily sleep seven. Those who tire of the tranquil woods-and-water setting (Is that even possible?) can venture to nearby Highway 3 with its lively lobster pounds, shopping outlets, and the surprisingly entertaining Great Maine Lumberjack Show.

BLACKWOODS CAMPGROUND

🚐 60 no hookup, 🏕 221

155 Blackwoods Drive, Otter Creek, ME 04660
Open: May to October ▪ Rate: RV/ tent $30 ▪ Amenities: Dump station, restrooms, picnic tables, fire rings, potable water, shuttle bus ▪ ADA sites: Yes

With Cadillac Mountain rising behind and the Atlantic raging out front, Blackwoods offers an iconic Acadia camping adventure. One of only four spots where visitors can camp inside the national park, it's also the closest campground to Bar Harbor, Jordan Pond, and the Park Loop Road scenic drive. Although much of the campground is set aside for tent camping, it can also accommodate self-sufficient RVs. From any site, it's a short walk to Otter Cove and its rocky shoreline. Heading in the opposite direction, campers can hike the Cadillac Ridge Trail to the park's highest point (1,530 feet/ 466 m) and its spectacular coastal views. Blackwoods doesn't offer showers, but the public bathhouse in Otter Cove village is walking distance. The village also harbors a general store with camping supplies, deli counter, Maine souvenirs, and boiled lobster dinners.

COBSCOOK BAY STATE PARK

🚐/🏕 48 no hookup, 🏕 58

40 South Edmunds Road, Dennysville, ME 04628
Open: May to October ▪ Rates: RV/ tents $20/$30 (state resident/non-resident) ▪ Amenities: Dump station, showers, picnic tables, fire rings with grills, potable water, boat ramp, playground ▪ ADA sites: Yes

Catch America's earliest sunrise at this small but captivating state park near the nation's easternmost point. Located just 8 miles (12.8 km) from West Quoddy Head and the open Atlantic Ocean, Cobscook gets its name from a local Native American

Don't forget the kayaks when packing for camping in Cobscook Bay State Park.

Sunrise on the coast of Mount Desert Island in Maine's Acadia National Park

term for "boiling tides." And that aptly named ebb and flow is extreme—high tide reaches up to 28 feet (8.5 m) or nearly the height of a three-story building. Campers can watch the rise and fall from sites located along Broad Cove, Burnt Cove, and Whiting Bay. With your eye on the tide charts, the bay is a great place for canoeing, kayaking, or paddleboarding. There are two short trails inside the park and a nearby route to the fire tower lookout in neighboring Moosehorn National Wildlife Refuge, which also offers a 6-mile (9.6 km) wilderness loop trail. More than 200 bird species have been spotted in the area, including Maine's largest concentration of bald eagles.

AROOSTOOK STATE PARK

🚐/🏕 5 partial hookup, 23 no hookup

87 State Park Road, Presque Isle, ME 04769

Open: Year-round ▪ Rates: RV/tents partial hookup $25/$35 (state resident/nonresident), RV/tents no hookup $15/$25 ▪ Amenities: Kitchen shelter, showers, picnic tables, fire pits, potable water, playground, boat ramps, beach, canoe/kayak rentals ▪ ADA sites: Yes

Maine's oldest state park (established 1938) lies about as far north as you can travel on America's Eastern seaboard, a region that nearly wound up in Canada and where an estimated 10 to 15 percent of residents speak French at home. The campground and most other facilities sit between Echo Lake and Quaggy Jo Mountain, although the park's hiking, cross-country skiing, and snowmobile paths extend into the wooded wilderness beyond the landmark peak. Aroostook is especially attractive in the autumn when its maples, beech, and other deciduous trees burst with color. About a mile from the park entrance, a monument marks the spot where *Double Eagle II* lifted off in 1978 to start the first successful transatlantic balloon crossing.

WILDERNESS EDGE CAMPGROUND

🏚3, 🚐/🏕 33 partial hookup, 🏕 70

Come winter, Gorman Chairback Lodge is reachable only by ski, snowshoe, or dogsled.

71 Millinocket Lake Road, Millinocket, ME 04462

Open: May to October ▪ Rates: RV/tent partial hookup $39.95, tent $11.50 per person, cabins from $50 ▪ Amenities: Dump station, camp store, showers, picnic tables, fire rings, swimming pool, playground, canoe/kayak rentals, laundry, shuttle service, firewood, ice, potable water, internet, tent and RV rental ▪ ADA sites: Partial

Located deep in the heart of the state's Katahdin region, this private campground offers a great base for exploring Baxter State Park and the myriad rivers and lakes of Katahdin Woods and Waters National Monument. Nearly all of the RV and tent sites are heavily shaded. Those who didn't haul along their own shelter can overnight in three rustic cabins or hire a tent or RV from the campground. Wilderness Edge offers guided moose and wildlife tours and wilderness ATV adventures daily during the season. The front desk can also arrange white-water rafting and canoe trips, scenic flights, and fly-fishing.

DAICEY POND CABINS
🏠10

Daicey Pond Road, Baxter State Park, Millinocket, ME 04462

Open: May to October ▪ Rates: From $57 ▪ Amenities: Restroom, picnic tables, fire pits, firewood, canoe rental, library ▪ ADA sites: Yes

The last overnight before reaching the northern end of the Appalachian Trail (AT) on Mount Katahdin, Daicey Pond offers a handful of log cabins that sleep anywhere from two to six people. Beds with bare mattresses, gas lights, and woodstoves are provided with each cabin, but campers need to bring their own blankets/sleeping bags, pillows, towels, and cooking gear to prepare meals on the fire pit outside. The only water source is Daicey Pond, which means it has to be treated before human consumption. In addition to a ranger station, the camp boasts a canoe landing and a log library with books and board games. The AT runs right behind the camp, Mount Katahdin in one direction, Little Niagara and Big Niagara waterfalls in the other as the trail snakes its way south through Baxter State Park.

AMC GORMAN CHAIRBACK LODGE & CABINS
🏠12

Gorman Chairback Camp Road, Greenville, ME 04441

Open: May to October and December to March ▪ Rates: From $249/$299 all inclusive (AMC member/nonmember) ▪ Amenities: Bathhouse, sauna, woodstoves, gas lamps, picnic tables, fire pits, boat dock, snowshoes, fishing gear ▪ ADA sites: Yes

Founded in 1876 with a mission to advocate outdoor recreation and preserve wilderness areas in the Northeast states, the Appalachian Mountain Club (AMC) is one of the nation's oldest conservation organizations. Among its many projects is a lodge-to-lodge cross-country ski traverse with four overnight stops that stretches across the AMC 100 Mile Wilderness Conservation Area in north-central Maine. Newest of the lodges along this wilderness route, Gorman Chairback is reachable only by ski, snowshoe, or dogsled (if you happen to bring your pack) during the winter, but by vehicle during the summer and fall when the traverse morphs into a long-distance hiking route.

Overlooking Long Pond, Gorman Chairback offers two types of cabin. Basic units feature nothing more than beds, woodstove for heat, and gas lamps for illumination—no running water or power outlets. However, the deluxe cabins come with private bathrooms and showers. The all-inclusive rate includes three meals per day in the lodge dining hall and use of canoes, kayaks, and paddleboards. Fishing gear is available for those who want to cast for trout and salmon in the local lakes and streams. ▪

SOMETHING SPECIAL

Lighthouses

Because of its rocky coastline, Maine is famous for its lighthouses. There are more than 60 of them peppering the state up and down its shoreline. The oldest lighthouse in Maine is the Portland Head Light in Cape Elizabeth, on what was once the site of Fort Williams, which was in service from 1898 to 1962.

Construction of a lighthouse at this spot began in 1787, and the original tower was first lit in 1791. The lighthouse looks out over Portland Harbor and Casco Bay and offers views of four other towers: Spring Point Ledge Light (built in 1897), Ram Island Ledge Light (built in 1905), Halfway Rock (first lit in 1871), and the Cape Elizabeth light (first lit in 1874).

Maryland

Maryland offers the chance to tent-camp with wild ponies, park your RV a short distance from the sites and monuments of Washington, D.C., and glamp near a wild and scenic river.

HOLLOFIELD CAMPGROUND

🚐/⛺ 28 partial hookup, 43 no hookup

8020 Baltimore National Pike, Ellicott City, MD, 21043

Open: April to October ▪ Rates: RV/tent partial hookup $24.50, RV/tent no hookup $18.50 ▪ Amenities: Dump station, showers, picnic tables, fire rings with grills, firewood, potable water, amphitheater ▪ ADA sites: Yes

You would never know it today given the pristine woods and water, but the Patapsco Valley was once an environmental disaster area, its forests denuded by logging, its namesake river polluted by erosion, factories, and sewage. The vale has become a poster child for successful renewal, a campaign that started in 1907 when it became Maryland's first state park. Set along the western edge of the Baltimore metro area, the state park is split into five units along a 32-mile (51 km) stretch of the Patapsco River. Hollofield Campground spreads across a thickly wooded area beside the river near the elongated park's midway point.

Unlike other parts of the valley where the terrain is more inviting,

There's nothing like camping with the wild ponies that live on Assateague Island National Seashore.

Hollofield's steep topography limits hiking to a few short paths including the Ole Ranger Trail through the nearby woods and the Union Dam Trail to riverside remains of Union Dam, erected in 1810 to power a nearby cotton mill. Two of the park's other landmarks are a short drive away: a 300-foot-long (91 m) pedestrian-only, swinging suspension bridge and the Thomas Viaduct, a 612-foot (187 m) behemoth that is the world's oldest and largest multiarched stone railroad bridge.

ELK RIVER CAMPING AREA

🏠15, 🚐/⛺ 28 full hookup, 19 partial hookup, 124 no hookup, ⛺ 23

4395 Turkey Point Road, North East, MD 21901

Open: April to October ▪ Rates: RV/tent full hookup $36.50, partial hookup $27.50, no hookup and tent only $21.50, cabins from $50.50 ▪ Amenities: Camp store, dump station, showers, picnic tables, fire rings with grills, lantern posts, potable water, playgrounds, boat ramp, fishing pier, nature center ▪ ADA sites: Partial

Floating near the top end of the Chesapeake Bay, Elk Neck State Park straddles a narrow peninsula crowned by the historic Turkey Point Lighthouse (built in 1833). The camping area comprises more than 200 sites

spread across seven loops between Beaver Marsh and Wapiti Pond on the peninsula's eastern side. North East Loop boasts the only full hookups, and Bohemian Loop is reserved for tent campers. Only a handful of sites overlook the water, the rest hunkered down beneath a thick canopy of trees behind the shore. However, many of the cabins are sited along the Elk River, a wide tidal tributary of the big bay. A tad farther down the shore, Rogues Harbor offers a boat ramp and fishing pier. Elk River's best hikes are the loop around Beaver Marsh and the well-worn footpath to the lighthouse, which crosses a raptor viewing field.

OCEANSIDE CAMPGROUND

🚐/⛺ 41 no hookup, ⛺ 63

Bayberry Drive, Berlin, MD 21811

Open: Drive-in year-round, tent-only March to November ▪ Rate: $30 ▪ Amenities: Dump station, showers, picnic tables, fire rings with grills, beach ▪ ADA sites: Partial

If you dream about wild horses splashing through the surf along a pristine shore, Assateague Island should be on your bucket list because one morning you might wake up to find such ponies grazing next to your beachside campsite. An undeveloped barrier island along the Atlantic side of the Delmarva Peninsula, Assateague divides its sandy expanse between a small Maryland state park and the much larger Assateague Island National Seashore, which spills across the state line into Virginia. The latter offers overnight spots on both sides of the peninsula, including the Oceanside Campground with RV-friendly drive-in sites and a walk-in portion reserved for tent campers right along the beach. It's dry camping all the way—no hookups here. Just the dunes, the waves, and the island's legendary ponies, which have called the island home since at least the 17th century.

JANES ISLAND STATE PARK

🚐/🏕 49 partial hookup, 52 no hookup

26280 Alfred J. Lawson Drive, Crisfield, MD 21817
Open: March to November ▪ Rates: RV/tent partial hookup $27.50, no hookup $21.50 ▪ Amenities: Camp store, dump station, showers, picnic tables, fire rings with grills, lantern posts, potable water, boat rental, boat ramp, fish cleaning station ▪ ADA sites: Yes

Located on the opposite side of the Delmarva Peninsula from Assateague, this water-oriented state park lies along the eastern edge of the Chesapeake Bay. Rather than wild horses and raging surf, Janes Island is celebrated for terrific bird watching and paddling terrain through a warren of wetlands. And it just might boast the best sunsets in all of Maryland. The park's campsites and camper cabins sit along the Daugherty Creek Canal, a waterway that connects the Big Annemessex River estuary and Crisfield Harbor with its historic waterfront. On the opposite side of the canal are 2,900 acres (1,173 ha) of salt marsh with canoe and kayak trails that lead to excellent birding spots and remote beaches on tiny barrier islands along the outer edge of the marsh.

GREENBELT PARK CAMPGROUND

🚐/🏕 107 no hookup, 🚐 35, 🏕 30

6565 Greenbelt Road, Greenbelt, MD 20770
Open: Year-round ▪ Rate: $20 ▪ Amenities: Dump station, showers, picnic tables, fire rings with grills, potable water, playground, beach, amphitheater ▪ ADA sites: Yes

It's camping in the burbs rather than true wilderness, but the white-tailed deer and beaver, the abundant trees and silence, make it feel like the back of beyond. Managed by the National Park Service, the park takes its name from the town of Greenbelt on the outskirts of Washington, D.C. Located near the University of Maryland's huge College Park campus, the NASA Goddard Space Flight Center, and three major malls, it's an offbeat place for a campground. But don't tell that to the folks who cherish the park as a quick, easy overnight escape from big-city life.

CHERRY HILL PARK

🏠 15, 🚐/🏕 400 full hookup, 🏕 19, 🛖 3

9800 Cherry Hill Road, College Park, MD 20740
Open: Year-round ▪ Rates: RV/tent full hookup from $85, tent only from $65, cabins from $149, yurts from

Along with spots for RVs and tents, Cherry Hill Park offers cabins and glamping pods.

You'd never guess the woodsy campsites at Greenbelt Park Campground are just minutes from the nation's capital.

$169 ■ Amenities: Restaurant, snack bar, camp stores, dump station, showers, laundry, picnic tables, fire rings with grills, potable water, firewood, ice, propane, swimming pools, splash park, hot tub, sauna, playgrounds, basketball, miniature golf, fitness center, game room, fishing pond, outdoor theater, dog run, campground shuttle, golf cart rental, cable TV, internet ■ ADA sites: Yes

Few other RV parks anywhere on the continent boast this many amenities, let alone one in a major metropolitan area that started life 100 years ago as a chicken farm. But Cherry Hill Park (CHP) nearly has it all, starting with a location that's right outside the Washington, D.C.,

beltway (Interstate 495). The resort complements its full-hookup RV pads with premium tent sites outfitted with hammocks, gazebos, brick patios, and Adirondack chairs. Indoor accommodation includes traditional log cabins and smaller, less expensive glamping pods. From a dog-walking service and summer outdoor movie nights to tractor rides and a kids' gem-mining sluice, CHP offers all sorts of extra services and amenities. Campers who want to venture into the nation's capital can hop a Metro bus to the College Park commuter rail station from right outside the resort front gate. Or they can purchase tickets at the front desk for four different sightseeing tours that depart from

Cherry Hill, including the resort's own guided ride around the District.

OWENS CREEK CAMPGROUND

🚐 / ⛺ 50 no hookup
15882 Foxville-Deerfield Road, Sabillasville, MD 21780
Open: April to November ■ Rate: $30
■ Amenities: Showers, picnic tables, fire rings with grills, lantern poles, firewood, potable water, amphitheater ■ ADA sites: Yes

Make like the many world leaders who have sojourned in the Maryland wilderness over the past century by overnighting at Catoctin Mountain Park, location of both the Camp

For easy entry to the trails, canal, and cascades at historic C&O National Historic Park, make your camp at Antietam Creek.

David presidential retreat and Owens Creek Campground. Managed by the National Park Service, the campground offers 50 primitive sites for tents, camper vans, and smaller RVs in a thickly wooded area near the park's northern extreme. Other than chillaxing beside Owen Creek, hiking is really the only activity. However, the campground is convenient for visiting nearby sights like Gettysburg Battlefield, Eisenhower National Historic Site, and historic Frederick, Maryland.

ANTIETAM CREEK CAMPGROUND

🏕 20 no hookup

Canal Road, Sharpsburg, MD, 21782
Open: Year-round ▪ Rates: From $10 ▪ Amenities: Restrooms, picnic tables, fire rings with grills, playground, beach, boat rental, basketball courts, bike repair station, amphitheater ▪ ADA sites: No

Campers need to trek a short portion of the Chesapeake & Ohio Canal Towpath to reach this small tent-only campground beside the Potomac River. Located around 90 minutes from Washington, D.C., the campsites are well spaced across a grassy shoreline shaded by big trees. The C&O Canal Ferry Hill Visitor Center and historic Shepherdstown are about an hour's hike upstream from the campground. As the name implies, it's also close to Antietam National Battlefield, and Harper's Ferry is a short way downstream.

SAVAGE RIVER LODGE

🏚 18, 🏚 8

1600 Mount Aetna Road, Frostburg, MD 21532
Open: Year-round ▪ Rates: Cabins from $250, yurts from $270 ▪ Amenities: Restaurant, bar, gift shop, ski

shop, guest services desk, library, private bathrooms, toiletries, minifridges and coffeemakers, bedding and towels, fireplaces, private deck, electric vehicle charging station, internet ▪ ADA sites: No

"Good things come in round packages" is the motto of this upscale glamping resort in the Maryland panhandle. If that's not enough of a hint, they're referring to their spacious yurts. Outfitted with king beds, breakfast nooks, beverage centers, private decks, and bathrooms with double sinks and supersized showers, the circular abodes seem more like upscale studio apartments than backwoods escapes. Yet that's exactly what Savage River is: an ultra-comfy base for exploring the 700 acres (283 ha) of state forest that surround the lodge and hiking routes like the Great Allegheny Passage. Glampers can dine at the resort's gourmet restaurant or order room service.

WILD YOUGH GLAMPING HUTS

🏕 5 huts

1976 Herrington Manor Road, Oakland, MD 21550
Open: Year-round ▪ Rate: $90 ▪ Amenities: Bathhouse, cooktop and cooking gear, blankets and pillows, propane heater, picnic tables, fire rings with grills, firewood, private porch, board games, lawn games, communal barbecue grill, USB station, dishwashing station ▪ ADA sites: No

Sure, the glamping huts are cool. But what really makes this Maryland panhandle property extraordinary was its transformation from a coal-mining site into an ecofriendly wilderness escape after the current owners purchased the property in 1994. The name comes from the wild and scenic Youghiogheny River that flows through the 400-acre (161 ha) resort; the huts were christened for places the owners have visited, like the Ardennes Forest in Belgium and Okavango Delta in Botswana. Each hut comes with a double bed and convertible sofa, dining table, food preparation area with propane stove, and an outdoor area with picnic table and fire pit. ▪

SOMETHING SPECIAL

Assateague Island National Seashore

Encompassing a 37-mile-long (59.5 km) barrier island at the Maryland-Virginia state line, Assateague Island National Seashore welcomes those who enjoy beautiful beaches and the recreational opportunities they offer, as well as lovers of nature and wildlife.

The most popular animal on Assateague isn't part of the native wildlife at all. The island's famed ponies inhabit both the national seashore and

Chincoteague refuge, delighting visitors with their appealingly shaggy charm. The horses are descended from stock brought to the island in the 1600s by colonists. Over the years, they've adapted well to the often harsh seaside environment: dining on salt marsh, cordgrass, salt meadow hay, and beach grass. Their chubby look comes from the amount of fresh water they drink to offset their salt intake.

While the horses are undoubtedly delightful to look at, they are genuinely wild. Enjoy them from a distance to avoid bites and kicks.

Massachusetts

Multiple forests—including the Berkshires and Mohawk Trail—offer woodsy refuge, along with more famous beach spots such as Cape Cod and Martha's Vineyard.

LEE CAMPGROUND, OCTOBER MOUNTAIN STATE FOREST

🚐 / 🏕 43 partial hookup, 🏚 3
256 Woodland Road, Lee, MA 01238
Open: Mid-May through mid-October ▪ Rates: RV/tent $17/$55 (state resident/nonresident), yurts from $45 to $120 ▪ Amenities: Dump station, showers, grills, picnic tables ▪ ADA sites: Partial

The fabled Berkshires provide a rugged, woodsy setting for the largest state forest in Massachusetts. Located along the park's western edge near Lenox village, the campsite blends RV/tent camping and comfy yurts beneath a canopy of maple, birch, larch, ash, beech, spruce, and other common New England trees. Needless to say, the campground transforms into a multicolored collage each fall. Trails fan out across the forest to Washington Mountain Marsh, October Mountain, and several other high viewpoints, as well as a pioneer cemetery, beaver habitat, and more than a dozen ponds. A portion of the Appalachian Trail cuts across the western side of the park. Although Lee Campground is closed in winter, the state forest maintains snowshoe, snowmobile, and cross-country ski trails. The

Experience quintessential New England fall colors on an autumn camping trip to Mohawk Trail State Forest.

campsite is also close to author Edith Wharton's historic home, the Norman Rockwell Museum in artsy-crafty Stockbridge, and Tanglewood with its Boston Symphony concert series in the summer.

MOHAWK TRAIL STATE FOREST

🏯 6, 🚐 / 🏕 50 no hookup
Cold River Road, Charlemont, MA 01339
Open: Mid-May through mid-October ▪ Rates: Tent sites $17/$55 (state resident/nonresident); cabins from $50/$130 ▪ Amenities: Dump station, showers, grills, picnic tables, food storage lockers, dishwashing station, potable water ▪ ADA sites: Partial

Old-growth trees are the stars of a state forest that hugs the ancient and modern path of the Mohawk Trail through western Massachusetts. The original way was a busy Native American trade route between New England and upstate New York blazed long before Europeans settled the region; the modern way is Route 2, a scenic 62-mile (100 km) drive through the Berkshire hills. Perched along the Deerfield River, the campsite offers RV/tent sites and historic log cabins constructed during the 1920s by the Civilian Conservation Corps shortly after the state forest was established. Campers can hike the Mahican–Mohawk Recreation Trail into an ancient forest where some of the eastern hemlocks are more than 500 years old and a good number of maples, birches, oaks, and spruce were saplings three centuries ago. The forest also boasts many of the state's tallest trees, including white pines that tower more than 160 feet (49 m). The Deerfield River offers catch-and-release fishing and designated swimming areas.

TULLY LAKE CAMPGROUND

🏕 36
Doane Hill Road, Royalston, MA 01368
Open: April to October ▪ Rates: from $35 ▪ Amenities: Showers, grills, picnic tables, firewood, fire pits with grills, ice, cornhole, volleyball, horseshoes, canoe/kayak rental ▪ ADA sites: Yes

A forest-flanked lake in the North Quabbin region of central Massachusetts provides a bucolic setting for a tent-only campground that appeals to those who really want to get away from it all. Hiking, fishing, swimming, paddling, and afternoon naps are the main activities during the warmer months. The 22-mile (35 km) Tully Trail awaits those with more energy.

BOSTON MINUTEMAN CAMPGROUND

🏠 7, 🚌 51 full hookup, 42 partial hookup

264 Ayer Road, Littleton, MA 01460
Open: May to October ▪ Rates: RV full hookup from $62, RV partial hookup $52, tents from $52, cabins $72 ▪ Amenities: Dump station, showers, camp store, laundry, cable TV, recreation room, swimming pool, internet, picnic tables, fire pits, potable water ▪ ADA sites: Partial

Just 20 minutes from Concord and Walden Pond and only 45 minutes from the Boston Common and the Freedom Trail, Minuteman Campground affords history buffs an ideal location to delve into the Revolution and other early American

history. Surrounded by thick woods and small farms, the campground gives a hint of the landscape that Paul Revere famously rode through in 1775 and Henry David Thoreau immortalized in the 1840s. The campground features a heated pool (summer only), playground, bocce and volleyball courts, movie library, and other pastimes. But there's also plenty to amuse in the immediate area—horseback riding, canoeing and kayaking, fruit picking, and the Nashua River Rail Trail for hiking and biking.

BOSTON HARBOR ISLANDS

⛺ 33, ⛺ 12

Long Wharf North, Boston, MA 02110 or Hingham Shipyard, 28 Shipyard Drive, Hingham, MA 02043 (ferry terminals)
Open: Mid-June to September ▪ Rates: $8/$10 (state resident/nonresident) ▪ Amenities: Composting toilets, picnic tables, grills, shade structures, potable water (Peddocks only) ▪ ADA sites: No

Jointly managed by state and federal park services, this national recreation area embraces 34 islands and peninsulas in Massachusetts Bay. Four of the islands—Bumpkin, Grape, Lovells, and Peddocks—offer beachside camping during the summer and early fall. Three of the isles tender tent-only camping, while Peddocks offers both tent sites and yurts. The only way to reach these insular campsites is boat: either your own watercraft or inter-island ferries from Hingham or downtown Boston (via Georges Island). Campers must bring everything they need for their island sojourn: drinking water, camp stove or charcoal, and trash bags. Besides swimming, paddling, fishing, hiking, and beachcombing, the islands also boast historic sites like Fort Standish (Lovells) and Fort Andrews (Peddocks).

WAQUOIT BAY NATIONAL ESTUARINE RESEARCH RESERVE

⛺ 9

131 Waquoit Highway, East Falmouth, MA 02536
Open: Mid-June to September ▪ Rates: $8/$20 (state resident/nonresident) ▪ Amenities: Composting toilets ▪ ADA sites: No

It's not all about science. This esteemed research facility on Cape Cod's south shore is also open to recreation, including overnight camping on secluded Washburn Island. Established in 1987 on land once occupied by the Wampanoag people, the reserve protects 12,700 acres (5,140 ha) of wetlands, barrier beaches, and open water. Washburn is far and away Waquoit Bay's largest island. Accessible only by private boat, its primitive campsites are

The Boston Harbor Islands feel like a nature escape—with skyline views.

Nothing says Cape Cod like the National Seashore's historic lighthouses. Explore the sandy shores and famous towers from Dunes Edge Campground.

spread among the trees behind a beach on the island's east side. Hiking trails meander through the woods to wetlands and Eel Pond on the western shore. The rest of the reserves—including the beaches and boardwalk on Nantucket Sound—can be explored by boat. It almost goes without saying that campers need to bring along all food and supplies.

AUTOCAMP CAPE COD/ FALMOUTH
🏕 10, 🚐 88
836 Palmer Avenue, Falmouth, MA 02540
Open: Year-round ▪ Rates: From $179 ▪ Amenities: Camp store, fire

pits, Ursa Major bath products ▪ ADA sites: Yes

Opened in 2021, AutoCamp introduces Cape Cod to glamping via brand-new Airstreams. Built exclusively for the Falmouth resort, the 31-foot (9.4 m) travel trailers feature large, private bedrooms and expansive living and kitchen areas, plus custom-designed outdoor living spaces with designer fire pits and handmade lounge furniture. The resort revolves around a retro midcentury modern clubhouse with fireplace, lounge areas, and a shop that dispenses beverages, apparel, and grab-and-go meals. Rounding out the AutoCamp amenities are

morning yoga sessions, happy hour beer and cider tastings, and live music evenings. Stationed at the cape's southwest corner, the resort is a short drive from Woodneck Beach, the historic Falmouth waterfront, and Woods Hole Ocean Science Discovery Center.

MARTHA'S VINEYARD FAMILY CAMPGROUND
☎ 27, 🚐 46 full hookup, 🚐/🏕 77 partial hookup, 🏕 4
569 Edgartown Road, Vineyard Haven, MA 02568
Open: Mid-May to mid-October ▪ Rates: RV from $70, tents from $59, cabins $155 ▪ Amenities: Dump station, showers, camp store, laundry,

Retro Airstreams get a modern twist at Autocamp Cape Cod, where glamping is made easy.

recreation room, sports field, Wi-Fi hot spots, potable water ▪ ADA sites: Partial

The island's only campground offers RV and tent sites and rustic cabins in a forested area near Vineyard Haven town and Lagoon Pond. Managed by the third generation of the Feeney family, the campground was founded in 1968 on a plot of land where aerospace engineer Chuck Feeney could take his own family island camping. Since then, the complex has grown to more than 150 choices, ranging from primitive walk-in tent sites with no utilities to cabins and premium RV sites with cable TV. True to its creed, the campground offers plenty of family-friendly amenities, from basketball court and bike rental to playground and volleyball/badminton court. The campground is just a six-minute drive from the Vineyard Haven ferry pier, with service from Woods Hole, and a 15-minute drive from Oak Bluffs ferry terminal with service to Hyannis and Nantucket.

NICKERSON STATE PARK, CAPE COD

🚐 / 🏕 404 no hookup, 🏚 6
3488 Main Street, Brewster, MA 02631
Open: May to October ▪ Rates: Tent/ RV sites $22/$70 (state resident/ nonresident); yurts $45/$120 ▪ Amenities: Dump station, showers, camp store, grills, fire rings, picnic tables, playground ▪ ADA sites: Yes

Cape Cod's biggest campground (more than 400 sites) nestles among scrub pines and kettle ponds between Orleans and Brewster. The park takes its name from Gilded Age tycoon Samuel Nickerson, a

descendant of the area's Puritan settlers, who funded an opulent estate on the site. In 1934, a large tract of woodlands and wetlands on the estate became the first Massachusetts state park. RV and tent sites and yurts are scattered around seven camping areas near the park's four largest ponds. The camps are connected by hiking, biking, and bridle trails (which transition into cross-country ski routes come winter). Boat ramps expedite paddling, while the park's northern neck extends to Linnell and Crosby beaches on Cape Cod Bay. The state park segment of the Cape Cod Rail Trail (25 miles/41 km) harbors a bike rental station. During the summer, the park amphitheater hosts interpretive programs and kid-friendly shows ranging from magicians to animal encounters.

DUNES EDGE CAMPGROUND, CAPE COD

🚐 45 partial hookup, 🏕 63
386 U.S. 6, Provincetown, MA 02657
Open: Mid-May through late September ▪ Rates: RV partial hookup

from $63, tents $53 ▪ Amenities: Dump station, showers, camp store, laundry, picnic tables, ice, potable water ▪ ADA sites: Yes

Managed by the Trustees of Reservations, a nonprofit dedicated to historic preservation and conservation in Massachusetts, Dunes Edge is one of the few places to pitch a tent adjacent to Cape Cod National Seashore. While the wooded, rustic location is a plus, the campground's trump card is a location near Race Point Beach, the Beech Forest, and the Province Lands Bike Trail. Heading in the other direction, it's about a half-hour walk or five-minute bike ride to the Provincetown waterfront with its many eateries, bars, art galleries, and historic sights. Creative types who want to stay longer at the Cape can apply for an art or writing residency at the nearby Dune Shacks of Peaked Hill Bars Historic District, where Eugene O'Neill, Tennessee Williams, Jackson Pollock, Willem de Kooning, Norman Mailer, and Jack Kerouac contemplated and created over the years. ▪

SOMETHING SPECIAL

Cape Cod National Seashore

Serving as an oasis of still-wild lands at the edge of urbanized eastern Massachusetts, Cape Cod National Seashore protects about 40 miles (64.4 km) of beautiful beaches, as well as salt marshes, freshwater wetlands, and scattered woodlands. The shape of Cape peninsula has often been compared with that of a bent arm, culminating in a clenched fist, stretching out in the Atlantic Ocean from the mainland of southeastern

Massachusetts. The relentless Atlantic continues to sculpt the Cape: In the 1990s several historic structures had to be moved inland, away from coastal areas eroded by wave action, including the historic Highland Light and Nauset Light.

While many visitors are simply intent on enjoying a sunny summer day along the Atlantic and Cape Cod Bay beaches, there's much more to do here than swimming and sunbathing—from bicycling along paved trails to exploring historic lighthouses to enjoying flocks of seabirds skimming the waves.

Michigan

Camping in Michigan? Must bring boat. Or rent one if you can, because these sites offer plenty of lakeside and on-lake adventures.

WILD CHERRY RESORT

🏚 2, 🚐/🏔 75 full hookup, 🏠 1
8563 East Horn Road, Lake Leelanau, MI 49653
Open: May to September ▪ Rates: RV/tent full hookup from $55, cabins from $115, yurts from $99, tent-only sites from $35 ▪ Amenities: Fire pits, picnic tables, internet, golf driving range, firewood; no restrooms or showers ▪ ADA sites: Yes

Set in the heart of Michigan's cherry country, this bucolic resort is the perfect spot for exploring the northwest coast of the state's Lower Peninsula. The camp's full-hookup sites are spread around the edge of a small pond and a grassy hillside flanked by trees resplendent in the fall. Many have fire rings and concrete patios where you can read the free local newspaper delivered by the hosts each morning (they also fetch your garbage daily). While the resort primarily caters to RVs, it also offers log cabins, a yurt, and pitch-your-own tent sites. Wild Cherry's strategic location makes it easy to roam the region. Traverse City and its popular riverside boardwalk, Sleeping Bear Dunes National Lakeshore, various Lake Michigan beaches, and two dozen wineries are within short driving distance.

Just a few hours from Chicago and Detroit, the Fields of Michigan offers a glamping retreat from big cities.

PLATTE RIVER CAMPGROUND

🚐/🏔 96 partial hookup, 58 no hookup, 🏔 25
5685 Lake Michigan Road, Honor, MI 49640
Open: Year-round ▪ Rates: RV/tent partial hookup $31, RV/tent no hookup $26, tent only $22 ▪ Amenities: Dump station, showers, fire pits with grills, picnic tables, food storage lockers, firewood, potable water, amphitheater, internet ▪ ADA sites: Yes

The sandy shoreline of Lake Michigan is only a short walk (1.2 miles/ 1.9 km) along the Railroad Grade Trail from the largest campground at Sleeping Bear Dunes National Lakeshore. Located in a heavily forested area along its namesake river, the campground provides plenty of shade and a good deal of privacy between spaces. One of the few Michigan campgrounds that's open year-round, Platte River offers aquatic activities during the warmer months and cross-country skiing and snowshoeing during the winter. If you didn't bring your own craft, nearby Riverside Canoes lays on canoe, kayak, tubing, paddleboard, and raft rentals for journeys of up to four hours along the placid Platte.

THE FIELDS OF MICHIGAN

🏕 10
154 68th Street, South Haven, MI 49090
Open: May to October ▪ Rates: From

$329 ▪ Amenities: Dining hall, fire rings, firewood, games, berry picking ▪ ADA sites: No

If you're into homemade blueberry pie—and munching berries straight from the bush—this is the place for you. Michigan's hippest glamping spot is over on the west coast, a three-hour drive from Detroit but just a two-hour scoot from Chicago. The resort's spacious safari-style tents are furnished with king beds, writing desks, sofas, wood-burning stoves, area rugs, and bathrooms with hot-water shower and high-end amenities. Guests can cache their own food and drinks in Yeti coolers or mosey over to the Willows, an old deer blind converted into a covered kitchen and dining area where farm-fresh breakfast is served each morning. Besides berry picking, Fields offers spa treatments and an evening communal campfire with storytelling and s'mores. South Haven and its Lake Michigan beaches is just a

10-minute drive, and the Kal-Haven hike/bike trail is only half a mile (0.8 km) away. The camp concierge can recommend or arrange fishing, boating, hiking, wine tasting, and other activities.

PORT CRESCENT STATE PARK

☎ 7, 🚐/🏕 142 partial hookup, 🔯 2

1775 Port Austin Road, Port Austin MI, 48467

Open: April to October ▪ Rates: RV/tent $33, geodesic domes $160, cottages/cabins $52-$160 ▪ Amenities: Dump station, restrooms, showers, fire rings, picnic tables, potable water, beach, playground, horseshoes, internet ▪ ADA sites: Yes

Michigan's thumb—the peninsula that juts into Lake Huron around 100 miles (160 km) north of Detroit—provides a low-key location for a state park that offers campsites, cabins, cottages, and geodesic domes. The elongated campground shape offers numerous sites along the park's 3-mile (4.8 km) shoreline. Paneled in spruce, the geodesic domes feature skylights and lake-view windows, kitchenettes, and queen beds but no bathrooms. Hiking trails (that double as cross-country ski routes in winter) meander through the woods behind the shore, while the slow-flowing Pinnebog River is ripe for tubing, swimming, and various paddle sports. After dark, Port Crescent transforms into a dark sky preserve.

AU SABLE LOOP CAMPGROUND

🚐/🏕 5 no hookup

Federal Trail 4366, Cadillac, MI 49601

Open: April to November ▪ Rate: $10 ▪ Amenities: Restroom, potable water, boat ramps; no dump station or showers ▪ ADA sites: No

With just five campsites, this Huron-Manistee National Forest campground caters to RV and car campers who loathe large motorhome resorts and the often crowded national park campsites. Hunkered beneath hardwood forest in the middle of Michigan's Lower Peninsula, Au Sable takes its name from a huge bend in its namesake river. Set near the river's eastern end, the campground makes an awesome embarkation point for paddle trips along the Au Sable National Scenic River as it flows toward Lake Huron; canoe/kayak rentals are available in four nearby towns. And bring your bait and tackle: The Au Sable is also known for brown trout angling.

MACKINAW MILL CREEK CAMPING

☎ 27, 🚐/🏕 600 full, partial, and no hookup

9730 U.S. Highway 23, Mackinaw City, MI 49701

Open: May to October ▪ Rates: RV full hookup from $23, RV/tent partial or no hookup from $19, cabins from $29 (three-night minimum stay) ▪ Amenities: Dump station, showers, fire pits, picnic tables, playgrounds, basketball courts, game room, camp store, propane, internet ▪ ADA sites: Partial

Located at the top end of the Lower Peninsula, this colossal campground offers more than 600 options ranging from full-hookup RV pads to tent-only spots and lakeside cabins. It's little more than a stone's throw (five minutes) from Colonial Michilimackinac and the epic Mackinaw Straits Bridge, and a short ferry ride from historic Mackinaw Island. Family owned and operated since it opened in 1964, the campground features a beach, camp store, heated swimming pool, miniature golf, antique fire engine and hayrides, bike rentals, and free shuttle to the ferry pier in town.

These secluded cabins overlook the St. Marys River on Lime Island.

From Twelvemile Beach Campground, take a paddling tour of Pictured Rocks National Lakeshore.

LIME ISLAND STATE RECREATION AREA

🏠 7, ⛺ 6

De Tour Village, MI 49725

Open: June to September ▪ Rates: Cabins $74, tents $22 ▪ Amenities: Restrooms, picnic tables, potable water, boat ramps ▪ ADA sites: No

Visitors need their own boat to reach the secluded cabins and campsites on Lime Island in the St. Marys River, a wide waterway that connects Lakes Superior and Huron and also separates Michigan from Ontario province in Canada. The closest place to launch your craft is the boat ramp in Raber, Michigan, 2 miles (3.2 km) across the river.

Cabins are aligned on a grassy bluff that overlooks the St. Marys River toward Raber Bay; tent platforms stretch south along the shore from the docks. Tent camping is also allowed at South Beach on the island's southeast side, a 2.25-mile (3.6 km) hike from the village. Whether cottages or campsites, visitors need to bring their own food, drinks, cooking equipment, and sleeping gear. Bathrooms are primitive and cabins are rustic. Hiking, hunting, and paddling are the main activities. The village offers a historic schoolhouse, Victorian-era house museum, and 18th-century lime kilns. But the coolest thing about Lime Island is watching the big

Great Lakes freighters moving up and down the river.

TWELVEMILE BEACH CAMPGROUND

🚐 / ⛺ 36 no hookup

Twelvemile Beach Road, Grand Marais, MI 49839

Open: May to October ▪ Rates: $20 (seniors $10) ▪ Amenities: Restrooms, fire rings with grills, picnic tables, potable water, amphitheater; no showers or hookups ▪ ADA sites: Yes

Overlooking the big lake the Ojibwe once called Gichi-Gami ("Great Sea"), Twelvemile Beach offers the largest and arguably the most spectacular of the three campgrounds

Take in sweeping views of Lake Michigan and Sleeping Bear Dunes National Lakeshore from viewing platforms.

that grace Pictured Rocks National Lakeshore on Michigan's Upper Peninsula. It's pretty basic living: no hookups, showers, or camp store. The nearest place to purchase food and other supplies is the little town of Grand Marais, a half-hour drive to the east. But the location more than makes up for any inconvenience: Lake Superior in all its glory, the world's largest freshwater lake in surface area and third largest in water volume. No wonder Native Americans considered it a sea.

Campers reach the lakeshore via wooden stairs down a sandy slope. Water temperature normally ranges between 55°F (13°C) and 65°F (8.5°C) in summer, which makes kayaking and other paddle pursuits more inviting than swimming. On its long trek between North Dakota and upstate New York, the North Country Trail runs through the middle of the campground, giving campers the option of day hikes to other Painted Rock landmarks like Au Sable Light Station (founded in 1874), the 300-foot (91 m) Au Sable Dunes, and the wildlife-rich Beaver Basin. The White Birch Interpretive Trail meanders through the woods behind the campground, and during the warmer months, rangers take the stage for interpretive talks at the Twelvemile Beach amphitheater.

UNION BAY MODERN CAMPGROUND

🚐 / 🏕 100 partial hookup, 🏠 2
107th Engineers Memorial Highway, Ontonagon, MI 49953
Open: May to October ▪ Rates: RV/ tent partial hookup $28, yurts $68 ▪ Amenities: Dump station, showers, fire rings, picnic tables, firewood, ice, potable water, boat launch ▪ ADA sites: Yes

Porcupine Mountains Wilderness, Michigan's largest state park, is home to a marvelous waterfront campground on Lake Superior. The rocky, driftwood-strewn shoreline is more conducive to beachcombing than sunbathing. But depending on the weather, the offshore waters invite kayaking, canoeing, and other aquatic pastimes. A jetty-protected boat ramp expedites quick and easy lake access. In addition to food and beverages, the camp store offers boat and bike rentals. Union Bay lies within walking distance of the visitors center and warm-weather events like the Porkies Music Festival staged at the Porcupine Mountain Ski Area. Beyond the campground, the 60,000-acre (24,281 ha) park is a mosaic of woods and wetlands, rivers and waterfalls, mountains and lakeshore laced with hiking and biking routes. In addition to the largest grove of old-growth northern hardwood forest west of the Adirondacks, the park harbors creatures that have largely disappeared elsewhere in the Midwest—black bears, moose, wolves, lynx, beaver, river otters, and the park's namesake porcupines.

ROCK HARBOR LODGE

🏠 20, 🚐 2

Rock Harbor, Isle Royale National Park, MI 49931
Open: May to September ▪ Rates: Housekeeping cabins from $227, camper cabins $52 ▪ Amenities: Bathrooms, kitchenettes, towels and bedding, electric heaters, bellhop service, camp store, restaurants, boat docks ▪ ADA sites: Yes

The only indoor accommodation on Isle Royale, Rock Harbor traces its roots to the early 20th century, nearly 40 years before the remote Lake Superior landfall became a national park. Visitors can choose from motel-style rooms, comfy housekeeping cabins within walking distance of the lodge, or rustic camper cabins at Windigo near the island's west end. Housekeeping cabins offer the option of cooking your own meals and dining at the Greenstone Grill or Lighthouse Restaurant. Campers can explore Isle Royale's many trails on their own or join guided hikes and boat trips. Rental canoes, kayaks, and motorboats, as well as fishing charters, are available at Rock Harbor Marina. Ferries and seaplanes link both the lodge and its Windigo satellite with mainland Michigan and even closer Minnesota. ▪

SOMETHING SPECIAL

Isle Royale National Park

Located in the northwestern portion of Lake Superior, 56 miles (90.1 km) from Michigan's Upper Peninsula, Isle Royale National Park preserves the largest island in the world's largest freshwater lake, as well as more than 450 surrounding islands. For more than 50 years, Isle Royale's isolation made it the perfect place for scientists to study its wolves and their predator-prey relationship with moose—and a secret spot for you to explore.

Experience the farthest boundaries of the park on Passage Island, located about 3.5 miles (5.6 km) off the northeast end of the main island. Visitors can reach here via their own boats or the excursion boat M.V. *Sandy*, operated by the Rock Harbor Lodge.

Minnesota

In addition to all those lakes, Minnesota campgrounds offer an array of outdoor spaces to explore: prairie, rivers, beaches, and bluffs, just to name a few.

BLUE MOUNDS STATE PARK

🚐/🏕 40 partial hookup, 33 no hookup, 🏕 14, 2 tipis

1410 161st Street, Luverne, MN 56156

Open: Year-round ▪ Rates: RV/tent partial hookup from $26, no hookup/tent only from $18, tipis $35 ▪ Amenities: Dump station, showers, picnic tables, fire rings with grills, gift shop, firewood, ice, potable water, playground, volleyball, horseshoes, internet ▪ ADA sites: Yes

Closer to the Missouri River and the Badlands than the Mississippi and Great Lakes, Blue Mounds is situated in Minnesota's wild west. Unlike the state's iconic woods-and-water image, this is die-hard prairie, with campgrounds and other facilities floating amid a sea of endless grass. The frontier vibe is complemented by a large bison herd that roams the range just south of the park's two overnight spots. One campground features power-only pads and dry camping; the other offers tent-only sites and tipis that pay homage to the Native Americans that still call this region home. Other than watching the buffalo, campers can rock-climb on lofty Sioux quartzite formations that give the park its name or visit the interpretive center inside the distinctive prairie-style house where noted

Breezy Point Cabins are set on the rocky coast of Lake Superior.

Western author Frederick Manfred once lived and wrote.

PRAIRIE VIEW RV PARK & CAMPGROUND

🚐/🏕 26 full hookup, 16 partial hookup

5590 Prairies Edge Lane, Granite Falls, MN 56241

Open: April to October ▪ Rates: RV/tent full hookup from $40, partial hookup from $35 ▪ Amenities: Dump station, showers, laundry, picnic tables, fire rings, playground, basketball court, firewood, propane, indoor swimming pool, internet ▪ ADA sites: Yes

Located in the Minnesota River Valley about 2.5 hours due west of Minneapolis, this excellent RV park was created by the region's Upper Sioux community on land they traditionally called Pejuhutazizi Kapi ("the place where they dig for yellow medicine"). Nearly every pad offers expansive prairie views (and killer sunsets), and now that many of the campground trees are reaching maturity, many of the pads are partially shaded. A short trail links the campground with a gas station, convenience store, and half a dozen restaurants inside the nearby Prairie Edge Casino Resort, which is also owned and operated by the tribe. More camping and overnight tipis are available five minutes down Highway 67 at Upper Sioux Agency State Park, a historic site and sacred

gathering place for Dakota Sioux from around the region.

ITASCA STATE PARK

🛖 39, 🚐/🏕 160 partial hookup, 63 no hookup, 🏕 11

36750 Main Park Drive, Park Rapids, MN 56470

Open: Camping year-round, cabins May to October ▪ Rates: RV/tent partial hookup from $26, no hookup/tent only from $18, cabins from $110 ▪ Amenities: Dump station, showers, picnic tables, fire rings with grills, firewood, ice, potable water, playgrounds, fish cleaning station, boat and bike rentals, restaurants ▪ ADA sites: Yes

Camping at Itasca has special meaning. This was Minnesota's first state park (founded in 1891) and only the second state park in the entire nation after Niagara Falls. The park's namesake lake is considered the ultimate source of the Mississippi River—although any one of the five streams that empty into the lake could also claim that title. Itasca also offers a vast number of ways to spend the night: two large campgrounds with both drive-up and walk-in sites, plus an array of cabin choices, some of them built by the Civilian Conservation Corps during the 1930s.

All of the organized campsites and most of the cabins are located along the east arm of Lake Itasca. But the park also boasts a vast backcountry with trails leading to remote primitive campsites. Even if you're not backpacking, it's worth trekking Itasca's trails to experience the unique "knobs and kettles"—a glacier-carved landscape of moraines and depressions—and old-growth forest with red pines more than 200 years old.

The official headwaters of the Mississippi River is located at the north end of Lake Itasca. Really more a stream at its birth, the river is shallow enough to walk across on stepping-stones. Campers also know the state park as the starting or ending point of several epic journeys: the Great River Road vehicle route, the Mississippi River Water Trail for boaters, and the Mississippi River Bikeway, as well as a leg of the North Country Trail between North Dakota and Vermont.

NORWAY BEACH RECREATION AREA
🏚11, 🚐/🏕 55 partial hookup, 124 no hookup
Norway Beach Road Northwest, Cass Lake, MN 56633
Open: May to September ▪ Rates: RV/tent partial hookup $26, no hookup $21, cabins from $165 ▪ Amenities: Dump station, camp store, showers, picnic tables, fire rings, firewood, potable water, boat rental, beach, boat ramps ▪ ADA sites: No

The great north woods are in full force at this lakeside camping spot in Chippewa National Forest. Set at the bottom end of Cass Lake, the recreation area features four separate campgrounds near a visitors center with naturalist programs and a beach with a dedicated swimming area. Adjacent to the campgrounds, privately run Norway Beach Resort offers fully furnished waterfront cabins built in the 1920s, with kitchens, private bathrooms, and their own docks for boating or fishing. The resort rents pontoon boats for angling trips or sightseeing on Cass Lake. Boaters can overnight at a primitive Forest Service campsite on Star Island that harbors its own small lake-within-a-lake and 6 miles (9.7 km) of hiking trails through red and white pine woods.

PINES OF KABETOGAMA RESORT
🏚5, 🚐/🏕 30 full hookup, 🚐 1
12443 Burma Road, Kabetogama, MN 56669
Open: May to October ▪ Rates: RV/tent full hookup from $75, cabins from $229, glamping trailer from $199 ▪ Amenities: Camp store, showers, laundry, picnic tables, fire rings, firewood, ice, boat rental, boat slips, live bait, cable TV, internet ▪ ADA sites: Call ahead

Although it's world renowned for canoe and kayak camping, Voyageurs National Park also offers spots where landlubbers can pitch a tent or park an RV. Set on 54 acres (21 ha) along the south shore of its namesake lake, the Pines offers waterfront cabins and campsites in a woodsy setting just a mile from the main visitors center. All of the RV pads are full hookup, but the "Premium" sites come with a complimentary golf cart and dock space for one boat. The spacious cabins feature two to four bedrooms, plus kitchen, private bathroom, and wooden deck. There's also a single fully equipped, fifth wheel "glamping" trailer.

Voyageur Canoe Outfitters makes a weekend of paddling and camping.

Itasca State Park, Minnesota's first state park, offers loads of recreation along its lake.

VOYAGEUR CANOE OUTFITTERS

🏠 7

189 Sag Lake Trail, Grand Marais, MN 55604

Open: Year-round ▪ Rates: $88-$400 ▪ Amenities: Kitchens, gas or wood stoves, bedding, towels; some cabins have outdoor picnic tables and barbecues ▪ ADA sites: No

Make like the French traders and trappers who pioneered the Great Lakes region at a remote retreat deep in Boundary Waters Canoe Area (BWCA) of northern Minnesota. While the primary service is outfitting canoe camping expeditions through the region's watery wilderness and neighboring Quetico Provincial Park in Canada, they also offer drive-up accommodation in cabins that range from basic digs to premium abodes with private bathrooms, decks, docks, and a complimentary canoe for forays into the BWCA. Voyageur rents all necessary canoeing and camping equipment and will help plan your routes. They also offer outfitting packages with canoe, tent, sleeping bags, mess kit, stove, and even toilet paper.

BREEZY POINT CABINS

🏠 12

540 Old North Shore Road, Two Harbors, MN 55616

Open: Year-round ▪ Rates: From $177 ▪ Amenities: Kitchens, fireplaces, firewood, board games, DVD movies, s'mores, snowshoe rental, lakeside fire pits, internet ▪ ADA sites: Call ahead

With a comfy couch, a bottle of wine, the fireplace ablaze, and jaw-dropping views of Lake Superior through the picture windows, you may never want to leave these cabins along the shore of the largest Great

Take a break from cross-country skiing in Great River Bluffs State Park for hot cocoa within view of the Mississippi River.

Lake. Located 24 miles (38 km) from Duluth, Breezy Point offers a dozen spacious, comfortable, and well-decorated cabins ranging from studios to two bedrooms. All of them feature king or queen beds, full kitchens, private bathrooms, fireplaces, and patios or balconies with lake views. Those who tire of chilling out can trek a portion of the Superior Hiking Trail or venture into nearby Two Harbors for restaurants, museums, and fishing charters.

PETE'S RETREAT FAMILY CAMPGROUND & RV PARK
🚐 / 🏕 99 full hookup

22337 State Highway 47, Aitkin, MN 56431
Open: May to September ▪ Rates: From $47 ▪ Amenities: Camp store, snack bar, showers, picnic tables, fire rings, swimming pools, playgrounds, horseshoes, game room, sports courts, fish cleaning station, ice, firewood, internet ▪ ADA sites: Partial

Family fun is the forte of this eclectic campground near Mille Lacs Lake, the third largest of the state's 11,842 lakes (yes, officially it's way more than 10,000). Situated on 40 acres (16 ha) of forest and field, all of the pads are full hookup. Like many other full-service RV parks, Pete's has a swimming pool, game room, and sports courts. But it also has a BMX bike track, its own fishing pond, weekend hayrides, and daily family-oriented events and activities during the summer. Farther afield, the Mille Lacs region boasts seven golf courses and fishing in the "walleye capital of the world."

KAMP DELS
🏕 7, 🚐 / 🏕 175 full hookup,

45 partial hookup

14842 Sakatah Lake Road, Waterville, MN 56096
Open: May to September ▪ Rates: RV/tent from $50, cabins from $179 ▪ Amenities: Dump station, snack bar, swimming pools, showers, laundry, picnic tables, fire rings, playground, fitness center, boat rental, internet, tornado shelters ▪ ADA sites: Partial

Just an hour's drive south of the Twin Cities, Kamp Dels offers an iconic Minnesota summer camp experience that includes a multi-pool water park, lake boating and swimming, catch-and-release fishpond, golf driving range, and even good old-fashioned shuffleboard. One of the largest RV/camping resorts in the Midwest, it has more than 200 sites for short-term campers (four- or five-night minimum stay) and another 200-plus sites for long-term seasonal visitors. Most are full hookup RV pads, but there are also power and water sites and a handful of cabins overlooking Sakatah Lake. A free shuttle moves campers around the sprawling grounds. The restaurants and shops of downtown Waterville and Sakatah Lake State Park are

about a 1-mile (1.6 km) hike from the Kamp Dels front entrance.

GREAT RIVER BLUFFS STATE PARK
🚐 / 🏕 31 no hookup, 🏕 4, 5 bike paths

43605 Kipp Drive, Winona, MN 55987
Open: Year-round ▪ Rate: RV/tent, tent only, and bike only from $16 ▪ Amenities: Showers, picnic tables, fire rings, firewood, potable water ▪ ADA sites: Partial

Hovering more than 1,200 feet (365 m) above the river—around the same height as the observation deck atop the Empire State Building—there's not a better place to contemplate the mighty Mississippi along its entire length. Shaded by big trees at the end of a gravel road, the Great River Bluffs State Park campground sits about a five-minute walk from the lofty East and Orchard overlooks, where you can peer down on barges and other watercraft making their way along America's greatest river. You'll also find more than six miles (9.7 km) of hiking trails to explore. There's also a cart-in/walk-in area for tent campers and a bike camping site along Highway 61, just outside the state park. ▪

SOMETHING SPECIAL

Blue Mounds State Park

When the sun set on the prairies of 1800s Minnesota, pioneers trekking west saw a blue haze in an outcrop of Sioux quartzite and named it Blue Mound. This park is one of the rare places where today's visitors can see what the travelers in covered wagons saw: bison, wildflowers, and summer bluestem grasses taller than a pioneer.

For wildflowers and a spectacular view, hike the Upper Mound Trail, which crosses the Rock Alignment, a 1,250-foot (381 m) ridge running east to west. The unknown builders aligned it with the sunrise and sunset on the first day of spring and fall. Also atop the mound, the 0.7-mile (1.3 km) Burk Oak Trail runs through wooded habitat friendly to birds and butterflies.

Mississippi

Whether you're looking for a forest-shaded campsite or a waterfront spot on the bayou, Mississippi is particularly friendly for RVers in search of a nature retreat.

DAVIS BAYOU CAMPGROUND

🚐 / 🏕 52 partial hookup

3500 Park Road, Ocean Springs, MS 39564

Open: Year-round ▪ Rate: $22 ▪ Amenities: Dump station, showers, picnic tables, fire pits with grills, potable water, beach, boat ramp, amphitheater ▪ ADA sites: Yes

Sun, sea, and sand may be the main events at Davis Bayou. But this Mississippi coast hot spot has plenty of other ways for campers to pass a day or even a couple of weeks. One of two land-based campgrounds at Gulf Islands National Seashore (the other is in Florida), Davis spreads beneath live oaks in the mix of coastal forest and wetlands just east of Biloxi.

Wildlife photographers can snap dolphins, sea turtles, alligators, ospreys, and even the occasional black bear that wanders through the park. Hikers can meander down the Nature's Way Loop, the CC Spur Trail, or a third route that leads to the visitors center and fishing pier. Bikers can undertake a 15.5-mile (25 km) round trip on a Live Oaks Bicycle Route that links Davis Bayou and the adjacent town of Ocean Springs, where fans of cutting-edge architecture can visit

Jeff Busby Campground is a great spot to overnight along the Natchez Trace Parkway.

the town's Charnley-Norwood House, created in 1890 by star architects Frank Lloyd Wright and Louis Sullivan. The campground doesn't have its own patch of sand, but Ocean Springs East Beach lies within walking distance.

If that's not wild enough for your liking, consider bringing your own boat, packing it with provisions and camping gear, and flitting across Davis Bayou to the Gulf of Mexico barrier islands that give the park its name. Primitive backcountry camping is possible on Horn, Cat, Petit Bois, and West Petit Bois.

BIG BILOXI RECREATION AREA

🚐 / 🏕 25 partial hookup

19551 Desoto Park Road, Saucier, MS 39574

Open: Year-round ▪ Rate: $20 ▪ Amenities: Dump station, showers, picnic tables, fire pits with grills, potable water ▪ ADA sites: Yes

Don't let the name fool you. This DeSoto National Forest campground takes its name from the slow-flowing Biloxi River rather than the sunny Gulf Coast city, which lies more than 20 miles (32 km) away. Longleaf pines shade campsites arrayed around an open grassy area beside the river. Catfish, bass, and bream lure anglers to the waterfront, while the sinuous river is perfect for a laid-back paddle with your own boat or rentals from Biloxi

River Kayak & Canoe. Campers with a hankering for surf and sand can cruise a half-hour down U.S. Highway 49 to Gulf Port and its white-sand strands.

TURKEY FORK RECREATION AREA

🚐 / 🏕 20 partial hookup, 🏕 8

746 Turkey Fork Lake Road, 968 Highway 15 South, Laurel 39443, MS

Open: Year-round ▪ Rates: RV/tent $20, tent only $7 ▪ Amenities: Dump station, showers, picnic tables, fire pits with grills, lantern posts, boat ramp, beach ▪ ADA sites: Partial

Another easy-going Forest Service campground, Turkey Fork lies along the western shore of its namesake lake near Hattiesburg. Power and water hookup pads and primitive tent-only areas hunker beneath towering pines along the lakeshore. You have to bring your own boat, but there's a ramp to help you slide it into the water for fishing and wildlife watching that might include the alligators that inhabit the lake or bald eagles that sometimes perch in the pines. The nearest gas and groceries are available at The Store at Turkey Fork, around 5 miles (8 km) from the campground. They also sell bait, peach cobblers, and pulled-pork sandwiches.

CAMPGROUND AT BARNES CROSSING

54 full hookup

125 Campground Road, Tupelo, MS 38804

Open: Year-round ▪ Rate: $45 ▪ Amenities: Showers, laundry, picnic tables, ice, nature trail, dog runs, self-service RV wash, cable TV, internet ▪ ADA sites: No

Be sure to pack your blue suede shoes for this RV resort on the north side of Tupelo, the iconic birthplace of Elvis Presley and, by extension, modern rock 'n' roll. Well-spaced with a fair amount of shade and privacy, the full hookup pads feature gravel drives and cable TV. Nearly half of the sites are pull-throughs, able to accommodate even the largest motor homes. But you're likely

here to do more than just park the RV and camp. And you won't be disappointed. The Elvis museum and birthplace are around a 10-minute drive from the campground. When you've had enough of the King, there's plenty else to do. Also nearby the campground are Tupelo National Golf Course (18-holes, semi-private), the Natchez Trace Parkway Visitor Center, and The Mall at Barnes Crossing with its myriad shops and restaurants.

TISHOMINGO STATE PARK

7, / 61 partial hookup, 17 no hookup

105 County Road 90, Tishomingo, MS 38873 (Milepost 304 on the Natchez Trace Parkway)

Open: Year-round ▪ Rates: RV/tent partial hookup $22, RV/tent no hookup $16, cabins from $60 ▪ Amenities: Dump station, showers, picnic tables, fire pits with grills, potable water, chapel, boat ramp, playground, disc golf, swimming pool ▪ ADA sites: Yes

Enveloped by the southernmost foothills of the Appalachians, Tishomingo bears more of a wilderness mien than just about any other park in Mississippi. The flatness that characterizes so much of the state gives way to a landscape of pristine creeks, springs, and waterfalls framed by massive boulders, sandstone cliffs, and limestone outcrops.

The Natchez Trace Parkway divides the park and its overnight spots into two units. The RV and tent campground wraps around Haynes Lake with its fishing, boating, and waterfront wedding chapel. The cabins squat on the other side of the parkway beside Bear Creek and an old swing bridge that kicks off the 2-mile (3.2 km) Outcroppings Trail along the cliffs. Rock climbing is allowed only with a permit from the park office.

Archaeological digs confirm that humans have lived in the area for around 9,000 years. The Paleo-Indians were the ancient ancestors of the Chickasaw who inhabited the region when Euro Americans first arrived. The park takes its name from Chickasaw chief Tishu Minco, who was born nearby and known to hunt and fish among the park's celebrated outcrops.

PINEY GROVE CAMPGROUND

/ 141 partial hookup, 10

County Road 3550, New Site, MS 38859

Open: Year-round ▪ Rates: RV/tent $22, island tent only free ▪ Amenities: Dump station, showers, laundry, picnic tables, fire pits with grills, lantern posts, playgrounds, sports courts, beach, boat ramp, fishing piers, fish cleaning station, amphitheater, internet ▪ ADA sites: Partial

Fort Pickens Campground sits along the largest loop of the Gulf Islands National Seashore.

As the sun rises, it burns the fog off a pond within Tishomingo State Park.

Developed by the U.S. Army Corps of Engineers when the agency created Bay Springs Lake, Piney Grove rides the back of a woodsy peninsula with numerous coves and capes. This beautiful spot along the Tennessee-Tombigbee Waterway is great for families. The main campground offers power and water sites, many of them tucked into trees along the shore. Those with a boat can also camp on Piney Grove Island, where 10 primitive sites feature picnic tables and barbecue grills. Piney Grove's pride and joy is an awesome little beach with a roped-off swimming area, picnic tables, and a sand volleyball court. Between Memorial and Labor Days, the campground amphitheater hosts live music, nature programs, and other special events.

EZ DAZE RV PARK
🚐 87 full hookup
536 W. E. Ross Parkway, Southaven, MS 38671
Open: Year-round ▪Rates: From $45 ▪ Amenities: Dump station, showers, laundry, picnic tables, ice, propane, swimming pool, hot tub, massage, fitness room, playground, dog run, cable TV, internet ▪ ADA sites: Partial

Whether you're revisiting Highway 61 à la Bob Dylan or making the obligatory once-in-a-lifetime pilgrimage to Graceland, EZ Daze offers a convenient place to park your motor home, camper van, or travel trailer. Situated on the southern outskirts of Memphis just over the state line, EZ Daze complements its full-hookup sites with an outdoor swimming pool, indoor hot tub, and on-site massage therapist to prep campers for a crazy night on Beale Street or a cruise down the Delta Blues Highway. Right down the road is Landers Center, a big-time venue for concerts, consumer trade shows, and the weekend Southern Flea Market between March and December. Also nearby, you'll find plenty more Memphis history including Sun Studios (where greats like Jerry Lee Lewis and Johnny Cash recorded their record-breaking albums), the National Civil Rights Museum, the Gibson Guitar Factory, and the Sharpe Planetarium. For a different kind of fun, head into Tunica, called the "South's Casino Capital" and boasting nine resorts as well as fine dining restaurants and entertainment venues.

At one of many sites within the DeSoto National Forest, find a pitcher plant bog amid slash pine trees.

JEFF BUSBY CAMPGROUND

🚐 / ⛰ 18 no hookup

Milepost 193.1 Natchez Trace Parkway, Ackerman, MS 39735

Open: Year-round ▪ Rate: Free ▪ Amenities: Picnic tables, fire pits with grills, potable water ▪ ADA sites: Yes

Named for the Mississippi congressman who lobbied for the federal government to survey the Old Natchez Trace, construct the 444-mile (715 km) modern parkway, and include it in the National Park System, Jeff Busby Campground offers a tranquil spot to overnight about halfway between Jackson and Tupelo. Campers can drive or hike to the summit of Little Mountain, one of the highest points in Mississippi and a great place to survey the heavily forested landscape of north-central Mississippi. The trail to the summit and back is 1.6 miles (2.6 km) round trip, but doable for most casual hikers. There's also an easy half-mile (0.8 km) nature trail that loops through the park, as well as 22 picnic tables for a nice spot to lunch within the scenic setting. The campground is especially attractive in fall when the trees burst into a range of autumn hues. Like all the other National Park Service campgrounds along the parkway, Jeff Busby is first come, first served and free of charge. Anyone hoping to overnight there needs a combination of good planning and perfect timing to snag one of the 18 spots, especially during the spring and fall high seasons and any holiday weekend.

ROCKY SPRINGS CAMPGROUND

🚐 / ⛰ 22 no hookup

Milepost 54.8, Natchez Trace Parkway, Hermanville, MS 39086

Open: Year-round ▪ Rate: Free ▪ Amenities: Picnic tables, fire pits with grills, potable water, amphitheater ▪ ADA sites: Yes

Arguably the best campground along the Natchez Trace Parkway, Rocky Springs flaunts its own natural and man-made attractions: hiking the 7-mile (11 km) Rocky Springs segment of the Natchez Trace National Scenic Trail, rambling along a portion of the original trace, or visiting the Rocky Springs townsite, cemetery, and the 1837 Methodist Church, which continued to hold Sunday service into the 21st century. The roadside campground also attracts Civil War buffs to half a dozen nearby battlefields, including Port Gibson, Raymond, Grand Gulf, Champion Hill, and Vicksburg—clashes that turned the tide of the War Between the States in 1863. There are only 22 sites here, and they fill up on a first come, first served basis.

NATCHEZ STATE PARK

🏠 10, 🚐 / ⛰ 6 full hookup, 44 partial hookup, ⛰ 8

230B Wickcliff Road, Natchez, MS 39120

Open: Year-round ▪ Rates: RV/tent full or partial hookup $22, tent only $15, cabins from $67 ▪ Amenities: Dump station, showers, laundry, picnic tables, fire pits with grills, firewood, boat ramp, playground, disc golf, nature trail ▪ ADA sites: No

Not to be confused with Natchez National Historical Park and its elaborate antebellum mansions, this southern Mississippi park lies around 13 miles (22 km) inland along the Natchez Trace Parkway. The park's waterfront cabins come with kitchens, bedding and towels, air-conditioning, and screened porches to keep those pesky summer bugs at bay. The park lake is small but well stocked for anglers and famous as the place where the largest bass in state history was hooked in 1992. Besides its proximity to historic Natchez and the Mississippi River, the park is also close to parkway landmarks like the ancient Emerald Mound and Mount Locust Historic House. ▪

SOMETHING SPECIAL

Natchez Trace National Scenic Trail

The 444-mile-long (714.5 km) scenic Natchez Trace Parkway runs from Natchez, Mississippi, to Nashville, Tennessee, following a corridor of trails once used by Native Americans, soldiers, and post riders, as well as flatboatmen returning north after taking their boats to New Orleans. In the early 19th century, the Natchez Trace was one of the most important "highways" of the American frontier.

Natchez Trace National Historic Scenic trail allows hikers and horseback riders to recall the experience of travelers on the original Trace. Five unconnected segments of the trail have been completed, totaling about 67 miles (107.8 km). The trail runs parallel to the parkway and never strays far from it. In several places, hikers and riders today can travel the exact path of the old Trace, often along paths worn deeply by decades of boots and hooves. Hardwood and pine forests, creeks, and swamp wetlands make up some of the habitats traversed on the trail.

Missouri

Find plenty of family fun, as well as relaxing glamping getaways, in the natural wonders of Missouri's landscape, including the celebrated Ozarks.

WORLDS OF FUN VILLAGE

🏠 42, 🚐/🏕 82 full hookup

8000 Northeast Parvin Road, Kansas City, MO 64161

Open: March to October ▪ Rates: RV from $34, cabins from $179 ▪ Amenities: Camp store, swimming pool, hot tub, showers, laundry, picnic tables, grills, satellite TV, internet, theme parks ▪ ADA sites: Yes

Ask kids to create their ideal campground, and it would probably resemble this sprawling RV village in Kansas City. It's not the large L-shaped swimming pool or the woody copse you can ramble around, but the fact that it's part of the same vacation complex as two theme parks: Worlds of Fun, with its giant roller coasters and other thrill rides, and summertime Oceans of Fun water park. While fully tricked out RV pads predominate, the village is well stocked with family-friendly holiday cabins and cottages. Sleeping as many as six each, the tiny houses come with kitchens and private bathrooms, all bedding and towels, heating and air-conditioning, and outdoor patios or decks with charcoal grills. The best perk of all? Campers are entitled to the best admission prices and free parking at the theme parks.

Along the Ozark National Scenic Riverway, stop by the historic Alley Spring and Mill.

HAWLEY FARM GLAMPING

 3

3406 NE Hardy Drive, Hamilton, MO 64650

Open: Year-round ▪ Rates: From $165 (two-night minimum stay) ▪ Amenities: Breakfast, private bathrooms, showers, fans, bedding and towels, picnic tables, grill, fire pit, firewood, gardens, trails, pond ▪ ADA sites: No

"Down on the farm" takes on a whole new meaning at Hawley, a smart glamping resort with just three tents and very personalized service. The overnight digs include two classic safari tents and the yurt-like Big Bear, all of them with modern "outhouse" bathrooms featuring toilets and solar-heated showers. Outdoor seating areas with tables, chairs, fire rings, and barbecue grills are also part of the package. Relaxation would seem to be the main pastime. Trails fan out across the property's 210 acres (84 ha), and there's a pond for fishing, swimming, or rowing. Set amid the rich farmland of north-central Missouri, the farm lies about an hour's drive northeast of Kansas City near the historic town of Hamilton (birthplace of J.C. Penney and the globe's self-proclaimed "quilting capital"). Although it's most designed for couples, glampers 14 years of age and older are welcome.

LAKE OF THE OZARKS STATE PARK

🏠 8, 🚐/🏕 126 partial hookup, 84 no hookup, 🏚 2

257 Public Beach Road, Brumley, MO 65017

Open: Year-round ▪ Rates: RV/tent partial hookup from $19, no hookup from $12, cabins and yurts from $50 ▪ Amenities: Camp stores, dump stations, showers, laundry, picnic tables, playgrounds, potable water, firewood, amphitheater, marina, boat ramps, beaches ▪ ADA sites: Yes

Whether you're visiting over wild and crazy spring break or chilling in the depths of winter, Lake of Ozarks offers one of the ultimate Missouri camping experiences. Born of the Great Depression, "Puff the Magic Dragon" (as locals like to call the serpentine lake) is one of the premier aquatic destinations in the Midwest. Set on a big bend in the lake's Grand Glaize Arm, the campground boasts its own marina, boat ramps, and beaches, as well as stores that stock fishing and boating supplies and the area's best ice cream. With no more motor restrictions, the lake is popular for waterskiing, wakeboarding, and personal watercraft. There's also an official aquatic trail that connects the campground with the Grand Glaize Beach area at the western end of the arm. Away from the water, equestrian and hiking trails wind through the park's Ozark wilderness.

COOPER CREEK RESORT & CAMPGROUND

🏠 22, 🚐 / 🏕 75 full hookup

471 Cooper Creek Road, Branson, MO 65616

Open: Year-round ▪ Rates: RV from $42.60, cabins from $105 ▪ Amenities: Camp store, swimming pools, showers, laundry, picnic tables, horseshoes, basketball court, boat ramp, fishing supplies, dog park, cable TV, tornado shelter, firewood, ice ▪ ADA sites: Yes

Branson is world-famous for live country music, but the southern Missouri resort area also offers some pretty fine angling. That's the major lure (pun intended) of Cooper Creek, a bona fide fishing resort on Lake Taneycomo with everything you need to fly-fish or trawl for trout, bass, and other species on the warren of local waterways. Cooper Creek's marina offers motorboat and pontoon rentals, as well as slip rentals. They can also set you up with a local fishing guide, Missouri fishing license, or the state's online boating safety course. Those arriving without their own rigs can book a fully equipped, 30-foot (9.1 m) trailer through Ozark Mountain Camper Rentals.

RIVER OF LIFE FARM

🏠 4, 🎪 16

1746 River of Life Drive, Dora, MO 65637

Open: Year-round ▪ Rates: From $239 (two-night minimum stay) ▪

Amenities: Restaurant, camp store, kitchens, private bathrooms, air-conditioning, fireplaces, barbecue grills, towels and bedding, internet ▪ ADA sites: No

Tree house cabins are the forte of an Ozarks resort that specializes in fly-fishing and river trips, family vacations, and romantic weekends. No two are the same—all of the lofty lodges feature individual designs and decor. Sturdy wooden, four-poster beds are standard, as are kitchens, private bathrooms, whirlpool tubs, stone fireplaces, and front porches looking down on the North Fork River. The resort can arrange various outdoor activities, from trout fishing and float trips to hiking and horseback riding in surrounding Mark Twain National Forest.

ALLEY SPRING CAMPGROUND

🚐 / 🏕 26 partial hookup, 124 no hookup

State Highway 106, Eminence, MO 65466

Open: Year-round ▪ Rates: RV/tent partial hookup $15, RV/tent no hookup $12 ▪ Amenities: Camp store, dump station, showers, picnic tables, fire rings with grills, lantern posts, potable water, amphitheater, river access ▪ ADA sites: Yes

Created in 1964 as the first national park to protect an entire river system, Ozark National Scenic Riverways offers impromptu, primitive camping on gravel bars during float trips along the Jacks Fork and Current Rivers, as well as developed waterfront campgrounds like Alley Spring. Largest of the park's seven overnight spots, Alley unfolds as a

Book a cabin at one of the best water getaways in Lake of the Ozarks State Park.

Just half an hour from the bustle of St. Louis, park your RV at KOA Route 66 St. Louis West for a green escape.

great place to camp at the end of a short float from Blue Spring or the start of a downstream journey to the confluence at Two Rivers or even all the way down to Van Buren town. Those who didn't haul their own watercraft can rent canoes, kayaks, or rafts or join a guided float trip at Harvey's Alley Springs Canoe Rental down Highway 106 from the campground.

MERAMEC STATE PARK
🏠11, 🚐/🏕 21 full hookup, 138 partial hookup, 50 no hookup
115 Meramec Park Drive, Sullivan, MO 63080
Open: May to October ▪ Rates: RV/tent full hookup $24, partial hookup

$21, no hookup $12, cabins from $125 ▪ Amenities: Restaurant, camp store, showers, laundry, picnic tables, fire pits with grills, playgrounds, boat ramp, boat rental, amphitheater, potable water, firewood ▪ ADA sites: Yes

With more than 6,400 known caverns, Missouri is rightly called the Cave State. About an hour beyond St. Louis along Interstate 44, Meramec State Park boasts at least 40 of the underground marvels, including famous Fisher Cave with its resident bats, prehistoric bear claw marks, and incredible hellectite formations. The campground is conveniently located between the Fisher

Cave entrance and the park's other star attraction: a meandering Meramec River ripe for swimming, fishing, and boating. A concessionaire offers float trips in canoes, kayaks, or rafts along a 5-mile (8 km) stretch of the river. Away from the water, the park offers hiking trails through thick hardwood forest and a 19th-century historic district that includes the old Hamilton Ironworks.

ST. LOUIS WEST/ HISTORIC ROUTE 66 KOA
🏠30, 🚐 39 full hookup, 29 partial hookup, 🏕 28, 1 caboose
18475 Old Highway 66, Eureka, MO 63069

Visitors to Onondaga Cave State Park can take a cave tour, camp, hike, or canoe the Meramec River.

Open: Year-round • Rates: RV full hookup from $36, RV partial hookup from $30, tent only from $25, cabins from $40, caboose from $99 • Amenities: Camp store, dump station, swimming pool, showers, laundry, picnic tables, fire rings, playground, sports courts, bike rental, dog park, propane, cable TV, internet, wedding site • ADA sites: Partial

Around a half hour from downtown St. Louis, this full-service RV resort offers everything campers have come to expect from Kampgrounds of America (KOA) since its founding in 1962. The resort's top-shelf RV pads feature a nicely paved patio and lawn area with gas grill, Adirondack chairs, and fire pit. Deluxe tent sites come with water and power hookups and a mulch-woodchip base. Cabins range from upscale units with kitchens and private bathrooms that sleep as many as eight, to basic camper cabins for four people. Or give the kids a thrill by camping in a revamped train engine. There's a single bright-red railroad caboose, totally renovated with three beds, a bathroom, and cable TV. Six Flags St. Louis theme park lies on the other side of the interstate, and there are plenty of family-friendly eateries in nearby Eureka.

GLAMPING ST. LOUIS
🏠 2, 🏕 3
800 Wilson Road, St. Charles, MO 63301
Open: March to November • Rates: Glamping tents from $340, cabins from $300 • Amenities: Communal outdoor kitchen, bathhouse with outdoor showers, bedding and towels, heating and air-conditioning,

picnic tables, fire rings, camp chairs, potable water • ADA sites: No

Make like Tom Sawyer and Huck Finn and overnight on a raft on the Mississippi River—albeit far more comfy than those skippered by the iconic Mark Twain characters. Located at River Island Marina, Glamping St. Louis offers two floating tents moored to a dock on a side channel of the Big Muddy, as well as a single landbound tent and two unique glamping cottages tucked into the riverside greenery. Located about 30 miles upstream from the Gateway Arch, the waterfront resort invites guests to bring along their own canoes, kayaks, pontoon boats, or Jet Skis for modern adventures on the Mississippi.

MARK TWAIN CAVE CAMPGROUND
🚐 / 🏕 59 full hookup, 19 partial hookup, 🏕 16
300 Cave Hollow Road, Hannibal, MO 63401
Open: April to October • Rates: RV full hookup $38, RV partial hookup from $33, tent only from $22 •

Amenities: Restaurant, winery, camp store, dump station, showers, laundry, picnic tables, playground, horseshoes, dog walk, ATM, internet • ADA sites: Partial

This popular show cave near Twain's boyhood home in Hannibal is featured in at least five of the author's beloved books. But it wasn't until 2019, when researchers discovered his signature scribbled on a cavern wall, that it was established that young Samuel Clemens (the author's real name) had frequented the limestone cavern as a child. Located near the main entrance, the campsites are shady and for the most part well spaced. In addition to cave tours (the Mark Twain Cave holds 200 years of history within its walls, explained during a walking tour of some of its 260 passageways), the complex includes a tasting room that showcases Missouri wines made and served at the Cave Hollow West Winery, a humorous *Life & Times of Mark Twain* one-man show, and a "Stick, Stones & Bones" gemstone panning sluice for kids of all ages. ∎

SOMETHING SPECIAL

Ozark National Scenic Riverways

Some of the most ruggedly beautiful landscapes in the central United States are found within the region known as the Ozark Plateau, largely located in southern Missouri and northern Arkansas. A once flat terrain, shaped by millennia of erosion, the plateau now features forested highlands, steep-sided valleys, and—most notable for many people—clear, cool, rocky creeks and rivers, many of them perfect for canoeing and swimming.

A number of Ozark rivers have been dammed to create expansive reservoirs, but several have been protected in their free-flowing form. Parts of two of those rivers in southern Missouri, the Current and Jacks Fork, were designated as the Ozark National Scenic Riverways in 1964, creating the first national U.S. park area to protect a wild river system.

Canoeing, kayaking, rafting, and other forms of boating make up the most popular activity on the Current and Jacks Fork. Many boaters enjoy fishing for smallmouth bass and other game fish.

Montana

With plenty of national parks, state parks, national forests, and stunning mountain ranges, the Big Sky State is the perfect place to pitch a tent or park your RV and retreat into nature.

ST. MARY CAMPGROUND

🚐 / ⛺ 148 no hookup

Going-to-the-Sun Road, St. Mary, MT 59417

Open: Year-round ▪ Rates: RV/tent sites $10-$20 (spring and fall), $23 (summer) ▪ Amenities: Dump station, showers, picnic tables, fire rings, potable water, food storage boxes, amphitheater ▪ ADA sites: Yes

Located at the eastern end of Going-to-the Sun Road, the large campground offers an excellent base for exploring the fjord-like valleys on the rain shadow side of Glacier National Park. Like many older national park camping spots, it could use a little more TLC. But the location is hard to beat. East Flattop and other mighty mountains of the Lewis Range loom right behind the campsites. Trailheads for the various hiking routes around St. Mary Lake are nearby. It's little more than a five-minute walk via a wooden footbridge to St. Mary Visitor Center, where campers can delve into interpretive programs and guided tours. St. Mary Village offers colorful "tiny homes" across the road from the main lodge, as well as several bars and restaurants, two general stores, and a gas station. For those who cherish quiet, the campground's Loop A is generator free, but most

Find restored log cabins in Bannack State Park.

would agree that sites along Loops B and C offer better panoramic views.

HOLLAND LAKE CAMPGROUND

🚐 / ⛺ 40 no hookup

Holland Lake Lodge Road, Condon, MT 59826

Open: May to October ▪ Rate: $20 ▪ Amenities: Dump station, restrooms, picnic tables, fire rings with grills, potable water, boat ramp ▪ ADA sites: Yes

High in the Swan Range of western Montana, this Flathead National Forest campground offers awesome lake and forest views far away from the crowds that often flood the region's celebrated national parks. Camping is dry: no hookups of any kind. But the gravel beach affords quick and easy access to Holland Lake for canoes, kayaks, and paddleboards. A mantel of ponderosa pines, tamaracks, and Douglas firs provides ample shade at most of the campsites. Holland Falls National Recreation Trail lies nearby. Meals, microbrews, and Moscow mules are available down the shore at Holland Lake Lodge.

THE RESORT AT PAWS UP

☎ 28, ⛺ 36

40060 Paws Up Road, Greenough, MT 59823

Open: Glamping May to October, cabins year-round ▪ Rates: Glamping

tents from $1,530, cabins from $1,588 (per day, all inclusive) ▪ Amenities: Camp butler, camp chef, heating and air-conditioning, daily housekeeping, laundry, internet, spa, yoga, fitness center, fitness trail, restaurants, bar, live music ▪ ADA sites: Yes

Whether it was Paws Up or another resort that coined the term *glamping* in the 1990s, this posh all-inclusive Montana retreat was one of the first places in North America to offer luxury camping. "Nature served on a silver platter" is the resort's motto, and Paws Up does its best to deliver on that promise. Dispersed through six small camps along the Blackfoot River and Elk Creek, the safari-style tents feature one to three bedrooms, bathrooms with heated floor, and private porches. The decor is out of this world: handcrafted wooden beds, copper bathtubs, wrought-iron chandeliers, Montana-inspired artwork, and other rustic chic furnishings. Each of the six camps includes a dining pavilion and outdoor

MORE TO CONSIDER

• **Under Canvas:** The upscale glamping folks have established two seasonal camps in Montana: one near West Yellowstone and the other near Glacier National Park's west entrance. *undercanvas.com*

• **Apgar Campground:** The largest overnight spot on the west side of Glacier National Park sprawls beneath tall trees along the shore of Apgar Lake and within walking distance of restaurants, shops, and boating activities in Apgar Village. *nps.gov/applications/glac/cgstatus/camping_detail.cfm?cg=Apgar*

• **Medicine Rocks State Park:** One of Montana's easternmost state parks offers camping among the Badlands where the Northern Cheyenne people gathered medicinal plants and conjured magical spirits before hunting. *stateparks.mt.gov/medicine-rocks/*

• **Collective Yellowstone:** In-tent massage, gourmet meals, and private bathrooms with rain showers are a few of the ways that glampers are pampered at this chic retreat in the Moonlight Basin at Big Sky. *collectiveretreats.com/retreat/collective-yellowstone/*

seating area around a fire pit where guests can enjoy their meals, cocktails, or conversation. Paws Up also boasts luxury cabins in five styles from cozy one bedrooms to a veritable log mansion with four bedrooms and three baths. Set on a 37,000-acre (15,000 ha) working cattle ranch, Paws Up offers equestrian pursuits like horseback riding and horse whispering, carriage rides, and wagon team driving. Among the many other activities are fly-fishing, hot-air ballooning, rappelling, whitewater rafting, fat tire electric biking, and biathlon.

DOWNSTREAM CAMPGROUND

🚐/🏕 70 partial hookup, 🏕 15 Yellowstone Road, Nashua, MT 59248

Catch the sunset over snowcapped peaks from the shore of St. Mary Lake.

Open: May to October ▪ Rates: RV/tent partial hookup from $18, tent only $14 ▪ Amenities: Dump station, showers, picnic tables, fire rings, potable water, playground, horseshoes, basketball court, bike path, fish cleaning station, fishing ponds, nearby boat ramps ▪ ADA sites: Yes

Extending more than 130 miles (209 km) along the Missouri River in eastern Montana, the nation's fifth largest reservoir offers nearly two dozen campgrounds, most of them created and managed by the U.S. Army Corps of Engineers (USACE). One of the largest and best equipped, Downstream lies in a grove of shady cottonwoods just below the huge earthen dam and right beside the Fort Peck Interpretive Center & Museum. This is the only USACE campground at Fort Peck that accepts reservations. Three other lakeside campgrounds offer partial hookups: Fort Peck Marine, Rock Creek Marina, and Hell Creek State Park.

7TH RANCH RV PARK

🚐 48 full hookup, 22 partial hookup 514 Reno Creek Road, Garryowen, MT 59031

Open: May to October ▪ Rates: Full hookup from $48, partial hookup from $43 ▪ Amenities: Showers, laundry, grills, picnic tables, potable water, laundry, playground, disc golf, horseshoes, book exchange, internet ▪ ADA sites: Partial

It's impossible to underestimate the historical significance of the park's location: You are literally camping on ground where the Battle of the Little Bighorn unfolded in summer 1876. Named after Custer's cavalry regiment, the park lies near the ford where Captain Benteen and his troops crossed the Bighorn River to

A chic way to experience Yellowstone National Park, Under Canvas offers a safari-style lobby along with glamping tents.

start the ill-fated attack and right below the bluffs where Benteen and Major Reno endured the counter-attack that led to Custer's Last Stand. History aside, this RV-only resort is a pretty cool place to biv-ouac: full hookups, hot showers, artesian water, and proximity to Little Bighorn Battlefield National Monument, Custer Battlefield Museum, and Sitting Bull's Camp.

TINY TOWN CAMPGROUND
🏠 5, ⛺ 4

9 Counts Lane, Emigrant, MT 59027
Open: Year-round ▪ Rates: From $50 ▪ Amenities: Common kitchen, bathhouse, fire pit, heating and air-conditioning, bed linens ▪ ADA sites: Partial

Located in gorgeous Paradise Valley of south-central Montana, Tiny

Town presents A-frame cabins and glamping tents just a half-hour from Gardiner and the north entrance to Yellowstone National Park. Adiron-dack chairs out front offer an ideal perch for contemplating the snow-capped Absaroka Range. And with so little ambient light, the stars are bright each night. Opened in 2020, this nifty little resort is also conve-nient for sampling the healing waters, spa treatments, and gourmet cuisine at nearby Chico Hot Springs, as well as white-water rafting and fly-fishing on the Yellowstone River. Guests can prepare their own meals in the common kitchen or dine at the Wildflower Bakery & Café or the Old Saloon in Emigrant village.

DREAMCATCHER TIPI HOTEL
⛺ 10 tipis

20 Maiden Basin Drive, Gardiner, MT 59030
Open: May to September ▪ Rates: From $339 ▪ Amenities: Bathhouse, breakfast, internet, room safes, lug-gage storage, activities concierge, car rental desk, massage services, daily housekeeping, firewood, picnic tables, fire pits, outdoor lounge areas ▪ ADA sites: No

This chic little glamping retreat fea-tures large, fully furnished tipis along the Yellowstone River on the outskirts of Gardiner. Memory foam beds, down pillows, plush duvets, and oriental rugs raise the bar on warmth and comfort, while the bathhouse pampers campers with rain showers, organic bath products, and heated floors. Nightly campfires include complimentary drinks and s'mores with fellow glampers.

Choose between lake or forest views at the Holland Lake Campground, located in the Flathead National Forest.

Don't be surprised if you find elk grazing outside your tipi each morning. Gardiner with its myriad restaurants, bars, and shops is just eight minutes up the road, and the north entrance to Yellowstone National Park is just a bit farther.

GRIZZLY RV PARK & CABINS
🏠 9, 🚐 227 full hookup
210 South Electric Street, West Yellowstone, MT 59758
Open: May to October ▪ Rates: RV from $44.95, cabins from $167.95 ▪ Amenities: Camp store, dump station, showers, picnic tables, laundry, playground, game room, dog runs, ice, RV supplies, internet ▪ ADA sites: Yes

Fangs bared and paw raised, a life-size grizzly figure greets visitors to this bear of a campground in West Yellowstone. With more than 200 total pads, Grizzly is one of the region's largest and best-equipped RV parks. All sites are full hookup, and tents are strictly forbidden. However, there's a handful of log cabins—all with heating, some with kitchens and private bathrooms—for those who don't drive their accommodation. Yellowstone Aerial Adventure Park is right across the street, while restaurant row along Canyon Street and Grizzly & Wolf Discovery Center (real bears this time) are a 10- to 15-minute walk.

BAR W GUEST RANCH
🏠 2, 🏔 4
2875 U.S. Highway 93, Whitefish, MT 59937
Open: Glamping May to October, cabins year-round ▪ Rates: Glamping doubles from $891 per person (three-night minimum stay), cabins from $1,109 per person (three-night minimum stay) ▪ Amenities: Daily

housekeeping, airport shuttle, internet, children's program ▪ ADA sites: No

Dude ranching goes glamping at this spread near Whitefish on the west side of Glacier National Park. Guests at this family-run retreat can choose between roomy safari-style tents with queen beds and large private porches or log cabin suites with kitchenettes and private bathrooms with showers. Many of the ranch activities involve horses: trail rides, wagon rides, and rodeo skills like barrel racing and pole bending. Bar W also organizes cattle drives and special photography, adults-only, and cowgirl (women-only) glamping weeks. Among other ways to pass the time are swimming or boating at Spencer Lake, skeet shooting and archery, cookout dinners, and cowboy dancing. Rates include all meals and ranch activities.

BANNACK STATE PARK
🚐/🏔 23 no hookup, 🏔 1 tipi,
1 bike camping
Bannack Road, Dillon, MT 59725

Open: Year-round ▪ Rates: RV/tent from sites $14/$24 (state resident/nonresident), bike-in site $6/$12, tipi from $26/$36 ▪ Amenities: Restrooms, picnic tables, fire pits with grills, potable water, firewood ▪ ADA sites: Yes

While you're camped along Grasshopper Creek in this secluded Rocky Mountains state park, think of the prospectors who pitched their tents along the same watercourse in the early 1860s when gold was first discovered in the streambed. More than 60 structures remain from those halcyon days in Bannack ghost town, which resurrects its glorious past through living-history weekends, haunted walks, gold panning, and ice skating on the old dredge pond. Located side by side at the west end of town, Vigilante and Road Agent campgrounds cater to travelers with RVs, tents, and even bikes. Some sites are shady; some are not. Either way it's a short walk to the state park visitors center and gold rush relics like the Masonic Lodge, Meade Hotel, and Methodist Church. ▪

SOMETHING SPECIAL

Bannack State Park

In 1862, a group of prospectors made the first significant gold discovery in Montana when they sank their shovels into the bed of Grasshopper Creek. Within a year, a new town of more than 3,000 people mushroomed into existence. In 1864, Bannack was declared the territorial capital and seemed to be headed for bigger things, but bigger discoveries soon drew attention elsewhere.

Bannack survived for nearly a century and produced millions in gold by various techniques. The hand-operated pans and sluices of the original miners gave way to hydraulic jets and great dredges that scoured the gravel to bedrock.

Today, with its more than 90 original buildings, Bannack reveals much about frontier mining town life. The bawdy houses, saloons, and tumble-down shacks were built at a time when the sheriff himself led a gang of murderous road agents called the Innocents. Bannack also reveals the gentler side of human nature: the desire to establish home, church, school, and community. Bannack is truly America's best ghost town.

Nebraska

Geological wonders, natural landmarks, and rolling prairie are among the sites where you'll park your RV, pitch your tent, or cozy up in a cabin in the Cornhusker State.

NIOBRARA STATE PARK

☎ 20, 🚐/⛺ 80 partial hookup, ⛺ 30

89261 522 Avenue, Niobrara, NE 68760

Open: Year-round ▪ Rates: RV partial hookup $25-$30, tents $10-$15; cabins from $150 ▪ Amenities: Internet, dump station, laundry, potable water, playground, showers, picnic tables, fire rings, grills, horse corral ▪ ADA sites: Partial

Make like Lewis & Clark in 1804 and camp at the confluence of the Missouri and Niobrara Rivers in north-central Nebraska. This stellar state park offers RV pads, tent sites, and cabins scattered through riverside woodlands and meadows near the spot where the Corps of Discovery bivouacked on September 4, 1804.

In his diary, Meriwether Lewis describes feasting on silver buffalo berries they foraged near their Niobrara camp: "a pleasant burry to eat—it has much the flavor of the cranbury, and continues on the bush throughout the winter." They also looked for signs of missing expedition member George Shannon, but, having found none, moved farther downriver the next day.

Camping at Niobrara now offers far more than flavorsome berries. In addition to 14 miles (22.5 km) of

Take in the majestic scenery of short-grass prairie and iconic views of Chimney Rock.

hiking and biking trails, the park has fishing, swimming, horseback riding, wildlife watching, and summer Saturday "buffalo cookouts" with cowboy poets and storytellers. Learn more about Lewis & Clark and the Ponca Indians at the J. Alan Cramer Interpretive Center or walk the disused Chicago Northwestern Bridge (now a rail trail) over the Niobrara River.

PONCA STATE PARK

☎ 27, 🚐/⛺ 135 partial hookup, ⛺ 50+

88090 Spur 26 East, Ponca, NE 68770

Open: Year-round ▪ Rates: Cabins from $100, RV partial hookup $25-$30, tents $15 ▪ Amenities: Internet, dump station, potable water, showers, picnic tables, fire pits, grills, playground, boat ramp, kayak rental, amphitheater ▪ ADA sites: Partial

Set on bluffs above the Missouri River, Ponca offers what are arguably the state's best cabins. More than half are four-bedroom minilodges, and all are equipped with kitchens, fireplaces, wireless internet, cable TV, gas barbecue grills, and outdoor seating with views of river, lake, or forest.

Even without its roomy cabins, Ponca is a spectacular park. Its eclectic activities range from hiking, biking, and horseback riding on 22 miles (35 km) of trail to a nine-hole golf course, new aquatic center, and

boating on the Mighty Mo. Ponca also hosts annual special events like the Missouri River Outdoor Expo, Christmas in the Woods, and Haunted Hayrides before Halloween.

Ponca is the eastern gateway to Missouri National Recreational River (MNRR), one of the longest stretches of untamed river in the contiguous 48 states. A dozen primitive riverside campsites are scattered along an MNRR Water Trail that takes as long as a week to traverse by canoe or kayak.

TWO RIVERS STATE RECREATION AREA

🚃 10 cabooses, 🚐 144 partial hookup, 🚐/⛺ 165 no hookup

27702 F Street, Waterloo, NE 68069

Open: Year-round ▪ Rates: RVs $25-$30, tents $10-$15, caboose $75 ▪ Amenities: Dump stations, potable water, camp store, showers, playground, picnic tables, fire rings with grill, equestrian campground ▪ ADA sites: Yes

HIGHLIGHTS

Capital: Lincoln

Total National Parks: 0

Total State Parks: 8 (Largest is Fort Robinson State Park)

State Bird: Western meadowlark

State Flower: Goldenrod

State Mammal: White-tailed deer

Wildlife Spotting: Bison; pronghorns; antelopes; coyotes; jackrabbits; prairie dogs; bald eagles; sandhill cranes; violet-green swallows; western meadowlarks; snapping turtles; bull snakes; glass lizards; rare Blanding's turtles; American bullfrogs; Great Plains toads; western tiger salamanders

Two Rivers State Recreation Area offers a one-of-a-kind experience: camping in an authentic retired caboose train.

Only a 30-minute drive from downtown Omaha, Two Rivers renders the closest camping to Nebraska's largest city. Visitors can bivouac right beside the Platte River or overnight in a fully restored Union Pacific caboose with air-conditioning, kitchen, and hot-water shower.

Between the river and five small lakes, the recreation area features fishing, boating, and swimming, as well as hiking and horse trails. A historic marker honors the Oto Indians who occupied earth-lodge villages in the Two Rivers region when Spanish and French explorers and the Lewis & Clark expedition passed this way. Between Memorial Day and Labor Day, float trips along a 6-mile (9.6 km) stretch of the Elkhorn River are available at

Tubing & Adventures, a seven-minute drive from the rec area.

KIMBERLY CREEK RETREAT

🏚 4, 🏕 2, ⬡ 2

30010 Kimberly Drive, Ashland, NE 68003

Open: Year-round ▪ Rates: From $215 geodesic domes, $175 cabins, $125 glamping pods ▪ Amenities: Kitchenettes, full bathrooms, propane barbecues, breakfast packs, s'more packages ▪ ADA sites: Yes

Geodesic domes, stylish cabins, and futuristic glamping pods are your overnight choices at Nebraska's premier glamping destination. Situated on the south side of the Platte River about 30 miles (48 km) south of Omaha, the new retreat (opened in

2019) sprawls across 20 wooded acres with hiking trails and picnic areas.

All of the glamping units come with air-conditioning and heating, hot-water showers, kitchenettes, bedding and pillows, as well as outdoor grill, fire pit, picnic table and seating area. The largest cabin also boasts an outdoor hot tub big enough for eight people.

Nearby attractions include the Strategic Air Command & Aerospace Museum, hiking and biking in Maloney State Park, and native North American critters at the Omaha Zoo's Lee G. Simmons Wildlife Safari Park.

PRAIRIE OASIS CAMPGROUND & CABINS

🏚 1, 🚐 31 full hookup, 🏕 7

913 Road B, Henderson, NE 68371
Open: Year-round ▪ Rates: RVs
$39-$42.50, tents $30, cabin $52 ▪
Amenities: Internet, dump station,
showers, laundry, potable water,
camp store, tornado shelter, recreation hall ▪ ADA sites: Yes

Located right off Interstate 80, Prairie Oasis offers a convenient overnight stop between Omaha and western Nebraska. The resort is engulfed by miles of perfectly square wheat, corn,and soybean farms established since the area was first pioneered after the Civil War.

Full hookups are complemented by recreational pastimes like volleyball and badminton, horseshoes and a beanbag toss, as well as fishing and paddleboating on a small lake that curls around the southern side of the campground. A single red-roofed cabin features a front porch with rocking chairs for contemplating sunset over the prairie.

Campers who aren't in a rush can discover local attractions like Lee's Legendary Marble Museum & Collectibles or Wessels Living History Farm in York (the county seat) and the Mennonite Heritage Park in Henderson.

FORT KEARNY STATE RECREATION AREA

🚐 / 🏕 120 partial hookup, 7 no hookup

Fort Kearny State Recreation Area Road, Gibbon, NE 68840
Open: Year-round ▪ Rates: Partial hookup $25-$30, no hookup $15 ▪ Amenities: Dump stations, potable water, showers, picnic tables, fire rings, grills, playground, disc golf ▪ ADA sites: Partial

Whether you're an avid birder or history buff, camping at Fort Kearney affords a chance to explore the natural and human history of central Nebraska. The surrounding wetlands attract the world's largest concentration of sandhill cranes (and millions of other waterfowl) each spring, while nearby Fort Kearny once served as a vital U.S. Army post on the western frontier.

Shaded by cottonwood trees and surrounded by eight small sandpit lakes, the park's two campgrounds are ripe for recreation and relaxation. With many sites right on the water, fishing, swimming, and boating are literally right outside your RV door or tent flap. Starting from the park, the Fort Kearny Hike-Bike Trail crosses the Platte River on an old railroad bridge that doubles as an excellent bird-watching platform.

BESSEY RECREATION COMPLEX & CAMPGROUND

🚐 / 🏕 40 including 29 with electric hookup

40637 River Loop, Halsey, NE 69142

Open: Year-round ▪ Rates: RV electric hookup $20, no hookup $15 ▪ Amenities: Internet, dump station, potable water, showers, picnic tables, fire rings, ball field, rec building, tornado shelter ▪ ADA sites: Yes

Bessey makes it possible to stay and play in two of Nebraska's natural landmarks: the Sandhills that roll across the middle of the state and the woodlands of the U.S. Forest Service's Bessy Ranger District—which has grown into the nation's largest hand-planted forest since the first seedlings were planted on the local short-grass prairie in 1902.

Hiking, swimming, fishing, biking, bird watching, and ATV riding are among the many outdoor activities at this Forest Service campground. Trees provide plenty of shade. Campers can also schedule a guided tour of Bessey Nursery, where thousands of saplings are raised annually.

Make yourself cozy in one of two geo domes at Kimberly Creek Retreat.

Find the quintessential tent camping experience in Niobrara State Park in Knox County, Nebraska.

CHIMNEY ROCK PIONEER CROSSING CAMPGROUND

🏠 1, 🚐 / ⛰ 16 full hookup

10012 Road 75, Bayard, NE 69334

Open: Year-round ▪ Rates: RVs $38, tents $30, cabin $60 ▪ Amenities: Dump station, showers, picnic tables, souvenir shop, ice cream counter ▪ ADA sites: Call ahead

Located right off the original route of the combined Oregon, California, and Mormon trails in western Nebraska, this small RV park takes full advantage of its historic location. With the short-grass prairie rolling to the horizon and iconic Chimney Rock hovering above, Pioneer Crossing makes it easy to imagine the days when it was Conestoga wagons rather than motor homes and travel trailers camped at this very spot. The camp store offers cold beer and tasty ice cream, as well as Chimney Rock souvenirs and local handicrafts. Chimney Rock National Historic Site visitors center, pioneer cemetery, and hiking trail to the base of the legendary spire are just up the road from the campground.

ROBIDOUX RV PARK

🚐 17 full hookup (19 with cable), 5 partial hookup

585 Five Rocks Road, Gering, NE 69341

Open: Year-round ▪ Rates: Full hookup $32, full hookup with cable $35, partial hookup $29, tents $13 ▪ Amenities: Internet, dump station, laundry, showers, playground, picnic tables, grills ▪ ADA sites: Partial

Another place to sleep beside the old Oregon Trail, Robidoux is named for the nearby pass that once took wagon trains around the western end of rugged Scotts Bluff. Concrete pads at every site ensure your rig is always dead level, and a number feature four-way hookups: water, power, sewer, and cable TV. The park also offers a play structure, basketball court, and large, grassy play area for kite flying, Frisbee, and other ball games—in other words, ideal for families.

A strategic location right next to Five Rocks Amphitheater makes this municipal RV park a perfect base for catching country, blues, and rock concerts as well as summertime "Movies at the Rocks." Legacy of the Plains Museum and Scotts Bluff National Monument (where visitors can hike an original, deeply rutted portion of the Oregon Trail) are only a short drive from Robidoux.

TOADSTOOL GEOLOGICAL PARK AND CAMPGROUND

🚐 / ⛰ 6 no hookup

FS Road 902, Harrison, NE 69346

Open: Year-round ▪ Rate: $15 (May to November) ▪ Amenities: Vault toilets, shade structures, picnic tables, fire rings, grills ▪ ADA sites: Partial

Surrounded by the endless plains of Oglala National Grassland in Nebraska's remote northwest corner, Toadstool Geological Park defines "middle of nowhere." But for those who make the effort—on their way to or from the Black Hills or Rocky Mountains—it's a special place to spend a few days. The park takes its name from the unusual mushroom-shaped sandstone formations.

With just six sites located around a teardrop-shaped loop, the Forest Service–managed campground is never crowded; visit midweek in the off season and you're likely to have it all to yourself. Three hiking routes radiate from the campsite including the 3-mile (4.8 km) Bison Trail to the Hudson-Meng archaeological site, where more than 600 *Bison antiquus* mysteriously perished around 10,000 years ago. A reproduction sod house near the campsite offers a hint of pioneer life in the Great Plains. ▪

SOMETHING SPECIAL

Fort Robinson State Park

Fort Robinson, the largest of Nebraska's state parks, nestles beneath the stark rugged bluffs of the White River. Its main attraction is its military history, from its role in 1873 as an Indian agency to its use as a German prisoner-of-war camp during World War II. The park complex takes in the original site of the Red Cloud Agency, established as a reservation for the Sioux under Chief Red Cloud.

Fort Robinson and the agency were among the most important staging areas for the 19th-century Indian interactions in the West, as the U.S. Army tried to entice the Sioux people to join Red Cloud on the reservation. Many Sioux refused, remaining on the plains with Crazy Horse and later joining the Cheyenne to defeat Lt. Col. George Armstrong Custer at the 1876 Battle of the Little Bighorn. When Crazy Horse surrendered in 1877, he was eventually taken to Fort Robinson and imprisoned in the guardhouse, where a soldier fatally stabbed him during an altercation.

Beyond the fort complex and its complicated history, the park's 22,000 acres (8,8903.1 ha) include an extensive plains environment complete with a bison herd.

Nevada

Nevada may be best known for Sin City, but there's much more to this western state, including the camping sites in the Mojave Desert, eco-resort glamping, and wildlife refuges.

BOULDER BEACH CAMPGROUND

🚐/🏕 148 no hookup

268 Lakeshore Road, Boulder City, NV 89005

Open: Year-round ▪ Rate: $20 ▪ Amenities: Dump station, restrooms, picnic tables, fire rings, grills, potable water, boat ramp, fishing pier, boat rental, swimming beach, internet ▪ ADA sites: Partial

The shaded, oasis-like setting of Boulder Beach makes it the coolest of the dozen camping spots at Lake Mead National Recreation Area. The location is also primo: close to the area's swimming and personal watercraft beaches; near the Boulder Beach boat ramp, fishing pier, and Las Vegas Marina; a 15-minute drive from Hoover Dam; and a 40-minute cruise to the Las Vegas Strip. The campsite shade comes courtesy of the many palms and cottonwood trees. Down at ground level, the native vegetation provides a reasonable amount of privacy between sites. While the campground is open to everything from tents to large RVs, campers in need of hookups can opt for the adjoining Lake Mead RV Village.

Otherworldly sandstone formations are the focal point of Valley of Fire State Park.

OASIS LAS VEGAS RV RESORT

🚐 935 partial hookup

2711 West Windmill Lane, Las Vegas, NV 89123

Open: Year-round ▪ Rates: RV full hookup from $54.95 ▪ Amenities: Camp store, restaurant, fitness center, swimming pools, putting course, cable TV, internet, 24-hour security, dump station; some sites have picnic tables and fire pits ▪ ADA sites: Partial

The camping equivalent of a Vegas mega-hotel, Oasis offers more than 900 concrete pads and all the bells and whistles one expects from a full-service RV resort. Wedged between Interstate 15 and Las Vegas Boulevard on the city's south side, the resort is just a 10-minute drive from the Strip and also well placed for visiting Hoover Dam, Lake Mead, Red Rock, and other attractions in the surrounding desert. The copious palm trees don't offer much shade, and the sites are rather closely spaced, but the resort's many amenities more than compensate. The restaurant, store, and fitness center are located in a large, air-conditioned pavilion beside the double swimming pools (one is adults only) and an 18-hole putting course. The resort concierge can score show tickets, restaurant reservations, and more.

VALLEY OF FIRE STATE PARK

🚐/🏕 21 partial hookup, 51 no hookup

Valley of Fire Highway, Moapa Valley, NV 89040

Open: Year-round ▪ Rates: RV/tents partial hookup $30, RV/tents no hookup $20 ▪ Amenities: Dump station, restrooms, showers, picnic tables, grills, potable water, internet, shade structures ▪ ADA sites: Yes

About an hour from Las Vegas in the Mojave Desert, Valley of Fire offers two adjacent overnight spots engulfed by awesome rock formations, prehistoric artifacts, and the vivid Aztec sandstone landscapes that give the park its name. Atlatl Campground is the larger and better equipped of the two, but neighboring Arch Rock Campground is quieter and slightly more secluded. Both camps lie within short walking distance of Atlatl Rock and its ancient petroglyphs, the aptly named Beehive formations, and 225-million-year-old petrified logs. Nearby trailheads mark the start of longer hikes like the 4.6-mile (7.4 km) Prospect Trail, 4.5-mile (7.2 km) Pinnacles Loop, and the Old Arrowhead Road (an abandoned 1930s motoring route). Keep a sharp eye out for desert bighorn sheep clambering over the higher rocks around the camps. Elvis footnote: The famous race scene from *Viva Las Vegas* was largely filmed on the highway leading to the campgrounds.

WHEELER PEAK CAMPGROUND

🚐/⛺ 37 no hookup
Wheeler Peak Scenic Drive, Great Basin National Park, Baker, NV 89311
Open: June to October ▪ Rate: $15 ▪ Amenities: Dump station, restrooms, picnic tables, fire pits, grills, potable water, amphitheater ▪ ADA sites: Yes

Perched at nearly 10,000 feet (3,000 m) in the South Snake Mountains, Wheeler Peak is the most remote and spectacular of the seven campgrounds inside Great Basin National Park. But it's not for everyone. If the possibility of altitude sickness doesn't dissuade you, the drive just might: 12 miles (19 km) of wicked switchbacks and a steep 8 percent grade need to be traversed to make it to your campsite. The Park Service recommends that RVs and trailers longer than 24 feet (7.3 m) camp elsewhere. There's also the weather to consider: Even during the height of summer, Wheeler Peak can experience snowfall and intense lightning storms. But for those who make the climb, this campground is stunning: daytime views that seem to run forever and night skies filled with a billion stars. It's also a great base for hiking the park: shorter jaunts like the Alpine Lakes Loop and Bristlecone Pines Trail or more

challenging treks like the 16-mile (26 km) round trip to the summit of Wheeler Peak.

MUSTANG MONUMENT ECO-RESORT & PRESERVE

🏠 10, ⛺ 10 tipis
Great Basin Highway (U.S. 93), Wells, NV 89835
Open: June to September ▪ Rates: Cabins $2,600 all inclusive, tipis $2,400 all inclusive ▪ Amenities: Restaurant, bar, housekeeping, butler service, spa and beauty treatments, heating and air-conditioning, culinary classes, adventure activities ▪ ADA sites: No

The high desert of northeast Nevada provides an apt setting for luxury glamping on a ranch dedicated to rescuing wild horses. Established in 2010 by Madeleine Pickens, the resort offers close encounters of the mustang kind (in the saddle or safari-style vehicles) with the 600-plus wild horses that Pickens has saved. The ranch offers other Wild West–flavored endeavors like roping lessons, archery and shooting ranges, horse-drawn wagon rides, and Native American craft workshops, as well as chef-led culinary experiences ranging from homemade pasta to mastering barbecue. All of this is offered with creature comforts in mind, of course, because Mustang Monument is designed for those who really don't need to ask the price. Housed in luxury log cabins or roomy tipis, guests at the all-inclusive resort are treated to three gourmet meals per day and pampering spa treatments. Guests with their own (small) private jet can touch down at Wells Municipal Airport, 27 miles (44 km) to the north; otherwise it's a three-hour drive from Salt Lake City.

At Mustang Monument Eco-Resort, make your way to Western-themed Tommy's Saloon.

Camp within iconic Zephyr Cove, the largest waterfront camping spot on Nevada's side of Lake Tahoe.

SOUTH RUBY CAMPGROUND

🚐/🏕 34 no hookup

Ruby Valley, NV 89833

Open: Year-round ▪ Rates: RV/tent from $17 ▪ Amenities: Restroom, picnic tables, fire pits, potable water, fish cleaning station, firewood ▪ ADA sites: Yes

Set amid pinyon pines and juniper trees in Humboldt-Toiyabe National Forest, this rugged little campground lures wildlife watchers, anglers, and winter sports enthusiasts to northeast Nevada. But there's also something for Western history buffs. Mule deer and pronghorn antelope are among the larger animals that occasionally wander through the camp, while

the best place for birding and fishing (bass and trout) is nearby Ruby Lake National Wildlife Refuge. The flat terrain of Ruby Valley is ideal for cross-country skiing and snowmobiling come winter, and the Ruby Mountains are the state's hot spot for heli-skiing. A new interpretive trail meanders through the ruins of Fort Ruby, built in 1862 to protect a stretch of the Pony Express and overland mail trail.

BERLIN-ICHTHYOSAUR STATE PARK

🚐/🏕 14 no hookup

State Route 844, Austin, NV 89310

Open: Year-round ▪ Rate: $15 ▪ Amenities: Dump station, picnic tables, fire pits, grills, potable water ▪ ADA sites: Yes

Two for the price of one is an apt description of this family-friendly central Nevada campground that offers both a ghost town and dinosaur dig. Arrayed around a loop sprinkled with sagebrush and pinyon pines, the campsites are just a half-mile (0.8 km) hike from an A-frame structure that shelters the fossils of several ichthyosaurs (*Shonisaurus popularis*), a massive marine reptile that swam the inland sea that covered Nevada more than 200 million years ago. For history of another kind, campers can hike or drive to Berlin ghost town, the remains of a gold mining camp inhabited between 1892 and 1911. Guided tours of the Fossil House are offered by park rangers during the summer months, while three

Pitch a tent or park your RV along Lake Tahoe's beach at the family-friendly Nevada Beach Campground.

self-guided interpretive trails spin tales of bygone Berlin.

WALKER RIVER RESORT

5, 72 full hookup, 55 partial hookup

700 Hudson Way, Smith, NV 89430
Open: Year-round ▪ Rates: Cabins from $164, RV full hookup from $59, RV partial hookup from $57 ▪ Amenities: Dump station, camp store, bar, swimming pool, showers, picnic tables, beach, clay shooting, gaming machines, golf course, dog run, horseshoes, internet ▪ ADA sites: No

One of Nevada's best-kept camping secrets, this RV and cottage getaway sits along its namesake river about an hour's drive from Carson City and two hours from Reno. The site's cottages include air conditioning, private patios, and outdoor barbecues, while the RV pads boast shaded pull-through sites as well as back-in sites for privacy. While the resort showcases its own attractions—like a swimming pool, large clubhouse with a cliff-side lounge, full service bar, clay shooting range, and slot machines—the main lures are the river and desert. Campers who bring their own kayaks or tubes can float 6 miles (9.6 km) of the Walker River downstream from the resort. Or you can cast for rainbow trout fly-fishing in Wilson Canyon right off the campground's private beach. The resort also caters to 4x4, ATV, and dirt bike devotees exploring the vast Bureau of Land Management tracts of west-central Nevada.

NEVADA BEACH CAMPGROUND

/ 54 no partial hookup

Bittlers Road, Zephyr Cove, NV 89448

Open: Year-round ▪ Rates: From $36 ▪ Amenities: Dump station, picnic tables, fire pits, grills, potable water, firewood, food lockers, beach ▪ ADA sites: Yes

One of the few places where you can pitch a tent or park an RV beside a Lake Tahoe beach, this Forest Service campground offers access to three totally different worlds. Pick your favorite: boating, swimming, or fishing on one of the world's most iconic lakes; Sierra Nevada hiking or biking; or the neon-studded gambling, entertainment, and dining scene of nearby Stateline. A wide, sandy strand and waterfront picnic areas shaded by towering pines are just steps away from campsites. It's a short hike (and even shorter drive) to a supermarket, sushi bar, pizza parlor, and Mexican restaurant across Lincoln Highway (U.S. 50) from Nevada Beach.

ZEPHYR COVE RESORT

28, 93 full hookup, 47, 10 tent-only drive-in, 3

760 U.S. Highway 50, Zephyr Cove, NV 89448

Open: Year-round ▪ Rates: RV full hookup from $42, tent only from $30, cabins from $99 ▪ Amenities: Restaurant, camp store, dump station, showers, picnic tables, fire rings, laundry, propane, cable TV, internet, marina, stables, beaches ▪ ADA sites: Yes

The largest waterfront camping resort of the Nevada side of Lake Tahoe offers several ways to spend the night, from full-hookup RV pads to tent-only camping among the pines, and brand-new Airstream trailers. Located close to the lakeshore, the studio and one- and two-bedroom cabins come with private bathrooms, full kitchens, fireplaces, and daily housekeeping. RV/tent sites are scattered through the woods on the east side of Highway 50. Campers have full access to Zephyr Cove's two beaches and various activities offered by the resort, including scenic and dinner cruises, sportfishing, parasailing, watercraft and buoy rental, horseback riding, and snowmobile tours. ▪

SOMETHING SPECIAL

Valley of Fire State Park

The Valley of Fire seems otherworldly, a surreal realm of stone formations with evocative names like Cobra Rock, Indian Marbles, and Grand Piano. Indeed, the area is named for a phenomenon of cosmic scale: In the morning and the evening, the low, slanting sun touches the ancient red sandstone like a torch, setting it ablaze.

Here the past is laid bare. You have entered a basin of Aztec sandstone that formed during the age of dinosaurs from vast dunes of sand. In this stone, water carved canyons, spires, domes, and spiny ridges. Wind scoured the exposed walls of buttes and canyons, gouging them into odd textures and shapes, including arches and balancing rocks. Upon these sculptures, chemical reactions created tints across the entire warm spectrum: ruby, rosé wine, terra-cotta, apricot, copper, gold.

On some of the sandstone walls, prehistoric Native Americans left petroglyphs depicting lizards, eagles, mountain sheep, snakes, and other symbols of desert life. The park still offers a habitat for these creatures.

New Hampshire

Pitch your tent on a mountainside idyll, cozy up in a cabin set in a romantic New England forest, or dock your RV near rock formations that challenge Yosemite.

HAMPTON BEACH STATE PARK

28 full hookup

160 Ocean Boulevard, Hampton, NH 03842

Open: May to October ▪ Rate: $30 ▪ Amenities: Camp store, showers, picnic tables, fire pits, firewood, beach ▪ ADA sites: Partial

New Hampshire's coastline is shorter than that of any other state: just 13 miles (21 km) of Atlantic shore. The only place to camp along that small but lovely stretch is Hampton Beach near the New Hampshire–Massachusetts state line. Located along the Hampton River in the park's South Beach section, the campground is RV only; no tents or pop-ups allowed. And RVs must be fully self-contained, able to plug into water, power, and sewer. It's just a few steps to the gorgeous white-sand strand for swimming, surfing, and shore fishing. And right across Ocean Boulevard is busy little Hampton Harbor, where campers can step aboard deep-sea fishing or whale-watch cruises, purchase bait and tackle, or feast on locally caught seafood at Smitty's State Pier Lobster Pound.

Dolly Copp Campground offers forest, lakes, and rivers to its visitors.

GETAWAY BLAKE BROOKE

43

76 Mountain Road, Epsom, NH 03234

Open: February to November ▪ Rates: From $199 ▪ Amenities: Camp store, private bathrooms, mini-kitchens, air-conditioning and heating, bedding and towels, two-burner stoves, cell phone lockboxes, outdoor chairs, picnic tables, fire pits with grills ▪ ADA sites: No

Although it was originally aimed at Bostonians craving a rustic escape, Getaway attracts fans from near and far to one of New England's best glamping experiences. The designer-savvy cabins are dispersed through 20 acres (9 ha) of woods, affording loads of privacy and even a feeling that you're all alone in the southern New Hampshire forest. Each unit comes with one or two queen beds, private bathroom, and mini-kitchen, as well as an outdoor space where you can cook and dine alfresco. Romance and relaxation are the main activities in camp. But there's plenty nearby for those who want to work up a sweat or sample the local amber nectar. Epsom Town Forest is about a 15-minute walk, and Northwood Lake, Bear Brook State Park, and the Blasty

Bough Brewing Company are but a short drive away.

SAVOIE'S LODGING & CAMPING

13

396 Daniel Webster Highway (Route 3), Center Harbor, NH 03226

Open: Year-round ▪ Rates: Singles from $55, doubles from $70, $85 in winter ▪ Amenities: Private bathrooms with showers, mini-fridge, towels and bedding, fans, picnic tables, fire pits, playground, volleyball, televisions, internet ▪ ADA sites: No

While Savoie's little red, white, and blue cabins appeal to any traveler seeking quirky one-off lodging rather than a cookie-cutter experience, they're especially cherished by the motorcycle fraternity and car-racing fans. That's because it's just up the road from New Hampshire Motor Speedway, where NASCAR and other races take place each year, as well as ground zero for Laconia Bike Week, one of the nation's oldest and largest annual motorbike rallies. In fact, it's only during Bike Week that Savoie's offers actual camping—on the lawn for $20 a night. Cabins are outfitted with one or two double beds, three-quarter bathrooms, and mini-refrigerators, plus an outdoor picnic table and communal fire pit. During winter, the resort offers easy access to the snowmobile trail between Meredith and Holderness/Squam Lake.

LAFAYETTE PLACE CAMPGROUND

98 no hookup

Styles Bridge Highway (I-93), Franconia Notch State Park, Franconia, NH 03580

Open: May to October ▪ Rate: $25 ▪ Amenities: Camp store, showers, picnic tables, fire pits, potable water, dishwashing stations ▪ ADA sites: Yes

The Old Man of the Mountain may have crumbled in 2003, but Franconia Notch is plenty awesome even without its iconic rock formation. With granite walls towering nearly 2,000 feet (609 m) above a narrow valley laced with lakes and rivers, forest and meadow, the notch is often compared to Yosemite Valley. Located about halfway between Echo Lake and Flume Gorge, Lafayette Place is the park's largest campground, as well as a hub of hiking, biking, and other outdoor activities. In addition to hosting the park's Hiker Information Center, several popular trails start at or near the campground. It's also a stop on a hiker shuttle with nine stops along the valley, including the Old Man Museum and Cannon Aerial Tramway. Lafayette Place offers only dry camping.

PARTRIDGE CABINS

7

3 Partridge Road (off U.S. Route 3), Pittsburg, NH 03592

Open: Year-round ▪ Rates: From $145 ▪ Amenities: Private bathrooms, kitchens, fireplaces, gas heaters, satellite TV, kayak/canoe rental, ice cream stand ▪ ADA sites: Yes

Listen to the haunting call of the loons on First Connecticut Lake at this small, family-owned resort in New Hampshire's far north. With a lakeside setting beneath spruce and fir trees, the resort's housekeeping cabins can sleep as many as eight people. All feature private baths, heating, and full kitchens. Guests are also entitled to a complimentary ice cream from the resort's own Moose Alley Cones.

Visit the flume gorge in Franconia Notch State Park during the autumn for beautiful foliage.

Partridge offers more than 600 feet (182 m) of lakeshore and rental canoes or kayaks for those who want to explore the headwaters of the Connecticut River. Anglers can cast for salmon or trout during the warmer months or try their luck at ice fishing during the winter. There's plenty of hiking too, with starting points for the Falls in the River Trail, Moose Alley Trail, and Magalloway Mountain Loop just a short drive from Partridge. For those who want to venture into Quebec, the Pittsburg U.S.-Canada border crossing is 14 miles (23 km) up Daniel Webster Highway.

Getaway Blake Brook offers designer cabins throughout its woodlands.

DOLLY COPP CAMPGROUND

🚐/⛺ 18 partial hookup, 80 no hookup, ⛺ 26

Dolly Copp Campground Road (off Route 16), Gorham, NH 03581
Open: May to October ▪ Rates: RV/tent partial hookup $37, no hookup/tent only $25 ▪ Amenities: Restrooms, picnic tables, fire pits with grills, potable water ▪ ADA sites: Yes

One of the largest campgrounds in the entire National Forest system, Dolly Copp spreads along the banks of the Peabody River along the northern edge of the White Mountains. Nearly 200 campsites are dispersed along nine loops and lanes. The sylvan setting sets a laid-back tone that may or may not include casual river fishing. Otherwise, campers can set off along the Daniel Webster Trail into the Presidential Range or the Great Gulf Wilderness or navigate the historic Auto Road to the summit of Mount Washington. Camping and fishing equipment are available at Gorham Hardware & Sport Center in the nearby town of Gorham, which also

offers groceries, fast food, and a lively local pub.

DRY RIVER CAMPGROUND

🚐/⛺ 29 no hookup, ⛺ 7, 3 lean-tos

1464 U.S. Route 302, Crawford Notch State Park, Harts Location, NH 03812
Open: May to October ▪ Rates: RV/tent $25, lean-tos $25-$29 ▪ Amenities: Camp store, showers, laundry, picnic tables, fire rings with grill, potable water, firewood ▪ ADA sites: Yes

It's a rather mundane name for a glorious location—a White Mountains campground set below the Frankenstein Cliff and beside a river that runs the length of Crawford Notch. The area is especially lovely in the fall when the leaves are changing color, although the interplay of the deep green forest and the gray granite walls that frame the valley is equally intriguing in summer. Complementing the dry RV sites are a

handful of tent platforms and wooden lean-to structures where all you really need is a sleeping bag to spend the night. Six backcountry trails are easily accessed from Dry River, most of them steep and rated hard. One leads to Arethusa Falls, another to the top of a Frankenstein Cliff named for a 19th-century landscape painter rather than the literary monster. There's also a link to the easy, valley-bottom Saco River Trail that leads to a general store, post office, and Willey House Historical Site.

SACO RIVER CAMPING AREA

🏠 14, 🚐/⛺ 180 full hookup, 40 partial hookup

1550 White Mountain Highway, North Conway, NH 03860
Open: May to October ▪ Rates: RV/tent from $51.75, cabins from $60.75 (two-night minimum stay) ▪ Amenities: Camp store, dump station, swimming pool, showers, laundry, playgrounds, sports courts,

Huttopia White Mountains offers everything from wooden chalets to glamping tents in the picturesque New Hampshire woods.

laser tag, golf cart rental, bike rental, kayak/canoe/tube rental, dog park, propane, internet ▪ ADA sites: Partial

Forest meets fairground at a tricked-out campground on the edge of North Conway, the self-proclaimed gateway to the White Mountains. Given how much there is to do around the property—including float trips down the Saco River—campers may never stray far from their pad. But the temptation is there to explore a town with everything from factory outlets and year-round Christmas stores to escape rooms, an indoor water park, and a pirate-themed miniature golf course. The shadier campsites are right along the river or the resort's boundary with the neighboring Audubon Dahl Sanctuary with its trails through native woodland inhabited by many native birds. Those with less shade are closer to the swimming pool and sports courts. In addition to food and drink, the camp store offers a selection of local products.

HUTTOPIA WHITE MOUNTAINS
🏨 10, ⛺ 87

57 Pine Knoll Road, Albany, NH 03818
Open: May to October ▪ Rates: Glamping tents from $85, cabins from $200 ▪ Amenities: Camp store, restaurant, picnic tables, fire pits, swimming pool, beach, playground, sports courts, game room, boat rental, potable water, boat dock ▪ ADA sites: Partial

Born in France and raised in Quebec, Huttopia brings its unique blend of savoir-faire and plein-air camping to the White Mountains. Dedicated to helping its guests

"disconnect from everyday life to reconnect with nature," the resort offers wooden chalets and three types of glamping tents near the eclectic Conways and scenic Kancamagus Highway. The camp's crème de la crème, the two-bedroom Trappeur tent features a private bathroom with shower, a fully outfitted kitchen, indoor dining area, and outdoor space with fire pit and picnic table. At the other end of the spectrum is the petite Bonaventure tent with a single queen bed, small cooking area, and use of a communal bathhouse. The tents are arrayed around a "village" with a swimming pool, camp store, lounge, and Airstream trailer converted into a bistro kitchen that serves crepes, pizzas, salads, gourmet coffees, and other goodies. Glampers can pass the time paddling or fishing on Iona Lake, joining an outdoor yoga session, and attending evening campfire programs.

BEAVER POND CAMPGROUND
🚐 / ⛺ 101 no hookup

600 Lower Road, Deerfield, NH 03037

Open: May to October ▪ Rate: $25 ▪ Amenities: Camp store, dump station, showers, picnic tables, fire pits with grills, potable water, playground, softball diamond, beach, boat dock, boat rental, firewood, ice ▪ ADA sites: Yes

With a location near urban Concord and Manchester, Bear Brook State Park is extremely popular with locals. But it's big enough to handle the human load: around 10,000 acres (4,046 ha) of forest, marsh, ponds, and rocky summits ripe for both summer and winter fun. The park's only campground lies along Beaver Pond on the east side, well-shaded sites served by a camp store with canoe and kayak rental, coin-operated showers, and a small sandy beach area with a dock to slip your canoe into the water. Forty miles (64 km) of trail meander through the park to half a dozen other ponds, an archery range, the Old Allenstown Meeting House (built in 1815), and the New Hampshire Snowmobile Museum. ▪

Mount Washington

The 6,288-foot (1,916.6 m) summit of Mount Washington is lashed with weather reputed to be the worst in the world. In 1934, meteorologists recorded on its summit one of the highest wind velocities ever measured on Earth—231 miles an hour (371.8 km/h). Winds in excess of hurricane force sweep across the mountain more than 100 days per year. So why venture to the top? Simple: the views. On a clear day (fewer than 180 days per year), you can see more than 90 miles (144.8 km) to Vermont, Massachusetts, Maine, Quebec, and the Atlantic Ocean.

Today, several hiking trails, including parts of the Appalachian Trail, lead up the steep slopes (only expert hikers should attempt an ascent; there's a road for others to drive). At the summit, visit the Mount Washington Observatory's museum, featuring historical exhibits about the peak. At the observatory, staff monitor harsh weather.

New Jersey

The Garden State has plenty to offer beyond the Jersey Shore (though there's camping there too), including two state forests and numerous parks that make it worthwhile to pack your tent.

SAWMILL LAKE CAMPGROUND

🏕 50

1480 State Route 23, High Point State Park, Sussex, NJ 07461
Open: April to October ▪ Rates: $20/$25 (state resident/nonresident) ▪ Amenities: Restrooms, picnic tables, fire rings, potable water, boat ramp ▪ ADA sites: No

They call it the Garden State. But New Jersey can get pretty wild at times, especially the Kittatinny Mountains in the state's northwest corner, where High Point State Park offers a tent-only campground beside Sawmill Lake. The little water body lends itself to canoeing and kayaking, swimming, or angling for trout and bass. Hiking routes head off in several directions from the campground, including a short connector to the mighty Appalachian Trail. You can hike, bike, or drive to the park's High Point Monument and its panoramic views of three states (New Jersey, New York, and Pennsylvania). Those states and the Delaware River converge in nearby Port Jervis, where campers can snap selfies while standing or sitting on a marble slab that marks the spot where the three states rendezvous.

Riders should take advantage of the Burnt Mill equestrian trail in Wharton State Forest.

AMC MOHICAN OUTDOOR CENTER

🏠 7, 🏕 75

50 Camp Mohican Road, Blairstown, NJ 07825
Open: Year-round ▪ Rates: Cabins from $39/$46, tent sites from $28/$33 (AMC member/nonmember) ▪ Amenities: Meal service, restrooms, showers, food storage containers, picnic tables, shared fire ring with grill, boathouse ▪ ADA sites: Yes

Delaware Water Gap National Recreation Area provides an apt setting for a backwoods Appalachian Mountain Club lodge that offers both tent sites and self-service cabins. All of the sites are walk-in; some have wooden platforms, others bare ground. Picnic tables and fire rings are shared. The camp's big advantage is a deli and meal service in the lodge dining room (May to October). The lodge also offers a demonstration center with various brands of summer and winter outdoor gear and clothing. Mohican is a popular stopover on the New Jersey portion of the Appalachian Trail, which leaps across the camp access road just a third of a mile from the lodge. It's also an ideal base for paddling down or hiking beside a refreshingly unspoiled stretch of the Delaware River, which is just a 2.3-mile (3.7 km) downhill hike from AMC.

THE GREAT DIVIDE CAMPGROUND

🏠 10, 🚐 130 full hookup, 88 partial hookup, 🏕 19, 🏚 1, 2 wagons

68 Phillips Road, Newton, NJ 07860
Open: April to October ▪ Rates: RV full hookup from $60, RV partial hookup from $58, tents from $48, cabins from $110, covered wagons from $99, yurts from $79 ▪ Amenities: Dump station, showers, camp store, laundry, picnic tables, fire rings, swimming pool, beach, playground, game room, sports courts, firewood, ice, propane, internet, cable TV, dog park ▪ ADA sites: Partial

Family camping in the Jersey hills at this full-service RV resort is located a little over an hour's drive from New York City and two hours from Philadelphia. The campground occupies the one-time site of Hazy Vale Dairy Farm. The Holsteins are long gone, replaced by a blend of full-hookup and power/water RV pads, tent sites, wooden cabins, and even a couple of covered wagons. A dedicated family campground, Great Divide presents a wide range of daily activities and special event weekends with live entertainment that can range from British Invasion and Fairy Tale to Masked Singer and Living Dead (before Halloween).

CAMP GATEWAY

🏕 20

Hartshorne Drive, Gateway NRA, Highlands, NJ 07732

Open: May to September ▪ Rate: $30 ▪ Amenities: Restrooms, picnic tables, fire rings with grills, potable water, some shade structures ▪ ADA sites: Yes

Set on the Sandy Hook peninsula at the southern end of Gateway National Recreation Area, Gateway offers a quick and easy seaside escape from the Big Apple and its Jersey burbs. The tent-only campground doesn't offer many bells and whistles, but the location is sublime: walking distance to beaches on both the open Atlantic and Sandy

Hook Bay. There's history too: a retired Nike missile site, Battery Arrowsmith, and the ruins of Fort Hancock—facilities that once protected New York Harbor from enemy attack. Camp Gateway can be reached by car; it's about 90 minutes from Manhattan and an hour from Newark Airport. But the carefree way to get there is the summertime Seastreak Ferry from Manhattan to Highland and then a short bus transfer into the park.

ALLAIRE STATE PARK

🚐 / 🏕 45 no hookup, 6 shelters

Atlantic Avenue (Route 524), Howell Township, NJ 07731

Open: Year-round ▪ Rates: RV/tents $20/$25, shelters $48/$60 (state resident/nonresident) ▪ Amenities: Dump station, showers, picnic tables, fire rings, potable water, playground ▪ ADA sites: Partial

The remains of a 19th-century bog-iron factory town are the focus of a state park that features living history programs, vintage buildings, and a

working steam train. Allaire is divided into two sections by Interstate 195. The campground is located on the north side beside Long Swamp Pond and its eponymous wetlands, the restored town on the south side along the Manasquan River. The 2.5-mile (4 km) Canal Trail provides an easy way for campers to explore the swamp or reach the park's historic quarter. Those who bring their own canoe or kayak can paddle down the slow-flowing river. From spring to fall, Allaire Village offers old-time cooking, sewing, blacksmithing, and other historical demonstrations and rides on the narrow-gauge Pine Creek Railroad.

ATSION CAMPGROUND

🏚 9, 🚐 / 🏕 50 no hookup

Atsion Road, Wharton State Forest, Shamong, NJ 08088

Open: April to October ▪ Rates: RV/tents $20/$25, cabins from $55/$65 (state resident/nonresident) ▪ Amenities: Dump station, showers, picnic tables, fire rings, potable water ▪ ADA sites: No

Immerse yourself in Pinelands legend and lore at this state forest campground and cabins along the north shore of Atsion Lake in Wharton State Forest. You probably won't spot the Jersey Devil—a mythological beast with wings, cloven hooves, a forked tail, and the head of a horse that allegedly dwells in the Pinelands. But there are plenty of other creatures that roam the state's largest park, including beavers, otters, deer, foxes, and dozens of bird species. The camping is pretty basic. But with so much to see and do elsewhere in the state forest, you're probably not going to spend a lot of time around the

Discover nature at the AMC Mohican Outdoor Center, along the Appalachian Trail.

Allaire State Park offers living history programs and vintage buildings honoring its bog-iron factory history.

campfire. Among Wharton's other attractions are historic Batsto Village and its 33 historic structures, the 19-mile (30 km) Penn Branch biking trail, the 12-mile (19 km) Burnt Mill equestrian trail, and the 50-mile (80 km) Batona Trail hiking route.

BAKER'S ACRES CAMPGROUND

🏠 5, 🚐/⛺ 83 full hookup, 175 partial hookup, ⛺ 40
230 Willets Avenue, Little Egg Harbor Township, NJ 08087
Open: May to October ▪ Rates: RV/tent full hookup from $48.60, RV/tent partial hookup from $45, tent sites from $39.60, cabins from $110 ▪ Amenities: Dump station, camp store, showers, laundry, picnic tables, swimming pool, playgrounds,

propane, firewood, ice, sports courts, game room, nature trail, DVD/video library, internet ▪ ADA sites: Yes

Located about halfway down the New Jersey coast and not far from the Garden State Parkway, Baker's lies within easy striking distance of Surf City, Long Beach, and other Atlantic strands. Depending on your mood (and vacation priorities), the woodsy location can also make it feel like a million miles from the shore. Very much family oriented, the resort organizes a wide range of daily activities, from Fourth of July decoration and cannonball diving contests to scavenger hunts, movie nights, and the annual Music Fest at the Boondocks. And for the record, Baker's is located on 60 acres (24 ha).

BASS RIVER STATE FOREST

🏠 6, 🚐/⛺ 176 no hookup, 9 lean-tos, 6 shelters
Stage Road, Tuckerton, NJ 08087
Open: Year-round ▪ Rates: RV/tent $20/25, cabins $75/$85, shelters $48/$60, lean-tos $40/$45 (state resident/nonresident) ▪ Amenities: Dump station, showers, laundry, picnic tables, fire rings, potable water, beach, playground, boat rental, boat ramp, sports field ▪ ADA sites: Partial

New Jersey's oldest state forest (founded in 1905) offers campers two very different ways to spend their time. Created by the Civilian Conservation Corps during the Great Depression, Lake Absegami affords a cool escape from the state's hot, humid summers. Campsites, cabins,

Standing tall above river and forest, iconic High Point Monument at High Point State Park is a sight to be seen.

and shelters line both the north and south shores, making it easy for campers to swim, boat, or fish. The park's other gem is the bizarre Pygmy Forest, with stunted pitch pines and blackjack oaks that rarely reach more than four feet (1.2 m) in height. The miniature trees—together with an understory of heather, moss, lichen, and berry plants—form a unique wildlife habitat that nurtures a dozen moth species. Bass River also offers 13 hiking trails and summer activities that range from bluegrass concerts and scavenger hunts to stargazing and ranger campfire talks about local natural and human history.

BELLEPLAIN STATE FOREST

🚐 / 🏕 169 no hookup, 5 wooden shelters, 14 lean-tos

Champion Road, Woodbine, NJ 08270

Open: Year-round ▪ Rates: RV/tent no hookup $20/25, wooden shelters $48/$60, lean-tos $40/$45 (state resident/nonresident) ▪ Amenities: Dump station, showers, laundry, picnic tables, fire rings with grills, potable water, playground, canoe rental ▪ ADA sites: Partial

A remnant of the wetlands and oak, pine, and cedar forest that once covered much of southernmost New Jersey, Belleplain offers a range of outdoor activities and a choice of three overnight spots. Constructed by the Civilian Conservation Corps (CCC) in the 1930s, the campgrounds book-end Lake Nummy, an old cranberry bog the CCC transformed into a popular swimming, boating, and fishing venue. In addition to regular RV/tent sites, Belleplain features cabin-like wooden shelters with bunk beds and partially enclosed lean-tos that can sleep up

to eight. And don't be afraid to bring the pup along, as pet-friendly sites are available (dogs and cats only, with updated vaccinations, for an additional $5 fee). The park's two dozen trails lure hikers in summer and cross-country skiers and snowshoers during the winter months. The park's single-track mountain biking trail offers more than 9 miles (14.4 m) of rugged terrain. Belleplain also makes a perfect base for paddling the nearby Great Egg Harbor and Maurice Wild and Scenic River or visiting the Delaware Bay Museum & Folklife Center in Port Norris.

HOLLY SHORES CAMPING RESORT

☎ 40, 🚐 / 🏕 300+, 🏕 6

491 U.S. Highway 9, Cape May, NJ 08204

Open: April to October ▪ Rates: RV/tent from $58, cabins from $134, glamping tents from $144 ▪ Amenities: Camp store, showers, picnic tables, fire rings, laundry, swimming pool, hot tubs, game room, playgrounds, sports courts, kayak rental,

golf cart rental, dog park, internet, cable TV, propane ▪ ADA sites: Yes

A selection of 10 different cabin types and a location near Cape May and its fabulous beaches help Holly Shores stand out from all the other places you can bunk down in South Jersey. Indoor digs range from the two-person Hideaway Cottage and tiny houses that sleep four to ultradeluxe cabins with full kitchens and the Starfish House that can accommodate as many as eight people. All of them feature private bathrooms, heating and air-conditioning, and some sort of outdoor seating area. Holly Shores also offers safari-style glamping tents with kitchenettes and half baths and more than 300 shady RV/tent sites with full or water/power hookups. The Atlantic surf of Wildwood and Diamond Beach is just 15 minutes away. The Cold Springs Bike Path along an old railroad right-of-way starts across the street from the resort's front gate. A caveat for camping at Holly Shores: Your RV cannot be more than three years old. ∎

SOMETHING SPECIAL

Allaire State Park

If you like prowling around relics of the past, enter this park in the heart of a forest, where the narrow Manasquan River meanders toward the sea. On the river's north bank sits the remains of a company town that thrived by smelting bog iron ore over a century and a half ago. Yet from the looks of the carpenter shop, blacksmith shop, general store, bakery, chapel, and houses, the citizens just left on the train you might hear chuffing through the woods to the west.

Allaire village traces its roots to an early 19th-century iron forge. During the second quarter of the 1800s, the property was expanded and rebuilt into a community of 400 people. But when the iron business closed in 1846, the town declined. During the 1940s, the state began to develop the park and preserve the historic village. On weekends in the spring and fall, Allaire village comes alive with historical interpreters. The season for taking a quick loop on the Pine Creek Railroad (set up in the 1960s) is from April through October.

New Mexico

Find backcountry camping in the otherworldly setting of one of the newest national parks or make your camp in vintage trailers near the Rio Grande on a New Mexico excursion.

CHACO CANYON GLAMPING

🏕 10

Chaco Culture NHP, Nageezi, NM 87037

Open: Four times per year, as available ▪ Rates: From $1,199 per person ▪ Amenities: Restroom, bedding and towels, toiletries, flashlight, potable water, gift pack, transfers to and from Albuquerque ▪ ADA sites: No

Chaco affords a rare chance to overnight amid the ruins of an ancestral Puebloan settlement that ranked among the largest and most important in the Four Corners region 1,000 years ago. Declared a UNESCO World Heritage site in 1987, the park preserves monumental structures like Pueblo Bonito and Chetro Ketl renowned for both their size and exceptional architecture. Four times per year—on the spring and fall equinox and over two full moon weekends—Heritage Inspirations creates an all-inclusive glamping experience with fully furnished bell tents, gourmet meals, and top-notch guides.

STONE HOUSE LODGE

🏠 5, 🚐 25 full hookup, ⛺ 5, 2 mobile homes

1409 State Highway 95, Los Ojos, NM 87551

Hotel Luna Mystica offers camping stays in vintage trailers in Taos.

Open: Year-round ▪ Rates: From $100 cabins, $150 trailers; RVs $50, tents $15 ▪ Amenities: Full kitchens, showers, laundry, general store, café, boat rental ▪ ADA sites: Partial

Located on the edge of the Jicarilla Apache Nation in far northern New Mexico, Stone House features an eclectic range of accommodation and outdoor activities. Fully equipped stone or wooden cabins are its forte, but the lodge also has mobile homes, RV sites, and tent sites. Among the aquatic activities on nearby Heron and El Vado Reservoirs are fishing, power boating, waterskiing, and sailing. The lodge offers boat and fishing gear rental, as well as professional fishing guides. On summer weekends, Stone House Café serves New Mexico specialties.

HOTEL LUNA MYSTICA

🚐 22

25 ABC Mesa Road, El Prado, NM 87529

Open: Year-round ▪ Rates: From $90 ▪ Amenities: Internet, kitchenettes, showers, decks, fire pits ▪ ADA sites: No

The high plains between Taos and the Rio Grande Gorge provide a dramatic setting for Luna Mystica and its 22 super-cool vintage travel trailers. All are lovingly restored with modern amenities (like hot-water showers and full kitchens),

unique decor, and distinct personalities.

A 1958 Twilight trailer called Frida channels the spirit of the legendary Mexican artist; a 1961 Airstream Sovereign Land Yacht dubbed Sundance pays homage to outlaws Butch Cassidy and the Sundance Kid; and a 1957 Spartan Imperial Mansion called Sands sleeps eight in four bunk beds. Many of the trailers also boast wooden decks with seating for contemplating dusk and dawn over the Sangre de Cristo range. After dark, the staff can stoke a log blaze in the fire pit outside your trailer. Pets are welcome.

Luna Mystica is the official overnight spot for neighboring Taos Mesa Brewery, a craft beer and entertainment venue with live music on an outdoor stage. During special events, the resort opens up the sagebrush flats out back for primitive tent and no-hookup RV camping. In addition to the celebrated Rio Grande Gorge Bridge (which hovers 600 feet/182 m above the Rio Grande), Luna Mystica lies within easy striking distance of the Millicent Rogers Museum (4.7 miles/ 7.5 km), Taos Plaza (7.8 miles/ 12.5 km), Taos Pueblo (8.4 miles/ 13.5 km), and the winter sports of Taos Ski Valley (18 miles/29 km).

CLIFF RIVER SPRINGS

⌂ 7 casitas

283 State Highway 111, La Madera, NM 87539

Open: Year-round ▪ Rates: From $120 ▪ Amenities: Full kitchens, breakfast foods, swimming hole, horse boarding, private decks and patios ▪ ADA sites: No

Transitioning from cattle to accommodation, Palovista hacienda has refurbished many of its old ranch buildings into this modern glamping resort. Instead of longhorns, the oval plaza in the heart of the 1,200-acre (485 ha) spread is now surrounded by cool New Mexico–style casitas. Hiking and equestrian trails lead to Tecolote Peak, the Rio Ojo Caliente, and other landmarks. Stables are available for those who

bring their own horses. The soothing waters of Ojo Caliente Mineral Springs are just a 10-minute drive down the valley.

JUNIPER CAMPGROUND

🚐 / ⛺ 66

15 Entrance Road, Bandelier National Monument, Los Alamos, NM 87544

Open: Year-round ▪ Rate: $12 ▪ Amenities: Dump station, potable water, flush toilets, amphitheater, picnic tables, grills ▪ ADA sites: Partial

True to its name, Bandelier National Monument's only campground sprawls amid copious junipers and piñon pines on a mesa high above the park's ancient pueblo ruins. The trees provide a reasonable amount of shade and privacy at campsites arrayed along three loops named after the park's iconic creatures: Coyote, Black Bear, and Albert's Squirrel. All sites are first come, first served; Bandelier does not offer campground reservations. Perched at nearly 7,000 feet (2,133 m), the altitude keeps Juniper Campground

At Bandelier National Monument, a great spangled fritillary pauses on a blooming butterfly weed.

relatively cool in summer compared to the nearby Rio Grande Valley and cold enough in winter for the occasional snowfall.

"What Did the Ancients Weave" and "Ecotones: Where Ecosystems Meet" are two of the evening ranger programs presented at the campground amphitheater. Starting behind the theater, the 1.5-mile (2.4 km) Frey Trail drops into Frijoles Canyon and the park's namesake ruins. Although humans have occupied the canyon for around 10,000 years, the current cliff dwellings were built between A.D. 1150 and 1550 prior to the Spanish arrival in New Mexico. Footpaths, steel stairs, and wooden ladders arrayed along the canyon floor lead to adobe structures, residential caves, petroglyphs, and kiva ceremonial circles. Tyuonyi Overlook Trail also kicks off from the campground, a 2.2-mile (3.5 km) loop to viewpoints along the upper edge of Frijoles Canyon. The park offers two winter cross-country ski trails.

Juniper Campground is well positioned for visiting other human-made and natural sites in central New Mexico like Valles Caldera National Preserve (18 miles/20 km) and Manhattan Project National Historical Park in Los Alamos (12.5 miles/29 km).

RANCHO GALLINA

⌂ 2 casitas, ⛺ 1, 3 rooms/suites

31 Bonanza Creek Road, Santa Fe, NM 87508

Open: Year-round ▪ Rates: From $160 (two-night minimum stay) ▪ Amenities: Internet, kitchens (in most units), hammocks, hot tub ▪ ADA sites: No

The historic Turquoise Trail between Santa Fe and Albuquerque is the

Rancho Gallina offers incredible campgrounds, and guests can also host celebrations at its barn.

backdrop for a classic adobe inn. Rancho Gallina started life as a ranch house before serving as a glass artist's workshop and its current incarnation as an offbeat eco-retreat and special events venue. Accommodation includes two roomy casitas off a central courtyard, a secluded Lotusbelle glamping tent, and three guest rooms in the main house, including one decorated in a Moroccan style.

Scattered around the grounds are a cedarwood hot tub for nighttime stargazing and a circular patio area, "Woodhenge," strung with hammocks for an afternoon nap. Solar panels, geothermal generators, and an organic garden are part of the ranch's devotion to sustainability. Ziggy the Cat roams the grounds like he owns the place.

Santa Fe Plaza, with its abundant shops and restaurants, lies about a half-hour drive to the north of Rancho Gallina. Heading in the other direction, the Turquoise Trail (State Route 14) meanders through old mining towns like Los Cerrillos and Madrid, where hangouts like the Black Bird Saloon and the Holler provide great grub and local color. Located down the road from Santa Fe Studios, the rancho lies in the heart of a Tamalewood region renowned for movie and television production. Many celebrities have learned how to ride at the neighboring stables, and movie crews occasionally crash at Rancho Gallina.

ENCHANTED TRAILS RV PARK & TRADING POST

🚐 115 full hookup, 20 partial hookup, 🚐 7 vintage

14305 Central Avenue Northwest, Albuquerque, NM 87121
Open: Year-round ▪ Rates: From $30 RVs, $56 trailers ▪ Amenities: Internet, laundry, mail service, clubhouse, swimming pool, gift and food store, showers ▪ ADA sites: Partial

Sprawling right beside Interstate 40 and historic Route 66 on the western outskirts of the state's largest city, Enchanted Trails has all the bells and whistles one expects of a top-shelf RV park, including full hookups, swimming pool, game room, RV supplies, and general store. Built in the 1940s, the adobe Trading Post features Native American jewelry and crafts. Campers pondering a new home on wheels

A window at Pueblo de Arroya looks out on the beautiful landscape of Chaco Culture National Historical Park.

can browse the selection at neighboring Camping World. The museums, historic sites, restaurants, and bars of Old Town Albuquerque are just 10 minutes down the interstate.

WHITE SANDS NATIONAL PARK
🏕 10

Dunes Drive, White Sands National Park, Alamogordo, NM 88310
Open: Year-round ▪ Rate: $3 per person ▪ Amenities: Restroom and shaded picnic structure in the trailhead parking lot ▪ ADA sites: No

The rolling dunes of White Sands seem like something from an alien world rather than a landscape found on Earth. Most visitors come for the day—to glide down the bright white slopes on discs or toboggans, picnic among the dunes, or snap Instagram-worthy photos. But there's only one way to spend the night inside the park: primitive backcountry camping at 10 sites arrayed along a sandy trail through the dunes. The backcountry loop can close at a moment's notice due to testing at adjacent White Sands Missile Range, which means it's not possible to reserve sites. Campers must obtain a permit from the visitors center on the day they arrive and must return to renew the permit for each night they intend to stay. Permit in hand, campers leave their vehicles at the Backcountry Loop trailhead and set off along a path marked by thin red posts. Full moon nights—when lunar light almost mimics the day—and moonless nights when the stars are at their brightest are the best times to camp at White Sands.

AGUIRRE SPRING CAMPGROUND
🚐 / 🏕 55

Aguirre Springs Road, Las Cruces, NM 88011
Open: Year-round ▪ Rate: $7 ▪ Amenities: Pit toilets, shade structures, picnic tables, fire rings ▪ ADA sites: Partial

Situated in Organ Mountains–Desert Peaks National Monument in southern New Mexico, Aguirre Spring provides a remote, rustic place to overnight near Las Cruces. All sites are first come, first served. Set amid dramatic Chihuahuan Desert scenery, the park is sprinkled with juniper, oak, and mountain mahogany trees nurtured by natural springs and seasonal streams. Several hiking trails start from the campground, including routes to Indian Hollow, Baylor Canyon, and the Pine Tree Loop. The steep, twisting entrance road makes Aguirre Springs a no-go for longer RVs.

FAYWOOD HOT SPRINGS
🏠 9, 🚐 15 full hookup, 5 partial hookup, 5 no hookup, 🏕 18

165 State Highway 61, Faywood, NM 88034
Open: Year-round ▪ Rates: From $21 camping, $28 RV, $60 cabin ▪ Amenities: Dump station, potable water, showers, changing rooms, clubhouse, camp store ▪ ADA sites: Yes

Warm, healing water is the main attraction of natural hot springs that were known to Native Americans, Spanish explorers, and westward-bound American pioneers hundreds of years ago. Appealing to all who frequent hot springs today, Faywood offers clothing-mandatory and clothing-optional camping areas and bathing pools. The overnight lodging is also diverse with options that include furnished wooden cabins, tent camping, and full-hookup RV sites. Among the resort's hot-water options are outdoor private and group pools, an indoor bathhouse pool, and healing geothermal mineral showers. Out of the water, the nearby City of Rocks State Park provides plenty of scope for desert hiking, while Silver City (30 miles/48 km) offers restaurants, bars, and Wild West history. ▪

SOMETHING SPECIAL

White Sands National Park

The redesignation of White Sands from a national monument to a national park in December 2019 was in part acknowledgment of a simple geological fact: The vast sparkling white landscape here contains the world's largest expanse of gypsum dunes. The unlikely series of events that formed this spectacular terrain date back more than 250 million years when the region was covered by a shallow sea that deposited thick layers of gypsum as it continually rose and fell.

Driving the 8-mile (12.9 km) Dunes Drive is an immersive experience in itself, but hiking the easy Play Trail or Dune Life Nature Trail provides a much more intimate look at White Sands. The best time to visit the dunes is during the sunset, when reds and oranges mix with the long shadows created over the rolling white dunes. And if you look east, you'll see alpenglow of the Sacramento mountains.

New York

Camp within view of the Manhattan skyline or retreat into other parts of New York State for woodsy locales, lakefront campgrounds, and even Niagara Falls–adjacent destinations.

HIGHLIGHTS

Capital: Albany

Total National Parks: 0

Total State Parks: 180 (Largest is Allegany State Park)

State Bird: Bluebird

State Flower: Rose

State Tree: Sugar maple

Wildlife Spotting: Black bears; bobcats; moose; weasels; raccoons; skunks; golden eagles; peregrine falcons; wild turkeys; blue jays; cardinals; woodpeckers; snapping turtles; diamond back terrapins; queen snakes; eastern hellbender salamanders

HITHER HILLS STATE PARK

🚐/🏕 189 no hookup

164 Old Montauk Highway, Montauk, NY 11954

Open: Year-round ▪ Rates: RV/tents $35/$70 (state resident/nonresident) ▪ Amenities: Dump station, showers, picnic tables, camp store, snack bar, interpretive programs, playground, sports fields ▪ ADA sites: Yes

Fall asleep to the sound of Atlantic surf at this beachside campground near the eastern end of Long Island. Located about halfway between the posh Hamptons and moody Montauk Point, the park offers almost 200 dry campsites set along two loops, none of them more than 250 feet (76 m) from the beach. Although beach sports—swimming, surfing, fishing, paddleboarding—are far and away the main attraction, Hither Hills offers a sizable hinterland that includes "walking" (constantly shifting) dunes along Napeague Harbor, a bird conservation zone, large pond, forested areas, and another entire shoreline on Block Island Sound. Park trails cater to hikers, bikers, and horseback riders during the warmer months and cross-country skiers and snowshoers in winter. In addition, Hither Hills serves as the de

Camp Rockaway is a beachy glamping spot just outside bustling New York City.

facto campground for three nearby day-use state parks: Camp Hero and claims of its military time travel experiments during the Cold War (which allegedly inspired the television series *Stranger Things*), nature- and history-suffused Montauk Point, and Montauk Downs with its legendary golf course.

CAMP ROCKAWAY

🏕 5

Fort Tilden, Davis Road, Breezy Point, NY 11697

Open: May to October or early November ▪ Rates: Safari tents from $149, pup tents $99 extra ▪ Amenities: Showers, communal grill and fire pit, picnic area, potable water, camp store, linen service, internet ▪ ADA sites: Call ahead

Tucked between the golf course and Artists Alliance galleries at Fort Tilden, Camp Rockaway brings glamping to New York City's Atlantic shore. Although it's privately run, the camp lies inside Gateway National Recreation Area on the Rockaway Peninsula near Jamaica Bay and Coney Island. Set on raised wooden platforms, the safari-style tents include sunny front decks with lounge chairs and hammock-strung back porches. And in case you bring the kids, each safari tent comes with an adjoining pup tent with twin cots. Potted palms add a touch of the tropics. Queen-size beds are

complemented by side tables, electric fans, and charging stations; bedding and towels are provided. Camp Rockaway operates another summer-only glampground beside the Champlain Canal in Schuylerville, New York.

COLLECTIVE GOVERNORS ISLAND

🏠 4, 🏕 37

Governors Island National Monument, New York, NY 10004

Open: May to October ▪ Rates: Glamping tents from $829, cabins from $899 ▪ Amenities: Restaurant, bar, clubhouse, bathhouse, concierge, communal campfires, s'mores station, spa bath products, Frette robes, internet ▪ ADA sites: Yes

Imagine pulling back your tent flap each morning with the Statue of Liberty and Manhattan skyline right outside. That's what makes this glamping spot in New York Harbor one of the most audacious places to overnight anywhere on the planet. Reached by private water taxi from the Manhattan waterfront, the camp features glamping tents and "outlook shelters," all of them with king or double twin beds, temperature control, and daily breakfast in bed; most also feature bathrooms with rain showers. The camp boasts its own restaurant and alfresco bar (with jaw-dropping Big Apple views), as well as yoga and meditation sessions and a great lawn for sunbathing, picnics, and outdoor games. Glampers are free to explore the rest of Governors Island National Monument, a military bastion established in 1794 and now a venue for art and culture events and guided history tours.

NORTH-SOUTH LAKE CAMPGROUND

🚐 / 🏕 219 no hookup

County Route 18, Haines Falls, NY 12436

Open: June to October ▪ Rates: $22/$27 (state resident/nonresident) ▪ Amenities: Dump station, showers, fire pits, picnic tables, boat ramp, boat rentals, playground, sports field, firewood, beaches, horseshoes, volleyball ▪ ADA sites: Yes

Set deep in the forest near artsy Tannersville, North-South offers a classic Catskills summer vacation experience: lakeside camping with

swimming, boating, and beach volleyball inside a forest reserve, with trails leading to vistas that helped inspire America's first home-grown art movement (the Hudson River school). The sites at this large campground are nicely spaced along seven loops. While smaller RVs and trailers can fit, North-South is most appropriate for tent camping.

WHITE PINE CAMP

🏠 13

White Pine Road, Paul Smiths, NY 12970

Open: Year-round ▪ Rates: From $95 ▪ Amenities: Bowling, billiards, table tennis, boathouse, rock garden, nature tours ▪ ADA sites: Call ahead

In 1908, well-heeled Big Apple banker Archibald White established a posh private "great camp" on a gorgeous site overlooking Osgood Pond in the northern Adirondacks. In addition to attracting New York high-society guests, it famously served as the summer White House for Calvin Coolidge in 1926. More than a century later, White Pine is fully restored and available for overnight stays in cozy waterfront cabins outfitted with rustic furnishings, private bathrooms, kitchens, and either a stone fireplace or wood-burning stove. There's no longer a camp dining room, but nearby towns offer plenty of culinary choices. White Pine offers numerous ways to pass the time: swimming, fishing, canoeing, hiking, bowling in a vintage alley, and guided walks with resident naturalist Ed Kanze, who also dishes on various scandals that have unfolded there over the years—like a 1914 dalliance between the German ambassador and Mrs. White in the Japanese Tea

Book a stay in the cozy King Tent at Ithaca by Firelight glamping campground.

Collective Governors Island offers private cabins with views of the Manhattan skyline, as well as the Statue of Liberty.

House that may have affected the outcome of World War I.

WELLESLEY ISLAND STATE PARK

🏕 22, 🚐/⛺ 56 full hookup, 81 partial hookup, 295 no hookup
Lake of the Island Road, Wellesley Island, NY 13640
Open: Year-round ▪ Rates: RV/tent sites $18-$36/$23-$41 (state resident/nonresident), cabins from $66.50/$73.50 ▪ Amenities: Dump station, showers, picnic tables, fire rings with grills, camp store, laundry, recreation barn, boat ramps, beach, playgrounds, fish cleaning station ▪ ADA sites: Yes

The St. Lawrence River between Canada and the United States offers a stunning location for an insular campground set amid the Thousand Islands of upstate New York. With more than 400 sites, Wellesley is the region's biggest place to bunk for the night. But with the campsites and cabins dispersed across nine areas, it doesn't feel nearly that crowded. During summer, the park's Minna Anthony Common Nature Center offers birds-of-prey demonstrations, arts and crafts, Voyageur Canoe trips, and guided hikes along 10 miles (16 km) of trail, which are open in winter for cross-country skiing and snowshoeing. In addition to rental dock space, the marina boasts a maritime gas station and sewage dump. The park also harbors a nine-hole golf course.

ITHACA BY FIRELIGHT CAMPS

⛺ 21
1150 Danby Road, Ithaca, NY 14850
Open: May to October ▪ Rates: From $189 ▪ Amenities: Restaurant, bar, bathhouse, camp store, communal campfire, beverage station, potable water, game library, bocce, cornhole, ecofriendly bath products ▪ ADA sites: Call ahead

Located on the grounds of La Tourelle Hotel & Spa near Ithaca, this low-key glamping destination is all about romance in the woods. Outfitted with king or queen beds, writing desks, and private porches, the glamping tents are ready-made for couples. Farm-fresh breakfast is served each morning in the lobby, and there's bar service in the evening with wines, spirits, and craft beers to sip around the campfire. Guests can easily plug into everything else the Fingers Lakes region has on tap, from wineries and farmers markets

There's a reason Sunset Rock is a beloved lookout near North-South Lake Campground: The views go on for miles.

to waterfalls and wilderness trails. While Firelight isn't exclusively for adults, it'll cost you extra to bring the kids.

HIGHBANKS CAMPGROUND
🚐/🏕 270

Park Road, Mount Morris, NY 14510
Open: May to October ▪ Rates: From $24/$29 (state resident/nonresident) ▪ Amenities: Dump station, showers, picnic tables, fire ring with grill, camp store, laundry, recreation building ▪ ADA sites: Yes

True to its name, the only campground in Letchworth State Park sits high atop the Genesee River in western New York. It's a big one—nearly 300 sites with power and water—arranged around eight loops near the park's north end. But don't expect to spend much time in your RV or tent. One of the state's great nature areas offers multiple hiking, biking, and horseback trails along Letchworth Gorge, a 550-foot-deep (167 m) chasm with three spectacular waterfalls. Calmer stretches of the Genesee River facilitate whitewater rafting and kayaking. The park's hot-air balloon pad launches flights above the gorge, while the new Humphrey Nature Center offers a butterfly garden, birdwatching station, and year-round programs that focus on the park's natural and human history.

BRANCHES OF NIAGARA CAMPGROUND RESORT
🏚 15, 🚐 59 full hookup, 28 partial hookup, 🏕 12, 🛖 2

2659 Whitehaven Road, Grand Island, NY 14072
Open: April to October ▪ Rates: RV/tent full hookup from $79, RV/tent partial hookup from $68, cabins from $109, yurts from $143,

tent-only sites from $52 ▪ Amenities: Dump station, picnic tables, fire rings, showers, camp store, laundry, activities center, fishing piers, boat rental, chapel services, playground, sports courts, daily activities, beach, pedal bikes, dog park, ice ▪ ADA sites: Partial

Just upstream from the famed falls, Branches is one of the largest and best-equipped camping resorts in the Niagara-Buffalo region. Zip lines, laser tag, miniature golf, wildlife shows, outdoor movies, heated swimming pools, and canoeing and kayaking on the resort's lake are some of the activities available at Branches. The overnight digs are equally varied: full and power/water hookups, cabins, yurts, and tent-only sites. A strategic location on Grand Island puts the campground little more than 10 minutes from the American side of Niagara Falls and 15 minutes from downtown Buffalo.

ALLEGANY STATE PARK CABIN TRAILS
🏚 374

Allegany State Park Route 1, Salamanca, NY 14779
Open: Year-round ▪ Rates: $38.50/$45.50 (state resident/nonresident) ▪ Amenities: Varies from cabin to cabin ▪ ADA sites: Yes

The Allegany Mountains of western New York shelter a state park with unique "cabin trails"—rustic accommodations along unpaved roads in the park's Quaker and Red House areas. Built in batches since the park was created in the 1920s, the cabins vary in size and features. They can be anywhere from a single room to four bedrooms. Some have private bathrooms and showers, while others cluster around a central bathhouse. Some boast kitchens and electricity, and some do not. More than 150 of the cabins are winterized for year-round use. Yet even the most basic ones make a great base for exploring the hiking and biking trails and cross-country skiing and snowmobile routes, lakes and creeks of Allegany State Park. In addition to the cabin trails, the park offers three campgrounds with more than 300 total RV and tent sites. ▪

SOMETHING SPECIAL

Niagara Falls

Visitors beware: The mist, thunder, breadth, and height of Niagara Falls may overwhelm you. Yet each year, millions of people come to Niagara Falls, the oldest state park in America and one of the most popular. Few other parks claim so many attractions in such a small area, but the essence remains the sound and fury of the Niagara River rushing downhill from Lake Erie toward Lake Ontario.

At the heart of this drama lies Goat Island, where the river splits to plunge more than 175 feet (53.3 m) over the brinks of Horseshoe, Bridal Veil, and American Falls at a rate of 750,000 gallons per second. Wooded, with landscaped trails and bridges that follow the rapids to islets and all three falls, Goat Island is the largest of the isles in the mid-river archipelago above the falls. The river and shore west of here lie in Canada, while the Prospect Park section is on the eastern shore, or what is commonly called the "American side."

North Carolina

Find a spot on the sandy dunes across the Outer Banks, park your RV on an island nestled in a national seashore, or take to mountain campgrounds throughout North Carolina.

CAROLINA BEACH STATE PARK

🏠 4, 🚐/🏕 9 full hookup, 70 no hookup

State Park Road, Carolina Beach, NC 28428

Open: Year-round ▪ Rates: RV/tent full hookup $33, no hookup $23, cabins from $55 ▪ Amenities: Camp/marina store, snack bar, dump station, showers, picnic tables, fire pits with grills, potable water, marina, boat ramp, fishing deck, fitness trail ▪ ADA sites: Yes

Contrary to the name, this state park doesn't actually have a beach. Instead, it offers boating and fishing along the Intercoastal Waterway beside the town of Carolina Beach. Treacherous currents and steep drop-offs mean that swimming is prohibited in the park's waterways. Campers can rent a Jet Ski or pontoon boat at the park marina for a maritime adventure on the Cape Fear River, Myrtle Grove Sound, or even the open Atlantic via Snow's Cut. Landlubbers can trek nine trails through pocosin wetlands or tidal cypress-gum swamp, longleaf pine forest or savanna, evergreen forest or coastal fringe sandhill forest, and other Carolina shoreline habitats. There's also a self-guided TRACK Trail for kids that starts

Campgrounds along Cape Hatteras National Seashore offer views of the famous Bodie Lighthouse.

beside campsite 20. In addition to RV and tent sites, Carolina Beach offers two-room camper cabins with bunk beds, heating and air-conditioning, picnic tables, charcoal grills, and fire rings.

GREAT ISLAND CABINS

🏠 23

South Core Banks, Cape Lookout National Seashore, Davis, NC 28531

Open: March to November ▪ Rates: From $80 ▪ Amenities: Private bathrooms with hot-water showers, table and chairs, kitchens, barbecue grills, ice, gasoline (for generators), beach, boat docks ▪ ADA sites: Yes

True seclusion is the trademark of seaside cabins at Cape Lookout National Seashore on an island that can only be reached by boat. The vehicle and passenger ferry from Davis on the North Carolina mainland takes less than an hour and is available year-round. The cabins are located along a sandy lane within walking distance of the ferry landing on South Core Banks island. But if you're bringing lots of gear, it's wise to bring some kind of motorized transport across on the ferry.

The cabins are fairly basic, and you need to be largely self-sufficient. They sleep four to 12 people in bunk beds; there's a thin mattress on each bed, but no blankets or other bedding. Kitchens are equipped with a propane stove (gas provided), and there's a barbecue

grill on the porch outside. However, there is no fridge, and campers need to bring their own cooking utensils and dinnerware. Each has a bathroom with shower, but the hot-water heater and other electrical appliances need to be powered by a generator that campers need to bring themselves.

Anyone with four-wheel-drive can car-camp between March and November on the wild beaches of South Core Banks and North Core Banks islands in the national seashore.

OREGON INLET CAMPGROUND

🚐/🏕 47 partial hookup, 30 no hookup, 🏕 30

12001 State Highway 12, Nags Head, NC 27959

Open: Year-round ▪ Rates: RV/tent partial hookup $35, no hookup/tent only $28 ▪ Amenities: Dump station, showers, picnic tables, grills, potable water, beach, boat ramps, marina ▪ ADA sites: Yes

Set along a pristine beach on Bodie Island, this Cape Hatteras National Seashore campground is for anyone who digs sand, sun, and sea. Body or board surfing, shell hunting, bird watching, and surf fishing are just steps away from every campsite. Campers can also cross the highway to Oregon Inlet Fishing Center, where more than 40 charter boats offer guided angling trips into the open Atlantic. If the ocean's a little rough for your liking, consider kayaking or paddleboarding, clamming or crabbing on Pamlico Sound on the island's leeward side. Outer Banks OBX offers guided horseback rides along the shore. And with an off-road vehicle (ORV) permit from the Park Service, campers can drive up and down the beach. By the way, Oregon Inlet was created by an 1846 hurricane and named for the sailing ship that discovered the newborn passage after the storm.

Camp among the trees, and in style, at Pilot Cove Forest Lodging.

HANGING ROCK STATE PARK
🏠10, 🚐/⛺ 73 no hookup
1790 Hanging Rock Park Road, Danbury, NC 27016
Open: Year-round ▪ Rates: RV/tent no hookup from $19, cabins $110 ▪ Amenities: Gift shop, snack bar, showers, picnic tables, grills, potable water, boat rental, swimming, amphitheater ▪ ADA sites: Yes

Don't just picnic at Hanging Rock; camp there too at a state park in the Sauratown Mountains about a 40-minute drive north of Winston-Salem. While it's tempting to consider these rugged highlands as an outlier of the Blue Ridge or Appalachians, it's actually a separate range renowned for its impressive quartzite outcrops and some of the best rock climbing in the mid-Atlantic region. Campsites and cabins are arrayed along two loops between Cascade Creek and Park Lake. The 4.7-mile (7.5 km) Moore's Wall Loop Trail traverses the middle of the campground on its way to the park's

highest point. That's just one of Hanging Rock's 17 hiking or biking routes, including a segment of the long-distance Mountains to Sea Trail that runs the length of North Carolina. Flowing along the park's northern edge, the Dan River invites paddling or tubing, either on your own or with local companies like Dan River Outfitters.

CAROWINDS CAMP WILDERNESS RESORT
🏠15, 🚐/⛺ 140 full hookup
14609 Carowinds Boulevard, Charlotte NC 28273
Open: Year-round ▪ Rates: RVs from $44, cabins from $79 ▪ Amenities: Camp store, dump station, showers, laundry, picnic tables, fire pits with grills, swimming pool, game room, sports courts, theme park tram, ATM, internet ▪ ADA sites: Yes

A compelling contrast to North Carolina's coast and mountain campgrounds, Camp Wilderness offers an urban camping experience inside the limits of the state's largest city. The resort's campsites and cabins sit beside a sprawling entertainment complex that includes a thrill-ride heavy Carowinds theme park and Carolina Harbor warm-weather water park. Truth be told, there's not an awful lot to do at the campground other than recover from a day in the theme parks that might include a death-defying 325-foot (99 m) plunge on the Fury 325 roller coaster, a sprint down the Boogie Board Racer, or a whirl on the Scream Weaver big wheel. A shuttle bus links the resort and theme parks, and campers can purchase packages that include overnight fees and theme park admission.

Take in sweeping forest views—especially in the colorful fall months—from lookouts at Hanging Rock State Park.

PILOT COVE FOREST LODGING

🏠 15

319 Gateway Junction Drive, Pisgah Forest, NC 28768

Open: Year-round ▪ Rates: From $150 ▪ Amenities: Kitchens, private bathrooms, washer/dryers, bedding and towels, heating and air-conditioning, flat-screen TVs, bike washing station, communal barbecue area ▪ ADA sites: Yes

Stylish modern cabins are the forte of a forest lodge in the Blue Ridge foothills near Brevard. With their sloping roofs and timber-braced balconies, the green-and-gray cabins blend easily into the woodland setting. Sleeping two to six people each, the cabins offer full kitchens and bathrooms and a living area with wide-screen TV; the rooms are adorned with locally flavored artwork and photography. Outside there's a spacious patio, parking area, and a washing station for trail-muddied bikes and boots. Pilot Cove boasts two of its own trails. But the 64-acre (25 ha) property borders on Pisgah National Forest and more than 100 miles (160 km) of nearby hiking and biking routes. It's also a short walk into town and eateries like Sora Japanese and Hawg Wild Barbecue.

PISGAH GLAMPING

⛺ 12

375 Wesley Branch Road, Asheville, NC 28806

Open: March to November ▪ Rates: From $130 ▪ Amenities: Bathhouse, bedding, picnic tables, fire rings with grills, firewood, ice, potable water, swimming, fishing pier ▪ ADA sites: No

This new glamping camp in Pisgah National Forest offers the best of both worlds. On one hand, a location in Lake Powhatan Recreation Area means easy access to the lake's sandy swimming beach and an extensive network of hiking and biking trails. Ranger-led interpretive programs are offered on weekends between Memorial and Labor Days. And the North Carolina Arboretum—with its Blue Ridge Quilt Garden and National Native Azalea Repository, and Bonsai collection— is just down the road. On the other hand, campers craving an urban rush can easily zip into Asheville, less than 20 minutes away, for the city's copious craft breweries, art galleries, and music joints. Pisgah's fully furnished glamping tents come with queen beds and a foldable cot for a child or third grown-up. For

The Carolina portion of the Great Smokies offers plenty of hiking opportunities within the popular outdoor destination.

larger families or groups, there's also enough space under canvas for multiple sleeping bags.

PAINT ROCK FARM

⛺ 10, 🏠 1

1295 Paint Rock Road, Hot Springs, NC 28743

Open: April to November ▪ Rates: Glamping cabins from $100, tiny house from $125 ▪ Amenities: Bathhouse, bedding and towels, communal kitchen, sketchy internet ▪ ADA sites: Partial

This rustic glamping site is on a working farm on bluffs beside the French Broad River in the mountains along the North Carolina–Tennessee border. Arrayed around a grassy meadow, the cabins are small but comfy, with double or queen beds, a sitting area, and private porch. The new bathhouse boasts heated floors and solar-powered hot-water showers. The restored barn doubles as an indoor game room and dining space, with meals prepared in the communal catering space. Glampers can chill on the farm or explore a surrounding region that includes a portion of the Appalachian Trail and rafting on the French Broad. Or head down to Bridge Street in Hot Springs for suds at Big Pillow Brewing, breakfast or burgers at Hillbilly Market & Deli, or gourmet coffees, smoothies, and ice cream at Iron Horse Station.

CATALOOCHEE CAMPGROUND

🚐 / ⛰ 27 no hookup

Cataloochee Entrance Road, Waynesville, NC 28785

Open: April to October ▪ Rate: $25 ▪ Amenities: Restrooms, picnic tables, fire pits with grills, potable water, food storage container ▪ ADA sites: No

Escape the crowds, parking woes, and bumper-to-bumper traffic that afflict other parts of Great Smoky Mountains National Park by camping in the Cataloochee Valley near the park's eastern extreme. Set along a creek in the valley bottom, the campground welcomes RVs, tents, and even hammocks, although larger motor homes will discover that the twisty routes into Cataloochee from Interstate 40 aren't very user friendly. With the nearest stores around 40 minutes away in Waynesville, campers should stock up on everything they need for their Smoky Mountain getaway before venturing into the valley. Don't be surprised if an elk wanders past your pad: The big beasts were released in the valley 20 years ago as part of an experimental reintroduction program. Give them their space and they will give you yours. Historic structures like Palmer chapel and Beech Grove School are scattered along the valley, remnants of a remote 19th-century pioneer settlement that gradually faded away after Great Smoky became a national park in 1934.

RIVER'S EDGE TREEHOUSE RESORT

♀ 6

195 Old U.S. Highway 129, Robbinsville NC 28771

Open: April to October ▪ Rates: From $150 ▪ Amenities: Kitchenettes, private bathrooms, bedding and towels, toiletries, heating and air-conditioning, barbecue grills, communal fire pit, lawn games, fishing gear, car-washing supplies, satellite TV, internet ▪ ADA sites: Yes

River's Edge is set high in the mountains at the western end of the state, and revolves around half a dozen romantic tree houses perched above the Cheoah River. With king beds, comfy sofas, roomy bathrooms, and very private decks, they're ideal for couples relishing an escape into the woods. While glampers might be tempted to hang out in their tree houses, the area offers plenty of outdoor adventure: boating on Lake Santeetlah, hiking the old-growth woods of Joyce Kilmer Memorial Forest in Nantahala National Forest, white-water rafting on half a dozen local rivers, or traditional mountain music at the Stecoah Valley Center. ▪

SOMETHING SPECIAL

Great Smoky Mountains National Park

Its location, within a day's drive for tens of millions of Americans, helps make Great Smoky Mountains the most popular national park in the United States. The 800-square-mile (2,072 sq km) international biosphere reserve is split about evenly between Tennessee and North Carolina, and it protects some of the oldest mountains in the world.

More than 1,500 species of flowering plants and 60 species of native mammals, including deer, black bears, and elk, live within these often mist-shrouded mountains. The 384 miles (618 km) of hiking trails make it easy to stroll along a rushing stream without straying far from your car. Or join a ranger-led program to discover, among other things, a few of the park's 30 species of salamanders, the world's most diverse population for an area this size.

North Dakota

Campgrounds across the Peace Garden State offer fishing (ice, shore, and boat), swimming, canoeing, hiking, and biking, among other outdoor adventures.

WOODLAND RESORT

🏠 9

1012 Woodland Drive, Devils Lake, ND 58301

Open: Year-round ▪ Rates: Cabins from $149 ▪ Amenities: Restaurant, bar, bedding and towels, picnic tables, grills, internet, cable TV ▪ ADA sites: Yes

Whether you're into winter ice fishing or casting from boat or shore on a bright-blue summer day, Woodland offers an ideal place to base an angling expedition to Devil's Lake. The resort's modern cabins range from one to three bedrooms and come with private bathrooms, full kitchen, and cable TV. But don't expect to spend much time indoors with all of that water to try. Perch, pike, and walleye are among the game fish that populate the state's largest natural lake. Woodland offers motorboat, pontoon, and heated ice-fishing huts, as well as boat repair, bait-and-tackle shop, fish cleaning station, and the Perch Patrol pro fishing guides.

LINDENWOOD CAMPGROUND

🚐/⛺ 47 partial hookup

1955 Roger Maris Drive, Fargo, ND 58103

Open: May to October ▪ Rate: RV/tent partial hookup $30 ▪ Amenities:

Pitch a tent at Cottonwood Campground, nestled within Theodore Roosevelt National Park.

Dump station, fire pits, picnic tables, potable water, showers, firewood, playgrounds, ball fields, bike and kayak rental ▪ ADA sites: Partial

Located along the Red River, this outstanding municipal campground offers overnight digs for those making the long cross-country drive on Interstate 94 or anyone hanging out in Fargo. All sites are equipped with water and power. Campers can choose from a selection of quirky novelty bikes and cruise the riverside Lindenwood Bike Path or hire a kayak for a paddle along the river that divides North Dakota and Minnesota. Campers can also use Lindenwood as a base for exploring the Fargo-Moorehead twin cities. The Roger Maris Museum, Red River Zoo, Plains Art Museum, and three universities are all within a 15-minute drive of the campground.

BISMARCK KOA JOURNEY

🏠 4, 🚐 65 full hookup, 31 partial hookup, ⛺ 20

3720 Centennial Road, Bismarck, ND 58503

Open: Year-round ▪ Rates: RV full hookup from $43, RV partial hookup from $39, cabins from $60, tent-only sites from $28 ▪ Amenities: Dump station, showers, picnic tables, snack bar, camp store, laundry, dog park, firewood, propane, potable water, tennis court, basketball, fire pits (on request), bike rental, internet ▪ ADA sites: Partial

Tucked behind suburban housing tracts on the northeast side of the state capital, Bismarck Journey offers everything that campers have come to expect of a KOA campground, including a swimming pool, playground, camp store, and spanking clean (heated) restrooms with showers. An abundance of trees enhance privacy in the full hookup pads, but the less expensive RV sites are cheek-by-jowl in grass fields. Cabins and tent-only sites beneath the trees round out the sleeping options.

FORT ABRAHAM LINCOLN STATE PARK

🏠 2, 🚐/⛺ 82 partial hookup, 19 no hookup, 2 tipis

4480 Fort Lincoln Road, Mandan, ND 58554

Open: Year-round ▪ Rates: RV/tent partial hookup $25, RV/tent no hookup $17, cabins $60, tipis $35 ▪ Amenities: Dump station, fire pits, picnic tables, showers, amphitheater, playground, coffee shop, gift shop ▪ ADA sites: Partial

North Dakota's oldest state park (established in 1907) lies on the opposite side of the Missouri River from Bismarck, but its frontier ambience offers a dramatic contrast to modern city life. A reconstructed Mandan Indian village and the restored U.S. Army post where Custer and the Seventh Cavalry were based before their ill-fated day at Little Bighorn speak of the site's rich history, while the natural surroundings offer a hint of how much of the Dakotas once looked. Overlooking the muddy confluence of the Heart and Missouri Rivers, the campground offers primitive waterfront sites and inland pads with water and power. A few camping cabins and Cheyenne-style tipis are also available. The state park maintains 6.75 miles (11 km) of hiking routes, including an interpretive trail along the river and a big loop around the entire grounds, as well as a paved bike trail that leads to the nearby town of Mandan. During summer, guided tours are offered of the Custer family home and On-A-Slant Indian Village.

CROSS RANCH STATE PARK

3, / 36 partial hookup, 21 no hookup, 4, 1 tipi
1403 River Road, Center, ND 58530
Open: Year-round ▪ Rates: RV/tent partial hookup $25, RV/tents no hookup $17, cabins from $80, yurts from $65, tipi $35 ▪ Amenities: Dump station, fire pits, picnic tables, showers, playground, amphitheater, boat ramp ▪ ADA sites: No

About an hour's drive north of Bismarck, Cross Ranch lies along one of the last pristine, dam-free sections of the Missouri River. Like many other spots along the Big Muddy, Lewis & Clark passed this way on their epic journey to the Pacific Coast and would probably be astounded at the accommodation available today: not just RV hookups, but comfy cabins, yurts, and even a solitary Cheyenne-style tipi named after their guide, Sacagawea. Many of the overnight sites lie within a stone's throw of the river. The Missouri is a little rough for swimming but perfect for fishing and boating. Rental canoes and kayaks are available during the warmer months and cross-country skis and snowshoes during the winter. And there are 13 miles (21 km) of hiking trails through a riverine landscape little changed from when the Corps of Discovery wintered nearby in 1804-05. Campers with an affinity for American history can call on local sights like Fort Mandan, Knife River Indian Villages National Historic Site, and the Lewis & Clark Interpretive Center in Washburn.

COTTONWOOD CAMPGROUND

/ 64 no hookup, 12
East River Road, Theodore Roosevelt National Park, Medora, ND 58645
Open: Year-round ▪ Rates: $7-$14 ▪ Amenities: Restrooms, grills, picnic tables, potable water, amphitheater; no showers or dump station ▪ ADA sites: Yes

Make like Teddy Roosevelt (during his youthful cowboy days) and camp along the banks of the Little Missouri River in the national park that reflects both his name and legacy. Set among riverside cottonwoods not far from the park's main entrance, the campground is a great place for wildlife watching, including a nearby prairie dog town and the occasional bison or wild horse that wanders through. There's not much in the way of amenities at Cottonwood; although most of the sites are drive-up, the campground is basically primitive. But location is hard to beat: right beside the

Take your mountain bike for a ride along Maah Daah Hey Trail in the Sather Lake Recreation Area.

The 3.65-square-mile (9.5 sq km) International Peace Garden is located adjacent to the Canada–United States border.

36-Mile Scenic Drive through the park's South Unit and just a short drive or hike to the visitors center and Roosevelt's historic Maltese Cross Cabin (where the future 36th president bunked in 1883). And it's just 5 miles (8 km) from Medora, with all of its restaurants, shops, and historic attractions. Cottonwood offers special campsites for paddlers making the week-long float trip down the Little Missouri. Cross-country skiing is possible on the frozen-over river during the winter months.

WANNAGAN CREEK CABINS

🏠 4

2440 East River Road, Medora, ND 58645

Open: Year-round ▪ Rate: Cabins $200 (two-night minimum stay) ▪

Amenities: Picnic tables, barbecue grills, river views ▪ ADA sites: No

Huddled amid the Badlands between the north and south units of Teddy Roosevelt National Park, these modern cabins are about as remote as it gets in a part of North Dakota that's already secluded. Each of the two-bedroom units features a full kitchen, furnished living room, air-conditioning and heating, and bathroom with shower, washer, and dryer. Bedding is not provided, and it's best to stock up on food and beverage in Medora before heading out to the ranch. Wannagan is most convenient for exploring the national park and nearby Little Missouri National Grassland. At low water, you can venture across the river to hike or bike the portion of

the Maah Daah Hey Trail between Medora and Roosevelt's historic Elkhorn Ranch. Wannagan can arrange horseback riding, bike rentals, and other outdoor activities.

SATHER LAKE CAMPGROUND

🚐 / ⛺ 18 no hookup

State Highway 16, Alexander, ND 58831

Open: Year-round ▪ Rate: RV/tent $10 ▪ Amenities: Restrooms, fire pits, picnic tables, potable water, fishing pier; no showers or dump station ▪ ADA sites: Yes

Come for the fishing, stay for the fresh air, wide-open spaces, and absence of other human beings. Managed by the U.S. Forest Service, Sather Lake offers a handy place to

Rangers offer a look into history at Fort Abraham Lincoln State Park through artifacts and stories.

spend the night in Little Missouri National Grassland. Campers can angle for rainbow trout, bluegill, and bass from their own boats or a floating dock, although winter probably means poking a hole through the frozen surface. Be forewarned: This is dry camping, with no hookups of any kind and no dump station. The closest grocery stores, restaurants, and gas stations are 20 miles (34 km) away in Sydney, Montana.

LAKE METIGOSHE STATE PARK

☎ 4, 🚐/🏕 84 partial hookup, 🏕 39, 🏠 1

East Shore Park Road, Roland, ND 58318

Open: Year-round ▪ Rates: RV/tent partial hookup $25, tent only $17, cabins from $60, yurt $65 ▪ Amenities: Dump station, fire pits, picnic tables, showers, potable water, playgrounds, amphitheater, boat ramp, dog park, beach, fishing docks, paddle and snow rentals ▪ ADA sites: Yes

A stark contrast to the rolling prairies that cover so much of North Dakota, Lake Metigoshe rests in the timbered Turtle Mountains and its glacial lakes, a mosaic of woods and water created around 10,000 years ago when the last ice age retreated. Although the park boasts two RV/tent areas—Washegum and Maid O'Moonshine—they're close enough to each other to share facilities like the playground, amphitheater, and dump station. Primitive camping is allowed at three sites along the lakeshore. And there's a handful of indoor digs, including yurts and cabins. While aquatic activities are the main attraction, the park offers 8 miles (13 km) of hiking trails and

an outdoor learning center with nature and history programs. Big Lake Metigoshe is complemented by a dozen smaller water bodies, including several that straddle the U.S.-Canada border. Rentals include canoes and kayaks in summer and cross-country skis and snowshoes in winter.

INTERNATIONAL PEACE GARDEN

🚐/🏕 27 partial hookup, 🏕 7

10939 U.S. Highway 281, Dunseith, ND 58329

Open: May to September ▪ Rates: RV/tent partial hookup from $30, tent only $15 ▪ Amenities: Dump station, fire pits, picnic tables, showers, potable water, firewood, playground, restaurant, gift shop, tornado shelter ▪ ADA sites: Partial

Created in 1932 along the world's longest undefended international boundary, the Peace Garden straddles the U.S.-Canada border between North Dakota and

Manitoba. From a formal garden with a huge floral clock and cacti and succulent greenhouse to hiking and biking trails through 2,400 acres (971 ha) of woodlands and prairie, there's plenty to see and do. The gardens also boast multiple lakes where kayakers and canoers can take a paddle, or anglers can cast a line. For families, kid-friendly programs including scavenger hunts and geocaching are on offer. Located in a grove of aspens and oaks, the campground lies between the North American Game Warden Museum and a historic Civilian Conservation Corps lodge built in the 1930s. Four kinds of power and water pads are available, as well as tent-only campsites. It's about a half-hour hike from the campground to the Boardwalk Café and the international frontier. As long as they stay inside the park, visitors can walk or drive between the United States and Canada without going through customs or immigration. ■

SOMETHING SPECIAL

Theodore Roosevelt National Park

Few other national parks besides Theodore Roosevelt in North Dakota offer such a combination of epic scenery, wildlife, and history yet remain so overlooked by the average American. Only some 750,000 people experienced this park in 2018 (in contrast to the more than 11 million who visited the Great Smoky Mountains National Park that year), and the numbers would be even lower if it weren't for the interstate highway running right through the park. (You can exit I-94 and be at the visitors center in less than five minutes.)

An easily accessible scenic drive lets visitors cruise through, stop at a couple of overlooks, and be on their way again. That's a nice attribute for people in a hurry, but why rush? Take time to see the complete park and explore a landscape that inspired the nation's greatest conservationist president. Divided into North and South Units, there are a number of hikes, including the easy quarter-mile (0.4 km) Wind Canyon Trail that offers panoramas of the Badlands landscape at the southern end of the park, and the longer 5.7-mile (9.2 km) Caprock Coulee Trail, which showcases a bit of everything the North Unit has to offer.

Ohio

From lighthouses at Cedar Point to tree houses in Mohican County, there's a bit of everything for every type of camper in the Buckeye State.

SOUTH BASS ISLAND STATE PARK

☎ 5, 🚐/🏕 10 full hookup, 51 partial hookup, 34 no hookup, 🏕 39

1523 Catawba Avenue, South Bass Island, OH 43456

Open: April to October ▪ Rates: RV/tent full hookup $26, RV/tent partial hookup from $20, tent only $14 ▪ Amenities: Dump station, showers, picnic tables, fire pits with grills, beach, boat rental, boat ramp, fish cleaning station, playground ▪ ADA sites: Yes

Flanked by the lakeshore and glacial grooves that reveal the Lake Erie isle's ice age formation, the campground and cabins sprawl across around 70 percent of the park's area. The overnight digs range from full-hookup RV and tent sites to octagonal "cabents" (half cabin, half tent).

The park also offers a rocky beach, fishing pier, boat ramp, and ruins of the Victory Hotel, one of the world's largest summer resorts until destroyed by fire in 1919. Out-in-Bay Watercraft Rentals beside the pier has paddleboards, Jet Skis, power boats, and kayaks for playing on the lake. Campers can walk to other south shore hot spots like Saunders Golf Club, the Lake Erie Islands Nature & Wildlife Center,

Stay in one of nine glamorous treetop cabins at the Mohicans Treehouse Resort.

and Joe's Bar. Or hire wheels from Duffs Golf Cart Rental and explore the rest of South Bass.

LIGHTHOUSE POINT AT CEDAR POINT

☎ 156, 🚐/🏕 120 full hookup

1 Cedar Point Road, Sandusky, OH 44870

Open: May to October ▪ Rates: RV from $93, cabins from $239 ▪ Amenities: Camp store, showers, laundry, picnic tables, grills, swimming pool, boat ramp, fish cleaning station, beach, water sports rentals, playgrounds, tornado shelter, shuttle service, ATM machine, internet ▪ ADA sites: Yes

This full-service campground lies beside the most renowned theme park in the Great Lakes region. Founded in 1870, Cedar Point boasts 17 roller coasters and 50 other rides, plus indoor and outdoor water parks and a mile-long (1.6 km) beach. Two of those adrenaline junkie attractions—Steel Vengeance and Magnum XL-200—book-end the campground. The most desired digs are the posh Ultimate Patio RV pads and the waterfront cottages with their private decks overlooking Lake Erie. Campers can purchase special Cedar Point ticket packages.

COLUMBIA WOODLANDS

☎ 4, 🏕 4

6608 Rieger Drive Northwest, Dover, OH 44622

Open: Glamping April to October, cabins year-round ▪ Rates: From $317 ▪ Amenities: Restaurant, private bathrooms with showers, bedding and towels, heating and air-conditioning, private patios, spa treatments, wine tasting, yoga, bikes, canoes, lawn games ▪ ADA sites: No

While exploring the 400 acres (161 ha) of wilderness that envelop this luxury cabin and glamping resort, you realize it's something of a miracle that it escaped devastation during the 19th-century Industrial Revolution that remade so much of northern Ohio. The once bustling Ohio & Erie Canal runs along the eastern side of the forest, and old factory hubs Canton and Akron are just up the road. Long removed from those smoke-choked days, Columbia Woodlands attracts wedding parties, couples, and anyone cherishing a quiet walk in the woods or a paddle across a secluded pond.

Ranging from two to five bedrooms, the luxury cabins are arrayed around the camp's largest lake. The Meadows glamping camp is deeper in the woods, a cluster of tents that share a communal dining space, indoor lounge, and outdoor fire pit with chef-prepared gourmet meals.

BERLIN RV PARK & CAMPGROUND

🚐/⛺ 46 full hookup, 5 partial hookup

5898 Amish County Byway (State Route 39), Millersburg, OH 44654
Open: April to November ▪ Rates: RV/tent full hookup $42, RV/tent partial hookup $37 ▪ Amenities: Dump station, showers, laundry, picnic tables, fire pits, firewood, playground, sports courts, herb garden, internet ▪ ADA sites: Partial

Deep in the heart of Ohio's Amish Country, this easy-going RV park makes a great base for browsing the area's traditional bakeries, quilters, cheese makers, antique shops, and custom furniture factories. Right across the road is the Peach Barn, which offers fresh fruit during the summer. And it's a short drive into the town of Berlin, with its famous Amish flea market and old-timey variety shows at the Amish Country Theater. The campground is spanking clean, offers walking trails in the adjoining woods, and features an herb garden that campers can harvest for whatever they're cooking in their microwave, on stovetop, or a fire ring.

THE MOHICANS TREEHOUSE RESORT

🏠 6, 👤 9, 🚐 1

23164 Vess Road, Glenmont, OH 44628
Open: Year-round ▪ Rates: Tree houses/travel trailer from $374, cabins from $300 ▪ Amenities: Kitchens, private bathrooms, bedding and towels, heating and air-conditioning, DVD players and screens, private decks, barbecue grills, electric vehicle charger ▪ ADA sites: Partial (cabins)

The Mohican Country of central Ohio provides a sylvan setting for a luxury tree house and cabin collection that also embraces a single vintage Airstream. Glampers could easily while away a day trying to identify the different species of trees in the surrounding forest (at least nine). They can climb even higher into the forest at nearby Tree Frog Canopy Tours or paddle the Mohican River on guided float trips organized by various outfitters. In September, Native Americans from around the country attend the Great Mohican Pow-Wow at a riverside park about a seven-minute drive from the tree houses.

THE WILDS AT COLUMBUS ZOO

🏠 7, 🏕 15

14000 International Road, Cumberland, OH 43732
Open: Yurts May to October, cabins year-round ▪ Rates: Yurts from $325, cabins from $359 ▪ Amenities: Private bathrooms with showers, bedding and towels, heating and air-conditioning, private decks; cabins also have kitchens, barbecue grills, rowboats ▪ ADA sites: Yes

The largest wildlife conservation center in North America offers three ways to spend the night among some of the planet's rarest and most endangered creatures. Nomad Ridge offers roomy yurts with decks overlooking the open-range wildlife habitats. The waterfront Cabins at Straker Lake come with rowboats for exploring the water. Those who want to get even closer to nature can opt for WildNights at the Outpost,

Take the plunge at Lighthouse Point, just minutes from the iconic Cedar Point amusement park.

The adults-only Nomad Ridge offers private yurts with sweeping views of The Wilds from a secluded balcony.

a small tent camp in the middle of an African animal habitat.

Wild animal observation and photography is the main attraction, The Wilds also offers hiking trails, horseback riding, fishing, and zip-line adventure. Located on land once strip-mined for coal, this sprawling satellite campus of Columbus Zoo shelters creatures like the dhole wild dog, one-horned Asian rhino, Persian onager, Sichuan takin, and eastern hellbender sala-mander that are rarely seen in zoos, let alone their natural habitats.

OLD MAN'S CAVE CAMPGROUND

🏠 3, 🚐 / 🏕 47 full hookup, 109 partial hookup, 13 no hookup
19852 State Route 664, Logan, OH 43138
Open: Year-round ▪ Rates: RV/tent full or partial hookup from $29, no

hookup from $25, cabins $70 ▪ Amenities: Restaurant, snack bar, camp store, dump station, showers, laundry, picnic tables, fire pits with grills, swimming pool, volleyball, horseshoes, archery, amphitheater, wildlife observation blind ▪ ADA sites: Yes

Hocking Hills State Park lies around an hour south of Columbus. The hills don't rise very far—the highest point is a mere 1,220 feet (372 m) feet above sea level—but the dra-matic cliffs, gorges, and waterfalls more than compensate for any lack of altitude. The campground lies near its namesake cavern and the new visitors center, as well as other landmarks like Sphinx Head and the old bridge that leaps Upper Falls. The bridge connects the Grandma Gatewood Trail, a 6-mile (9.6 km) route along the gorge bottom to

Whispering Cave, Cedar Falls, and spectacular Ash Cave. Campers can observe the night sky at the park's John Glenn Astronomy Park or scramble up Black Hand Sandstone cliffs at a dedicated rock climbing and rappelling area in adjoining Hocking State Forest.

LAKE VESUVIUS RECREATION AREA

🚐 / 🏕 48 partial hookup,
🏕 11 no hookup
6518 Ellisonville-Paddle Creek Road (State Route 93), Pedro, OH 45659
Open: April to October ▪ Rates: RV/tent partial hookup $20, tent only $15 ▪ Amenities: Dump station, showers, picnic tables, fire pits with grills, potable water, beach, boat rental, boat ramp ▪ ADA sites: Yes

Two outstanding Forest Service campgrounds lie on either side of

Old-growth forest lines the walking and hiking trails throughout Hocking State Forest, near Hocking Hills State Park.

the park's namesake lake in Wayne National Forest. Iron Ridge Campground is tucked into thick woods on a hilltop above the lake's eastern shore, and Oak Hill is in an equally elevated position above the western shore. They're about the same size, but Iron Ridge is more conducive for those who prefer quiet and a walk in the woods and Oak Hill for those who want to be close to the Lake Vesuvius Beach and boating facilities. Named for the historic Vesuvius Iron Furnace, the park offers several unique routes, including a long-bow archery trail, over-the-water boardwalk trail, and the Whiskey Run Trail through an old-time bootleg bastion. Kountry Kayaks offers canoe and kayak rental during the warmer months, while equestrians can explore 46 miles (74 km) of horse trails around the lake.

SHAWNEE STATE PARK CAMPGROUND

🏠 25, 🚐/🏕 94 partial hookup, 12 no hookup
4404 State Route 125, West Portsmouth, OH 45663
Open: Year-round ▪ Rates: RV/tent partial hookup from $23, no hookup from $19, cabins from $109 ▪ Amenities: Restaurant, bar, dump station, showers, laundry, picnic tables, fire pits with grills, potable water, boat rental, boat ramp, playground, sports courts, archery, miniature golf, amphitheater, internet (at cabins) ▪ ADA sites: Yes

This woodsy state park and its campground sit in the state's Little Smokies region, a nickname inspired by the area's dreamy mist-shrouded landscape and the fact that it's considered the westernmost reach of the vast Appalachian uplands. The campsites are scattered along Turkey Creek in Long Hollow, a short walk from the nature center and boating or fishing on little Roosevelt Lake. The park's modern family cabins huddle in the woods beside Shawnee Lodge and its Smokehouse Restaurant, Tecumseh cocktail lounge, and summertime Tiki Bar beside the swimming pool. Campers who want to explore beyond the state park will find the Ohio River Scenic Byway just a 10-minute drive to the south. There's also hard-core hiking on the 40-mile (64 km) Shawnee Backpack Trail, which includes portions of the cross-state Buckeye Trail and multistate North Country Trail.

HUESTON WOODS STATE PARK

🏠 37, 🚐/🏕 20 full hookup, 228 partial hookup, 137 no hookup
6301 Park Office Road, College Corner, OH 45003
Open: Campground April to September, cabins year-round ▪ Rates: RV/tent full or partial hookup from $25, RV/tent no hookup from $23, cabins from $109 ▪ Amenities: Camp store, dump station, showers, laundry, picnic tables, fire pits with grills, potable water, playground, miniature golf, sports courts, archery, beach, boat rental, boat ramp, fishing pier, dog park, internet ▪ ADA sites: Yes

A short drive from Dayton and Cincinnati, this southeast Ohio park boasts one of the state's largest campgrounds (nearly 400 sites) and more than three dozen cabins. The campground sits toward the west end of Acton Lake near the park's various water sports outlets, including a marina with canoe, kayak, and pontoon boat rental, as well as summertime docks for those who bring their own watercraft. The cabins are along the north shore, close to Hueston Woods Lodge with its restaurant, bar, and poolside snack bar.

Campers are free to collect found fossils of marine animals that lived around 500 million years ago when the region was covered by an ancient inland sea. The state park's nature center includes a Raptor Rehabilitation Center where visitors can observe and learn how injured or orphaned eagles, owls, and hawks are fostered for release back into the wild. ▪

SOMETHING SPECIAL

Hocking Hills State Park

Richard Rowe so loved the overhangs along the creeks of Hocking Hills that he moved into one, or under one, which became known as Old Man's Cave. Almost two centuries later, the recesses of the twisting gorge where Rowe lived (and is buried) still tempt those seeking refuge.

Water cutting through the black hand sandstone of these hills created a cluster of streams that drop through potholes and waterfalls, beribboned with ferns and hemlocks. Trails rise from the side to top cliffs and then tunnel beneath overhangs. The park is composed of six separate areas, each with a distinctive feature: Rock House, Cantwell Cliffs, Cedar Falls, Conkles Hollow, Ash Cave, and, of course, Old Man's Cave. These units fit into a patchwork of state forest and natural areas that comprise more than 10,000 acres (4,046.9 ha), linked by trails and roads.

Oklahoma

Campgrounds in Oklahoma are more than OK, with options that range from Great Plains retreats to lakeshore spots to base camps in the foothills of the Ozarks.

TWIN FOUNTAINS RV RESORT

🚐 205 full hookup

2727 Northeast 63rd Street, Oklahoma City, OK 73111

Open: Year-round ▪ Rate: $55 ▪ Amenities: Restaurant, bar, camp store, showers, laundry, fire pits, swimming pool, playground, miniature golf, salon and spa, fitness center, clubhouse, propane, tornado shelter, dog run, RV wash, shuttle service, ATM, internet ▪ ADA sites: Yes

This full-service RV resort might be situated inside the Oklahoma City beltway, but retains a genuine rural feel thanks to copious trees, well-spaced sites, and a lodge-like hub that wouldn't look out of place in a national park. Despite its large size, big pads and wide lanes eliminate crowding at a resort developed by a Marine Corps veteran of the Korean War. From miniature golf and a swimming pool, to a hair salon/day spa and the Semper Fi Bar & Grill, there's lots to do on the property. Twin Fountains also offers a few services rarely seen at campgrounds, like dog grooming, an RV wash, and limousine shuttle service to nearby sights like the National Cowboy & Western Heritage Museum.

Wildflowers bloom at the foot of the Wichita Mountains.

ROMAN NOSE STATE PARK

🏚 11, 🚐/⛺ 12 full hookup, 31 partial hookup, ⛺ 36

3236 State Highway 8A, Watonga, OK 73772

Open: Year-round ▪ Rates: RV/tent full hookup from $29, RV/tent partial hookup $25, tent only from $18, cabins from $105 ▪ Amenities: Restaurant, camp store, gift shop, dump station, showers, picnic tables, fire rings, grills, playground, swimming pool, miniature golf, sports courts, boat ramp, bait shop; bike, boat, horse, and fishing gear rental ▪ ADA sites: Yes

It seems an odd name for a geological landmark on the woodlands of central Oklahoma. It lauds the legacy of Henry Roman Nose, a Cheyenne-Arapaho chief who lived in the park area until his death in 1917. One of Oklahoma's first state parks, it offers both wilderness adventure via hiking, biking, and horseback trails and modern amenities like a swimming pool, an 18-hole golf course with pro shop, and an eye-catching midcentury-style lodge with a restaurant and hotel rooms. The park's twin lakes invite swimming, fishing, and paddle sports. Seven campgrounds are scattered along the main park road, while the cabins cluster farther west near the Three Springs area. The park's interpretive program includes a talk on local history and Chief Roman Nose.

BOBCAT CREEK RV PARK

🚐 30 full hookup

2005 Northeast Highway 66, Sayre, OK 73662

Open: Year-round ▪ Rate: $35 ▪ Amenities: Camp store with gas pumps, laundry, ice, propane, tornado shelter, playground, horseshoes, internet, mail service, picnic tables ▪ ADA sites: Call ahead

A chance encounter with a bobcat on the grounds sparked the owners of this tidy little RV park to rename it after the North American feline. You probably won't be lucky enough to spot a bobcat yourself because they're such elusive little cats, but there are many other ways to keep busy around the campground, like picnicking on grassy areas beneath the shade trees, sharing stories around the nightly communal campfire, or cooling your feet in the creek. Situated on Historic Route 66, Bobcat is convenient for those just passing through or anyone spending a few days discovering the eclectic attractions of western Oklahoma like the National Route 66 Museum and Washita Battlefield National Historic Site.

DORIS CAMPGROUND

23 partial hookup, 47 no hookup, 20

State Highway 49, Wichita Mountains National Wildlife Refuge, OK 73552

Open: Year-round ■ Rates: RV/tent partial hookup from $22, RV/tent no hookup $14, tent only $12 ■ Amenities: Dump station, showers, picnic tables, fire rings, grills, fishing ■ ADA sites: Partial

Wichita Mountains National Wildlife Refuge, one of the best all-around reserves managed by the U.S. Fish & Wildlife Service, is also home to an awesome campground. Located in the heart of the park near Quanah Parker Lake and the refuge visitors center, Doris offers a mix of power-only and dry pads as well as tent-only sites. Three short

trails take hikers along the lakeshore. But the real action lies in the red-rock highlands just west of the campground—in particular, the Dog Run Hollow Trail System and the rugged boulder-hopping route across the Charon's Garden Wilderness Area.

The park's other big allure is animals: feral longhorn cattle, cute little prairie dogs, and lots of bison. Transported from the Bronx Zoo to the Wichita Mountains in 1907 as part of an effort to save the American bison from extinction, the original herd of 15 bison has ballooned to more than 600 animals. Campers should venture into the old riverside resort town of Medicine Park (founded in 1908) to browse its many restaurants, bars, and Western-style shops.

BUCKHORN CAMPGROUND

42 partial hookup, 92 no hookup

Buckhorn Road, Chickasaw National Recreation Area, OK 73086

Open: Year-round ■ Rates: RV/tent partial hookup $22, no hookup $15 ■ Amenities: Dump station, showers, picnic tables, fire rings, grills, potable water, amphitheater, boat ramp, fishing pier ■ ADA sites: Yes

Overlooking the Lake of the Arbuckles, Buckhorn is far and away the largest of six campgrounds at Chickasaw National Recreation Area in south-central Oklahoma. With a mix of power/water and primitive sites, Buckhorn welcomes RV, car, bike, and even hike-in campers. Arranged around four loops, a number of campsites are directly on the water, which makes them mighty convenient for swimming, fishing, or paddle sports. The Rock Creek Multi-Use Trail for hiking and biking meanders through the woods to the Platt Historic District, bison pasture, and Chickasaw Nation Visitor Center. Historical footnote: The park was founded in the early 20th century as Platt National Park before it was combined with Arbuckle Recreation Area and renamed for the Chickasaw people in 1976.

LAKE MURRAY FLOATING CABINS

21

3323 Lodge Road, Ardmore, OK 73401

Open: Year-round ■ Rates: From $150 per night (two-night minimum stay) ■ Amenities: Kitchens, towels and bedding, heating and air-conditioning, cable TV and DVD player, propane grill, boat moorings ■ ADA sites: No

Oklahoma's largest state park is the venue for a giant V-shaped reservoir and an armada of aquatic cabins offering instant access to boating,

An ebony jewelwing damselfly finds a perch at Roman Nose State Park.

Camp in the hilly woodlands of the San Bois Mountains at Robbers Cave State Park, a favorite of hikers and cave explorers.

fishing, or swimming on Lake Murray. The floating abodes range from tiny Loaded Pods that can sleep two adults and two children to a massive Atrium Lodge where as many as 18 people can spend the night. All units are fully furnished with kitchens and private bathrooms; towels and bedding are provided. Boats are easily docked along the wooden decks that support each cabin, which also feature outdoor areas with barbecue grills and seating. Nearby Lake Murray Resort offers waterfront dining at Foggy Bottom Kitchen, as well as boat and floaty rental, miniature golf, and scenic lake cruises.

REBEL HILL GUEST RANCH

🏠 7

420175 East 1930 Road, Antlers, OK 74523

Open: Year-round ▪ Rates: From $120 ▪ Amenities: Kitchens and cooking utensils, private bathrooms with tubs or showers, towels and bedding, picnic tables, barbecues, fire rings, firewood, cable TV, swimming pool ▪ ADA sites: Call ahead

This working horse ranch in southeast Oklahoma has transformed half a dozen of its vintage structures into guest accommodations scattered across 500 acres (202 ha) of farmland and forest on the western edge of the Ouachita Mountains. The lodging ranges from the Bunkhouse, where the ranch cowpokes used to bed down, and a converted red barn, the Pavilion, to the three-bedroom Farmhouse that served as the family home for four generations of Rebel Hill's owners

and the secluded Cajun-style Hideout located on a small island reached by wooden footbridges. And oddly enough, there's also a vintage railroad passenger car with Victorian-era furnishings. It almost goes without saying that horse riding is the main activity. But the ranch also offers lake paddling and fishing, a swimming pool, and a barnyard full of farm animals.

BEAVERS BEND LOG CABINS

🏠 14

576 Split Shot Circle, Broken Bow, OK 74728

Open: Year-round ▪ Rates: From $195 ▪ Amenities: Kitchen, private bathrooms, laundry, fireplaces, firewood, fire pit, barbecue, towels

Take a canoe ride from the floating cabins on Lake Murray, a one-of-a-kind stay for water enthusiasts and anglers.

and bedding, satellite or cable TV, internet • ADA sites: Call ahead

Belying Oklahoma's reputation as a purely horizontal state, there's quite a bit of elevation out east—a rugged Ouachita range that tumbles across the border from Arkansas. Various parks and vacation resorts flank the region's Mountain Fork River, including this gathering of stylish log cabins near Broken Bow. Set in thick forest around a cluster of small lakes, the cabins vary greatly in size and architectural style. Some are made from stone rather than logs, but all of them feature king or queen beds, full kitchens, outdoor grills and indoor fireplaces, and hot tubs. Roads and trails across the heavily wooded property provide plenty of scope for hiking and biking, while fishing and boating are possible on the main lake. Just up the road is Beavers Bend State Park and its excellent Forest Heritage Center, with 14 dioramas depicting the Oklahoma Ouachita region's long and colorful history.

ROBBERS CAVE STATE PARK

🏚 26, 🚐/🛖 114, 🛖 73, 🏛 2
State Highway 2, Wilburton, OK 74578
Open: Year-round • Rates: RV/tent full hookup from $29, RV/tent partial hookup from $24, tent only $16, yurts from $88, cabins from $88 • Amenities: Dump station, camp store, gift shop, showers, picnic tables, grills, fire rings, swimming pool, playgrounds, disc golf, boat ramps; boat, bike, and horse rental • ADA sites: Yes

Jesse James and Belle Starr are among the legendary outlaws who

took refuge amid the park's sandstone cliffs. More than 140 years after the notorious James-Younger Gang was eradicated, those imposing palisades are still the main attraction. Challenging routes like Belle Starr Crack and Squeeze Chimney make this prime rock-climbing country. Overnight options range from full-hookup RV pads and primitive backcountry camping to cabins, yurts, and an equestrian campground spread across more than a dozen separate sites inside the park. In addition to climbing, Robbers Cave offers hiking, biking, and equestrian trails; a dedicated ATV off-road area; water sports on three lakes; and a nature center with interpretive programs. The park celebrates the advent of autumn color with its Fall Festival featuring food stalls, live music, carnival rides, and a classic car show.

RIVERSIDE RESORT

🏚 10, 🚐/🛖 6 full hookup,
🛖 12 no hookup
5116 State Highway 10, Tahlequah, OK 74464
Open: May to September • Rates: Cabins $95, RV $40, tents from $20 • Amenities: Kitchenettes, private bathrooms, air conditioning, picnic tables, grills, fire rings, showers, potable water, boat rental, swimming beach, sports courts • ADA sites: Call ahead

The sinuous Illinois River is the focus of this campground and float trip outfitter tucked up in the Ozark foothills of northeast Oklahoma. Those running the river during the day in rafts or kayaks can overnight at the Riverside base camp in RV or tent campsites or cabins equipped with private bathrooms, kitchenettes, and air-conditioning. Most cabins also boast their own docks. Out on the river, the company outfits overnight river camping trips with a shuttle service to fetch you at journey's end. Flowing through the Cherokee Nation, the upper stretch of the Illinois is an official Oklahoma Scenic River and a key location in the popular children's book *Where the Red Fern Grows*. ■

SOMETHING SPECIAL

Lake Murray State Park

Oklahoma's first and largest state park, Lake Murray State Park in southern Oklahoma, spans 12,496 acres (5,057 ha) over two counties. The park is a year-round visual feast of splendid colors—from the blended grays and browns of the limestone walls that line the roadways to the greens of native grasses and tan sand beds on the edge of the lake shoreline that disappear into the pristine aqua waters.

A rock-and-earth-walled dam holds in the clear waters of the

5,876-acre (2,377.9 ha) spring-fed lake with 95 miles (152.9 km) of shoreline. Built under the premise of the New Deal program in the 1930s that focused on revitalization and reforestation of lands, recreation was an important ingredient in this mix, and this remains true today. More than 100 structures built by the Civilian Conservation Corps (CCC) remain standing at Lake Murray; however, the most recognized building is Tucker Tower, refurbished and revitalized as a history center that houses displays dedicated to the CCC.

Oregon

Whether you're following the footsteps of Lewis and Clark or seeking refuge in Oregon's lakes and forests, there's a campground that fits your needs.

FORT STEVENS STATE PARK

🏠 11, 🚐/🏕 174 full hookup, 302 partial hookup, 🏕 6, ⛺ 15
1675 Peter Iredale Road, Hammond, OR 97121

Open: Year-round ▪ Rates: RV/tent full hookup from $34, partial hookup from $32, tent only from $22, yurts from $54, cabins from $98 ▪ Amenities: Dump station, showers, picnic tables, fire pits with grills, firewood, beach, boat ramp, playground, disc golf, bike rental, amphitheater ▪ ADA sites: Yes

Create your own encampment near the place where Lewis and Clark spent the winter of 1805-06 at the mouth of the Columbia River in northwest Oregon. Fort Stevens provides nearly 500 campsites, plus comfy yurts and cabins. The state park takes its name from a military base originally constructed during the Civil War. Part of the 19th-century earthworks has been reconstructed, and guided tours are available of a World War II gun battery and underground command center. The campground lies about a 20-minute walk from the nearest beach and the photogenic wreck of the *Peter Iredale*, a British sailing ship that ran aground in 1906. Campers can also swim in the park's freshwater lakes, watch wildlife around the

Ever dream of tiny house living? Try it out for a weekend at Caravan: The Tiny House Hotel.

edge of Swash Lake marsh, or join a guided paddle around Trestle Bay with Kayak Tillamook.

SUTTON CAMPGROUND

🚐/🏕 22 partial hookup, 58 no hookup
4840 Vista Road, Florence, OR 97439

Open: Year-round ▪ Rates: RV/tent partial hookup $29, RV/tent no hookup $24 ▪ Amenities: Restrooms, picnic tables, fire rings with grills, potable water, firewood ▪ ADA sites: Partial

Although it's close to the Oregon Dunes and all of those crazy quad bikes, Sutton reflects the quiet side of the Oregon coast. This laid-back campground in Siuslaw National Forest offers mostly dry camping on sites arrayed beneath a canopy of towering spruce, pines, and Douglas fir trees. It lies about midway between Sutton Lake, with its freshwater fishing and swimming, and wild Sutton Beach, with its pristine dunes and slow-flowing creek. From the campground, a network of hiking trails fans out through this unique coastal portion of the national forest. Dramatic Heceta Head Lighthouse and the Sea Lion Caves are just a 15-minute drive to the north of Sutton along the Oregon Coast Highway (U.S. 101). Florence and its historic waterfront are about the same distance to the south.

HONEY BEAR BY THE SEA RV RESORT & CAMPGROUND

🚐/🏕 64 full hookup, 26 partial hookup, 🏕 20
34161 Ophir Road, Gold Beach, OR 97444

Open: Year-round ▪ Rates: RV/tent full hookup from $55, partial hookup from $45, tent only $32 ▪ Amenities: Camp store, dump station, showers, laundry, picnic tables, fire rings, playground, game room, firewood, ice, library, cable TV, internet ▪ ADA sites: Partial

What's there not to like about a place called Honey Bear? It's right across the road from Ophir Beach and an uninterrupted stretch of sand that runs more than 6 miles (9.6 km) between Nesika and the Devil's Backbone rock formation. There's a meadow out back where campers can see elk grazing, especially in the early morning mist. The camp store stocks ice-cold beer, Oregon wines, ice cream, and the three items you need to make perfect s'mores. And Honey Bear has a wide range of overnight choices from full-hookup RV pads to lawn areas where you can pitch a tent.

CAVE CREEK CAMPGROUND

🚐/🏕 17 no hookup
15500 Caves Highway (State Route 46), Cave Junction, OR 97523
Open: May to September ▪ Rate: $10 ▪ Amenities: Restrooms, picnic tables, fire pits with grills, potable water ▪ ADA sites: No

The only overnight spot inside Oregon Caves National Monument & Preserve other than the historic Chateau Lodge, Cave Creek burrows deep inside an old-growth forest about 4 miles (6.4 km) from the show cave entrance. Limited space between the trees means this campground is only for tents, camper vans, and smaller RVs. It's all dry camping with few amenities other than the thrill that comes with sleeping beneath Douglas firs that were saplings several hundred years before Columbus. Campers can join guided jaunts of the marble caverns, including a historical candlelight tour, another for families with children, and a third that goes off-trail through narrow underground passages into the dark heart of Oregon Caves. The park also boasts six hiking trails including an 8-mile (12.8 km) loop to the summit of Mount Elijah and a 1.8-mile (2.9 km) route that links the campground with the Chateau and cave entrance.

MAZAMA CAMPGROUNDS & CABINS

🏚40, 🚐/🏕 93, 🏕 121
569 Mazama Village Drive, Crater Lake National Park, OR 97604
Open: June to September ▪ Rates: RV/tent full hookup from $42, partial hookup from $36, no hookup from $31, tent only $21, cabins $165 ▪ Amenities: Camp store, restaurant, gift shop, gas station, dump station, gas station, showers, laundry, picnic tables, fire rings with grills, food storage containers, potable water, firewood, ice, amphitheater, Tesla charger, internet ▪ ADA sites: Yes

Hovering at around 6,000 feet (1,829 m) above sea level, Mazama is one of two campgrounds inside Crater Lake National Park and the only one set up for RVs. Named for the ancient volcano that erupted and collapsed between 6,000 and 8,000 years ago to create the iconic lake, the campground offers a handful of electric sites, modern cabin accommodation, and several tent-only spaces, including a dedicated area for Pacific Crest Trail hikers. A location in Mazama Village means that campers can amble over to Annie Creek Restaurant, as well as a gift shop, grocery store, and gas pumps. From the campground, it's a 7-mile (11.2 km) drive or 8.3-mile (13.3 km) hike to the crater rim.

ELK LAKE RESORT & MARINA CAMPGROUND

🏚13 (3 camping cabins), 🚐 3 no hookup, 🏕 3, 🏕 6
60000 Southwest Century Drive, Bend, OR 97701
Open: Campground/glamping tents May to October; cabins/camping cabins year-round ▪ Rates: Cabins from $239, camping cabins $70, glamping tents $99, RV no hookup $35, tent only $25 ▪ Amenities: Restaurant, bar, showers, picnic tables, fire pits, potable water, bike rental, boat rental, boat ramp, wedding chapel, snowmobile and snowshoe rentals ▪ ADA sites: No

It's just 45 minutes from Bend, but Elk Lake seems light years from anything urban. Located in the heart of the Cascades range near Mount Bachelor and the Sisters Peaks, the resort blends hiking along the Pacific Crest Trail in Deschutes National Forest and diving into various lake pursuits from stand-up paddleboard (SUP) fitness classes to scenic cruises and floating day dock rental. The overnight digs are just as varied, with RV and tent sites, glamping tents,

Take a step back in time camping in one of 35 fully restored trailers at the Vintages.

Steps away from Gold Beach, Honey Bear by the Sea RV offers a family-friendly resort to enjoy Oregon's coast.

and vintage 1940s log cabins among the options. The resort bar offers tasty Oregon wines and craft brews, while raspberry chipotle smoked ribs, elk burgers, and beer-marinated bratwurst are among the restaurant specialties.

LOST LAKE RESORT & CAMPGROUND
🏚 9, 🚐 / 🏕 148 no hookup, 🛖 20

9000 Lost Lake Road, Hood River, OR 97031

Open: May to October ▪ Rates: RV/tent no hookup from $30, cabins from $107, yurts from $96 ▪ Amenities: Restaurant, camp store, showers, picnic tables, fire rings, firewood, ice, boat ramp, fishing dock, boat rental, fishing licenses ▪ ADA sites: Partial

One of Oregon's favorite photo spots, Lost Lake reflects perpetually snow-covered Mount Hood, a massive stratovolcano and the state's highest summit. But the lake is more than just a pretty reflection. It's also a chance to overnight at campsites, cabins, and yurts scattered inside a lush cedar and fir tree forest along the lake's north shore. You can drive right up to cabins equipped with a cooking area, wood-burning stove, bedding, and electrical outlets. The yurts are far more basic and require a walk of 100 to 300 yards (90 to 275 m) from the parking area. Lost Lake Grille specializes in old-fashioned diner fare and gourmet coffees. Food, beverages, camping items, and fishing gear are available at the Lost Lake General Store, while the boat shack rents nonmotorized watercraft. (Lost Lake is a quiet zone.)

THE VINTAGES TRAILER RESORT
🚐 35

16205 Southeast Kreder Road, Dayton, OR 97114

Take a nature retreat—and a ride through the woods of Crater Lake National Park—at the Mazama Campgrounds.

Open: Year-round ▪ Rates: From $75 ▪ Amenities: Camp store, bathhouse, laundry, swimming pool, clubhouse, heating, air-conditioning, barbecue grills, fire pits, cruiser bikes, flat-screen TVs, internet ▪ ADA sites: No

The name is a double entendre, referring to both the antique travel trailers that provide the digs at this hip resort and the fact that it's set amid the Willamette Valley wine country. Pinot Noir is the favorite libation among the area's 300 winemakers, with Stoller Family Estate, Winter's Hill, and Sokol Blosser just up the road. The resort makes it easy with a complimentary Tasting Passport for every guest (over 21). Some of the resort's restored trailers are rarities, like the 1949 Kit Chateau, the 1958 Ideal, and the 1963 Silverstreak Duchess. All of them are nicely spaced in a parklike setting of trees and lawns, each with an outside patio area with seating and cruiser bikes; some even come with a bathtub big enough for two. The Vintages also boasts two brand new Neutron trailers designed and built by Oregon's own Justin and Anna Scribner, who have hosted two Travel Channel shows about restoring travel trailers.

CARAVAN: THE TINY HOUSE HOTEL
🏠 5

5009 Northeast 11th Avenue. Portland, OR, 97211

Open: Year-round ▪ Rates: From $145 ▪ Amenities: Kitchenettes, private bathrooms, room service, bedding and towels, air-conditioning and heating, sound machine, internet ▪ ADA sites: Yes

Who says you can't glamp in the city? Caravan's cute little trailer/cabins inhabit Portland's funky Alberta neighborhood near a lively stretch of Alberta Street with abundant restaurants, bars, one-off shops, and entertainment via the restored Alberta Rose Theatre and Curious Comedy club. Fashioned from wooden shingles or clapboard, all of them look straight out of a fairy tale, with the bright-red Caboose and the teal-colored Amazing Mysterium among the favorites. Kitchens and bathrooms are standard in every cabin, and one is outfitted for ADA access.

WALLOWA ALPINE HUTS
 5

500 North River Street, Enterprise, OR 97828

Open: January to April (depending on the snow) ▪ Rates: From $1,000 per person all-inclusive or $250 per person otherwise (four days/three nights) ▪ Amenities: Propane stoves and cooking equipment, outside bathrooms, sleeping pads, woodstoves, firewood, flashlights and lanterns, wash basins and soap, axes, snow shovels, beer keg service ▪ ADA sites: No

With as much as 30 feet (9.1 m) of snow, the Wallowa Mountains of eastern Oregon have some of the nation's best backcountry skiing and snowboarding. Each winter, Wallowa Alpine Huts sets up three remote base camps—with accommodation for visitors set up in yurts or tents—in the Eagle Cap Wilderness Area. The "huts" aren't for those looking for a glamping or luxurious experience. But they will get the job done, as each are outfitted with cots, sleeping pads, and everything you need to make meals. Making it to Wallowa's huts is not for the faint of heart, or inexperienced skier. The only way to reach the camps is skiing in or being towed behind a snowmobile for at least part of the way. Campers need to bring their own sleeping bags, clothing, and sports equipment, and food if they're not going all-inclusive (food portage is available for an extra cost). The company can also supply a keg of beer. ▪

SOMETHING SPECIAL

Fort Stevens State Park

Since the early years of the republic, the nation's military has been prepared for attacks from foreign adversaries. From the Civil War until shortly after World War II, Fort Stevens helped defend our borders; along with Forts Canby and Columbia in Washington State, the artillery of Fort Stevens guarded the mouth of the Columbia River.

And it was right here at Fort Stevens that the continental United States came under fire during World War II. In 1942, a Japanese submarine shelled the fort, making it the only military installation in the lower 48 states to be fired on by a foreign power since the War of 1812.

Though the big guns are gone, the massive concrete bunkers remain atop the bluffs. Logically enough, the emplacements command a sweeping view of Columbia's mouth, which visitors today can enjoy without the added burden of scanning for enemy warships. The park also includes natural areas, such as a long beach that extends to the extreme northwestern tip of Oregon.

Pennsylvania

From the Laurel Highlands to Pennsylvania Dutch country, you'll find a wide variety of campsites to pitch your tent, park your RV, or nestle into nature.

KENTUCK CAMPGROUND

🏠 6, 🚐/🏕 55 partial hookup, 124 no hookup, 🏕 30, 🏘 4
400 Kentuck Road, Dunbar, PA 15431
Open: April to December ▪ Rates: RV/tent partial hookup from $26.25, RV/tent no hookup/tent only from $19.25, cabins from $41.60, yurts from $38.60 ▪ Amenities: Dump station, showers, picnic tables, fire rings with grills, firewood, ice, potable water, playgrounds, amphitheater ▪ ADA sites: Yes

The Laurel Highlands are home to Ohiopyle State Park, renowned for its waterfalls and natural waterslides that expedite a quick cool-off for campers during the region's hot, muggy summers. Down in the gorge, the rapid-laden Youghiogheny River churns up plenty of white water for rafters and paddlers. Kentuck Campground sits high above the river's west bank, close to trails that convert from hiking and biking to cross-country skiing come winter.

SARA'S CAMPGROUND ON THE BEACH

🚐/🏕 44 full hookup, 25 no hookup, 🏕 varies
50 Peninsula Drive, Erie, PA 16505
Open: April to October ▪ Rates: RVs $35-$40, tents $30-$35, bike campers $15 per person ▪ Amenities: Restaurants, camp store, gift shop, showers, laundry, picnic tables, fire rings, firewood, ice, playgrounds, basketball court, game room, beach, cable TV, internet ▪ ADA sites: No

It's the Great Lakes rather than an Atlantic shore. But with its own sandy strand, lakeside picnic tables, and old-time waterfront amusement park nearby, Sara's feels like an oceanfront resort. Campers have a choice of RV camping in the woods or pitching their tent directly on the beach. The campground also harbors a pizza parlor, a classic American diner, and a shop that hawks beachwear, boogie boards, floaties, and other aquatic accessories. Sara's sits beside the entrance to Presque Isle State Park with its lakeside hiking and biking trails, and Waldameer Park and Water World, which debuted in 1896.

COOK FOREST STATE PARK

🏠 20, 🚐/🏕 22 full hookup, 69 partial hookup, 116 no hookup, 3 sites canoe/kayak camping
State Highway 36, Cooksburg, PA 16217
Open: Campground April to October, cabins April to December ▪ Rates: RV/tent full hookup from $39.25, partial hookup from $26.25, no hookup from $19.25, cabins from $35.36, canoe/kayak camping from $4 ▪ Amenities: Dump station, showers, picnic tables, fire rings with grills, potable water, ball field, playground, amphitheater, dog run ▪ ADA sites: Yes

Located on the edge of the Pennsylvania Wilds, Cook Forest State Park preserves one of the largest groves of unlogged, old-growth hardwoods in the Northeast. Camping is available at two places inside the park. Ridge Campground offers a variety of sites near the Forest Cathedral area, where most of the oldest, biggest trees are, including a stand of 350-year-old hemlocks dubbed "The Ancients." Paddlers can overnight at three tent-only primitive campsites along the 13 miles (21 km) of the wild and scenic Clarion River that meanders through the park. Cook Forest also offers cabins at two spots above the river.

In addition to river trips, campers can hike, bike, horseback ride, cross-country ski, or snowmobile more than 40 miles (64 km) of trails. If you're visiting in winter, be sure to pack your skates; a frozen-over pond is converted into a lighted, outdoor

Cherry Springs State Park gives new meaning to sleeping beneath the stars.

ice rink. Local artisans create, display, and sell their wares at the park's Sawmill Center for the Arts, which also offers workshops in skills like wood-carving, quilting, and landscape painting. During the warmer months, the center stages musicals, comedies, and murder mysteries at Verna Leith Sawmill Theater.

CHERRY SPRINGS STATE PARK

🚐/⛰ 16 no hookup, ⛰ 14
4639 Cherry Springs Road, Coudersport, PA 16915
Open: April to October ▪ Rates: From $15.25 ▪ Amenities: Dump station, restrooms, picnic tables, fire rings with grills, lantern hangers, potable water, amphitheater ▪ ADA sites: Partial

As many as 10,000 heavenly bodies can be seen on any given cloudless night at the world's second oldest International Dark Sky Park, tucked amid the rugged hills and regenerated forest of the Pennsylvania Wilds region. Much of the park is a "light-free zone" that allows only flashlights with red filters after dark. Campsites are arrayed across a grassy area beside the Night Sky Public Viewing Area with its information kiosks and a back-lit electronic sky map of the planets and constellations. Across the road is the Overnight Astronomy Observation Field on the site of the old Cherry Springs Airport, which features concrete telescope pads and the park's only Wi-Fi.

Each summer, rangers and guest speakers present astronomy talks at the amphitheater. The park hosts overnight "star parties" several times every year. Cherry Spring's other claim to fame is the annual Woodsmen Show in August, a three-day extravaganza of logrolling, wood-chopping, and chain-saw competitions complemented by live music, craft vendors, and food stalls. Closer to the ground, the Cherry Springs Working Forest Interpretive Trail honors the region's legendary lumbermen and timber industry.

PINE CRADLE LAKE FAMILY CAMPGROUND

🏠16, 🚐/⛰ 74 full hookup, 4 no hookup
220 Shoemaker Road, Rome Township, PA 18850
Open: April to December ▪ Rates: RV/tent full hookup from $55, partial hookup $47, cabins from $90 ▪ Amenities: Camp store, snack bar, dump station, showers, laundry, picnic tables, fire rings with grills, propane, swimming pool, splash pad, boat rental, playgrounds, sports field, game room, dog run, golf cart rental, internet ▪ ADA sites: No

Pine Cradle in the Endless Mountains offers many ways you and the kids can while away a day without leaving the property. There's the lake, of course, well stocked for fishing and smooth as glass for paddling or pedal boats, and a big pool and splash pad beside a snack bar that specializes in hand-dipped, chocolate-covered ice cream cones. Many of the campsites and cabins are right on the lake, others tucked into the woods behind. From Muffins for Moms in the spring to Pumpkin Palooza in the autumn, Pine Cradle presents special weekend themes.

KEEN LAKE CAMPING & COTTAGE RESORT

🏠11, 🚐2 rentals, 🚐/⛰ 83 full hookup, 38 partial hookup, ⛰ 17, ⛺ 10
155 Keen Lake Road, Waymart, PA 18472
Open: April to October ▪ Rates: RV/tent full hookup from $69, partial hookup/no hookup from $54, tent only from $44, cabins from $214, glamping tents from $129, RV rentals from $189 ▪ Amenities: Camp store, snack bar, showers, laundry, picnic tables, fire rings with grills,

Chocolate-laden s'mores by the campfire are a must at the Hersheypark Camping Resort.

For more than 65 years, Keen Lake has offered tent and RV sites, as well as cottages, along the family-owned lake.

swimming pool, playgrounds, sports courts, playing fields, outdoor movie theater, game room, boat rental, boat ramp, fishing gear and bait, pet beach, ATM, cable TV, internet ▪ ADA sites: Yes

Owned and operated by the Keen family since it opened in 1954, this lakeside retreat does double duty as an old-fashioned Poconos summer camp and a newfangled glamping resort for couples and families. Vacationers can hook up a mobile home, pitch a tent, or overnight in an eclectic selection of cabins that includes the Pre–Civil War Barn and cottage on Hermit Island reached by rowboat. Located about 30 minutes from Scranton in the northern Poconos, Keen Lake lies close to the Upper Delaware Scenic and Recreational River and historic Honesdale, where America's first-ever train rumbled down tracks in 1829.

PICKEREL POINT CAMPGROUND

🏠 3, 🚐 / 🏕 12 full hookup, 25 partial hookup, 🏕 38
Pickerel Point Road, Greene Township, PA 18426
Open: Year-round ▪ Rates: RV/tent full hookup $41.25, partial hookup $28.25, tent only from $19.25, cabins from $38.60 ▪ Amenities: Dump station, showers, laundry, picnic tables, fire rings with grills, potable water, swimming beach, boat rental, boat ramps, fishing pier, amphitheater ▪ ADA sites: Yes

The only year-round campground at Promised Land State Park in the Poconos, Pickerel is situated on a finger-like peninsula surrounded by the park's namesake lake. That means it has more waterfront sites than any other campground in the park, plus a swimming beach, shoreline mooring, and a nearby boat ramp and fishing pier. Pickerel's small number of camping cottages are equipped with bunk beds, picnic tables, indoor heating, and outdoor cooking grill. The campground also hosts the Masker Museum and its exhibits on the Civilian Conservation Corps, which built many of the park facilities during the Great Depression. Between the state park and encircling state forest, campers have more than 50 miles (80 km) of trails to explore. Tiny Promised Land village offers a single restaurant, convenience store, and gift shop. The campground is about a two-hour drive from Philadelphia and New York City and around 30 minutes from Delaware Water Gap National Recreation Area.

LAKE IN WOOD CAMPGROUND & CABINS

🏠 25, 🚐 / 🏕 83 full hookup, 🏕 24, 🏚 1, 1 tipi, 1 covered wagon

Find swimming, sunbathing, tubing, and camping at Sara's Campground at the entrance to Presque Isle.

576 Yellow Hill Road, Narvon, PA 17555

Open: April to October ▪ Rates: RV full hookup from $62, tent only $50, cabins from $179, yurt $239, tipi $176, covered wagon $156 ▪ Amenities: Restaurant, camp store, dump stations, showers, laundry, picnic tables, fire rings, potable water, swimming pools, playground, basketball court, miniature golf, game room, bike/boat/golf cart rental, dog run, ATM, cable TV, internet ▪ ADA sites: Partial

Set in the Pennsylvania Dutch Country, Lake in Wood offers an array of overnight options, but it's the delightfully decorated cabins that really stand out. Its front end shaped like an old sailing craft, Pirate Inn boasts model ships and a suit of armor. Gnome Home provides shelter for garden gnomes large and small, both indoors and out. Frontier Log Cabin is adorned with horse tack and pioneer-style wooden bunks. Noah's Ark is inhabited by a wooden lion, chimp, and giraffe—but, ironically, doesn't allow pets. However, pups are welcome at Dog House and Woof Woof Hideway.

HERSHEYPARK CAMPING RESORT

🏠 43, 🚐/🏕 99 full hookup, 106 partial hookup, 42 no hookup
1200 Sweet Street, Hummelstown, PA 17036

Open: Year-round ▪ Rates: RV/tent full hookup from $59, partial hookup from $39, no hookup from $29, cabins from $59 ▪ Amenities: Camp store, snack bar, dump station, showers, picnic tables, fire rings with grills, firewood, ice, potable water, propane, swimming pools, playgrounds, movie theater, game room,

sports courts, pet kennel, ATM, cable TV, internet ▪ ADA sites: Yes

From roller coasters and wildlife habitats to gourmet tastings and a historic basketball arena, the Hershey universe seems to have just about everything under the sun. So why not a campground too? And like everything else at Hershey, it's a big one: around 300 spaces, from full hookups and tent-only campsites to both modern and rustic cabins. Among the many family-oriented activities are movie nights, puppet shows, live music, craft workshops, and three swimming pools. The only drawback is it's not within walking distance of the theme parks and chocolate attractions. However, campers can hop a shuttle to the "Sweetest Place on Earth."

ARTILLERY RIDGE CAMPGROUND & HORSE PARK

🏠 16, 🚐/🏕 111 full hookup, 20 partial hookup, 36 no hookup, 🏕 14
610 Taneytown Road, Gettysburg, PA 17325

Open: Year-round ▪ Rates: RV/tent full hookup from $79, partial hookup

$69, tent only $65, cabins from $109 ▪ Amenities: Camp, dump station, showers, laundry, picnic tables, fire rings, firewood, potable water, swimming pool, game room, playgrounds, lawn games, miniature golf, sports courts, dog run, fishpond, riding arena, internet ▪ ADA sites: Partial

Located along the eastern flank of Cemetery Ridge, this full-service camping resort is nearly enveloped by Gettysburg National Military Park. During the 1863 battle, the Union Army gathered its reserve cannons and ammunition trains at Artillery Ridge and used Taneytown Road to march reinforcements to the front. From full hookup pads and tent-only sites to cabins, the campground offers a variety of accommodation, plus an 80-stall horse camp for those who bring their steeds to ride on the battlefield equestrian trails. The battlefield visitors center and museum are a half-mile (0.8 km) up the Taneytown Road, where Lincoln delivered the Gettysburg Address. Little Roundtop, Big Roundtop, Devil's Den, and other places that saw fierce fighting are about a five-minute drive to the south. ▪

SOMETHING SPECIAL

Cook Forest State Park

Picture 200-foot-tall (61 m) stands of virgin timber on gentle slopes, and you will grasp the lure of Cook Forest and how it came to be nicknamed the "Black Forest of Pennsylvania." The first Pennsylvania state park acquired to preserve a natural landmark, Cook Forest lies south of the Allegheny National Forest, where an upheaval of Earth's crust created open valleys and rounded hills reaching 1,600 feet (487.7 m). Once a primary means of

shipping rafts of timber south to Pittsburgh, the shallow Clarion River has carved the valley that bounds the park to the east.

Follow the Longfellow Trail from the Learning Center to traverse the forest floor of pine needles. Giant hemlocks and white pines loom above the gently sloping trail until you arrive at a glade known as Forest Cathedral. A canopy of eastern hemlock and white pine more than 300 years old, here you will hear nothing but the songs of wind and bird.

Rhode Island

The smallest state in the United States has a robust number of camping options, including beachside docking spots, pine forest tent sites, and an RV park near posh Newport.

EAST BEACH

🚐 20 no hookup

East Beach Road, Charlestown, RI 02813
Open: May to September ▪ Rates: $28/$55 (state resident/nonresident) ▪ Amenities: Changing rooms, showers, beach ▪ ADA sites: No

Three miles (4.8 km) of pristine coast is the lure of this state-run campground near Quonochontaug village. RV dry camping amid the dunes is allowed at two spots along the shore. All units must be completely self-contained with a bathroom and have four-wheel drive for driving on the sand. Towed trailers and fifth wheels are prohibited. Campers are also required to obtain a beach vehicle permit. While swimming, surfing, and shore fishing are the main activities, East Beach is adjacent to a large wetlands area protected within the confines of state and federal conservation areas. Ninigret National Wildlife Area affords opportunities for paddling, wildlife viewing, and interpretive programs. Groceries, take-out food, and bait and tackle are available around 2 to 3 miles (3.2-4.8 km) from the campgrounds at outlets along the old Post Road (U.S. Highway 1).

The Point Judith Lighthouse stands tall near Narragansett.

BURLINGAME STATE CAMPGROUND

🏚 20, 🚐/🏕 692 no hookup, 🏕 1

75 Burlingame State Park Road, Charlestown, RI 02813
Open: April to October ▪ Rates: RV/tent no hookup from $18/$36 (state resident/nonresident), cabins $50/$75, camping shelters $18/$36 ▪ Amenities: Camp store, dump stations, showers, picnic tables, fire pits, potable water, boat ramp, playground, beaches, sports courts, athletic field, arcade, boat rental, firewood, ice ▪ ADA sites: Partial

One of Rhode Island's oldest state parks (founded in 1930) also boasts its single largest campground—more than 700 overnight sites scattered through the woods near Watchaug Pond. The park's rustic cabins are right on the water, while the RV/tent sites are scattered through dense woods behind the shore. All told, Burlingame offers 3,100 acres (1,254 ha) of wilderness home to a wide variety of flora and fauna, including deer, otters, muskrats, salamanders, and water snakes. The campground is convenient for hopping onto several hiking routes including the 8-mile (12.8 km) Vin Gormley Loop Trail around the entire pond and the 77-mile (124 km) North South Trail that stretches all the way across Rhode Island.

HIGHLIGHTS

Capital: Providence

Total National Parks: 0

Total State Parks: 15 (Largest is Burlingame State Park)

State Bird: Rhode Island red chicken

State Flower: Violet

State Tree: Red maple

Wildlife Spotting: Black bears; beavers; fishers; minks; raccoons; river otters; green herons; blue-winged warblers; common eiders; loons; harlequin ducks; northern redbelly and eastern smooth green snakes; blue-spotted salamanders; northern leopard frogs

ASHAWAY RV RESORT

🏚 4, 🚐 200 full hookup

235 Ashaway Road, Bradford, RI 02808
Open: April to October ▪ Rates: RV from $85, cabins from $195 ▪ Amenities: Swimming pool, hot tub, showers, laundry, picnic tables, fire rings, potable water, firewood, ice, propane, playground, sports courts, athletic field, arcade, radio-controlled car track, miniature golf, dog parks, cable TV, internet ▪ ADA sites: Yes

This RV-only retreat along the Pawcatuck River is buzzing between late spring and early fall with families questing a good-old-fashioned New England getaway. There are beaches, ponds, forest trails, and cute little villages within a 20-minute drive, but Ashaway is basically a self-contained resort flush with activities to keep both kids and their parents active and entertained throughout the day, with a swimming pool, miniature golf course, and radio-controlled car track. There's even a pioneer graveyard on the grounds, a reminder of the days when the area was part of the Colony of Rhode Island and Providence Plantations. Ashaway also offers a handful of Park Model cabin rentals.

WHISPERING PINES CAMPGROUND

🏠 4, 🚐 80 full hookup, 120 partial hookup, 🔺 10

41 Saw Mill Road, Hope Valley, RI 02832

Open: April to October ▪ Rates: RV full hookup from $45, RV partial hookup from $40, tent only from $35, cabins from $110 (two-night minimum stay) ▪ Amenities: Camp store, snack bar, dump station, swimming pool, showers, laundry, picnic tables, fire rings, potable water, firewood, ice, propane, playgrounds, sports courts, arcade, athletic field, miniature golf, fishpond, boating ▪ ADA sites: Yes

Theme events are the forte of a Hope Valley RV resort that invites guests to indulge in everything from a Decadent Dessert Weekend and Christmas in July to a country-western music festival and Disney character tribute. There's also a throwback Prom Night during which campers of any age are asked to don their old tux or poufed dress, a weekend that culminates with the crowning of a campground Prom King & Queen. At other times during the season, Whispering Palms offers 25 percent discounts to campers from Massachusetts or Connecticut and a similar discount to all teachers and current students. True to its name, the campground is set in 50 acres (20 ha) of pine forest with a spring-fed pond stocked for catch-and-release fishing. Regardless of the weekend, it also offers boating, tractor-pulled hayrides, and a tiny barrel train that chugs kids around the grounds.

Hathaway's Guest Cottages are nestled away in a country-like location minutes from the beach.

GEORGE WASHINGTON STATE CAMPGROUND

🚐 / 🔺 45 no hookup, 🔺 7

2185 Putnam Pike, Glocester, RI 02814

Open: April to October ▪ Rates: $18/$36 (state resident/nonresident) ▪ Amenities: Restrooms, picnic tables, fire rings with grills, potable water, boat ramp, beach ▪ ADA sites: Partial

Rhode Island's remote northwest corner provides a bucolic setting for a campground arrayed along the edge of Bowdish Reservoir. All sites are well shaded and within a short walk of the shore for boating, swimming, and fishing—or even ice skating if you happen to visit in winter when the lake is frozen over. It's primitive camping, which means no hookups and few amenities other than basic restrooms and drinking water. Away from the water, hiking is the main activity, with shore routes around the campground and a much longer loop trek through the 4,000-acre (1,618 ha) George Washington State Forest along a portion of the North South Trail. The closest place for groceries and restaurant meals, nearby Chepachet village, occupies a small niche in the horror/sci-fi world via *The X-Files* television series and the work of H. P. Lovecraft, the legendary science-fiction author.

MELVILLE PONDS CAMPGROUND

🚐 56 full hookup, 🔺 40, 🚙 2, 🏠 1

181 Bradford Avenue, Portsmouth, RI 02871

Open: April to October ▪ Rates: RV from $51, tents from $41, traveler trails from $125, mobile home from $150 ▪ Amenities: Camp store,

Take a boat out for a cruise or charter fishing at Charlestown Breachway State Park, located on Block Island Sound.

showers, laundry, picnic tables, fire rings, potable water, firewood, ice, playground, sports courts, dog park, cable TV, internet ▪ ADA sites: Partial

Newport may be renowned for its fancy waterfront mansions, but Rhode Island's illustrious seaside resort boasts a pretty cool campground too. Located on Aquidneck Island around 20 minutes from downtown Newport, Melville blends full-hookup RV and tent-only sites with restored Airstream travel trailers. From Cindy's Country Café and Ragged Island Brewing to the Newport Car Museum and Green Animals Topiary Garden, there's plenty to do in the immediate area without venturing into town. A small brook

runs along one side of the woodsy property, Narragansett Bay is just down the road, and the closest beach is 5 miles (8 km) away at Sandy Point. The campground is a long-time favorite for folks attending the Newport Folk Festival in July and other special events. Special conditions may apply—for instance, a four-day minimum stay over the folk fest weekend.

FORT GETTY PARK & CAMPGROUND

⛺ 26

1050 Fort Getty Road, Jamestown, RI 02835

Open: May to September ▪ Rate: $30 ▪ Amenities: Dump station, showers, picnic tables, fire rings,

potable water, boat ramp, overnight boat parking ▪ ADA sites: No

An early 20th-century naval gun battery overlooking Narragansett Bay has morphed in modern times into an excellent municipal campground with a rocky beach and boat ramp. While most of the spaces are reserved for long-term seasonal RV use, two sections are tent only even for campers spending just a single night. About a 15-minute drive from Newport via the Claiborne Pell Bridge and Jamestown, the campground lies on Dutch Island, which also hosts Beavertail State Park and its landmark lighthouse. Campers can hike a short trail around the edge of Fox

On the shores of the Bowdish Reservoir, George Washington State Campground offers rustic tent camping.

Hill Salt Marsh or launch a longer trek to Conanicut Battery Historic Park and the remains of defense works that stretch back to the Revolutionary War.

FISHERMEN'S MEMORIAL STATE PARK & CAMPGROUND

🚐 / 🏕 180

1011 Point Judith Road, Narragansett, RI 02882

Open: April to October ▪ Rates: RV/tent full hookup $28/$55 (state resident/nonresident), partial hookup $24/$45, no hookup $18/$36 ▪ Amenities: Dump station, showers, picnic tables, fire rings, potable water, firewood, playground, sports courts, boat ramp, beaches, electric vehicle charging station, internet ▪ ADA sites: Yes

Poised on Point Judith, this seaside park honors all of those from the Narragansett area who have gone fishing over the years and never returned. The campground is located away from the shore, but just a short driving or walking distance from Scarborough, Roger Wheeler, and other state beaches, as well as restaurants and shops on Point Judith village. The Block Island ferry terminal is also nearby for campers who want to spend the day on the wild island at the mouth of Long Island Sound. Copious trees and grass lend the campground a parklike feeling; a handful of the sites in Area 1 overlook Buff Hill Cove. That giant concrete structure in the middle of the campground is Battery 109, a massive gun emplacement built during World War II. Between June and October, the campground hosts the Fishermen's Park Farmers Market every Sunday.

HATHAWAY'S GUEST COTTAGES

☎ 8

4470 Old Post Road, Charlestown, RI 02813

Open: May to October ▪ Rates: From $125 ▪ Amenities: Swimming pool, private bathrooms, air-conditioning, bedding and towels, outdoor and indoor games, communal fire pit and barbecue, cable TV, internet ▪ ADA sites: No

Take a trip down memory lane at these classic New England–style beach cottages on the Old Post Road in Charlestown. Although the whitewashed clapboard cabins look similar, all of them have distinct personalities. Some are extended-stay efficiency units, but most can be booked for the usual stays. Some have full kitchens and others just mini-fridges and microwaves. Some boast daily housekeeping, and others do not. And they may feature king, queen, or even twin beds. So there's plenty of room to customize your stay. There's a swimming pool on-site and loads to try nearby, including NBX Bikes, Exeter Country Club, Frosty Drew Observatory,

the Kayak Center, and Ocean House Marina boat rentals.

CHARLESTOWN BREACHWAY

🚐 75 no hookup

Charlestown Beach Road, Charlestown, RI 02813

Open: April to October ▪ Rates: $18/$36 (state resident/nonresident) ▪ Amenities: Restrooms, boat ramp ▪ ADA sites: No

It's RVs only at this beachside campground beside a man-made channel that links coastal lagoons and the open Atlantic. The breachway was dug in 1904, largely at the behest of lagoon oyster farmers who required fresh seawater to raise their tasty crop. By the 1950s, recreation had eclipsed shellfish as the area's main attraction. There's nothing the least bit fancy about Breachway: It's basically a large, unpaved parking lot. The best sites are located right beside the canal and its rocky shoreline. Because there are no hookups, all overnight RVs must be fully self-contained, including an onboard bathroom. ▪

SOMETHING SPECIAL

Newport

You may think of Newport, Rhode Island, as the home of famous wealthy American families (and their mansions)—for example, the Vanderbilts and Astors, who made it their summer getaways—but the quaint town is actually an adventure oasis if you know where to look. With a rocky coast and quiet beaches, as well as three vineyards, there's much to do in Newport.

For instance, the Newport Cliff walk is a stunning coastal trail that hugs the 70-foot (21 m) drop along the stony shore. Or take a day-long guided kayaking tour (hosted by Kayak Centre of Rhode Island) along the coast. More experienced paddlers can do this self-guided with full-day rentals.

If food and wine are more your style of adventure, a vineyard tour of Newport is the way to go, visiting three stops: Newport Vineyards, Greenvale Vineyards, and Carolyn's Sakonnet Vineyard.

South Carolina

South Carolina boasts coastal campgrounds that include maritime forests, thriving wetlands, white sandy beaches, and a taste of southern charm.

HILTON HEAD ISLAND MOTOR COACH RESORT

🚐 401 full hookup

133 Arrow Road, Hilton Head Island, SC 29928

Open: Year-round ▪ Rates: $90-$140 ▪ Amenities: Snack bar, showers, laundry, lounge/game room, fitness center, swimming pool, hot tub, picnic tables, fire rings, potable water, tennis/pickleball courts, playground, dog run and wash, first aid station, propane, cable TV, internet, RV detailing and mechanic available ▪ ADA sites: Partial

With more than 400 full-hookup sites, this South Carolina coastal retreat feels more like a village than a typical RV resort. All the pads are paved and attractively landscaped with patio-style tables and chairs, and 24 sites back into a small lake. From snack bar and fitness center to a parking valet and warm-water dog wash, the resort is better equipped than most other RV campgrounds. But perhaps the best thing is location: near the rotary in the middle of Hilton Head Island, close to beaches on the Atlantic side and marinas and seafood restaurants on the estuary. In addition, the resort is within walking distance of a supermarket, drugstore, bike rental and repair shop, and local eating institutions like Ruby Lee's South.

Follow the Cedar Creek canoe trail in Congaree National Park.

HUNTING ISLAND STATE PARK

🚐/🏕 102 partial hookup, 🏕 25

2555 Sea Island Parkway, St. Helena Island, SC 29920

Open: Year-round ▪ Rates: RV/tent partial hookup from $40, tent only from $28 ▪ Amenities: Dump station, camp store, showers, picnic tables, fire rings, playground, boat ramp, fishing pier, ice, firewood, potable water, internet ▪ ADA sites: Yes

Tap into the wild side of coastal Carolina at a state park campsite situated beside pristine maritime forest, wildlife-rich wetlands and 5 miles (8 km) of unspoiled Atlantic beach. The name derives from the fact the island was once a private hunting reserve for lowland plantation owners. Its historic lighthouse was destroyed by the Confederates and then rebuilt by the Yankees after the Civil War. The campground lies near the park's north end, a combination of power/water hookups and primitive walk-in tent sites all within easy reach of the beach. Beyond the deep blue sea, the park offers a dozen hiking trails, a wildlife viewing platform overlooking Johnson Creek, and the Nature Center with exhibits and weekly programs. Campers can also book maritime tours with Coastal Expeditions, including a Story River dolphin cruise or visit

to nearby St. Phillips Island, until recently the private seaside estate of tycoon Ted Turner.

CAROLINA HERITAGE OUTFITTERS

🛖 3

1 Livery Lane, St. George, SC 29477

Open: March to November ▪ Rates: From $160 per person ▪ Amenities: Hammocks, picnic tables, grills, gas stove, cooking utensils, lanterns, board games, drinking water ▪ ADA sites: No

One of the state's special camping encounters, Carolina Heritage offers two-day canoe trips down the Edisto River with an overnight in tree houses inside the private Edisto River Refuge. The paddle distance is 23 miles (37 km), almost evenly divided between the two days. And because it's downstream, the journey is more a float trip than a hard-core paddle. Arboreal accommodation ranges from a small tree house that sleeps two to three people, to a large unit that can handle as many as eight. All three feature a ground-floor dining deck with gas camp stove, outdoor grill, and kitchen utensils for preparing meals. Upstairs is a sleeping loft with one or more futons. There's no power or water, but outhouse facilities are nearby. Campers can linger in the cypress, cedar, and live oak woods by arranging a two- or three-night tree house stay.

EDISTO BEACH STATE PARK

🏠 7, 🚐/🏕 112 partial hookup, 🏕 5

8377 State Cabin Road, Edisto Island, SC 29438

Open: Year-round ▪ Rates: RV/tent from $26, tent only from $22, cabins from $112 ▪ Amenities: Dump station, showers, picnic tables, fire pits with grills, boat ramp ▪ ADA sites: Yes

Located within the ACE Basin estuarine reserve—one of the largest tracts of coastal wilderness along the Atlantic seaboard—Edisto Beach offers two vastly different camping experiences. As the name implies,

Beach Campground stretches along the sandy shore, many of the sites shaded by palmetto trees and within easy reach of the shoreline for swimming, surfing, fishing, and shelling. On the inland side of Scott Creek, Live Oak Campground meanders through thick maritime forest beside a salt marsh rife with birds and other creatures. An extensive hiking and biking trail network (including routes that are wheelchair accessible) links the campgrounds with other parts of the park, including the excellent Environmental Learning Center. Boaters can launch into Big Bay Creek to enjoy a day on the basin or try their luck casting a few fishing lines.

THE CAMPGROUND AT JAMES ISLAND COUNTY PARK

🏠 10, 🚐/🏕 116 full hookup, 6 partial hookup, 🏕 15

871 Riverland Drive, Charleston, SC 29412

Just 15 minutes outside Charleston, James Island County Park offers myriad outdoor activities.

Open: Year-round ▪ Rates: Full hookup from $59, partial hookup $55, tent only $35, cabins $169, $20/$25 (state resident/nonresident) ▪ Amenities: Dump station, camp store, activity center, showers, laundry, picnic tables, fire rings with grills, firewood, ice, propane, potable water, boat and bike rental, dog park, playground, shuttle service, internet ▪ ADA sites: Yes

Although the woodsy Low Country location and various outdoor activities are the main reasons for camping at James Island County Park, another huge plus is location—the campground is less than a 15-minute drive from Charleston's historic heart and beloved Southern fare restaurants, and only 20 minutes from laid-back Folly Beach. There's plenty to keep you busy in and around the campground itself, of course: a climbing wall, summertime water park, 18-hole disc golf course, bike paths, and kayak rental for exploring the Stono River along the park's western edge. The county provides a shuttle service to the beach and downtown Charleston, and it's just a short drive to the Wild Blue Ropes Adventure Park, McLeod Plantation Historic Site, and Charleston Municipal Golf Course.

MYRTLE BEACH TRAVEL PARK

🏠 41, 🚐 700+, 🚙 45

10108 Kings Road, Myrtle Beach, SC 29572

Open: Year-round ▪ Rates: RV full hookup and partial hookup from $46, cabins and travel trailers from $435 per week ▪ Amenities: Restaurant, tiki bar, camp store, snack bar, swimming pools, showers, picnic tables, shade structures, laundry, game arcade, playground, sports

Myrtle Beach Travel Park is a lively resort in the heart of South Carolina's most popular beach town.

courts, fishing, paddle boats, propane, dump station, internet ▪ ADA sites: Partial

An RV resort with its own clothing line and branded merchandise must be big. Myrtle Beach Travel Park— "MBTP" as it says on all that swag—fits the bill. Stretching across 125 acres (50 ha) in the heart of the state's most popular beach town, the resort offers more than 1,000 total sites, including full hookup and water/power RV pads, ocean villas, lake-view cabins, and 35-foot (10.6 m) travel trailers. Although it's located right next to the beach, MBTP also features indoor and outdoor swimming pools and a lazy

river. There's also a large pond for fishing and paddle boating, but no swimming because there could be gators. A year-round slate of activities stretches all the way from live music, line dancing, and pool parties to fitness classes, fishing tournaments, and a campground ministry with Sunday morning worship services and Bible study.

RIVER ISLAND ADVENTURES

🏕 4, numerous primitive tent sites
1249 Vera Road, Longs, SC 29568
Open: Year-round ▪ Rates: Glamping tents from $75, primitive tent sites $10-$20 per person ▪ Amenities: Restroom, showers, picnic tables,

fire rings, outdoor games, boat ramp, internet ▪ ADA sites: No

Set along the wild Waccamaw River, this veteran adventure outfitter offers paddle sports, pontoon boats, and tubing, as well as forest and riverside camping. Glamping tents on wooden platforms afford the most comfortable way to overnight at River Island. They come with queen beds (linens provided), propane heaters, deck chairs, and picnic tables, as well as access to a communal fire pit and barbecue grill, various yard games, boat ramp, and a restroom with a heated outdoor propane shower. The alternative is the primitive camping in a nearby field

Sway to sleep in a hammock beneath the stars at Hunting Island State Park.

or on a private island downstream from the main outpost. Primitive sites are equipped with fire rings and picnic tables; those who bring their own kayak get a discount on the overnight rate.

CONGAREE NATIONAL PARK

🔺 16

100 National Park Road, Hopkins, SC 29061

Open: Year-round ▪ Rates: Campgrounds $5-$10, backcountry camping free (with permit) ▪ Amenities: Restrooms (at Longleaf Campground), picnic tables, fire rings ▪ ADA sites: No

One of the nation's newest national parks (established in 2003) Congaree preserves the South's largest remaining tract of old-growth, bottom-land, hardwood forest. It also harbors the pristine watersheds of the Congaree and Wateree Rivers, as well as an incredible number of "champion trees" that are the tallest of their species anywhere in the world. Two primitive wilderness campgrounds near the visitors center allow tent and hammock camping but not RVs or trailers. Hikers and paddlers who obtain a free backcountry permit (the park recommends applying for backcountry permits at least 48 hours in advance) can camp along the park's trails and waterways, although open fires are not permitted.

MOUNTAIN BRIDGE WILDERNESS AREA

🔺 18

Geer Highway (U.S. 276), Cleveland, SC 29635

Open: Year-round ▪ Rates: $14-$30 ▪ Amenities: Fire rings, leashed pets allowed ▪ ADA sites: No

Created in 1996, Mountain Bridge embraces more than 13,000 acres (5,260 ha) of forest, granite outcrops, waterfalls, and remote valleys that seem little changed from the days when the Cherokee people roamed the region. The wilderness area doesn't have developed campgrounds. However, backpackers can trek more than 100 miles (160 km) of trail to 18 primitive backcountry campsites. Most have fire pits, but none of the wilderness camps provide water, power, or restrooms. Campers need to carry in all of their own equipment and supplies, and the "leave no trace" credo is strictly enforced. The bucket list hike is the Jones Gap–Caesars Head Loop, a 28.5-mile (46 km) route between two state parks with multiple waterfalls, overlooks, and trailside campsites along the way. All trails close one hour before dark, and campers are asked to reach their site two hours before sunset.

OCONEE STATE PARK

☎ 19, 🚐/🔺 140 partial hookup, 🔺 15

624 State Park Road, Mountain Rest, SC 29664

Open: Year-round ▪ Rates: RV/tent from $23, tent only from $16, cabins from $72 ▪ Amenities: Dump station, showers, camp store, picnic tables, firewood, ice, potable water, playground, boat rentals, fishing pier, miniature golf, internet ▪ ADA sites: Partial

Largely sculpted by the Civilian Conservation Corps during the Great Depression, Oconee lies along the state's lofty Blue Ridge Escarpment. In addition to RV pads with power and water, the park offers tent-only sites and overnights in vintage 1930s cabins (all of which are listed on the National Register of Historic Places) outfitted with screened porches, stone fireplaces, full kitchens, and beds with sheets, pillows, and blankets. Some of the cabins are set around the edge of a small lake, others tucked inside the nearby forest. There is a minimum stay of two nights for all campers within the park. Besides serving as a spot for drive-up campers, Oconee is a hub for long-distance backpackers trekking the 76-mile (122 km) Foothills Trail through South and North Carolina. ▪

SOMETHING SPECIAL

Congaree National Park

Located just 20 miles (32.2 km) from South Carolina's capital, Congaree National Park encompasses 27,000 acres (10,926.5 ha) of old-growth, bottom-land, hardwood forest, the largest such expanse remaining in the southeastern United States. With an average canopy height of more than 100 feet (30.5 m), the trees form one of the tallest temperate deciduous forests in the world.

Hiking trails are concentrated in the western section of the park, leaving access to the central part mostly by canoe or kayak. Entering at the Cedar Creek canoe access, committed paddlers can take a two-day trek following the creek through the center of the park to the Congaree River, which forms in the southern boundary. Trees overhang the narrow, black-water creek, and alligators bask in the sunshine on the broad river.

South Dakota

From camping on the Badlands of South Dakota to the Black Hills, there are ample opportunities for a nature escape in remote and stunning places.

ELKHORN RIDGE RV RESORT & CAMPGROUND

🏠 36, 🚐 185 partial hookup, ⛺ 20, 🏠 1

20189 U.S. Highway 85, Spearfish, SD 57783

Open: Year-round ▪ Rates: RV full hookup $45, tent only from $20, cabins from $108, historic home from $499 (two-night minimum stay) ▪ Amenities: Restaurant, camp store, gift shop, snack bar, swimming pool, hot tubs, showers, picnic tables, playground, sports courts, golf course, dog park, propane, cable TV, internet ▪ ADA sites: Partial

From hikers and history buffs to mild-mannered bikers attending the Sturgis Motorcycle Rally, full-service Elkhorn Ridge appeals to a wide variety of people visiting the Black Hills region. With nearly 200 full-hookup sites, it's also one of the largest RV camps on the Northern Plains. While the great outdoors might beckon, there's certainly no lack of activities around the campground, from a heated swimming pool and 4.5-mile (7.2 km) hiking/biking trail system to an espresso bar and tennis/pickleball courts. Elkhorn Ridge also boasts its own 18-hole golf course and the Miller Creek bar and restaurant on the historic Frawley Ranch, founded in the 1870s and once one of South

Spotting bison is not uncommon at Wind Cave National Park.

Dakota's largest cattle operations. As part of that heritage, an 1888 stagecoach stop and hotel, the Draper Roadhouse, is available for overnight rentals.

YAK RIDGE CABINS & FARMSTEAD

🏠 4

24041 Cosmos Road, Rapid City, SD 57702

Open: Year-round ▪ Rates: From $175 (two-night minimum stay) ▪ Amenities: Kitchens, private bathrooms, bedding and towels, air-conditioning, fireplaces, books and board games, barbecue grills, fire pits, internet ▪ ADA sites: No

Yep, they really do have Himalayan yaks at this offbeat Black Hills outpost that blends cabin camping and farm-stay hospitality. Fashioned by local artisans and craftspeople, the wooden cabins feature queen or twin beds, vintage furnishings, full kitchens and bathrooms, flat-screen TVs, and covered porches. The husband-and-wife owners are happy to guide campers around a sustainable farm that nurtures honeybees, free-range chickens, and the hairy beasts from highland Asia. Among nearby attractions are Mount Rushmore, Deadwood, the giant Crazy Horse memorial, Wind Cave, and Custer State Park. Come winter, find skiing and ice fishing throughout the nearby Black Hills for adventure seekers.

UNDER CANVAS MOUNT RUSHMORE

⛺ 75

24342 Presidio Ranch Road, Keystone, SD 57751

Open: May to December ▪ Rates: From $199 ▪ Amenities: Indoor/outdoor restaurant with bar service, gift shop, wood-burning stoves, firewood, communal fire pit, USB battery packs, organic bath products, activities concierge ▪ ADA sites: Yes

Having slept beneath canvas for so much of his life—in Africa, the Amazon, and San Juan Hill—Teddy Roosevelt would have appreciated the standard of these luxury tents near the granite mountain that bears his likeness. Like other Under Canvas compounds around the nation, the Mount Rushmore version raises the bar on wilderness glamping with excellent on-site food and beverage options, live entertainment and artsy workshops, yoga sessions, and a guest experience coordinator to help plan out your weekend's Black

Yak Ridge Cabins is an ideal stay in the Black Hills and just a few miles from Mount Rushmore.

Hills activities that range from driving tours, hiking and biking excursions, and kayaking or stand-up paddleboarding. Accommodation ranges from romantic stargazer tents for two with bathrooms to family suites and safari units that feature a smaller adjacent tent with twin beds for the kids.

GAME LODGE CAMPGROUND

🏠 11, 🚐 / ⛺ 59 partial hookup, ⛺ 15

U.S. Highway 16A, Custer State Park, East Custer, SD 57730

Open: Year-round ▪ Rates: RV/tent partial hookup $30, tent only $26, cabins $55 ▪ Amenities: Restaurant, camp store, dump station, showers, laundry, picnic tables, fire pits, potable water, gas station, gift shop, theater ▪ ADA sites: Yes

Take your pick—Wild West or U.S. presidential history, awesome hiking or radical rock climbing, wilderness landscapes or the annual wild bison roundup: Custer State Park has something for just about everyone, including one of South Dakota's best campgrounds. Located beside the State Game Lodge where President Calvin Coolidge vacationed in 1927, the overnight oasis is one of 10 campgrounds spread around the Black Hills park but the most strategically located. The historic Game Lodge and restaurant, the park visitors center, Peter Norbeck Outdoor Education Center, Tatanka Barn with its indoor interpretive programs, and the Buffalo Safari Jeep Tours base camp are all within a 15-minute walk of the campground. Grace Coolidge Creek meanders right behind the campground, and there are several nearby trailheads for exploring the state park backcountry.

ELK MOUNTAIN CAMPGROUND

🚐 / ⛺ 48 no hookup, ⛺ 14

26611 U.S. Highway 385, Hot Springs, SD 57747

Open: Year-round ▪ Rates: $18 (summer), $9 (winter) ▪ Amenities: Restrooms, picnic tables, fire rings with grills, potable water, firewood, amphitheater ▪ ADA sites: Yes

While most of the half-million people who visit Wind Cave every year come for the subterranean wonders, Elk Mountain highlights an entirely different aspect of the national park: the aboveground wildlife and scenery of the Black Hills. The campground occupies an island of ponderosa pines amid a vast sea of prairie grass where buffalo still roam, as well as elk, prairie dogs, burrowing owls, and many other indigenous creatures. The short, easy Elk Mountain Interpretive Trail makes a loop around the campground. But there are plenty of other nearby hiking trails, including the southernmost leg of the 111-mile (178 km) Centennial Trail across the Black Hills. The campground amphitheater stages regular ranger talks from May to September, including an elk bugling program that concludes with a caravan drive to spot (and hopefully hear) the big animals calling in the wild.

FRENCH CREEK CAMPING AREA

🚐 / ⛺ 4 no hookup

East French Creek Road, Fairburn, SD 57738

Open: Year-round ▪ Rates: RV/tent partial hookup $36, no hookup/tent only $28, primitive $18, cabins from $90, yurts from $120 ▪ Amenities: Restrooms, shade structures, picnic tables, grills ▪ ADA sites: No

Located amid the Badlands and rolling prairies of Buffalo Gap National Grassland, French Creek is small but remarkable. It's super secluded even by South Dakota standards and located near an extraordinary rock-hounding site that yields all kinds of geological treasures, including the occasional agate, rose quartz, banded jasper, and even a few meteorites. Officially, French Creek has just four campsites. But given the fact that camping is dispersed across a large lawn area, it can probably hold twice that many—not that you'll have much company. Sites are reserved on a first come, first served basis, for tents and camping trailers. Beyond the utter remoteness, the campground comes with few amenities other than vault toilets and shade structures. It's not everyone's camping cup of tea, but it's paradise for avid gemologists.

CEDAR PASS LODGE & CAMPGROUND

26, / 21 partial hookup, 75 no hookup
20681 State Highway 240, Interior, SD 57750
Open: Year-round ▪ Rates: RV/tent partial hookup $38, tent only $23, cabins $182 ▪ Amenities: Restaurant, gift shop, showers, picnic tables, shade structures, potable water, internet ▪ ADA sites: Yes

Cedar Pass makes the South Dakota Badlands better with comfy new cabins, electric RV sites, and tent-only camping sites in the heart of the bleakly beautiful national park. Adding to the campground's allure is the fact that it featured in the Oscar-winning movie *Nomadland*.

Located at the eastern end of the scenic Badlands Loop Road, the cabins and campground lie within walking distance of Ben Reifel Visitor Center and ranger talks at the park amphitheater, and it's just a short drive from trailheads for the Medicine Root, Castle, and other hiking routes through the fantastically eroded landscape. In good 21st-century fashion, the cabins are locally crafted and built to Gold Level LEED standards yet reflect the architecture of the lodge's original 1928 cabins. In addition to king or queen beds, they feature energy-saving kitchen appliances, flat-screen TVs with satellite service, bedding and towels, and ultra-quiet heating and air-conditioning, plus seating areas in front and out back.

Don't miss sunset views of the ridges at Badlands National Park when staying at nearby Cedar Pass Lodge.

Luxury tents at Under Canvas Mount Rushmore make a stay in the Black Hills National Forest an upscale wilderness retreat.

FORT SISSETON HISTORIC STATE PARK

🏚 3, 🚐/🏕 10 partial hookup, 🏕 4

11907 434th Avenue, Lake City, SD 57247

Open: Year-round ▪ Rates: RV/tent partial hookup $26, tent only $22, cabins $55 ▪ Amenities: Gift shop, showers, picnic tables, fire rings, potable water, boat rental, boat ramp, internet ▪ ADA sites: Partial

Like the troopers of old, Fort Sisseton offers a rare chance to camp on the grounds of a genuine U.S. Cavalry post established during the Civil War in the glacier-carved, lake-filled flatlands of northeast South Dakota. The tree-shaded campground lies beside the old barn and the only remaining blockhouse from the Civil War days. Campers can undertake a guided or self-guided tour that includes 14 original structures from the fort's late 19th-century heyday. The apex of the state park year is the Fort Sisseton Historical Festival in June, which features food, period music, and frontier military encampment.

NEWTON HILLS STATE PARK

🏚 10, 🚐/🏕 117 partial hookup, 🏕 9

28767 482nd Avenue, Canton, SD 57013

Open: Year-round ▪ Rates: RV/tent partial hookup $26, tent only $22, cabins from $55 ▪ Amenities: Dump station, showers, picnic tables, fire rings with grills, potable water, playground, boat ramps, amphitheater, concert stage, bike rental ▪ ADA sites: Yes

Just across the Big Sioux River from Iowa, Newton Hills presents an entirely different take on outdoor South Dakota: thick hardwood forest instead of cornfields and prairie grass. The park hovers atop the Coteau des Prairies plateau that marks the transition from the Great Lakes region to the Great Plains. In addition to RV and tent sites, the campground offers rustic camping cabins and a single "modern cabin" that features more amenities including a full kitchen, private bathroom, heating, and air-conditioning. There's plenty to do around the campground, too: Hiking, horseback riding, and cross-country skiing, as well as swimming and boating on Lake Lakota, are the park's top activities. Newton Hills is also huge on festivals, including the Sioux River Folk Festival in August and the FestiFall & Candlelight Walk in October.

LEWIS & CLARK RECREATION AREA

🏚 40, 🚐/🏕 409 partial hookup, 🏕 1

43349 SD-52, Yankton, SD 57078

Open: Year-round ▪ Rates: RV/tent partial hookup $26, tent only $15, camping cabins $55, deluxe cabins from $125 ▪ Amenities: Restaurant, dump stations, showers, picnic tables, fire rings, grills, potable water, marina, fishing docks, boat ramps, beaches, sports courts, playgrounds, fish cleaning station, bike repair station, horse and bike trails, amphitheater, internet ▪ ADA sites: Yes

Created in the 1950s with the completion of the Gavins Point Dam, Lewis & Clark Lake stretches 25 miles (40 km) along the Missouri River between South Dakota and Nebraska. The state's largest camping destination offers more than 400 sites spread across three large campgrounds, plus state-run camping cabins and private deluxe cabins at Midway Gulch and Lewis & Clark Resort. Many of the campsites and cabins are perched on the lakeshore. From boating, fishing, and swimming to biking, hiking, disc golf, and an archery trail, the rec area offers plenty of pastimes. Reservations are recommended, and most are booked at least a week in advance of your camping trip during the high summer season. ▪

SOMETHING SPECIAL

Newton Hills State Park

For the visitor heading across the corn and wheat field country of South Dakota and Iowa, timbered Newton Hills pops up ahead in sharp relief, the legacy of glaciers from the last ice age. This park preserves native countryside on the southern edge of the Coteau des Prairies. Extending along the eastern border of South Dakota, the plateau marks the western edge of the geographical province known as the Central Lowlands. To the west begin the Great Plains, extending to the Rockies.

Inside the park thrives a native upland forest, primarily oak but laced with other hardwoods. To get a flavor of the park in a short time, hike the Woodland trail that travels along the Sergeant Creek drainage, then up a hill to a peaceful niche of beautiful old oaks interspersed with small areas of preserve natural prairie. An excellent place for bird watching, the park has recorded more than 200 species.

Tennessee

A stay in the Great Smoky Mountains, a spot outside the bustling country music scene of Nashville, and a riverbank perch are just a few options on offer for camping in the Volunteer State.

ROAN MOUNTAIN STATE PARK

☎ 30, 🚐/🏔 86 partial hookup, 🏔 20

527 State Highway 143, Roan Mountain, TN 37687

Open: Year-round ▪ Rates: RV/tent $33, tent only $16, cabins from $93 ▪ Amenities: Camp store, gift shop, dump station, showers, picnic tables, fire pits, grills, swimming pool, sports courts, playgrounds ▪ ADA sites: Yes

Surrounded by national forest, this eastern Tennessee state park helps protect several of the most amazing natural habitats along the entire Appalachian chain: the world's largest natural rhododendron garden and heath-like areas called grassy balds. The campground and cabins are scattered through the hardwood forest along the Doe River deep in Bearwallow Hollow in the heart of the park. The adjacent recreation area offers tennis and basketball courts and a swimming pool (with diving boards). First staged in 1947, the Rhododendron Festival in June is the highlight of the state park year.

COSBY CAMPGROUND

🚐 8 no hookup, 🚐/🏔 11, 🏔 138

Rhododendrons bloom along part of the Appalachian Trail through the Roan Highlands.

127 Cosby Entrance Road, Cosby, TN 37722

Open: April to October ▪ Rate: $17.50 ▪ Amenities: Dump station, picnic tables, fire pits with grills, potable water, amphitheater, food storage container ▪ ADA sites: Yes

Set in a forest-filled valley along the eastern flank of the Great Smoky Mountains, Cosby offers all the natural splendor of America's most visited national park without the crowds and traffic that often afflict more popular areas along Highway 441. The campground offers a few spots for motor homes and trailers that are 25 feet (7.6 m) or less, but Cosby is primarily aimed at car, bike, and backpack campers dozing in tents or beneath the starry sky.

Rangers take the stage at the campground amphitheater for a "Celebrating Cosby" talk on Friday nights during the summer months. Otherwise, this secluded vale is all about entertaining yourself by reading a book, splashing in the creek, photographing the wildflowers, or hiking routes like Snake Den Ridge Trail or Low Gap Trail that climb into the highlands for rendezvous with the Smoky Mountains segment of the Appalachian Trail as it straddles the Tennessee/North Carolina border. Just outside the park— about a seven-minute drive from the campground—the town of Cosby offers groceries, camping

supplies, a gas station, and several restaurants.

LITTLE ARROW OUTDOOR RESORT

☎ 38, 🚐/🏔 76 full hookup, 🏔 19, ⛺ 8, 📶 1

118 Stables Drive (off State Highway 73), Townsend, TN 37882

Open: Year-round ▪ Rates: RV/tent full hookup from $165, glamping tents from $125, tent only from $42, cabins from $132, travel trailer $175 ▪ Amenities: Camp store, coffee lounge, food trucks, showers, laundry, picnic tables, fire rings with grills, firewood, ice, swimming pool, playground, basketball, dog park ▪ ADA sites: Yes

Fancy camping and food trucks are the heady mix at Little Arrow, an upscale RV and cabin resort near the Townsend entrance to Great Smoky park. Unveiled in 2021, the deluxe RV pads aren't just pull-through and full hookup; they've also got paved patios, covered cabana-like porches, and outdoor sinks with counter space. Indoor accommodation includes glamping tents as well as tiny homes and modern log cabins with kitchens, private bathrooms, cable TV, and outdoor seating. A wide variety of local food trucks—REO Cheesewagon, Bangin' Burgers, Meatball Madness, Lobster Dogs, and more—take up residence on weekends. The national park is the big draw, but the town of Townsend offers plenty of its own distractions, including river tubing, horseback riding, and the Little River Railroad Museum.

CHARIT CREEK LODGE

🏚 5

Fork Ridge Road, Jamestown, TN 37862

Open: Year-round ▪ Rates: From $120 per person (full service), from $50 per person (limited service), horses from $20, dogs $10 ▪ Amenities: Dining hall, bathhouse with showers, bedding, wood-burning stoves, firewood, lanterns, beer and wine, cakes and pies ▪ ADA sites: No

Make like Daniel Boone and blaze a trail across the Cumberland Plateau to this super-secluded lodge in Big South Fork National River & Recreation Area. It's no joke when it comes to blazing because the only way to reach these historic log cabins is by foot, bike, or horse along a 1.1-mile (1.7 km) trail from the parking area. The overnight digs include four vintage log cabins and a converted corn crib—all of them on the National Register of Historic Places and among the oldest structures being used for modern means in the entire national park system. Truly off the grid, the cabins don't have electricity, internet, refrigeration, or air-conditioning, and very limited cell phone reception. Lighting is by lanterns and flashlights. Campers can opt for full service, which includes dinner and breakfast, or limited service with no meals.

FALL CREEK FALLS STATE PARK

🏚 30, 🚐 / ⛺ 92 full hookup, 114 partial hookup, ⛺ 16

2009 Village Camp Road, Spencer, TN 38585

Open: Year-round ▪ Rates: RV/tent full hookup from $38, RV/tent partial hookup from $23, tent only from $16, cabins from $170 ▪ Amenities: Camp store, snack bar, restaurant, gift shops, dump station, showers, laundry, picnic tables, fire pits, grills, firewood, ice, playground, sports courts, golf course, boat rental, boat dock, amphitheater, internet ▪ ADA sites: Yes

Tennessee's largest state park offers more than 200 campsites spread across five zones in a wilderness renowned for deep canyons, precipitous trails, and awesome cascades. At 256 feet (78 m), Fall Creek Falls is the most stunning, one of the most photogenic waterfalls in the Southeast. The park also offers a scenic drive and recreation lake, as well as offbeat attractions like a treetop obstacle course, pedestrian suspension bridge, color-blind viewfinder, and even its own outdoor gear and clothing shop. The campground lies a short distance from Taft Village, where most of the amenities are located. The cabins are arrayed along the waterfront on the opposite side of Fall Creek Lake.

NASHVILLE KOA

🏚 42, 🚐 / ⛺ 255 full hookup, ⛺ 7

2626 Music Valley Drive, Nashville, TN 37214

Open: Year-round ▪ Rates: RV/tent full hookup from $69.99, tent only $40, cabins from $62.49 ▪ Amenities: Camp store, snack bar, dump station, showers, laundry, picnic

Little Arrow Outdoor Resort offers luxury cabins in the Great Smoky Mountains.

Like something out of *The Hobbit,* Forest Gully Farms offers a stay in an underground glamping Gully Hut.

tables, fire pits with grills, propane, swimming pool, hot tub, playground, sports courts, bowling, fitness room, dog runs, internet ▪ ADA sites: Yes

Pennington Bend on the Cumberland River provides a cozy venue for the capital city's premier camping resort. Like other KOA locations, the Nashville campus offers a variety of overnight choices, from deluxe RV pads with tricked-out patios to cabins and tent-only sites. The resort's Notes Café serves breakfast and lunch five days a week. Campers can whip up dinner themselves or mosey over to the neighboring Cock of the Walk Restaurant for catfish, hush puppies, and fried dill pickles. A location in Nashville's Music Valley affords KOA campers easy access to the Grand Ole Opry, Sound

Waves water park, and the Opry Mills outlet stores. A shuttle ($10 per person) provides transportation to and from Lower Broadway in downtown Nashville with its famous honky-tonks, the legendary Ryman Auditorium, and the Country Music Hall of Fame & Museum.

FOREST GULLY FARMS
🏕 3

6016 Fly Hollow Road, Santa Fe, TN 38482
Open: Year-round ▪ Rate: $325 ▪ Amenities: Kitchen and cooking utensils, gas grill, bathhouse with showers, laundry, bedding, heating and air-conditioning, potable water, chickens, gardens ▪ ADA sites: No

It's the middle of Tennessee rather than Middle Earth, but the Gully

Huts at this rural outpost could easily have been conjured in the mind of author J. R. R. Tolkien. With white cedar walls and bamboo flooring, the underground cabins include two sleeping units with several beds, plus heating and air-conditioning, and a communal hut with a full kitchen, sitting area, and long dining table that can seat four to six people. They are rented nightly as a trio on a 15-acre (6 ha) largely self-sustaining farmstead that includes chickens, an orchard, and a vegetable garden. Forest Gully is about a one-hour drive from Nashville and around 40 minutes from Franklin.

MERIWETHER LEWIS CAMPGROUND
🚐/🏕 32 no hookup
191 Meriwether Lewis Park Road

Take hiking trails to see one of 256 cascades within Fall Creek Falls State Park.

(Milepost 386 Natchez Trace Parkway), Hohenwald, TN 38462

Open: Year-round ▪ Rate: Free ▪ Amenities: Restrooms, picnic tables, fire pits with grills, potable water ▪ ADA sites: No

Meriwether Lewis National Monument marks the place on the Natchez Trace Parkway where the famed explorer died in 1809 during an overland journey to Washington, D.C. The National Park Service maintains a small campground near his grave and replica log cabin similar to the Grinder's Stand roadhouse, where Lewis passed away at the age of 35. In addition to paying their respects at the Lewis memorials, campers can hike a section of the original Natchez Trace or a trail along Little Swan Creek. With other nearby sights like Davy Crockett State Park, Devil's Backbone, and Gordon House Historic Site, the campground makes a great base for exploring this part of central Tennessee.

PARIS LANDING STATE PARK

🏚16, 🚐/🏕 39 partial hookup, 18 no hookup

16055 U.S. Highway 79N, Buchanan, TN 38222

Open: Year-round ▪ Rates: RV/tent partial hookup $26, no hookup $16, cabins from $185, camping cabins from $67 ▪ Amenities: Restaurant, bar, camp store, snack bar, dump station, showers, laundry, picnic tables, fire rings, grills, firewood, ice, swimming pool, golf course, sports courts, playground, marina, boat ramp, fish cleaning station, overnight dockage, marine fuel ▪ ADA sites: Yes

From water sports and wildlife to golf, tennis, margaritas, and cornbread pancakes, few other state parks can match the variety available at Paris Landing. The park's campsites and cabins rest along the western shore of Kentucky Lake, the largest man-made water body east of the Mississippi and by far the biggest lake created by the Tennessee Valley Authority. It almost goes without saying that boating is the park's most popular activity, with a full-service marina to serve watercraft.

Among the park's other outdoor pursuits are a swimming pool, golf course, bird watching, guided hikes, and ranger programs. Between March and October, the floating Marker 66 Grille is open for lunch and dinner, the fried calamari baskets, Philly beef, grilled cheese, and homemade beef stew complemented by a cocktail menu with margaritas and mojitos. Highway 79 leaps across the lake on a long bridge-causeway to Land Between Lakes National Recreation Area and the Civil War battlefield at Fort Donelson. Twenty miles (32 km) in the other direction is the town of Paris, known for both its scale model of the Eiffel Tower and the World's Largest Fish Fry in April.

REELFOOT LAKE STATE PARK

🏚7, 🚐/🏕 100 partial hookup, 🏕10

2595 State Highway 21, Tiptonville, TN 38079

Open: Year-round ▪ Rates: RV/tent $26, tent only $12, cabins from $236 (two-night minimum stay) ▪ Amenities: Dump station, showers, laundry, picnic tables, fire pits with grills, boat ramp, boat rental, fish cleaning station, internet ▪ ADA sites: Yes

Reelfoot's flooded forest ecosystem is a geographical curiosity, created in the early 1800s when the massive New Madrid earthquakes caused the Mississippi River to temporarily flow backward, drowning a portion of western Tennessee. The park's modern, roomy cabins and largest campground are spread along the lake's south shore. A smaller, more remote campground is at Airpark in the north. Paddling the sunken cypress forest is a must-do activity, especially during January and February, when thousands of bald eagles arrive at the park, and the autumn, when hundreds of white pelicans stop over on their south-bound migration. ▪

SOMETHING SPECIAL

Reelfoot Lake State Park

Named for a legendary Native American, this appealing lakeside park is composed of 10 segments situated among the 25,000-acre (10,117.1 ha) Reelfoot Lake Wildlife Management Area, 60 percent of it water and wetlands. Ancient cypress trees haunt the margins of Reelfoot Lake, while waterbirds and eagles add to a picture of primitive beauty. Only 5 miles (8 km) from the Mississippi River, the lake was born during the New Madrid earthquakes in the winter of 1811-12, when violent landslides and sinks reshaped the area's topography.

The Reelfoot Lake National Wildlife Refuge offers the chance to learn more about local flora and fauna. Thousands of mallard ducks, white pelicans, and other waterfowl stop here during winter migrations. A short excursion by foot or car brings you to an observation platform on Grassy Island, a great place for viewing the wildlife and sunsets.

Texas

Everything's bigger in Texas, including campgrounds sprawled across country landscapes, mountain retreats, and even canoe camping on the Rio Grande.

CADDO LAKE STATE PARK

10, 8 full hookup, /
18 partial hookup, /20,
7 screened shelters

245 Park Road 2, Karnack, TX 75661
Open: Year-round ▪ Rates: RV full hookup $20, RV/tent partial hookup $15, tents/trailers $10, screened shelters $25, cabins from $40 ▪ Amenities: Dump station, showers, picnic tables, fire rings, grills, potable water, fishing pier, amphitheater, canoe rental, boat ramp, playground, camp store ▪ ADA sites: Yes

The mulchy wetlands of the Red River watershed feel more like Louisiana bayou country than our typical image of Texas. Four camping areas and a cluster of wooden cabins are tucked into woods along the eastern edge of Saw Mill Pond and Big Cypress Bayou. While there are plenty of hiking trails to explore the forest, the main attraction is paddling a warren of moss-covered bald cypress and tupelo trees, lily pads, and floating lotus plants. The park and surrounding area offer more than 50 miles (80 km) of canoe and kayak trails along waterways inhabited by snakes, turtles, frogs, beaver, nutria, and even the occasional alligator.

COUNTRY WOODS INN

6, 4 vintage, 1 railroad car

Paddle by otherworldly cypress trees in Caddo Lake State Park.

420 Grand Avenue, Glen Rose, TX 75043
Open: Year-round ▪ Rates: Vintage trailers $150, railroad car from $200, cabins from $125 ▪ Amenities: Kitchens, private bathrooms, heating and air-conditioning, outdoor seating areas, picnic tables, community fire circle and barbecue grill, sports courts, fishing, internet ▪ ADA sites: No

It's only around an hour's drive from the Dallas–Fort Worth metro area, but this glamping resort on the Paluxy River seems a hundred years removed from modern Texas. Spread around a 40-acre (16 ha) farm, accommodation ranges from a 19th-century prairie house and a Santa Fe Railroad boxcar to vintage travel trailers and cabins. The adjacent river offers a quick way to cool off during the sweltering Texas summer. Guests can while away the day hiking, tossing horseshoes, playing volleyball, or cooling off in the adjacent river. Ideal for families, Country Woods comes with a barnyard full of farm animals and nearby attractions like Dinosaur World, the Granbury Drive-In Theater, and Snow Shack shaved ice stand.

PALO DURO CANYON GLAMPING

4

11450 Park Road 5, Canyon, TX 79015

HIGHLIGHTS

Capital: Austin

Total National Parks: 2 (Big Bend National Park and Guadalupe Mountains National Park)

Total State Parks: 89 (Largest is Big Bend Ranch State Park)

State Bird: Mockingbird

State Flower: Bluebonnet

State Large Animal: Texas longhorn

Wildlife Spotting: Black bears; armadillos; coyotes; cougars; jaguarundis (endangered); tiger salamanders; leopard frogs; screech owls; hummingbirds; broad-winged hawks; Acadian and great crested flycatchers; wood thrush; gray catbirds; American redstarts

Open: Year-round ▪ Rates: From $299 ▪ Amenities: Kitchenettes, grills, fire pits, heating and air-conditioning, luggage service, board games, bikes, hamburger kits, camp store ▪ ADA sites: No

From Comanche war parties to Charlie Goodnight of cattle-driving fame, people have been camping out in Palo Duro Canyon for centuries. Sleeping under the stars inside this massive gap in the Texas Panhandle is nothing new. But glamping is—comfy tent cabins with wooden walls and canvas roofs. All of them are equipped with sturdy wooden beds, kitchenettes, dining tables, lounge areas, heating and air-conditioning, and porches with rocking chairs. Located near the upper end of the 800-foot (243 m) deep canyon, the glampground is close to hiking, biking, and equestrian trails that meander through a red-rock landscape dubbed the "Grand Canyon of Texas." If glamping is full, Palo Duro

State Park offers seven campgrounds as well as the historic Rim and Cow Camp cabins.

DAVIS MOUNTAINS STATE PARK

🚐/⛺ 26 full hookup, 34 partial hookup, 33 no hookup

State Highway 118, Fort Davis, TX 79734

Open: Year-round ▪ Rates: RV/tent full hookup $25, RV/tent partial hookup $20, RV/tent no hookup $15 ▪ Amenities: Dump station, showers, picnic tables, grills and fire pits, gift shop ▪ ADA sites: Call ahead

Rising like a tree-filled island amid the Chihuahuan Desert, the Davis Mountains of West Texas offer a refreshing respite from the surrounding "No Country for Old Men" (yes, the movie was filmed nearby). The campground stretches along a valley shaded by a lush oak-juniper forest between the state park entrance and the historic Indian Lodge hotel, plus nearly 100

RV and tent sites with a blend of hookups. Skyline Drive snakes its way to a lofty viewpoint above the valley, as do hiking routes like the Montezuma Quail Trail and Limpia Creek Trail that start beside the campground. Human and natural history programs are offered at the nearby Interpretive Center and outdoor amphitheater, while a variety of birds are attracted to feeders at the Wildlife Viewing Area. Campers can dig into a hearty breakfast or lunch at the lodge's Black Bear Restaurant. Nearby attractions include night-sky shows at McDonald Observatory, the old cavalry post at Fort Davis National Historic Site, and an old-time soda fountain and burger joint called the Drug Store in Fort Davis town.

TERLINGUA GHOST TOWN CASITAS

🏠 3

100 Ivey Road, Terlingua, TX 79852

Open: Year-round ▪ Rates: From $245 ▪ Amenities: Kitchens, private

bathrooms, dining tables, fireplaces, heating and air-conditioning, barbecue grills, fire pits, internet ▪ ADA sites: No

For anyone who has ever dreamed of spending the night in a bona fide ghost town, this is your chance. Located in the wilds of West Texas, Terlingua was a quicksilver boom town until the 1930s when the ore petered out. Bill Ivey purchased the entire town in the 1980s, gradually transforming the adobe ruins into a variety of overnight digs that include three restored casitas with a blend of Southwest, Mexican, and Native American decor. Given the antique plumbing, the toilets and showers are detached (but fully modernized). Patios offer views over a town that once housed 3,000 souls, many of them refugees from the Mexican revolutions. Just down the road are the Terlingua Trading Company store (which includes a small museum), a cool little breakfast spot called Espresso Y Poco Mas, and the Starlight Theatre restaurant inside the old cinema. A self-guided tour leads to ghost town landmarks like the Perry Mansion and Santa Inez Church.

RIO GRANDE CANOE CAMPING

⛺ remote riverside

Rio Grande River, Big Bend National Park, TX 79852

Open: Year-round ▪ Rates: From $399 (two days) ▪ Amenities: Canoes and rafts, life jackets, dry bags, tents, potable water, all meals on the river, rental sleeping bags and sleeping pads ▪ ADA sites: No

Flanked by sheer 1,500-foot (457 m) cliffs on both the U.S. and Mexican sides, Santa Elena Canyon offers

Make camp on the beach of Padre Island National Seashore.

The Country Woods Inn offers lodging in vintage trailers, and even a refurbished railroad car.

the ultimate river camping adventure. The standard trip offered by Far Flung Outdoor Center and other local outfitters is a two-day, one-night voyage along the Rio Grande through the canyon, with a hike up Fern Canyon and overnight at Arches. The canyon supports plenty of bird life, as well as aoudad mountain sheep, Big Bend slider turtles, and catfish. With a put-in at Lajitas and a take-out near Cottonwood/Castolon in Big Bend National Park, the total journey is between 19 and 25 miles (30 and 40 km) depending on how far you paddle beyond the canyon mouth. During the winter dry season—when the Rio Grande is often shallow enough to wade across—a

"boomerang" trip is the best bet: venturing upstream on day one, downstream on day two. The choice of watercraft also varies with the seasons: rafts during high water, canoes or kayaks during low. Far Flung also offers longer, more ambitious river trips through Mariscal and Boquillas canyons farther down the river.

ROOSEVELT STONE COTTAGES
🏠6

Basin Junction Road, Big Bend National Park, TX 79834
Open: Year-round ▪ Rate: $176 ▪ Amenities: Private bathrooms, mini-fridges, microwaves, ceiling fans, heaters, dining tables, patios with chairs ▪ ADA sites: Call ahead

In the early 1940s, when Big Bend was still a state park, the Civilian Conservation Corps arrived in the secluded Chisos Basin and constructed a handful of sturdy stone-and-adobe cabins along the Lost Mine Trail. They christened the cabins for FDR, the president who established the agency to combat the Great Depression. Eighty years on, the Roosevelt Cottages are still the coolest place to overnight in the huge national park. The digs are modest but charming, with Western-style furnishings emblazoned with the Texas lone star. But the views of the Window, Casa Grande Peak, and other geological features around the ancient volcanic basin are spectacular. A trailhead beside the cabins

Follow trails through the high desert for scenic overlooks of Davis Mountains State Park.

offers quick and easy access to the Basin Loop, Pinnacles, and Laguna Meadow trails through the basin's distinctive fusion of evergreen forest and desert plants. If the cottages are booked, accommodation is also available at the motel-style Chisos Mountain Lodge or Basin Campground. Meals are available at the lodge restaurant and basin convenience store.

COLLECTIVE HILL COUNTRY
🏕 12

7431 Fulton Ranch Road, Wimberley, TX 78676

Open: Year-round ▪ Rates: From $269 ▪ Amenities: Restaurant, wine bar, private bathroom with shower, heating and air-conditioning, horseback riding, electric bikes, Pilates, yoga, meditation sessions ▪ ADA sites: No

In keeping with Austin's hipster image, the surrounding Hill Country offers more than its fair share of glamping options. Exceptional cuisine, posh safari tents, and a range of new age activities help Collective stand out from the crowd. But the thing that really makes it special is a location on Montesino Ranch, a 225-acre (91 ha) working spread that sprawls across the Wimberley Valley. Glampers can spend the day roaming the ranch on foot, bike, or horseback before returning to camp for "live sound" meditation with singing bowls or culinary treats like a charcuterie spread, champagne, or romantic fondue for two.

MALAQUITE CAMPGROUND
🚐/🏕 48 no hookup

20420 Park Road 22, Padre Island National Seashore, Corpus Christi, TX 78418

Open: Year-round ▪ Rate: $14 ▪

Amenities: Dump station, restrooms, showers, beach, picnic tables, grills, shade structures, potable water ▪ ADA sites: Partial

Less than an hour from downtown Corpus Christi, Malaquite is one of only two developed campgrounds at Padre Island National Seashore. On the island's Gulf of Mexico side, it's the park's most family-friendly overnight spot, within short walking distance of a visitors center with natural history exhibits, interpretive programs, and a Junior Ranger program. The beach beside the campground is one of the few in the park where vehicles are verboten. Beyond the paved RV and tent sites, tent camping is allowed along the sandy shore beside shade structures with picnic tables. Campers questing a more secluded experience can obtain a permit to bivouac primitive style along 60 miles (96 km) of South Beach stretching down the Gulf Coast.

STELLA MARE RV RESORT
🏠 2, 🚐/🏕 195 full hookup

3418 Stella Mare Lane, Galveston, TX 77554

Open: Year-round ▪ Rates: RV from $69, cabins from $400 ▪ Amenities: Clubhouse, swimming pool, hot tub, kids' splash pad, showers, laundry, TV lounge, playground, sports courts, dog parks, internet, community grills, fire rings, picnic tables ▪ ADA sites: Yes

Stella Mare sets a tropical holiday mood with palm trees, tiki huts, a spacious swimming pool, and a Galveston Island beach that's just steps away. The RV-only sites are a bit tight, especially for those who tow a vehicle behind their motor home. With the great outdoors all around, there's a temptation to spend as much time as possible beachcombing, sport fishing, shopping the Strand, or discovering local landmarks like the Galveston Pleasure Pier, 19th-century tall ship *Elissa*, or the 1894 Opera House. Stella Mare also rents two large vacation homes—Sunny Smile and Into the Blue—each equipped with four bedrooms, three and a half baths, wraparound decks, and full kitchens. ▪

SOMETHING SPECIAL

Padre Island National Seashore

Padre Island National Seashore, set on the southern Texas coast just minutes from the city of Corpus Christi, protects the largest tract of undeveloped barrier island in the world. The park safeguards the great majority of this fragile and beautiful strip of beach, dunes, and grassland from permanent intrusion of vacation houses, resorts, and towns.

Visitors crowd the park's easily accessible Malaquite Beach area in the warm months for swimming and sunbathing on the Gulf of Mexico. But beyond this popular sand-and-surf spot stretch miles and miles of undeveloped beach offering solitude for swimming, camping, fishing, walking, bird watching, and searching for seashells. Most of this beachfront is accessible only via an off-road vehicle and may require a permit.

Utah

With its plethora of national and state parks and wide array of landscapes—from snowcapped mountains to sandstone arches to sandy deserts—Utah is a camper's paradise.

CONESTOGA RANCH

🏕 27, 14 Conestoga wagons
427 North Paradise Parkway, Garden City, UT 84028
Open: May to September ▪ Rates: Wagons from $206, glamping tents from $186 ▪ Amenities: Restaurant, camp store, bathhouse, free bikes, campfire valet, luggage porter, linen service, internet, playground, lawn games, volleyball/badminton court, laundry, game tent, yoga, massage ▪ ADA sites: Yes

Time-travel back to pioneer days at a unique northern Utah glamping resort that offers overnights in modern versions of the Conestoga wagons that once rolled the American frontier. Truth be told, they're a tad larger than the 19th-century versions—big enough for a king-size bed and one or two bunk beds, plus a seating area. Like the Conestogas of old, these wagons are mobile; guests can have them relocated anywhere on the property, and groups of family or friends can even circle the wagons around a campfire. The ranch also boasts luxury glamping tents, some of them with en suite bathrooms with full-size showers and/or bathtubs. Conestoga Ranch overlooks Bear Lake in a part of Utah that's far more Rocky Mountains than Southwest desert. The resort can arrange power boating,

Under Canvas Moab is a glamorous way to spend a weekend in the desert.

sailing, kayaking, waterskiing, fishing, and other aquatic activities through partner Epic Recreation. Hiking, biking, horseback riding, cave exploration, and fossil hunting at Fish Dig Quarry count among the other options. Glampers can make their own meals at kitchen tents scattered around the property or dine at the Campfire Grill, where the menu includes steak, burgers, seafood, pizza, salads, and pulled pork biscuits.

BRIDGER BAY CAMPGROUND

🚐/🏕 26 no hookup
4528 West 1700 South, Syracuse, UT 84075
Open: Year-round ▪ Rate: RV/tent $20 ▪ Amenities: Dump station, showers, fire pits, picnic tables, potable water, firewood, shade structures ▪ ADA sites: Yes

Antelope Island affords a rare chance to sleep beside the Great Salt Lake. Largest of the island's three state park campgrounds, Bridger offers RV/tent sites within walking distance of the lakeshore. The environment is bleak: salt flats, sagebrush, and wild grass with a few scattered trees. But you're not there for the vegetation. The largest saltwater lake in the Western Hemisphere beckons campers who bring their own watercraft or pose for a classic photo of floating in the lake while reading a book or

newspaper. Connected to the mainland by a long causeway, the state park also offers hiking, mountain biking, the historic Fielding Garr Ranch House (built in 1848), and guided tours with Antelope Ebikes. Among the wildlife are bighorn sheep, Utah's biggest bison herd, and the pronghorn antelope that give the island its name.

MIRROR LAKE CAMPGROUND

🚐/🏕 78 no hookup
State Highway 150, Kamas, UT 84032
Open: July to September ▪ Rate: RV/tents $24 ▪ Amenities: Restrooms, picnic tables, potable water, boat ramp, nature trail, firewood; no dump station or showers ▪ ADA sites: Yes

It's only 90 minutes from downtown Salt Lake City, but feels like a million miles away, a waterfront Forest Service campground in the Uinta Mountains. Many of the sites are a stone's throw from the lake, which, true to its name, is often smooth as glass. Those who don't mind chilly alpine water might want to take a dip; otherwise, cast a fishing line or slide a kayak into the water. There's a trail around the lakeshore, and many more in Uinta-Wasatch-Cache National Forest. With feed boxes and hitching posts, a dozen campsites are reserved for equestrian use—horses, mules, donkeys, even llamas.

DEVILS GARDEN CAMPGROUND

 51 no hookup

Campground Road, Arches National Park, Moab, UT 84532

Open: Year-round ▪ Rate: RV/tents $25 ▪ Amenities: Restrooms, picnic tables, fire pits with grills, potable water, amphitheater, firewood ▪ ADA sites: Yes

---

MORE TO CONSIDER

- **Abajo Haven Guest Cabins:** Located just outside the Navajo Nation in southeast Utah, Abajo Haven offers a rustic ideal base for exploring Canyons of the Ancients and the Four Corners region. *abajohaven.com*

- **Sorrel River Ranch & Spa:** Celebrities flock to this upscale cabin resort on the Colorado River about 30 minutes from Moab. Posh waterfront cabins run $649 to $1,699. *sorrelriver.com/rooms/*

- **Coral Pink Sand Dunes State Park:** Pink, orange, and ocher dunes make this southern Utah state park a truly surreal place to camp. *stateparks.utah.gov/parks/coral-pink/*

- **Cataract Canyon:** Navtec Expeditions offers one- to four-night white-water camping trips down the Colorado River through Cataract Canyon in Canyonlands National Park. *navtec.com/*

Surrounded by colossal rock formations, Devils Garden lies in the deepest part of Arches National Park, 18 miles (29 km) from the entrance station. Many of the campsites rest between "fins"—narrow red-rock walls that will someday erode into the park's emblematic arches. Splashes of green against the ruddy stone, pinyon pines and juniper trees offer a modicum of shade. Spring through fall, rangers host presentations at the campground amphitheater. Given the high altitude and the super-clear skies of southeast Utah, Devils Garden is also an awesome place to ponder the night sky. The nearby Devils Garden Trail leads to some of the park's most astonishing landmarks, including Landscape Arch, the longest natural stone arch in North America at 306 feet (93.3 m).

WINGATE CAMPGROUND

🚐/🏕 20 partial hookup, 🏕 11, 🛖 4

State Highway 313, Moab, UT 84532

Open: Year-round ▪ Rates: RV/tent sites from $40, tent only sites from $35, yurts from $120 ▪ Amenities: Dump station, restrooms, fire pits, picnic tables, shade structures, dishwashing sinks ▪ ADA sites: Yes

Dead Horse Point State Park balances on a narrow stone escarpment along the eastern edge of Canyonlands. Wingate is the larger of its two campgrounds and the only one that features yurts in addition to RV and tent sites. It's a short walk from the campsites to vertigo-inducing rim overlooks along the western edge of the escarpment with their stunning sunsets and dramatic views down into Shafer Canyon. It's about a half-hour hike (or five-minute drive) to Dead Horse Point, poised

Mirror Lake offers scenic camping—and pet-friendly sites too.

How the West was fun! Relive it all at Conestoga Ranch, where you can glamp in covered wagons.

high above the Colorado River and the cliff where the final scene of *Thelma & Louise* was filmed. Wingate is a terrific alternative if the campgrounds in Arches and Canyonlands national parks are full.

UNDER CANVAS MOAB
🏕 41

13784 U.S. Highway 191, Moab, UT 84532

Open: March to October ▪ Rates: From $219 ▪ Amenities: Restaurant, daily housekeeping, organic bath products, adventure concierge ▪ ADA sites: Call ahead

Desert glamping doesn't get any better than this: high-end safari tents with king-size beds, private bathrooms, and stylish West Elm furnishings, some of them outfitted

with skylights for gazing at the stars and planets from the cozy comfort of your own bed. The kitchen tent creates tasty grab-and-go breakfast and lunch, while communal barbecues serve guests who want to rustle up their own grub. Another big plus is a strategic location between Arches and Canyonlands National Parks, and just up the road from Moab with its Colorado River activities and eclectic restaurant scene.

FRUITA CAMPGROUND
🚐/🏕 64 no hookup, 🏕 7

Camp Ground Road, Capitol Reef National Park, Torrey, UT 84775

Open: Year-round ▪ Rate: RV/tent sites $20 ▪ Amenities: Dump station, restrooms, fire pits and grills, picnic tables, potable water, amphitheater ▪ ADA sites: Yes

Nature and history combine in sublime form at this leafy campground in Capitol Reef National Park. Set along the Fremont River, the site was pioneered by Mormon settlers in the 1880s who planted the fruit trees that give the campground its name. The orchards are still there—campers can pick the apples, pears, and other fruit for free—as are historic structures like the Gifford House, Gifford Barn, and a one-room schoolhouse. Together they form the Fruita Rural Historical District. The Capitol Reef Natural History Association runs a store in Gifford House that sells reproduction pioneer items like cooking utensils, rag dolls, candles, and quilts, as well as pies, jams, and dried fruit made with items from the nearby orchards. Gifford House

Park the RV at Devils Garden Campground for a stunning spot surrounded by the sandstone structures of Arches National Park.

is also the meeting point for ranger-led porch talks and star walks. A trail along the river connects the campground with Ripple Rock Nature Center and the Capitol Reef Visitor Center, while the Cohab Canyon Trail climbs switchbacks to bird's-eye views of Fruita.

BASIN CAMPGROUND

🚐/🏕 15 full hookup, 21 no hookup

Cottonwood Canyon Road, Cannonville, UT 84718

Open: April to November ▪ Rates: RV/tent full hookup $35, RV/tent no hookup $25 ▪ Amenities: Dump station, showers, fire pits with grills, picnic tables, potable water, firewood, dishwashing station, laundry ▪ ADA sites: Yes

With so many amazing national parks, campers tend to forget that Utah also boasts a number of incredible state parks. One of those is Kodachrome Basin near Cannonville, named by members of a 1948 National Geographic Society expedition who figured the area's multicolored stone was just as vivid as the legendary slide film. Flanked by chromatic cliffs, Basin Campground lies near the head of a long canyon that forms the heart of the park. RV and tent spaces are well spaced and partially shaded by both the canyon walls and the pinyon pines and junipers scattered throughout the campground. Easily accessible from the campground, trails lead through a fantasyland of monolithic stone spires formed over the past 180 million years. Most are hiker only, but several of the longer trails allow mountain bikes and horses.

BRYCE CANYON LODGE WESTERN CABINS

🏠 15

State Highway 63, Bryce Canyon National Park, UT 84764

Open: April to October ▪ Rate: $231 ▪ Amenities: Restaurants, camp store, gift shop, horseback riding, heating and fan ▪ ADA sites: No

Designed by famed architect Gilbert Stanley Underwood and located near one of the most scenic points along the rim, these historic stone-and-log cabins were erected during the 1920s not long after Bruce Canyon was declared a national park. They've been modernized, of course, and each unit now features two queen-size beds, full bathroom with shower and tub, gas-log fireplace, microwave, and mini-fridge. Cabin dwellers can dine at the main restaurant, pizzeria, or coffee shop in the adjacent lodge, which also harbors a gift shop and a general store with groceries and grab-and-go meals.

ZION PONDEROSA RANCH RESORT

🏠 32, 🚐 13 full hookup, 3 no hookup, 🏕 55, 🏕 22, 6 wagons

Twin Knolls Road, Orderville, UT 84758

Open: Year-round ▪ Rates: Cabins from $151, glamping tents from $129, RV full hookup from $69, covered wagons from $149, tent sites from $29 ▪ Amenities: Restaurants, coffee bar, showers, grills, picnic tables, laundry, internet, swimming pool, hot tubs, miniature golf, climbing wall, game room, tennis courts ▪ ADA sites: Partial

Set at 6,500 feet (2,000 m) in the rugged high country just east of Zion National Park, this sprawling resort covers just about every base: upscale and rustic cabins, glamping tents, covered wagons, tent sites, and full-hookup RV sites. Adventure activities range from 4x4 tours, guided hikes, and canyoneering to horseback riding, paintball, skeet shooting, and sunset yoga sessions. For those who want to explore on their own, the ranch is close to trailheads for the national park's East Rim and East Mesa trails, as well as the upper reaches of the Narrows along the Virgin River. ■

SOMETHING SPECIAL

Zion National Park

Although other great canyons awe with their sheer size, Zion, a relatively small national park, stuns in a much more subtle manner, with artistry rather than magnitude—rock canvases and stone sculptures that seem crafted by some ancient Michelangelo rather than the whim and fancy of nature.

The Mormon settlers who pioneered southern Utah from the 1850s to 1860s thought the canyon was heaven sent. They named it after a biblical place of peace and endowed many of its natural features with spiritual appellations such as Great White Throne, Angels Landing, and Altar of Sacrifice.

The forces of nature—in particular, floods—kept the canyon from being heavily settled and retained its atmosphere of secrecy. President William Howard Taft gave it federal protection as Mukuntuweap National Monument in 1909; 10 years later it was renamed and elevated to national park status.

Vermont

Peek out of your tent to see the magical wonders of Vermont's rolling hills, stunning Lake Champlain, and Green Mountain vistas at these campgrounds.

LIMEHURST LAKE CAMPGROUND

🏚 3, 🚐/🏕 21 full hookup, 11 partial hookup, 🏕 10, 3 lean-tos
4104 State Route 14, Williamstown, VT 05679
Open: May to October ▪ Rates: RV/tent full hookup $50, RV/tent partial hookup $45, tent only $30, cabins from $69, lean-tos $37 ▪ Amenities: Camp store, snack bar, dump station, showers, laundry, picnic tables, fire rings with grills, propane, playground, game room, boat rentals, swimming beach, lawn games, dog run, cable TV ▪ ADA sites: No

In good New England fashion, the trees around the lakeshore at Limehurst Lake Campground are a riot of color come fall. But with a swimming beach, boat rentals, and full-hookup RV and tent-only sites right along the water, Limehurst Lake is a pretty cool place to camp in summer too. Nearly dead center in the middle of the state, it's also close to some of Vermont's most beloved vacation attractions, from the golden-domed state capitol building in nearby Montpelier and the granite quarries and museum in Barre to factory tours (and tastings) at Ben & Jerry's, the SkyRide gondolas at Stowe, and hiking in Green Mountain National Forest.

Book a stay in the Sugar Shack at Crofter's Green Cabins.

STERLING RIDGE RESORT

🏚 23
155 Sterling Ridge Drive, Jeffersonville, VT 05464
Open: Year-round ▪ Rates: From $155 ▪ Amenities: Full kitchens, private bathrooms, bedding and towels, woodstoves or fireplaces, air-conditioning, private porch, outdoor grills and fire pits, swimming pool, canoes and kayaks, flat-screen TVs, cable TV, internet ▪ ADA sites: No

Vermont's scenic Lamoille River Valley is the backdrop for a backwoods resort with a range of indoor camping options, from two-person log cabins to the two-bedroom luxury Field & Stream cabin originally built for a magazine feature in the eponymous periodical. Maple sap lines scattered around the grounds provide the raw ingredient for the resort's own brand of pure maple syrup and granular sugar. Open through all four seasons, Sterling Ridge is just minutes away from winter fun at Smuggler's Notch and Stowe, prime resort centers for fantastic East Coast skiing and snowboarding. During the warmer months, campers can mosey across the Grist Mill Covered Bridge to a swimming hole in Brewster River Park or hook up with Vermont Canoe & Kayak for a float trip down the Lamoille. Numerous hiking and biking trails also surround the campground.

CROFTER'S GREEN

🏚 5
2956 Mountain Road, Montgomery Center, VT 05471
Open: Year-round ▪ Rates: From $169 ▪ Amenities: Kitchens, private bathrooms, bedding and towels, flat-screen TVs, communal hot tub, communal barbecue grill and fire pit, lawn games, cable TV, internet ▪ ADA sites: No

Tucked up near the Quebec border, Crofter's Green offers a trip around the world in cottages decorated with Japanese, Irish, Santa Fe, Caribbean, and Vermont themes. Set around a large, grassy space, the units feature queen beds, kitchens, bathrooms, dining table, and deck seating. Guests share the communal hot tub, fire pit, and barbecue area. Beyond the green, Crofter's offers 25 acres (10 ha) of Vermont woods. More trails await in nearby Jay State Forest and Hazens Notch State Park. Or pack your passport and launch a day trip into Canada via the tiny North Troy border crossing.

TYLER PLACE FAMILY RESORT

🏠 45

175 Tyler Place, Swanton, VT 05488
Open: May to September ▪ Rates:
From $146 per person ▪ Amenities:
Restaurant, bar, kitchenettes, private bathrooms, screened porches, swimming pools, hot tubs, splash pad, sports courts, fitness center, arts and crafts studio, playgrounds, trampolines, driving range, miniature golf, climbing wall, yoga, boats, bikes, archery, skeet, spa treatments ▪ ADA sites: Yes

This all-inclusive cabin resort on Lake Champlain makes it easy for parents by providing all meals and a daily children's program divided into 10 age groups from babies to teens. Good-old hiking, biking, and swimming are complemented by modern activities like rock climbing, paddleboarding, and banana boats. In addition to a mile of private lakeshore, Tyler Place is surrounded by 165 acres (66 ha) of fields and forest for kids to run amok. From water sports and tennis to spa treatments and evening cocktails with live jazz, the resort also offers plenty of ways for parents to while away lazy days beside the lake. Cabins range from one to four bedrooms, and most include living rooms, kitchenettes, and screened porches.

GRAND ISLE STATE PARK

🏠 4, 🚐/⛺ 115 no hookup, 36 lean-tos

36 East Shore South, Grand Isle, VT 05458
Open: May to October ▪ Rates: RV/tent from $19/$21 (state resident/nonresident), lean-tos from $28/$30, cabins $51/$53 ▪ Amenities: Dump station, showers, picnic tables, fire rings with grills, potable water, sand volleyball, swimming beach, boat ramp ▪ ADA sites: Yes

Lake Champlain's largest island is home to the most popular campground in Vermont's state park system. While motor homes, camper vans, and tents are certainly welcome, Grand Isle is also bullish on lean-tos—three-sided huts on wooden platforms with bare floors to spread your sleeping bags and dirt "front yards" with picnic tables and fire pits. Unlike most of the campsites at Grand Isle, which are set back in the woods, about half of the lean-tos are right on the lakeshore. Like many other Vermont state parks, Grand Isle also boasts an official ranger interpreter in charge of arranging summertime family programs and answering questions about the park's natural and human history.

BUTTON BAY STATE PARK

🏠 4, 🚐/⛺ 53 no hookup, 13 lean-tos

5 Button Bay State Park Road, Ferrisburgh, VT 05491
Open: May to October ▪ Rates: RV/tent from $19/$21 (state resident/nonresident), lean-tos from $28/$30, cabins $51/$53 ▪ Amenities: Dump station, showers, picnic tables, fire rings with grills, firewood, potable water, swimming pool, playground, boat ramp, horseshoes ▪ ADA sites: Yes

Located around 30 miles (48 km) south of Burlington along the eastern shore of Lake Champlain, Button Bay is that rare Vermont state park that enhances an incredible natural setting with human contraptions—in this case, a swimming pool staffed by lifeguards during the season. Only a handful of cabins and premium campsites overlook the water, but none of them are far away from a bay

Campers can make the most of the shores of Lake Champlain at Grand Isle State Park.

Sterling Ridge Resort offers 370 acres (149.7 ha) to explore during your comfortable, woodsy cabin retreat.

named for the button-like clay concretions—many of them with perfectly round holes—that garnish the shore. For campers who want to flit over to the western shore (upstate New York), the bridge between Chimney Point and Crown Point is a pastoral 20-minute drive south of Button Bay.

ROBERT FROST MOUNTAIN CABINS

🏠 7

2430 North Branch Road, Ripton, VT 05766

Open: Year-round ▪ Rates: From $189 ▪ Amenities: Full kitchens, private bathrooms, bedding and towels, fireplaces, screened porches, barbecue grill, air-conditioning, DVD players and flat-screen TVs, laundry, communal hot tub, hammocks, snowshoes, internet ▪ ADA sites: Yes

"The woods are lovely, dark and deep," wrote Robert Frost in one of the poems he penned during 40-plus years of living and writing in Vermont. Right up the road from his long-time Ripton home, Robert Frost Mountain Cabins pays homage to the state's poet laureate and the Green Mountain nature manifest in so much of his work. All of the cabins are handcrafted to perfection, the trees milled on-site to construct the wooden floors, beamed ceilings, reading nooks, and other woodsy features. Guests gather in the morning and evening at The Loft, a common area with books, maps, games, puzzles, and stimulating conversation. Prebuilt campfires and complimentary firewood, along with Mountain Grove Coffee, tea, and hot cocoa are regularly supplied. And the campground offers flower gardens, berry bushes, and a frog pond to explore—not to mention snowshoes, YakTrax, and sleds for rent. Discount tickets to the Rikert Nordic ski area and Middlebury Snow Bowl are available. And everyone should make a point of visiting Homer Noble Farm to see the tiny wood-framed cabin where Frost penned five volumes of poetry, including the Pulitzer Prize–winning *A Witness Tree.*

Look out over Lake Dunmore from rocky outposts on the Rattlesnake Cliffs in Moosalamoo National Recreation Area.

MOOSALAMOO CAMPGROUND

🚐 / 🏕 19 no hookup

Forest Road 24, off the Goshen-Ripton Road, Salisbury, VT 05769

Open: May to October ▪ Rate: $15 ▪ Amenities: Restrooms, picnic tables, fire rings with grills, potable water, playing field, interpretive trail ▪ ADA sites: Partial

It's not the biggest or best-equipped campground in Green Mountain National Forest, but Moosalamoo is one of Vermont's most cherished overnight spots. That's because it lies in a national recreation area of the same name with more than 70 miles (112 km) of wilderness trails and a variety of outdoor activities that range from harvesting blueberries, raspberries, and wild apples to hiking, biking, and horseback riding. The well-shaded campsites can handle tents or RVs up to 20 feet (6 m) long. High above the campground, Mount Moosalamoo and the Rattlesnake Cliffs afford bird's-eye views of distant Lake Champlain and Lake George. And, yes, the name does refer to the big antlered creatures that occasionally wander through the campground, a derivation of the Abenaki word *mozalômo* ("moose call").

HALF MOON POND STATE PARK

📞 6, 🚐 / 🏕 52 no hookup, 11 lean-tos

1621 Black Pond Road, Hubbardton, VT 05743

Open: May to October ▪ Rates: RV/tent from $19/$21 (state resident/nonresident), lean-tos from $28/$30, cabins from $51/$53 ▪ Amenities: Dump station, showers, picnic tables, fire rings with grills, potable water, playground, boat rental, boat ramp, swimming beaches, volleyball, horseshoes ▪ ADA sites: Yes

Nestled away in the forests of 3,500-acre (1,416.4-ha) Bomoseen State Park, primitive campsites, a good number of RV and tent sites, wooden lean-tos, and cabins are the overnight options at this remote spot in the woods of southern Vermont. Or splash out on Tall Timbers Cottage, a two-story waterfront abode with a screened-in back porch overlooking the lake and its own boat dock. Canoes, kayaks, and other nonmotorized watercraft are available for rent at the park office for those who want to fish for perch, bass, and panfish or simply cruise around a tranquil water body that resembles the back-to-nature vibe of legendary Walden Pond. Two small beaches expedite swimming, and a couple of forest trails lead to ponds that are even more secluded.

GREENWOOD LODGE & CAMPSITES

🚐 / 🏕 40 partial hookup

311 Greenwood Drive, Woodford, VT 05201

Open: May to October ▪ Rates: From $40 ▪ Amenities: Dump station, showers, picnic tables, fire rings, firewood, ice, sports courts, playing field, rec room, boat rental, self-service RV wash, dog run, internet ▪ ADA sites: Partial

On the outskirts of Bennington, where the Green Mountain Boys battled the redcoats in 1777, Greenwood Lodge is enveloped by rugged woodland that seems little changed since Revolutionary War days. Campsites spread around the edge of a meadow that also harbors the lodge and two of the resort's three ponds. But the property is large enough (120 acre/48 ha) for quiet walks in a forest that blends spruce, fir, and birch trees. Or make time for fishing, boating, and swimming throughout the expansive property. Campers seeking a more strenuous hike can wander into neighboring George Aiken Wilderness Area or a stretch of the Appalachian Trail that runs its course through the Green Mountains. Out on Highway 9, Woodford General Store sells provisions and gas. ▪

SOMETHING SPECIAL

Island Complex

A string of bucolic islands in Lake Champlain, Vermont's island complex comprises three unusual state parks. Accessible only by state-run ferry or private boat, these three isles—Burton, Knight, and Woods—provide different levels of escape for day and overnight visitors.

Burton is the string's largest and most developed island, where most visitors head. If you're searching for a more remote experience, try Knight Island, dotted with small ponds and primitive camping sites, or undeveloped Woods Island—reachable only by private boat.

All three islands were farmed extensively from the early 1800s to early 1960s, when the state acquired the land. Original plans called for building a causeway, but plans were scrapped, and the islands have remained vehicle free. Today the former farm fields contain trails that pass by remnants of stone fences, evidence of abandoned corn and bean fields, and even old foundations and farm implements.

Virginia

These campgrounds put your RV or tent near many of Virginia's treasures, including the Luray Caverns, Colonial Williamsburg (and the nearby amusement park), Virginia Beach, and Shenandoah National Park.

FIRST LANDING STATE PARK

🏚20, 🚐/🏕 108 partial hookup, 🏕 80, 🛖 4

2500 Shore Drive, Virginia Beach, VA 23451

Open: March to December ▪ Rates: RV/tent partial hookup $40/$46 (state resident/nonresident), tent only $30/$35, cabins from $137/$158, yurts $75/$88 ▪ Amenities: Camp store, snack bar, dump station, showers, laundry, picnic tables, fire rings with grills, firewood, ice, potable water, playgrounds, beach, boat ramps, amphitheater ▪ ADA sites: Partial

The English settlers who would later establish Jamestown first stepped ashore in the Americas at Cape Henry on April 26, 1607. The state park preserves a patch of Virginia coastal wilderness similar to what those earlier colonists would have encountered during their three-day stay before sailing up the James River. The campground hugs the shore of Chesapeake Bay, its yurts perched atop bayside dunes. The state park cabins—built in the 1930s and on the National Register of Historic Places—are scattered through the woods on the other side of Shore Drive.

While the beach is undoubtedly the main attraction, campers can venture inland on trails through the

The tree houses at Primland Resort look out over the Kibler Valley.

park's mix of maritime forest, cypress swamp, and salt marsh. Running all the way across the park to Atlantic beaches, the 6-mile (9.6 km) Cape Henry Trail features displays on Native American life in Tidewater Virginia around the time of the First Landing.

CHIPPOKES PLANTATION

🏚4, 🚐/🏕 50 partial hookup, 🛖 3, 🏠1

695 Chippokes Park Road, Surry, VA 23883

Open: March to December ▪ Rates: RV/tent partial hookup $35/$40 (state resident/nonresident), cabins from $110/127, yurts $75/$88, historic house from $291/$334 ▪ Amenities: Camp store, snack bar, dump station, showers, picnic tables, fire rings with grills, firewood, potable water, lantern posts, swimming pool, playground, amphitheater ▪ ADA sites: Yes

Perched on the south bank of the James River opposite Jamestown, this state historic park preserves one of the nation's oldest continuously operating farms. From the wealthy planters who occupied the park's well-preserved plantation house to the workers who lived in the ruined slave quarters, people have been growing crops and raising livestock on the site since the early 17th century. A crop garden and heritage breed program maintained by the

park's Farm & Forest Museum showcase some of the foods and animals that early residents would have tended. The double-looped campground rambles through woods near the park's western edge, a short walk from the swimming pool complex, visitors center, and gift shop. Visitors can also overnight in one- to three-bedroom cabins, as well as the historic 1770 Walnut Valley House, which can sleep eight.

WILLIAMSBURG/BUSCH GARDENS AREA KOA

🏚44, 🚐/🏕 104 full hookup, 20 partial hookup, 🏕 17, 🛖 2

4000 Newman Road, Williamsburg, VA 23188

Open: March to December ▪ Rates: RV full hookup from $66, RV partial hookup from $62, tent only from $46, cabins from $70, yurts from $113 ▪ Amenities: Camp store, snack bar, dump station, showers, laundry, picnic tables, fire rings with grills, firewood, propane, swimming pool, splash pad, playground, sports courts, bike rental, disc golf, electric vehicle charging stations, dog park, cable TV, internet ▪ ADA sites: Yes

This sprawling KOA attracts two entirely different breeds of camper: individuals with an abiding interest in American history and families seeking theme-park fun at Busch Gardens. While most of the sites feature full hookups for even the largest RVs, the campground also offers nearly four dozen cabins, a tent-only area, and even a couple of yurts. The resort offers Kamp K9 dog sitting, as well as offbeat activities like a gem mining sluice and Gravity Rail playground attraction.

OAK RIDGE CAMPGROUND

🚐/🏕 67 no hookup, 🏕 33
6975 Oak Ridge Road, Triangle, VA 22172
Open: March to November ▪ Rate: $26 ▪ Amenities: Showers,

picnic tables, fire rings with grills, lantern posts, amphitheater ▪ ADA sites: Yes

Prince William Forest Park on the outskirts of the Washington, D.C., metro area provides a leafy venue for this laid-back National Park Service campground. The park boasts an interesting history, a one-time refuge for freed slaves and site of a World War II espionage training center. Oak Ridge campsites are totally dry (no hookups), with Loop C reserved exclusively for tents. Three hiking routes start beside the campground pay station: Farms to Forest Trail, South Valley Trail, and Oak Ridge Trail. Those in search of more solitude can trek to a small backcountry campground in the Chopawamsic Area.

#1 ROCK TAVERN RIVER KAMP

🏚2, 🏕 varies, 🏛 6
1420 South Page Valley Road, Luray, VA 22835

Open: Year-round ▪ Rates: Yurts from $131, cabins from $185, tents $45 ▪ Amenities: Kitchenettes, bathhouse, picnic tables, fire rings with grills, firewood, potable water, boat rental, playground, fishing, cornhole ▪ ADA sites: Yes

Rock Tavern combines glamping and water sports along the South Fork of the Shenandoah River. Yurts are their signature accommodation, but the bucolic resort also offers overnights in two vintage houses: Massanutten Springs built in the 1850s and Rock Tavern erected in 1947. A primitive camping area allows tent and even hammock camping. Canoes, kayaks, and tubes are available for floating down the Shenandoah, float trips that can stretch to two and a half hours if the river is running high and the resort shuttle drops you far enough upstream.

SKYLAND CABINS

🏚 12
Mile 41.7 Skyline Drive, Shenandoah National Park, Luray, VA 22835
Open: March to November ▪ Rates: Cabins from $121 ▪ Amenities: Restaurant, bar, snack bar, gift shop, bedding and towels, housekeeping, private bathrooms, ceiling fans, Tesla destination charger, ATM, internet ▪ ADA sites: Yes

Perched near the highest point along Skyline Drive in Shenandoah National Park, Skyland Resort lives up to its lofty name with panoramic views across the Shenandoah Valley and the endless ridges of the Appalachians beyond. Skyland features a variety of quarters, including modern motel-style rooms and vintage cabins with double or twin beds and private bathrooms. The larger units

Douthat State Park has a 50-acre (20.2 ha) lake perfect for fishing and boating.

The KOA Williamsburg/Busch Gardens is the perfect family retreat for a historic colonial experience or amusement park fun.

also feature sitting rooms and kitchenettes, although dwellers should consider at least one meal at the resort's excellent Pollack's Dining Room or evening drinks at the Mountain Taproom with its live mountain music. There's also a great deli counter. Guided horseback and pony rides hit the road from the Skyland stables, while hikers can take off down half a dozen trails that fan out from the lodge, including a short but steep path to the summit of Stony Man Mountain, the park's second highest point at 4,011 feet (1,223 m).

DOUTHAT STATE PARK

🏠30, 🚐/🏕️ 87 partial hookup
14239 Douthat State Park Road, Millboro, VA 24460
Open: Year-round ▪ Rates: RV/tent partial hookup $35/$40 (state resident/nonresident), cabins from $76/$87 ▪ Amenities: Restaurant, camp store, dump stations, showers, picnic tables, fire rings with grills, lantern posts, firewood, playground, beach, boat rental, boat ramp, fishing pier, amphitheater ▪ ADA sites: Yes

Three campgrounds and 30 cabins huddle around a lake in a highland park in the Appalachians around an hour's drive north of Roanoke. Although it's mostly a fair-weather park, Whispering Pines Campground is open through the winter. Other than the trees and mountains, nearly everything you see in the park, including its beloved lake, was created by Civilian Conservation Corps workers during the 1930s.

More than 40 miles of hiking, biking, and equestrian trails meander through hollows and over forested ridges to Blue Suck Falls, Tuscarora Overlook, Beards Mountain, and other landmarks. Cabins feature kitchens, bathrooms, heating, and air conditioning.

PRIMLAND COTTAGES & TREEHOUSES

🏠14, 🌳3
2000 Busted Rock Road, Meadows of Dan, VA 24120
Open: Year-round ▪ Rates: Cottages from $340, tree houses from $630 ▪ Amenities: Restaurants, bars, room service, housekeeping, kitchenettes, private bathrooms, fireplaces, bedding and towels, flat-screen TVs, private decks, private putting greens, golf course, spa, sport

Located on Skyline Drive, Skyland offers a stunning view of the Blue Ridge Mountains and Shenandoah National Park.

shooting, boating, biking, horseback riding, archery, disc golf, tennis, yoga and meditation, fly-fishing, internet ▪ ADA sites: Yes

"Fancy glamping in the Blue Ridge" is an apt description of the upscale cottages and tree houses at a posh mountain retreat founded by French Swiss billionaire Didier Primat. As the name suggests, Fairway Cottages with their cathedral ceilings are set along the resort's 18-hole championship golf course, the two-story Pinnacles Cottages on a forested slope beneath the jagged Pinnacles of Dan. But it's the three tree houses that really blow your mind—deluxe cabins in the sky with king beds, opulent bathrooms, and expansive decks with dreamy mountain views. As if that's not enough, Primland offers a range of offbeat activities like tomahawk throwing, guided tree climbing, air rifle and sporting clay-shooting ranges, and night-sky shows at its own observatory.

GRAYSON HIGHLANDS STATE PARK

🚐/⛺ 36 partial hookup, 28 no hookup, 🏕 4, 🐎 24 partial hookup

829 Grayson Highland Lane, Mouth of Wilson, VA 24363
Open: Campgrounds March to December, yurts May to November ▪ Rates: RV/tent partial hookup $35/$40 (state resident/nonresident), no hookup $25/$30, yurts $75/$88, equestrian from $8 ▪ Amenities: Camp store, craft gallery, dump station, showers, picnic tables, fire rings with grills, firewood, potable water, playground, amphitheater, gift shop ▪ ADA sites: Yes

Have horse, will travel? Then this equestrian-friendly park in the

Appalachians of southwest Virginia is your horsey holy grail. In addition to sites for ordinary campers, Grayson offers a horse camping area with power and water hookups, horse trailer parking, three different stall options, and five equine routes. Foremost among the routes is the 67-mile (107 km) Virginia Highlands Horse Trail, which skirts the northern edge of the park on an epic route through Jefferson National Forest. Along the way, riders might get a glimpse of the wild ponies relocated to the park in the early 1970s. Horseless campers can dive into other highland activities like hiking and mountain biking, fly-fishing the trout streams, or cross-country skiing and snowshoeing if your visit coincides with early winter snowfall. Grayson Highlands Mountain Craft Gallery at the visitors center sells a variety of items by local artists.

WILDERNESS ROAD CAMPGROUND

🚐/⛺ 41 partial hookup, 120 no hookup

854 National Park Road, Ewing, VA 24248
Open: Year-round ▪ Rates: RV/tent partial hookup $20, no hookup $14 ▪ Amenities: Dump station, showers, picnic tables, fire rings with grills, potable water, amphitheater ▪ ADA sites: Partial

Camping at Cumberland Gap National Historical Park summons visions of all those who have overnighted here in the past: the Native Americans who followed bison herds through this legendary cleave in the Appalachians, Daniel Boone and his men who blazed the Wilderness Trail in 1775, and the thousands of settlers who trekked the pass on their way to new homes in Kentucky and the Ohio River Valley. The campground sits about as far west as you can venture in Virginia before crossing into Tennessee or Kentucky. Sites are well shaded with red cedars, pines, hemlocks, and maidenhairs—like those old-time travelers would have camped under. The short, easy Colson/Boone Trail links the campground with the park visitors center and a more rugged Wilderness Road Trail along the original route that climbs up to Cumberland Gap. ▪

SOMETHING SPECIAL

Skyline Drive

Skyline Drive starts near Front Royal. Shenandoah National Park's north gate is just five minutes from downtown Front Royal. And not far beyond is Dickey Ridge Visitor Center with its information desk, small museum, swag shop, and 10-minute video about the park.

The stretch of Skyline between the visitors center and Thornton Gap provides some of the best views across the lush Shenandoah Valley and the higher, hazy Appalachian Mountains to the west.

The road continues to climb to Skyland—the highest point along the drive at 3,680 feet (1,121.7 m)— where the historic lodge provides food, drink, horseback riding, and overnight digs for both drivers and backpackers on the 100-mile (160.9 km) segment of the Appalachian Trail that runs through the park. Skyland also offers less challenging hikes, like the 1.6-mile (2.6 km) circuit to the top of Stony Man Summit and the ADA-accessible Limberlost Trail.

Washington

Take a dip in a crystal-clear lake, kayak with orcas, or hike beloved Mount Rainier on your next camping adventure in Washington State.

EXPEDITION OLD GROWTH

6 tree boat hammocks
Gifford Pinchot National Forest, Carson, WA 98648
Open: June to October ▪ Rates: $750 singles, $1,500 doubles ▪ Amenities: Climbing gear, dinner and breakfast, drinks, restrooms, picnic table, potable water, headlamps, LED lights, fireplace ▪ ADA sites: No

One of the more adventurous ways to spend a night in the Pacific Northwest wilderness, Expedition Old Growth offers camping 80 to 100 feet (24 to 30 m) off the ground in ancient Douglas fir and western red cedar trees. Campers arrive around midday at the remote location in Gifford Pinchot National Forest for an orientation and climbing equipment practice with owner Damien Carré and his crew. They spend a couple of afternoon hours climbing the 250-foot (76 m) conifers before dinner down at ground level around a campfire and then ascend back into the canopy for overnight in an individual "treeboat"—a strong, sturdy hammock used by arborists when they study trees. As an alternative, couples can camp in a portaledge hanging tent of the sort used by world-class rock climbers.

Look out for water worms on your paddle through Deception Pass State Park.

CAPE DISAPPOINTMENT STATE PARK

🏠 3, 🚐 / ⛰ 60 full hookup, 18 partial hookup, 137 no hookup, 🏚 14, 3 lighthouse keeper houses
244 Robert Gray Drive, Ilwaco, WA 98624
Open: Year-round ▪ Rates: RV/tent full hookup from $45, RV/tent partial hookup from $40, RV/tent no hookup from $30, yurts/cabins from $64, lighthouse keeper houses from $164 ▪ Amenities: Camp store, snack bar, dump station, showers, picnic tables, fire pits with grills, potable water, firewood, ice, beaches, boat ramp, amphitheater ▪ ADA sites: Yes

One of the best all-around, four-season parks in the Pacific Northwest, Cape Disappointment also boasts an extraordinary overnight option: three restored lighthouse keepers' residences beside the historic 1898 North Head Lighthouse. Whitewashed and crowned by a bright red roof, the two-story, fully furnished main house features three bedrooms, full kitchen with modern appliances, dining room, living room, and lawn area. On the other side of allegedly haunted Deadman's Hollow, the park campground ranges from full hookup RV/tent sites to yurts outfitted with bunk beds, tables, heaters, and outdoor cooking and seating areas. From local Native American groups and Lewis & Clark to Civil War forts and World War II gun batteries, the

HIGHLIGHTS

Capital: Olympia

Total National Parks: 3 (Mount Rainier, North Cascades, and Olympic National Parks)

Total State Parks: 140 (Largest is Mount Spokane State Park)

State Bird: Goldfinch

State Flower: Coast rhododendron

State Marine Mammal: Orca

Wildlife Spotting: Bighorn sheep; gray wolves; Olympic marmots; osprey; bald eagles; goldfinches; albatrosses; puffins; Pacific giant salamanders; Pacific chorus frogs; sharp-tailed snakes; pygmy short-horned lizards

park boasts a long and colorful history. The cape was named by disappointed British navigator John Meares who failed to locate the mouth of the Columbia River during a 1788 expedition.

LOG CABIN RESORT & CAMPGROUND

🏠 24, 🚐 / ⛰ 30 full hookup, ⛰ 7
3183 East Beach Road, Port Angeles, WA 98363
Open: May to September ▪ Rates: Cabins from $84, RVs $48.52, tents from $27.60 ▪ Amenities: Restaurant, camp store, kitchenettes, private bathrooms, bedding and towels, laundry, showers, picnic tables, fire rings with grills, swimming beach, bike, boat and paddleboard rental, internet ▪ ADA sites: Yes

Set along the north shore of Lake Crescent, Log Cabin Resort offers a great base camp for exploring the northern parts of Olympic National Park and nearby Port Angeles, as well as its own gorgeous location. The resort's A-frame chalets, camper cabins, and recently built log cabins are tucked beneath trees beside a rocky beach with the park's Olympic Mountains as a dramatic backdrop. Cabins equipped with kitchenettes feature a fridge, stovetop, microwave, cooking and eating utensils, and a kitchen table. The resort also offers waterfront RV and tent sites, as well as the Sunnyside Café and a well-stocked camp store. Canoes, kayaks, and paddleboards are available for campers who want to get out on the water, while the nearby Olympic Discovery Trail meanders along a roadless and uninhabited section of the lakeshore.

THE INN AT SALTWATER FARM

🏠 5

176 Sea Breeze Lane, Friday Harbor, WA 98250

Open: Year-round ▪ Rates: From $349 ▪ Amenities: Kitchenettes, breakfast, private bathrooms, decks, heating and air conditioning, bedding

and towels, community fire pit and hot tub, lavender field, electric car charger, internet ▪ ADA sites: Partial

What happens when a veterinarian with her own goat herd and her psychologist husband decide to relocate from helter-skelter Seattle to the laid-back San Juans? An idyllic getaway on the outskirts of Friday Harbor with upscale cabins overlooking a lavender field and the island-filled Salish Sea. Unveiled in 2018 as a glamping hub and wedding venue, Saltwater Farm features five upscale cabins set around "gathering spaces" like a communal dining/living area, fire pit, and hot tub. Large enough for four, the cabins feature a large master suite with king bed and floor-to-ceiling windows, private bathroom with shower or tub and heated floor, and a living area with fridge, microwave, and wet bar. Saltwater's emphasis on sustainability includes solar power, locally sourced building materials, compost, recycling, and organic gardening. The restaurants,

museums, and ferry terminal of downtown Friday Harbor are just a three-minute drive down the road. While the island's main outdoor sights—like Lime Kiln State Park and San Juan Island National Historical Park—are a short drive in the other direction.

CRANBERRY LAKE CAMPGROUND

🚐 / 🏕 83 partial hookup

41229 State Route 20, Oak Harbor, WA 98277

Open: Year-round ▪ Rates: RV/tent partial hookup from $30, no hookup from $20 ▪ Amenities: Camp store, snack bar, gas station, dump station, showers, picnic tables, fire pits with grills, potable water, ice, boat ramp, beach, fishing pier, bait and tackle, amphitheater, ATM ▪ ADA sites: Yes

Located on the south side of Deception Pass State Park, this Whidbey Island campground offers campers a rare choice of freshwater and saltwater swimming, fishing, and boating. Both loops are also within walking distance of the park's North and West beaches, sandy shores with calm waters, dreamy views, and gorgeous sunsets across the Puget Sound. A portion of the 1,200-mile (1,931 km) Pacific Northwest Trail takes campers onto historic Deception Pass Bridge, a photogenic steel-arch structure opened in 1935 and separated into two parts by rocky Pass Island. Those seeking more seclusion can rent the lone cabin on Ben Ure Island or paddle out to six primitive campsites on Hope Island.

TREEHOUSE POINT

🧑 7

6922 Preston–Fall City Road SE, Issaquah, WA 98027

Plant yourself at the Lodge at Stehekin for a weekend of hiking and fishing.

Cape Disappointment State Park is anything but disappointing, with cabin options and acres of nature to explore.

Open: Year-round ▪ Rates: From $300 ▪ Amenities: Bathhouse, breakfast, library, board games, bedding and towels, heating and air-conditioning, potable water, electric kettle, MP3 player/radio ▪ ADA sites: Yes

Washington State native Pete Nelson began to transform his lifelong obsession with tree houses into three-dimensional reality in 2004 when he purchased this heavily wooded tract in the Snoqualmie Valley near Seattle. Since then, Nelson and his family have designed, built, and outfitted seven arboreal dwellings in the property's mighty Sitka spruces. Reached by spiral wooden staircases or wooden foot bridges, the fully furnished tree houses come with queen beds,

sitting area, and heating for those chilly Cascade Range nights. Tree house Point guests can explore the surrounding forest or dive into yoga sessions, deep-tissue massage, hypnotherapy, or tai chi beneath the trees. While most of the tree houses sleep just two people, "Upper Pond" can accommodate four and "Ananda" is wheelchair accessible. But for sheer beauty, nothing tops two-story "Trillium" with its ample windows.

COUGAR ROCK CAMPGROUND
🚐/🏕 60 no hookup, 🏕 113 Paradise Valley Road, Mount Rainier National Park, Longmire, WA 98304
Open: May to October ▪ Rate: $20 ▪ Amenities: Dump station, showers, picnic tables, fire pits with grills,

firewood, potable water, amphitheater ▪ ADA sites: Yes

Set on the southern slopes of Mount Rainier, Cougar Rock offers more than 170 primitive tent and RV sites along six loops beside the Nisqually River. Thick evergreen forest blesses the sites with plenty of shade, a good amount of privacy, and shelter from the precipitation that keeps these woods so glaringly green. The 96-mile (154 km) Wonderland Trail that encircles the perpetually snowcapped, active stratovolcano runs right past Cougar Rock. And the campground is close to Longmire and Paradise, historic national park towns with restaurants, shops, and museums. July through September, there's a Junior Ranger program and evening ranger-led talks at the campground amphitheater.

Find epic views of Mount Rainier from your site at Cougar Rock Campground.

NORTH CASCADES LODGE AT STEHEKIN

🏠 8

#1 Stehekin Landing, North Cascades National Park, Stehekin, WA 98852

Open: Year-round ▪ Rates: From $214 ▪ Amenities: Restaurant, coffee shop, camp store, bedding and towels, housekeeping, private bathrooms, kitchens in some units, fans, private decks, boat rental, bike rentals, rec room, scenic tours, internet ▪ ADA sites: No

This classic cabin resort on the edge of North Cascades National Park can only be reached via a grueling overland hike, private floatplane charter, or ferry passage on the Lady of the Lake from Chelan. But at the end of the line is splendid isolation, one of the most remote towns in the lower 48 states. Although the lodge offers motel rooms, those craving a stroll down the wilderness version of memory lane will opt for a private cabin (with or without kitchen) or the two-story Lakehouse. Rent a cycle from Discovery Bikes or hop the famous Red Bus to local landmarks like Golden West Visitor Center, Buckner Homestead Historic District, or the Stehekin Garden & Pastry Company where you can buy goat cheese, organic fruit, honey, and baked goods for a picnic in the woods.

ROLLING HUTS

🏠 7

18381 State Highway 20, Winthrop, WA 98862

Open: Year-round ▪ Rates: From $145 ▪ Amenities: Private toilets, bathhouse, mini-fridges, microwaves, dishes and silverware, wood-burning stove, potable water, communal barbecue grills and picnic shelter, internet ▪ ADA sites: No

Pack your mountain bikes or Nordic skies for a sojourn at this all-weather resort in north-central Washington. Encircled by more than 120 miles (200 km) of summer-winter trails, Rolling Huts provides the perfect base for outdoor fun along the eastern edge of the Cascades. The name derives from the fact the huts are actually on wheels. Like updated versions of the sleek prairie style pioneered by Frank Lloyd Wright, the futuristic design of these steel, glass, and wood cabins offers stark contrast to a traditional three-bedroom farmhouse that can also be rented. Hut dwellers can rustle up their own meals at the communal barbecue shelter or cruise 10 minutes down the road to Wild West–flavored Winthrop for grub at Three Fingered Jacks, Rocking Horse Bakery, or the Old Schoolhouse Brewery.

PREMIER RV RESORT GRANITE LAKE

🏠 4, 71 full hookup

306 Granite Lake Drive, Clarkston, WA 99403

Open: Year-round ▪ Rates: RVs from $56, cabins $99 ▪ Amenities: Camp store, showers, laundry, picnic tables, fire rings with grills, ice, game room, book/DVD library, dog run, communal fire pits, satellite TV, internet ▪ ADA sites: Partial

The twin cities of Clarkston and Lewiston, named for the famed explorers, are home to this full-service RV park in Washington's extreme southeast corner. Yet with a location along the Snake River and the khaki-colored Palouse hills rising on the opposite shore, the campground feels far from urban. The Greenbelt Walkway runs right past Premier, providing campers with a paved hiking and biking path that runs 7 miles (11 km) upstream along the Snake. Shady waterfront pavilions with tables, barbecue grills, and Adirondack chairs provide pleasant spots for picnics, sundowners, and watching watercraft move up and down the river. At the same time, civilization is mere steps away in the form of big-box stores, fast-food outlets, and even a golf driving range. ▪

SOMETHING SPECIAL

North Cascades National Park

Less than three hours from Seattle, Washington's North Cascades National Park preserves a wide array of biodiversity, from its western temperate rainforest to its eastern dry ponderosa pine ecosystem. More than 300 glaciers can be found in the park's jagged, comparatively young mountains, with dramatic landscapes spread over 9,000 feet (2,743.2 m) of vertical relief.

Experienced backcountry travelers in search of solitude can take numerous trails such as Bridge Creek Trail into Upper Stehekin Valley, located in the park's southern section. The narrow, forested area is surrounded by glaciated peaks, crowned by Goode Mountain. A side trip along the Goode Ridge Trail takes hikers into a spectacular horseshoe surrounded by giant ridges that reveal the mountainous grandeur of the park.

West Virginia

West Virginia boasts roaring rapids, historic coal mines, lush forests, and heavenly mountain retreats among its robust array of campgrounds.

BATTLE RUN CAMPGROUND

🚐 / 🏕 110 partial hookup, 🏕 7

2981 Summersville Lake Road, Summersville, WV 26651

Open: May to October ▪ Rates: RV/tent partial hookup from $30, tent only $20 ▪ Amenities: Dump station, showers, laundry, picnic tables, fire rings with grills, potable water, boat ramp, fishing dock, beach, playground, sports courts ▪ ADA sites: Yes

Developed by the U.S. Army Corps of Engineers in the 1960s when they dammed the Gauley River to create a massive reservoir, this awesome waterfront campground expedites boating, swimming, and fishing on West Virginia's largest lake. Campers can explore 60 miles (96 km) of lakeshore flanked by forest and impressive cliffs. Summersville Lake Marina rents boats, while Sarge's Dive Shop expedites exploration of the lake's underwater rock formations. Battle Run Beach is located right across a cove from the campground. The lake area is also spangled with hiking and biking trails, and the upper put-in for rafting the wild and crazy Gauley River lies right below the colossal Summersville Dam.

COUNTRY ROAD CABINS

🏚 17, 🎪 2, 🏠 2, 🏕 1

1508 Sunday Road, Hico, WV 25854

Open: Year-round ▪ Rates: Cabins and yurts from $175, tree houses from $195, glamping tent from $225 ▪ Amenities: Kitchens, private bathrooms, bedding and towels, heating, air-conditioning, fireplaces, washer/dryers, satellite TVs and DVD players, hot tubs, barbecue grills, internet ▪ ADA sites: Yes

Country Road takes you home to cozy cabins, tree houses, and yurts in the woodsy wilderness that flows across the Allegheny Plateau. Overnight options range from romantic two-person abodes like the Love Shack yurt to the Pillow Rock and Insignificant cabins that sleep a dozen or more. During the warmer months, Country Road offers a great base for hiking or biking the surrounding summits or rafting the nearby New River and Gauley Rivers. During colder times, nearby Winterplace Ski Resort offers skiing and snowboarding.

ADVENTURES ON THE GORGE

🏚 160, 🚐 4 partial hookup, 🏕 30, 🏕 5

219 Chestnutburg Road, Lansing, WV 25862

Open: Year-round ▪ Rates: Cabins from $44.50, glamping tents from $159, RV no hookup from $80, tent only from $50 ▪ Amenities: Restaurants, bars, coffee shop, snack bar, camp stores, bathhouse, picnic tables, swimming pool, rafting,

fishing, kayaking, paintball, zip lines, rock climbing, guided hikes, mountain biking, horseback riding, kids' club, shuttle bus, ATM, internet ▪ ADA sites: Yes

New River Gorge, America's newest national park, is home to a wilderness camp and outdoor adventure outfitter that takes full advantage of the area's legendary white water. In addition to RV/tent sites and glamping tents, the resort offers a wide variety of cabins from modern two-story units with spiral staircases and private hot tubs to rustic log cabins with woodsy decor and outdoor fire pits. Campers can cook their own meals or dine at five food and beverage outlets. Meanwhile, adventure awaits. The premier activity is rafting some of the planet's most celebrated white water: the relatively calm New River or the totally outrageous Gauley River, with rapids

Adventures on the Gorge is the perfect stay for a weekend of white-water river rafting.

ranging up to class V. There are also a zip line and tree canopy course, guided rock climbing and rappelling, horseback rides, paintball, laser tag, fly-fishing, and a stroll along catwalks suspended beneath the 876-foot-high (267 m) New River Gorge Bridge.

BECKLEY EXHIBITION COAL MINE CAMPGROUND

🚐 17 full hookup

513 Ewart Avenue, Beckley, WV 25801

Open: April to December ▪ Rate: $30 ▪ Amenities: Gift shop, restrooms, picnic tables, fire pits, grills, playground, swimming pool, sports courts ▪ ADA sites: No

This is coal country, after all, so why not a campground at a coal mine— or, rather, a former pit transformed into a fascinating open air and underground museum. Located in the city's New River Park, the exhibition preserves early 20th-century coal camp structures, including the

school, church, homes, and company store. Visitors board a miniature train to descend into the old mine during guided tours conducted by former miners. The well-shaded campground behind is RV only and offers few amenities other than a restroom block and small playground. However, the city park boasts an Olympic-size swimming pool with water slide, tennis courts, and a fitness trail.

BUFFALO TRAIL CABINS

🏠 24, 🚐 / ⛺ 5 full hookup, ♋ 6

190 Buffalo Trail, Bluefield, WV 24701

Open: Year-round ▪ Rates: Cabins from $128.80, tree houses from $162.40, RV/tent full hookup from $53 (two-night minimum stay) ▪ Amenities: Restaurant, bar, gift shop, bathhouse, picnic tables, fire rings with grills ▪ ADA sites: No

Four-wheeler fans and avid dirt bikers use this rustic resort as a base camp for riding 57 miles (91 km) of local ATV trails and connectors

leading to other sections of a Hatfield-McCoy Trail system with more than 600 miles (965 km) of unpaved routes across the southern part of the state. Buffalo's combination of crash pads includes cabins, full-hookup RV sites, and tree houses with parking underneath where guests can stow their heavy-metal thunder machines.

PIPESTEM RESORT STATE PARK

🏠 26, 🚐 / ⛺ 31 full hookup, 51 partial hookup

3405 Pipestem Drive, Pipestem, WV 25979

Open: Year-round ▪ Rates: Cabins from $131, RV/tent full hookup from $42, partial hookup from $37 ▪ Amenities: Restaurants, bars, camp store, dump station, showers, laundry, picnic tables, fire pits with grills, swimming pools, playground, fitness room, golf courses, driving range, miniature golf, tennis courts, boat rental, boat ramp, fishing pier, stables, amphitheater, electric vehicle charging station, internet ▪ ADA sites: Yes

The word "resort" alerts campers to the fact that Pipestem is no ordinary state park. Whether you're sleeping in one of the comfy, modern cabins or are sacked out in your tent or motor home, get ready for adrenaline-pumping outdoor adventure. In addition to hiking, the park also offers vertiginous rock climbing and zip lines, various white-water adventures on the Bluestone River, and guided mountain bike excursions, as well as a new splash park and adventure lake for kids. There is also guided trout fishing, an aerial tramway with panoramic views of the Allegheny Mountains, and an 18-hole championship golf course. After all

Camp 20 feet (6.1 m) in the air in a tree house at Country Road Cabins.

Just outside the historic town, Harpers Ferry KOA is perfect for families looking for a nature retreat with nearby attractions.

that sweat, campers can cool off with ice cream or shakes at the park's 1950s-style soda fountain.

WATOGA STATE PARK

🏛 34, 🚐 / ⛺ 13 partial hookup, 25 no hookup

4800 Watoga Park Road, Marlinton, WV 24954

Open: Cabins year-round, campgrounds May to November/December ▪ Rates: RV/tent partial hookup $33, no hookup $28, cabins from $84 ▪ Amenities: Dump station, showers, laundry, picnic tables, fire pits with grills, lantern posts, potable water, boating, fishing, swimming pool, sports courts, disc golf, playgrounds ▪ ADA sites: Yes

The rugged Allegheny Highlands provide a lofty location for West

Virginia's largest state park—10,100 acres (4,087 ha) of woods and waterways—offering a variety of outdoor activities. Two campgrounds share the park's RV and tent sites. Most of the cabins are located in the heart of the park near Watoga Lake, the Civilian Conservation Corps Museum, and recreation center. The park is large enough to offer different trails for hiking, biking, and horseback riding and its own botanical garden. Founded in the 1930s and listed on the National Register of Historic Places, Fred E. Brooks Memorial Arboretum offers a lovely walk through native trees.

SENECA SHADOWS CAMPGROUND

🚐 / ⛺ 13 partial hookup, 25 no hookup, ⛺ 10

State Highway 28, Seneca Rocks, WV 26884

Open: April to October ▪ Rates: RV/tent partial hookup $30, no hookup $22, tent only $17 ▪ Amenities: Dump station, showers, picnic tables, fire pits with grills, beach, boat rental, boat ramp, fish cleaning station, playground, amphitheater ▪ ADA sites: Partial

The Potomac Highlands of Monongahela National Forest provide a lofty venue for a National Forest campground that attracts both hikers and rock climbers. Their goal is jagged Seneca Rocks, a 900-foot (274 m) quartzite outcrop with outstanding views across the Upper Potomac Valley and West Virginia's mountainous eastern panhandle. Many of the campsites offer views

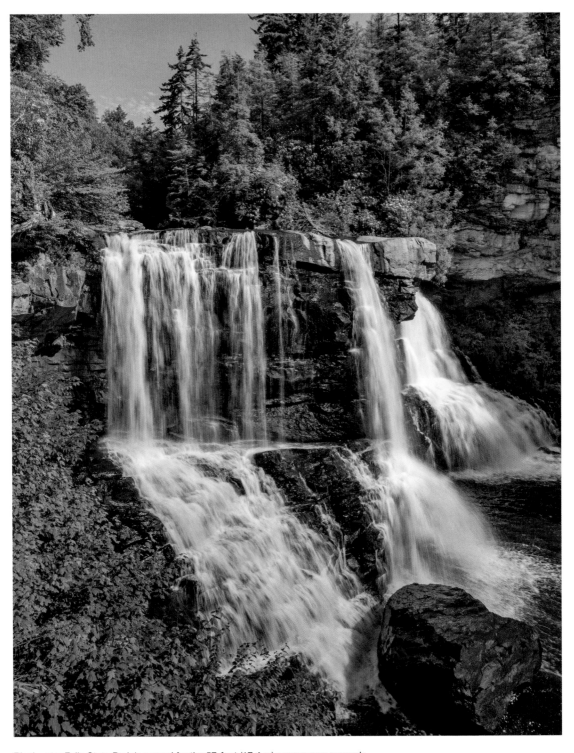

Blackwater Falls State Park is named for the 57-foot (17.4 m) eponymous cascade.

of the razorback summit. A trailhead across the road from Seneca Shadows takes campers to the Seneca Rocks Discovery Center and the base of the legendary rock. During the summer season, the park offers ranger talks, living history events, local artisans, and live mountain music.

CANAAN VALLEY RESORT STATE PARK

🏕 23, 🚐/🏕 34 full hookup, 🏕 2
230 Main Lodge Road, Davis, WV 26260

Open: Year-round ▪ Rates: RV/tent full hookup from $22/$35 (state resident/nonresident), tent only from $20, cabins from $199.99 ▪ Amenities: Restaurants, bars, gift shops, camp store, dump station, showers, laundry, picnic tables, fire rings with grills, firewood, ice, swimming pools, fitness center, games arcade, golf course, tennis courts, shooting range, winter sports area, internet ▪ ADA sites: Yes

Few state parks anywhere else in the nation welcome winter the way Canaan Valley does. Blanketed by an average 180 inches (4,572 mm) of snow, cabins and campsites are open throughout the colder months for visitors seeking the park's various winter activities. Cabins are equipped with heating but not air conditioning. There is full-fledged skiing and snowboarding with four lifts and 47 pistes. Equipment rentals and lessons are available. The tubing park features one of the longest runs on the East Coast.

Pack your skates too, because there's a covered ice rink. From their RV door or tent flap, campers can snowshoe or cross-country ski along 21 miles (35 km) of groomed paths and long snow-covered fairways on the 18-hole golf course. The ski area's Bear Paw Food Court and Quenchers Pub, as well as restaurant and cocktail lounge at Canaan Valley Lodge, serve throughout winter. That's not to say there isn't anything to do in summer: Hiking, biking, fishing, golf, archery, and clay shooting are just a few of the park's warm-weather activities.

HARPER'S FERRY/CIVIL WAR BATTLEFIELDS KOA

🏕 43, 🚐/🏕 173 full hookup, 11 partial hookup, 🏕 82
343 Campground Road, Harpers Ferry, WV 25425

Open: Year-round ▪ Rates: RV/tent full hookup from $47, partial hookup/tent only from $41, cabins from $76 ▪ Amenities: Camp store, snack bar, dump station, showers, picnic tables, fire pits with grills, firewood, propane, swimming pool, playground, miniature golf, sports courts, game arcade, craft room, bike rental, dog park, movie theater, ATM machine, cable TV, internet ▪ ADA sites: Partial

While people tend to think of KOAs as cookie-cutter campgrounds, sometimes you find one that's truly unique. For instance, the Harper's Ferry camp offers Grapes & Grinds, a specialty coffee and wine store with a variety of hot drinks each morning and wine tastings in the afternoon. That's not all that stands out. This KOA also boasts a 100-seat indoor movie theater, craft room, indoor basketball court, and all-you-can-eat free pancakes during the summer. It also organizes special family-oriented weekends that revolve around themes like Pirates & Mermaids, Chocolate Madness, Old Time Carnival, and Down on the Farm. An authentic Civil War trench runs through the property. Campers have easy access to the Murphy-Chambers Farm Trails system in Harpers Ferry National Historical Park. The park visitors center is next door, and right across the road is Bolivar Heights Battlefield. Campers can also hike a portion of the Appalachian Trail, white-water-raft the Shenandoah River, or bet on the horses at nearby Charles Town Races. ▪

SOMETHING SPECIAL

Canaan Valley Resort

Gazing for the first time upon Canaan Valley's rugged beauty, a group of fur traders in the 18th century were reminded of Canaan, the promised land of milk and honey. Hunters who later ventured into the valley, however, formed a different opinion. Filled with bears, panthers, tangled growth, and dangerous cliffs, the place literally swallowed humans whole. Visitors here still feel like explorers, enduring narrow, winding, mountainous roads to reach this isolated pocket in central West Virginia. But those who persevere discover a mecca for outdoor recreation, and in the heart of it all sits Canaan Valley Resort State Park.

The main reason people come here is to ski in winter and play in summer. Cradled by tall peaks of the Alleghenies, the valley catches storms and collects an abundance of snow, heralding long winters and skiing from Thanksgiving into April. The state park boasts a ski area with 34 runs, plus a cross-country ski center and many miles of trails. Mountain biking, hiking, golfing, and canoeing on the Blackwater River take precedence in other seasons.

Wisconsin

Wisconsin offers a variety of overnight options, from tree house resorts to travel trailers to yurts, along with traditional RV and tent destinations.

HIGHLIGHTS

Capital: Madison

Total National Parks: 0

Total State Parks: 66 (Largest is Devil's Lake State Park)

State Bird: American robin

State Flower: Wood violet

State Animal: Badger

Wildlife Spotting: Badgers; black bears; moose; white-tailed deer; muskrats; porcupines; flying squirrels; downy woodpeckers; eastern bluebirds; purple finches; red-winged blackbirds; robins; milk snakes; snapping turtles; eastern red-backed salamanders; American bullfrogs; mink frogs

INTERSTATE STATE PARK

🚐/🏕️27 partial hookup, 53 no hookup, 🏕️2

1275 State Highway 35, St. Croix Falls, WI 54024

Open: Year-round ▪ Rates: RV/tent partial hookup $28, no hookup and tent only $15 ▪ Amenities: Camp store/gift shop, dump station, showers, picnic tables, fire rings with grills, firewood, ice, potable water, fishing pier, boat ramp, ball field, amphitheater ▪ ADA sites: Yes

One of several state-managed segments of St. Croix National Scenic Riverway, this park lies on the east bank of a waterway that defines much of the boundary between Wisconsin and Minnesota. RV and tent sites are divided between North and South campgrounds, with the former boasting more amenities and electric hookups. Located at the western end of Ice Age National Scenic Trail, the park is a worthy example of the glacier-carved terrain that formed much of the Upper Midwest. Foremost among the park's natural features is the Dalles of St. Croix, a gorge with vertical cliffs that plunge straight into the river. Campers can snatch a bird's-eye view of the gorge along the River Bluff, Pothole, and Summit trails. Downstream from the Dalles,

Visit the Meyers Beach Sea Caves at Apostle Islands National Lakeshore during the icy winter months.

a boat launch offers paddlers easy access to the river. Alternatively, they can step aboard vintage Taylors Falls paddle wheelers on narrated scenic cruises along St. Croix.

NATURA TREESCAPE RESORT

🏠15, 🚐/🏕️10 full hookup, 10 partial hookup, ⛺ 12

400 County Road A, Wisconsin Dells, WI 53965

Open: Tree houses and cabins year-round, campsites May to September ▪ Rates: Tree houses from $69.99, cabins from $39.99, RV from $19.99 ▪ Amenities: Restaurant, bar, gas station, convenience store, bathhouse, microwaves, fridge, heating and air-conditioning, widescreen TV, picnic tables, fire ring, lagoon, beach, swimming pools, hot tubs, internet ▪ ADA sites: No

Natura is a textbook example of how to transform a tired older campground into a modern outdoor resort by revamping the existing tree house units, adding tiny homes, and replacing the worn-out tennis court with a swimming lagoon, sandy beach, and waterfall. Unveiled in 2019, the revamped resort lures families visiting theme parks, water parks, magic shows, carnival sideshow attractions, and other amusements in Wisconsin Dells. Natura guests get free admission to Noah's Ark Waterpark and Timbavati Wildlife Park. Right beside the

campground is Hot Rocks, a South Pacific tiki–themed restaurant where diners cook their own meat and seafood over simmering lava stones.

QUARTZITE CAMPGROUND

🚐/🏕️75 partial hookup, 25 no hookup

S5975 Park Road, Baraboo, WI 53913

Open: Year-round ▪ Rates: RV/tent partial hookup $35, no hookup $20 ▪ Amenities: Camp store, gift shop, dump station, showers, picnic tables, fire rings, firewood, ice, potable water, playground, beach, boat rental, boat ramps, amphitheater ▪ ADA sites: Yes

Although the water is certainly tempting, it's the 500-foot-high (152 m) quartzite bluffs that make Devil's Lake State Park such a guilty pleasure. The bluffs lend their name to Quartzite Campground, one of four overnight spots inside the state park but the only campground open year-round and the one best suited for larger RVs. Another feather in its cap is a location within walking distance of the nature center, with its many guided outdoor adventures and family-oriented learning activities, as well as boat rental, camp store, and swimming beach along the north shore. Nearly everyone gets around to hiking the dramatic glacier-carved heights that flank the lake. East Bluff Trail takes campers to three of the park's geological oddities: Elephant Rock, Balanced Rock, and Devil's Doorway. Across the lake, West Bluff Trail leads to super-slender Cleopatra's Needle (aka Prospect Point).

MAUTHE LAKE CAMPGROUND

🚐 / 🏕 51 partial hookup, 77 no hookup, 🏕 7

N1490 County Road GGG, Campbellsport, WI 53010

Open: Year-round ▪ Rates: RV/tent partial hookup $28, no hookup and tent only from $15 ▪ Amenities: Dump station, showers, picnic

tables, fire rings with grills, firewood, potable water, playground, beach, boat ramps, fishing pier, vending machines ▪ ADA sites: Yes

Little more than an hour's drive north of downtown Milwaukee, Mauthe Lake provides a quick and easy escape from the big city. A location in Kettle Moraine State Forest ensures that the waterfront campground is well shaded in summer and picture perfect in winter, when the leafless trees frame the frozen-over lake. Ice fishing is one of the park's favorite cold-weather activities, although the terrain is also ideal for Nordic skiing, snowshoeing, fat-tire biking, and snowmobiling along Kettle Moraine's 60 miles (96 km) of trails.

CANDLEWOOD CABINS

🏚 7

29493 State Road 80, Richland Center, WI 53581

Open: Year-round ▪ Rates: From $135 ▪ Amenities: Kitchenettes, full

bathrooms, bedding and towels, fireplaces, air-conditioning, barbecue grills, firewood, private decks or patios, internet ▪ ADA sites: No

Chic shacks are the hallmark of this swish retreat in the Lower Wisconsin River valley west of Madison. The digs range from designer-savvy wooden dwellings like the two-story Woodland House to the modern, glass-wrapped Meadow House that draws inspiration from the Prairie school. It's not just the structure that stands out: Each cabin is decorated with stylish furnishings and surprising one-off touches like the loft soaking tub in the Log Cabin and the huge open kitchen in the Barn. For a look at the early 20th-century architecture movement that inspired the cabins, visit Taliesin, Frank Lloyd Wright's masterwork in nearby Spring Hill.

NICOLET BAY CAMPGROUNDS—PENINSULA STATE PARK

🚐 / 🏕 54 partial hookup, 133 no hookup

Shore Road, Fish Creek, WI 54212

Open: May to October ▪ Rates: RV/tent partial hookup $35, no hookup $20 ▪ Amenities: Camp store, snack bar, clothing store, dump station, showers, picnic tables, fire rings, potable water, playground, beach, boat rentals, boat ramp, fishing pier, sand volleyball, bike rental, dog run, golf course, amphitheater ▪ ADA sites: Yes

Wisconsin's third largest state park is also its most popular, luring more than a million visitors every year to its montage of human and natural history and outdoor adventure throughout the four seasons. Located near the top of the Door

Sandhill cranes migrate through Kettle Moraine State Forest in the summer and fall.

Find cabins, vintage trailers, and glamping yurts at Coadys' Point of View, just minutes from Eagle River.

Peninsula between Green Bay and Lake Michigan, the park is often lauded as one of the most beautiful in the Midwest. Two of its five campgrounds stretch along the shore of Nicolet Bay, which means that swimming, boating, and fishing are mere minutes away from any of the 180-plus campsites. It's also easy for campers to hop onto the Nicolet Bay hiking trail, Sunset bike route, and other paths that meander through the woods to 1868 Eagle Bluff Lighthouse, Blossomburg Scandinavian pioneer cemetery, and an 18-hole golf course. Summertime campers can catch locally flavored musical comedies—like Packer Fans from Outer Space and Cheeseheads—at the park amphitheater.

PESHTIGO RIVER OUTPOST
🏠10, ⛰15, 🏠1

N12080 Allison Lane, Athelstane, WI 54104

Open: April to October ▪ Rates: Deluxe cabins from $150.95, rustic cabins and yurt from $89.95, tent camping from $28 ▪ Amenities: Kitchens, fireplaces, showers, picnic tables, satellite TV, picnic tables, fire rings, firewood, ropes course; guided raft, kayak, and paddleboard excursions ▪ ADA sites: No

Tucked deep in the woods of northern Wisconsin, this Wildman Adventure wilderness camp spikes your heart rate with white-water rafting, kayaking, and rope climbing by day, then eases you back into a mellow mood at night in cabins,

campsites, and a single yurt. The top-shelf deluxe cabins range from a one-bedroom perfect for two people, all the way through two- and three-bedroom units that can sleep as many as 15. Bedding ranges from queens and twins to sofa beds depending on the cabin. But all are outfitted with full kitchens, fireplaces, dining tables, sitting areas, satellite TV, and private bathrooms with showers. The resort's rustic cabins are basically one-room bunkhouses with a bathhouse down the road. Located along the Roaring Rapids section of the Peshtigo, the guided river trips are epic, class II through IV rapids along one of the longest stretches of white water in the Midwest.

Peninsula State Park offers 460 campsites, epic views of Green Bay, a summer theater, and an 18-hole golf course.

LOST LAKE RECREATION AREA

🏠 11, 🚐/🏕 27 no hookup
Lost Lake/Chipmunk Rapids Road, Tipler, WI 54121
Open: April to October ▪ Rates: RV/tent $15, cabins from $40 ▪ Amenities: Restrooms, picnic tables, fire rings with grills, potable water, firewood, ice, swimming beach, boat rental ▪ ADA sites: Yes

Chequamegon-Nicolet National Forest in northern Wisconsin is the leafy setting for an excellent Forest Service campground with an alluring choice of outdoor activities. The campground offers a small beach and ramp for launching nonmotorized watercraft for a laid-back cruise around the lake or angling for the trout, bass, and catfish. Canoes, kayaks, paddleboards, and rowboats are available for rent. The lakeshore is also great for spotting feathered friends ranging from loons to bald eagles. Among the park's other activities are table tennis, mushroom foraging, and a short interpretive trail through 150-year-old hemlocks and pines. The nearest place to stock up on supplies is Florence, 22 miles (35 km) to the east.

COADYS' POINT OF VIEW LAKE RESORT & CAMPGROUNDS

🏠 13, 🏕 2, 🏕 3, 🏕 1, 🚐 4
3932 North Primich Way, Phelps, WI 54554
Open: Year-round ▪ Rates: Cabins from $114, glamping tents from $130, travel trailers and yurt from $120, tents from $40 ▪ Amenities: Camp store, showers, laundry, picnic tables, fire rings with grills, firewood, ice, bait, boat rental, boat ramp, fish cleaning station, playground, rec room, swimming beach,

sports courts, space heaters, internet ▪ ADA sites: Yes

This lakeside resort is so far north it's basically an honorary member of the Upper Peninsula. Founded in 1897 as North Twin Lodge, the current name derives from the husband and wife who purchased the resort in 2018, transforming it from a rustic fishing outpost into the best glamping spot in the Wisconsin Northwoods region. Overnight options include cabins, safari tents, and restored vintage travel trailers, although it's also possible to tent beneath the shoreline trees. During the warmer months, Coadys' offers kayaks, canoes, and paddleboats free of charge but rents pontoon and fishing boats. After winter descends, the resort has special ice fishing and snowshoe packages and local partners that rent skis and snowmobiles.

APOSTLE ISLANDS NATIONAL LAKESHORE

🏕 58
415 Washington Avenue, Bayfield, WI 54814
Open: Year-round ▪ Rates: Terrestrial campsites and overnight docking

$15, sleeping on your anchored boat free ▪ Amenities: Picnic tables, fire rings with grills, toilets, food storage containers, docks/piers on some islands ▪ ADA sites: Yes

Travel back in time to camping at this gorgeous park along Wisconsin's Lake Superior coast. As the Park Service makes very explicit, there is no drive-up car, tent, or RV camping. Eighteen of the park's 21 islands offer waterfront campsites that can be accessed only with your own watercraft or local water taxi and shuttle services. Reaching the single mainland site requires a 6-mile (9.6 km) hike or paddle from Meyers Beach.

The experience varies from island to island. With 20 individual and two group sites, Stockton Island can feel downright crowded on summer weekends. Yet eight of the islands boast just a single site—like having your own private island retreat. The park's no-frill campsites are equipped with nothing more than a picnic table, fire ring, food storage container (yes, bears can swim), and a stump or moldering privy. But the adventure of having a wild island all to yourself is sublime. ▪

Apostle Islands National Lakeshore

The rugged beauty of the Lake Superior shore attracts visitors to this park on the northern tip of Wisconsin. Apostle Islands National Lakeshore encompasses 12 miles (19 km) of shoreline on the mainland, but when the parks' 21 islands are included, the total rises to 156 miles (251 km). With miles of beaches, more than 50 miles (80.5 km) of trails, and 42 square miles (108.8 sq km) of Lake Superior, it is best explored on foot or by boat.

Apostle Islands National Lakeshore is also known for its historic lighthouses, some of which can be explored on guided tours in summer, led by park rangers or volunteers. Camping is allowed on 19 of the islands and one mainland site. Black bears are present (they are especially common on Sand, Oak, and Stockton Islands), so campers and hikers need to follow rules for safety in bear country.

Wyoming

Valleys, rivers, mountains, and lakes are just some of the natural scenes awaiting campers, glampers, and RV enthusiasts in the Cowboy State.

BELLE FOURCHE RIVER CAMPGROUND

🚐 / ⛺ 46 no hookup

Devils Tower National Monument Road, Devils Tower, WY 82714

Open: May to October ▪ Rate: RV/tent $20 ▪ Amenities: Restrooms, fire rings with grills, picnic tables, potable water, amphitheater; no showers, hookups, or dump station ▪ ADA sites: Yes

Close encounters of the lava kind are the lure of a campground that sits in the shadow of Devil's Tower in northeast Wyoming. Tucked inside a bend in its namesake river, the RV and tent sites are arrayed around two loops, many of them shaded by cottonwood trees. It's a 1.3-mile (2.1 km) hike to the national monument visitors center near the base of the iconic tower, along the South Side Trail that passes the much-photographed "Wind Circle" sculpture and a prairie dog town. Campers can also hike the Valley View Trail along the Belle Fourche River to Devil's Tower Trading Post and Campstool Cafe just outside the park's entrance station. The park amphitheater (and its summer ranger programs) is right beside the campground.

See the majestic Grand Tetons during a stay at the Colter Bay Campgrounds.

THE HIDEOUT LODGE & GUEST RANCH

🏠 10, ⛺ 4

3170 County Road 40 1/2, Shell, WY 82441

Open: April to November ▪ Rates: From $2,300 per person, all inclusive (four nights) ▪ Amenities: Swimming pool, internet, hot tub, airport shuttle, laundry ▪ ADA sites: No

Into horses? This home-away-from-home on the range offers authentic riding and ranch adventures combined with gourmet meals and upscale lodging against a backdrop of the snowcapped Bighorn Range. The equestrian menu ranges from riding lessons and trail rides to cattle drives, stockmanship clinics, and other livestock tasks. But Hideout offers far more than horses: Fly-fishing, trap shooting, archery, 4x4 tours, and photo workshops count among other ranch activities. Guests sleep in plush log cabins and casitas with Western furnishings, roomy bathrooms, heating and air-conditioning, and other creature comforts. Chef Rachel Marks whips up gourmet meals at the lodge restaurant.

HORSESHOE BEND CAMPGROUND

🚐 / ⛺ 19 partial hookup, 29 no hookup

Horseshoe Bend Road (off Highway 37), Lovell, WY 82431

Open: Year-round ▪ Rates: RV/tent partial hookup $26.25, RV/tent no hookup $15.75 ▪ Amenities: Dump station, restrooms, fire rings with grills, picnic tables, shade structures, camp store, potable water, ice, amphitheater ▪ ADA sites: Partial

The desert-like terrain of north-central Wyoming provides a stark but alluring backdrop for the largest campground serving Bighorn Canyon National Recreation Area. It sits back from the shore, but it's only a five-minute downhill walk across sagebrush flats to Horseshoe Bend Marina and Bighorn Lake. In addition to food and drink, the marina offers fishing and boating supplies and varied watercraft rentals (pontoon boats, small motorboats, canoes, kayaks, paddleboards), as well as fishing expeditions and scenic Bighorn Canyon cruises through Hidden Treasure Charters (Memorial Day to mid-September).

MORE TO CONSIDER

- **Grant Village Campground:** Yellowstone's second biggest campground (430 no-hookup RV/tent sites) lies along the western edge of Yellowstone Lake and within walking distance of Grant Village shopping, dining, and boating. *nps.gov/yell/planyourvisit/campgrounds.htm*

- **Curt Gowdy State Park:** Named after the famed sports broadcaster, this southeast Wyoming state park lies about halfway between Cheyenne and Laramie in the foothills of the Laramie Mountains. *wyoparks.wyo.gov/index.php/places-to-go/curt-gowdy*

- **Headwaters Lodge, RV Park & Campground:** John D. Rockefeller Jr. Memorial Parkway between Yellowstone and Grand Teton provides a stunning location for RV/tent sites and cabins along the Snake River. *nps.gov/grte/planyourvisit/headwaterscg.htm* and *gtlc.com/lodges/headwaters-lodge-at-flagg-ranch*

- **Glamping of Jackson Hole:** All-inclusive luxury camping in Bridger-Teton National Forest about a half-hour south of Jackson; meals and horseback riding included in the rate. *glampingofjacksonhole.com/*

BUFFALO BILL STATE PARK

🚐 / 🏕 37 partial hookup, 34 no hookup, 🏕 11

4192 North Fork Highway, Cody, WY 82414

Open: Year-round (Lake Shore Campground only) ▪ Rates: RV/tent partial hookup from $16/$21 (state resident/nonresident), RV/tent no hookup from $6/$11 ▪ Amenities: Dump station, showers, fire rings with grills, picnic tables, potable water, playground, boat ramp ▪ ADA sites: Partial

Buffalo Bill Cody was instrumental in creating the imposing concrete dam in northwest Wyoming that bears his name, a barrier that formed a reservoir that's also named for the famed Wild West showman. More than a century later, that lake is the centerpiece of a state park with two splendid campgrounds.

Experience the American West at Brush Creek Ranch.

Located near the dam and visitors center, North Shore Campground is the smaller of the two but the only one that's open year-round and overlooks the lake. Another 10 minutes down the highway, North Fork Campground is larger but set back from the water and only open from May to September. Both offer a blend of electric/water, no hookup, and tent-only sites. Amenities are rather limited—North Shore boasts a boat ramp, North Fork a playground—but you're really there for the lake—and nearby Cody, founded by Buffalo Bill in 1896 and home to the excellent Buffalo Bill Center of the West (five museums at one location) and the summertime Cody Nite Rodeo.

MAMMOTH CAMPGROUND

🚐 / 🏕 85 no hookup

North Entrance Road, Yellowstone National Park, WY 82190

Open: Year-round ▪ Rates: Vehicles $20, hikers/bicyclists $5 ▪ Amenities: Restrooms, camp store, fire rings with grill, picnic tables, potable water, amphitheater, firewood, ice, food storage lockers; no showers, dump station, or hookups ▪ ADA sites: Yes

It's not easy choosing among the 12 campgrounds inside Yellowstone National Park. Do you want to be close to the geyser fields, the lake, the best wildlife areas? But the only one that's open year-round —including the months when the park is mantled in a lovely coat of snow—is Mammoth Campground in the far north. Its other plus is lying just 5 miles (8 km) from Gardiner, Montana, and activities like white-water rafting on the Yellowstone River. With no hookups, this

Bison graze just feet from tent and RV campers at Mammoth Campground in Yellowstone National Park.

campsite is mostly used by car campers. Spread across the sagebrush steppe that dominates this corner of the park, the campground is within easy walking distance of Albright Visitor Center, Mammoth Hot Springs Terraces, and Yellowstone Wilderness Outfitters.

COLTER BAY
☎ 208, 🚐 / ⛺ 112 full hookup, 13 partial hookup, 333 no hookup
100 Colter Bay Campground Road, Colter Bay RV Park, Moran, WY 83013
Open: May/June to September/October ▪ Rates: RV resort $69-$91, campground $7-$36, cabins from $70 ▪ Amenities: Dump station, camp store, laundry, showers, internet, food storage lockers, firewood, ice,

potable water, amphitheater, fire pits, picnic tables ▪ ADA sites: Yes

Perched on the eastern edge of Jackson Lake, Colter Bay offers picture-postcard views of the Grand Tetons and more than 600 spots to overnight, from full-hookup RV sites to cozy cabins scattered through the lodgepole pines. No matter where you lay your head, it's a short walk to the visitors center, marina, and restaurants in Colter Bay Village, as well as an easy drive into Yellowstone or Jackson Hole.

FIRESIDE RESORT CABINS
☎ 25, 🚐 / ⛺ 60 partial hookup
2780 North State Highway 390, Wilson, WY 83014
Open: Year-round ▪ Rates: Cabins

from $279, RV/tent from $59 ▪ Amenities: Dump station, showers, laundry, camp store, picnic tables, fire pits, internet, cable TV, potable water, Jeep and RV rentals ▪ ADA sites: No

You might as well call them chic shacks rather than cabins because the ecofriendly, LEED-certified living units at Fireside are like nothing the Wyoming wilderness has ever seen before. They come in four designer-savvy styles from a caboose cabin that vaguely resembles something a 19th-century homesteader might have lived in to the streamlined, largely glass-enclosed Road Haus with its high ceiling and slanted roof. Each is equipped with king or queen bed and private bathroom, plus

Sustainably built, LEED-certified cabins at Fireside Resort are a luxe way to camp with modern amenities and nature.

indoor and outdoor seating areas. Some feature fireplaces and wide-screen TVs. The resort also offers partial-hookup RV sites.

EAGLE RV PARK & CAMPGROUND

🏠6, 🚐/🏕34 full hookup, 🏕2
204 U.S. Highway 20 South, Thermopolis, WY 82443
Open: Year-round ▪ Rates: RV/tent full hookup from $41.50, cabins from $54, tents $22.73 ▪ Amenities: Restrooms, showers, picnic tables, fire pits, laundry, cable TV, internet, playground, propane, horseshoes, camp store, firewood, ice ▪ ADA sites: No

Located in Thermopolis, about half-way between Casper and Yellowstone, Eagle is a convenient spot to break up what's otherwise a fairly boring drive across the Badlands of central Wyoming. But it's also an easy place to get yourself into hot water—of the natural, mineral-suffused variety, of course, because Thermopolis is renowned for its geothermal springs. With full-hookup RV slots, rustic log cabins, and tent-only camping in a grassy area beneath shade trees, the resort offers several ways to overnight. The Bighorn River is right across the road, and Hot Springs State Park with its modern spas and historic State Bath House is about a 10-minute drive up U.S. Highway 20.

BRUSH CREEK RANCH

🏠29
66 Brush Creek Ranch Road, Saratoga, WY 82331
Open: Year-round ▪ Rates: Doubles from $2,070 (all inclusive) ▪ Amenities: Restaurants, bars, spas, swimming pools, library, fitness center, lawn games, wine cellar ▪ ADA sites: Yes

Wedged between the Medicine Bow Mountains and the Platte River Valley of southern Wyoming, this 30,000-acre (12,140 ha) spread offers the ultimate western dude ranch experience. The resort's lavish log cabins are divided between the historic Magee Homestead and the modern Trailhead Lodge & Spa. Every cabin boasts two to three bedrooms and comfy living areas decked out in smart Western decor; some are also equipped with kitchens, fireplaces, and private hot tubs. Activities run a broad gamut from spa treatments, yoga, and cooking classes to horseback rides, fly-fishing, rock climbing, and winter sports.

GUERNSEY STATE PARK

🚐/🏕245 no hookup, 🏠4
2187 Lake Side Drive, Guernsey, WY 82214
Open: Year-round ▪ Rates: RV/tent from $15/$25 (state resident/non-resident), yurts $60 ▪ Amenities: Dump station, restrooms, picnic tables, fire rings, potable water, boat ramps ▪ ADA sites: Partial

Located about 90 minutes north of Cheyenne and not far off Interstate 25, Guernsey is one of the better places to camp in southeast Wyoming. The park revolves around Guernsey Reservoir, with 13 camping spots around the lakeshore. Sandy Beach and Sandy Point are the only two with electric and water hookups. There's also a small yurt cluster along the road to the "Million Dollar Biffy"—a giant stone-and-log latrine construction by the Civilian Conservation Corps (CCC) in the 1930s when the park was first developed. Spread across three sites, Guernsey's National Historic Landmark District boasts more than a dozen other iconic "parkitecture" structures built during the same era. There's plenty of other history nearby: Oregon Trail wagon ruts, the names of 19th-century emigrants chiseled in sandstone at Register Cliff, and Fort Laramie National Historic Site. Among the park's outdoor activities are boating, fishing, swimming, and hiking/biking along 12 miles (19 km) of restored CCC trails. ▪

SOMETHING SPECIAL

Guernsey State Park

Located near the main route of the Oregon Trail, Guernsey State Park takes in a pleasant, serpentine canyon rimmed with sandstone cliffs and shaded by strands of ponderosa pine and juniper. The North Platte River, impounded as a reservoir here, laps placidly at the base of the cliffs and offers an inviting respite from the heat of the Wyoming plains.

The Evergreen Glade Nature Trail departs from the visitors center and wanders among grassy rolling hills dotted with wildflowers and animal tracks. To get to the Oregon Trail ruts, follow Wyo. 26 through the town of Guernsey and the signs across the North Platte River. A short trail climbs to the top of a ridge sandstone where you'll find unmistakable wagon ruts cup deep into the rock. Forced by a topographical bottleneck to come this way, hundreds of thousands of pioneers guided their creaking loads over this beautiful prairie highland. Their wagon wheels soon cut through the thin soil and eventually left the ruts you see today.

Eastern Canada

From Newfoundland and Ontario to Mont-Tremblant in Quebec, Eastern Canada provides a rich array of landscapes and campgrounds that are equally diverse.

BERRY HILL CAMPGROUND

🏠 6, 🚐/🏕 25 partial hookup, 41 no hookup, 🏕 3

Route 430, Rocky Harbour, Newfoundland A0K 4N0, Canada
Open: June to October ▪ Rates: RV/tent partial hookup C$33.01, RV/tent no hookup C$26.06, cabins C$122.64, glamping units C$122.64 ▪ Amenities: Dump station, kitchen shelter, showers, picnic tables, fire rings, potable water, firewood, playground, internet ▪ ACA sites: Partial

Set along the Viking Trail on the west side of Newfoundland, Gros Morne National Park offers dramatic mountain and seacoast scenery that seems more like Scandinavia than the stereotypical Canadian wilderness. Berry Hill is the park's largest and most centrally located campground, a blend of waterpower sites, rustic cabins, and oTENTik glamping huts that are half A-frame cabins, half canvas tents. Parks Canada's answer to glamping, the latter feature beds, tables, chairs, and an electric heater but no running water or bathroom. Cooking is outdoors on a barbecue or the campground's shared kitchen

Bel Air Tremblant offers camping in geo domes outfitted with private hot tubs.

shelter. Berry Hill is close to Lobster Cove Head Lighthouse with its visitors center, live music, and storytelling sessions. And it's just a 10-minute drive to Rocky Harbour, where outfitters offer scenic fjord boat tours and cod jigging cruises.

MURPHY'S CAMPING ON THE OCEAN

🚐/🏕 19 partial hookup, 🏕 26

308 Murphys Road, Murphy Cove, Nova Scotia B0J 3H0, Canada
Open: May to October ▪ Rates: RV from C$44, tents C$33 ▪ Amenities: Dump station, restroom, laundry, picnic tables, fire pits, playground, boat ramp, internet ▪ ACA sites: Partial

They aren't kidding when they say "camping on the ocean," because some of the RV pads and tent sites at Murphy's are just steps away from the sea and a coast that shelters Nova Scotia's 100 Wild Islands region (although there are more like 400 islands total). Founded in 1960 and still family owned, the campground revolves around a small harbor and its two-story, clapboard lobster tank. Given the shoreline location, activities are heavily water based, including scenic boat tours, sea kayaking, and drop-off picnics on an uninhabited wilderness island. Anyone who brings a tent and other camping gear

can arrange an overnight experience on a wild isle. Murphy's also organizes campground bonfires with freshly steamed mussels, live music, and storytelling. One percent of its annual sales is donated to the Nova Scotia Nature Trust and other nonprofits.

HEADQUARTERS CAMPGROUND

🚐/🏕 30 full hookup, 25 partial hookup, 47 no hookup, 🏕 10, 🏠 5

11 Headquarters Campground Road, Fundy National Park, New Brunswick E4H 4S7, Canada
Open: May to October ▪ Rates: RV/tent partial hookup from C$36.08, RV/tent partial hookup C$24.02, RV/tent no hookup C$16.05, yurts C$117.53, glamping units C$102.20 ▪ Amenities: Dump station, showers, laundry, picnic tables, internet ▪ ACA sites: Partial

HIGHLIGHTS

Capital: Ottawa

Total National Parks: 41 (Largest is Wood Buffalo National Park of Canada)

Total Marine Conservation Areas: 3 (Largest is Tuvaijuittuq Marine Protected Area)

Major Mountain Ranges: Rockies, Coast, Laurentian

Major Rivers: St. Lawrence, Mackenzie

Official Languages: English, French

Wildlife Spotting: Black bears; wolves; beavers; deer; mountain lions; bighorn sheep; raccoons; otters; rabbits; bison; pronghorn antelope; moose; caribou; musk ox; wolves; lynx; Atlantic fish

Fast Fact: Canada's lakes and rivers contain about 20 percent of all freshwater on Earth

Fundy National Park offers several camping spots, but the only one with full hookups within walking distance of restaurants and shops in Alma village is Headquarters Campground beside the visitors center. Despite its less-than-enticing name, it offers several overnight options from full-hookup RV pads to yurts and oTENTik glamping units. Local hot spots like Tipsy Tales lobster eatery, the Muddy Rudder Bar, and Holy Whale Brewery are just across the bridge. And it's near places where campers can experience the Bay of Fundy's world-record tides (as great as 52 feet/16 m) and the tidal bore that rushes up the Upper Salmon River.

PARC AVENTURES CAP JASEUX

🏕8, 🚐/🛶 13 partial hookup, 13 no hookup, 🏠 2, ⛺ 3, 5 coolboxes, 2 suspended spheres
250 Chemin de la Pointe aux Pins, Saint-Fulgence, Quebec G0V 1S0, Canada
Open: June to October ▪ Rates: Cabins from C$80, tree houses/coolboxes/domes/suspended spheres C$245, RV/tent C$40.50 ▪ Amenities: Private bathrooms, cooking/kitchen area, bedding rentals, heating and air-conditioning, potable water, dump station, laundry, bathhouse, laundry, picnic tables, fire pits ▪ ACA sites: Partial

This adventure resort along the north shore of the spectacular Saguenay Fjord pushes the outer edge of the envelope on wilderness lodging. In addition to traditional log cabins, Cap Jaseux offers tree houses, geodesic domes, translucent spheres suspended from the forest canopy, and prefabricated metal "coolboxes." While the indoor aspect is certainly intriguing, there's plenty to lure you from the comfy digs. Guests can undertake a treetop adventure course with zip lines and aerial bridges, scramble across a via ferrata rock climbing course, kayak a fjord renowned for its whale population, pick wild mushrooms, hike boreal forest trails, or pamper themselves with a massage on the beach.

ENTRE CÎMES ET RACINES FOREST LODGES

🏠14
80 Chemin Simard, Bolton-Est, Quebec J0E 1G0, Canada
Open: Year-round ▪ Rates: From C$115 ▪ Amenities: Bathhouse, kitchens, private toilets, wood-burning stoves, picnic tables, fire pits, firewood, candles, potable water, ice, snowshoe rental, bedding and towel rental, shop ▪ ACA sites: Yes

Inspired by fairy tales, legends, and fantasy stories, this romantic retreat features cabins with a wide array of architecture and decor. Le Hobbit really does look like somewhere Frodo Baggins might have lived, La Table Ronde honors King Arthur and his knights, and a Stone Age revival called La Pierre de Feu would make Fred Flintstone feel right at home. Located in Quebec's eastern townships region about an hour from Montreal, the lodges are scattered around a faux medieval structure called the Campanile, which hosts the reception, shop, bathhouse, and communal lounge. The property boasts more than 9 miles (15 km) of trails and forest roads for hiking and mountain biking. Guests can also forage for mushrooms, gaze at the night sky, or navigate a maze. Open throughout the year, Entre Cîmes et Racines offers snowshoeing, cross-country skiing, and tobogganing during the snow season.

BEL AIR TREMBLANT

⛺ 6, 6 pods , 4 mini-lofts, 11 chalets
80 Rue des Sept Sommets, Mont-Tremblant, Quebec J0T 1M0, Canada
Open: Year-round ▪ Rates: Domes from C$370, pods from C$330, mini-lofts from C$200, chalets from C$300

Entre Cîmes et Racines offers forest eco-lodges that blend into the scenery.

There are breathtaking views of Lake Superior from Ontario's Sleeping Giant Provincial Park.

■ Amenities: Restaurant, spa, fitness center, swimming pool, sports courts, bocce ball, archery, zip line, farm animals, winter sports rentals ■ ACA sites: Yes

Mont-Tremblant is Montreal's big backyard, a place to hike, bike, and paddle during the warmer months and downhill ski or snowboard come winter. From campsites and yurts inside Mont-Tremblant National Park to fancy ski hotels, there are scores of overnight options, but no others as intriguing as Bel Air, a designer-savvy cabin resort with a blend of geodesic domes, pods, chalets, and "mini-loft" cabins that could easily have been created for a sci-fi movie. Sleeping anywhere from two to eight people, the cabins range from Love Nest domes with an outdoor

hot tub and a futuristic wood-and-glass Ushuaia pod to a postmodern industrial-style Andorra mini-loft and boxy Cortina chalet that was surely inspired by Habitat '67, a revolutionary residential space at the 1967 Montreal world's fair. The clubhouse boasts a bistro for lunch and dinner, full-service spa and fitness center, outdoor swimming pool, and small cinema space for movie nights.

LONG POINT ECO-ADVENTURES
☎ 2, 🏠 2, 17 pods
1730 Front Road, St. Williams, Ontario N0E 1P0, Canada
Open: Glamping May to October, pods and cabins year-round ■ Rates: Glamping pods & tents from C$229, cabins from C$199 ■ Amenities: Restaurant, bar, fire pits,

bike and paddleboard rental, ax throwing, internet ■ ACA sites: Yes

Ax throwing, an apiary bee colony experience, foodie cycling tour, and kayaking on Lake Erie are just a few of the adventures on tap at this Turkey Point outdoor resort. Located about a two-hour drive west of Niagara Falls, Long Point lodges its overnight guests in "wilderness suite" glamping tents and half-barrel-shaped wooden glamping pods, as well as a vintage log cabin and farmhouse. The pods can be rented individually or in clusters for families or groups that want to glamp together. Marshview Patio serves fresh salads, burgers, vegetarian fare, and suds from the resort's own Hometown Brew Co. Glampers can also dive into excellent food, beverage, and live music at Burning Kiln Winery across the road.

Built in 1992, the 94-foot (29 m) Point Wolfe Covered Bridge offers a protected overpass through Fundy National Park.

CYPRUS LAKE CAMPGROUND

🚐/🏕 232 no hookup, 🏠 10

Cyprus Lake Road, Tobermory, Ontario N0H 2R0, Canada
Open: Year-round ▪ Rates: RV/tent from C$24.02, winter camping C$16.05 ▪ Amenities: Restrooms, picnic tables, fire pits with grills, potable water, firewood, beach, amphitheater ▪ ACA sites: Partial

One of Ontario's best-kept secrets, Bruce Peninsula National Park protects a swath of waterfront wilderness on a narrow slice of land between Lake Huron and Georgian Bay. Cyprus Lake, the park's only front-country campground, offers more than 200 dry RV/tent sites and comfy yurts along three loops beside its namesake lake. The big water is about a 20-minute walk from the campground on trails leading to Boulder Beach, Indian Head Cove, and the Grotto along the shore of Georgian Bay. Most of the campground is closed between November and April, but about a third of the Tamaracks loop is open for winter camping—the weather can be extreme and dangerous.

MEW LAKE CAMPGROUND

🚐/🏕 58 partial hookup, 65 no hookup, 🏠 8

Frank MacDougall Parkway (Route 60), Algonquin Provincial Park, Ontario, Canada
Open: Year-round ▪ Rates: RV/tent partial hookup C$53.68, no hookup C$47.46, yurts C$97.18 ▪ Amenities: Camp store, showers, laundry, picnic tables, fire pits, firewood, potable water, beach, bike rental and repair ▪ ACA sites: Partial

Disappear into Ontario's vast boreal forest at a wilderness campground in Algonquin Provincial Park. Around a three-hour drive from Toronto or Ottawa, Mew Lake offers a selection of electric and no hookup sites for RVs and tents, as well as a handful of yurts. A radio-free and dog-free camping zone on the west side of Mew Lake is reserved for those who prefer birdsong and the sound of wind whistling through the trees rather than loud music or barking. For those who want to get even farther off the grid—and test their wilderness skills at the same time—the park's Portage Store offers overnight guided canoe camping tours and multiday backcountry canoe and equipment rentals.

MARIE LOUISE LAKE CAMPGROUND

🏚 5, 🚐/🏕 53 partial hookup, 97 no hookup, 🏕 50

Route 587, Sleeping Giant Provincial Park, Silver Islet, Ontario P0T 2M0, Canada
Open: Camping May to October, cabins year-round ▪ Rates: RV/tent partial hookup C$43.75, RV/tent no hookup C$38.75, tent only C$38.75, cabins C$169.50 (two-night minimum stay) ▪ Amenities: Dump station, restrooms, picnic tables, fire pits, potable water, firewood, ice, amphitheater, beach, boat ramp ▪ ACA sites: Yes

Much of western Ontario is sparsely inhabited and protected within the confines of nature reserves like Sleeping Giant Provincial Park along the north shore of Lake Superior. Occupying most of the Sibley Peninsula near Thunder Bay, the park gets its peculiar name from its most prominent geographical feature: a long, flat-topped mountain that resembles a reclining human form. Campers can slumber beside the giant at Marie Louise Lake in the heart of the park. Electric hookup sites sit beneath trees away from the shore, while many of the tent-only plots are on a point that juts into the lake; the latter don't feature much protection from the wind, but that also means fewer midges and mosquitoes. Campers can reach the lofty Top of the Giant lookout via a 7.9-mile (12.8 km) path along Lake Superior. ▪

SOMETHING SPECIAL

Sleeping Giant Provincial Park

Offering sweeping views of Lake Superior (best seen from the Top of the Giant Trail and Thunder Bay Lookout), Sleeping Giant offers 62 miles (100 km) of hiking trails throughout its 60,293-acre (24,400 ha) landscape, as well as 31 miles (50 km) of well-groomed skate and classic cross-country skiing trails every winter.

Set on the southern tip of a rugged peninsula near Thunder Bay, the beloved park features boreal forests, lowlands, and of course access to Lake Superior, the largest freshwater lake in the world. In the park's boreal forest, you can look to the skies to spot more than 200 bird species, and keep an eye on the ground too for deer, wolf, fox, and lynx. For an easy hike in the park, tackle the Middlebrun Bay and Finlay Bay Trails, which take you to a secluded sandy beach and lead you to Finlay Bay. More serious hikers can tackle the Kabeyun Trail, an overnight trek along the coast that offers lookouts to Thundery Bay and paths along the beaches and coves of Lake Superior.

Western Canada

Western Canadian camping is all about the wild: glamping in North America's largest wilderness area, a cabin stay on Nimmo Bay, or tent camping in mountainous forests.

KATHLEEN LAKE CAMPGROUND

🚐/🏕 38 no hookup, 🏕 5

Kathleen Lake Road (off Haines Highway), Kluane National Park, Destruction Bay, Yukon Y0B 1H0, Canada

Open: May to September ▪ Rates: RV/tent C$22 per person, glamping tents C$122.64 ▪ Amenities: Restrooms, picnic tables, fire rings, firewood, food storage containers, fishing, guided walks, boat dock and ramp ▪ ACA sites: Partial

"Into the wild" is the theme of this Yukon campground, an overnight spot on the doorstep of Kluane National Park, one of North America's largest and least tamed wilderness areas. The sites are scattered through a mixed evergreen and deciduous forest near the eastern edge of its namesake lake. In addition to three dozen dry campsites, there are a handful of Parks Canada's popular oTENTik glamping tents. Whether it's paddling the lake against a backdrop of snowcapped Kathleen Peak or hiking nearby trails, campers can get a taste of Kluane's remarkable landscape without the need to hike for days or hop a bush plane into the park's nether regions.

Find epic thrills on rushing white water with REO Rafting and Yoga Resort.

REO RAFTING RESORT

 23

61755 Nahatlatch Forest Service Road, Boston Bar, British Columbia V0K 1C0, Canada

Open: May to September ▪ Rates: From C$320 per person ▪ Amenities: Restaurant, bathhouse, hammocks, guided hikes, rafting, yoga, archery, hot tub, massage, communal campfire ▪ ACA sites: No

Pampered glamping and rugged overnight rafting trips are the forte of this outdoor adventure resort in the Fraser Canyon region of south-central British Columbia. REO offers fully catered glamping in designer-savvy tents featuring king, queen, or twin beds and private balconies. Mornings are set aside for activities like cliff jumping, guided hikes, or river rafting, and afternoons are for yoga, hot tub soaking, a massage, or snoozing in the resort's hammock garden. There's a complimentary social hour with wine, cider, and appetizers, and every night there's a communal campfire.

NIMMO BAY WILDERNESS RESORT

🏠 9

100 Little Nimmo Bay, Mackenzie Sound, Mount Waddington A, British Columbia V0N 2R0, Canada

HIGHLIGHTS

Capital: Ottawa

Total National Parks: 41 (Largest is Wood Buffalo National Park of Canada)

Total Marine Conservation Areas: 3 (Largest is Tuvaijuittuq Marine Protected Area)

Major Mountain Ranges: Rockies, Coast, Laurentian

Major Rivers: St. Lawrence, Mackenzie

Official Languages: English, French

Wildlife Spotting: Black bears; wolves; beavers; deer; mountain lions; bighorn sheep; raccoons; otters; rabbits; bison; pronghorn antelope; moose; caribou; musk ox; wolves; lynx

Fast Fact: Canada's lakes and rivers contain about 20 percent of all freshwater on Earth

Open: May to November ▪ Rates: From C$1,495 per person, per day all inclusive (three-night minimum stay) ▪ Amenities: Restaurant, bar, gift shop, bedding and towels, organic bath and beauty products, Bose iPod dock, daily housekeeping, laundry service, sauna, hot tubs, massage, yoga, meditation, fitness center, game room, plunge pool, helipads, internet ▪ ACA sites: No

You're going to need a boat, helicopter, or floatplane to reach this super-secluded retreat along the British Columbia coast around 200 miles (321 km) north of Vancouver. Set on a fjord that reaches deep into the Great Bear Rainforest, the resort offers luxury cabins arrayed along the waterfront or tucked into the woods. Guests can paddle to a floating sauna or stroll through the woods to a spa with massage and aromatherapy, as well as alfresco meditation and an outdoor Gin & Yin session that combines yoga and cocktails. Nimmo Bay's restaurant serves modern Pacific Northwest dishes with many of the ingredients foraged from the surrounding forest or harvested in local waters. There's adventure too: paddling, hiking, personalized helicopter forays, and guided Zodiac trips to look for whales and bears.

CLAYOQUOT WILDERNESS RETREAT

🏕 25

Bedwell River Valley, Alberni-Clayoquot C, British Columbia V0R 2Z0, Canada

Open: May to September ▪ Rates: From C$1,700 per night, per person all inclusive (three-night minimum stay) ▪ Amenities: Restaurant, bar, private bathrooms with outdoor cedar shower, bedding and towels, woodstove fireplace, laundry and dry cleaning, helipad, fishing, paddling, horseback riding, spa, yoga, internet ▪ ACA sites: No

Vancouver Island's remote west coast provides a superb location for a fly-in glamping experience that revolves around posh tents rather than upscale cabins. Tucked into the temperate rainforest at the top of Clayoquot Sound, the resort takes full advantage of a wilderness area that was protected in the 1990s as a result of protests by environmentalists and First Nations people. After a day of hiking, paddling, heli-adventures, or wildlife photography, guests return to tents equipped with king beds, private bathrooms, plus a balcony with Adirondack chairs to read or contemplate the sunset over the sound. Rounding out the resort amenities are the Healing Grounds Spa, the Ivanhoe Bar and its extensive wine cellar, and the Cookhouse restaurant with floor-to-ceiling windows overlooking the water.

WHISTLERS CAMPGROUND

🚐/🏕 123 full hookup, 126 partial hookup, 531 no hookup, 🏕 21

Icefields Highway, Jasper, Alberta T0E 1E0, Canada

Open: May to October ▪ Rates: RV/tent full hookup from C$39.04/47.84, partial hookup from C$33.01, no hookup from C$23, glamping tents from C$122.64 ▪ Amenities: Dump station, showers, kitchen shelters, picnic tables, fire pits with grills, firewood, food storage containers, playgrounds, amphitheater ▪ ACA sites: Yes

Reopened in 2021 after a makeover that cost nearly C$50 million, Whistlers is one of Parks Canada's most modern and efficient campgrounds. The revamp included new washrooms and showers, wider roads, better hookups, and a registration office that doubles as a visitors center. With more than 780 sites along 48 loops, it's also one of the largest campgrounds in the Canadian national park system. A location along the Athabasca River in the middle of Jasper National Park makes it easy to escape into the park's vast wilderness by foot, bike, or car.

A spur trail near the campground's north end leads to the Jasper Sky Tram's lower terminal and a footpath that zig-zags to the summit of Whistler Peak with its panoramic views over the valley. Another hike/bike route heads for nearby Jasper village for shopping, dining, and outfitters for white-water rafting and other outdoor adventures, as well as the Jasper Park visitors center and Jasper Museum. And right outside the campground entrance is the legendary Icefields Parkway, a world-famous scenic drive flanked by glaciers, snowcapped peaks, and alpine lakes.

TUNNEL MOUNTAIN VILLAGE

🚐/🏕 321 full hookup, 188 partial hookup, 618 no hookup, 🏕 10

Beautiful Trapper's Tents at Sundance Lodges in the heart of the Canadian Rockies

Nothing beats a hammock break with a view, particularly of the majestic scenery within Banff National Park.

Tunnel Mountain Road, Banff, Alberta T1L 1B3, Canada

Open: Tunnel Mountain Village II year-round, others May to October ▪ Rates: RV full hookup C$38.20, RV/tent partial hookup C$32.30, RV/tent no hookup C$27.40, glamping tents C$120 ▪ Amenities: Restaurants, bars, dump stations, showers, picnic tables, fire pits, firewood, potable water, food storage containers, municipal bus service, RV wash ▪ ACA sites: Yes

With more than 1,100 sites, Tunnel Mountain Village often feels more like a small town than a wilderness retreat. But you can't knock a location in the heart of Banff National Park. The village divides into four separate and very distinct campgrounds: full hookup, power and

water, dry camping, and oTENTik glamping tents. Flush with evergreen trees, Village 1 offers more seclusion and shade. The Village Trailer Court boasts the most dramatic views over the Bow River Valley and majestic Mount Rundle. Village II is closest to Banff village. An easy trail loops through the woods around all four camping areas, another leads along the river, and a couple of short but steep trails take hikers to the summit of Tunnel Mountain.

SUNDANCE LODGES
🚐 / 🏕 8 no hookup, 🏕 42, 12 tipis
2 Sundance Road (off Highway 40), Kananaskis, Alberta T0L 2H0, Canada

Open: May to September ▪ Rates: Glamping tents from C$98.50, tipis

from C$79.50, RV/tent C$36 ▪ Amenities: Camp store, bathhouse, laundry, picnic tables, fire pits with grills, rental camping supplies and sports equipment, potable water, firewood, propane, sports courts ▪ ACA sites: No

Flanked by the Bow Valley and Elbow-Sheep Wildland Provincial Parks, family-friendly Sundance opens a door on the region's eclectic activities. That variety extends to the camp's overnight options: glamping in Trapper's tents or Sioux-style canvas tipis or a DIY at a small selection of dry RV and tent sites. You have to bring your own bedding, but the Sundance Trading Post sells groceries, the bathhouse has hot showers, and you can disappear into the wilderness in seconds on a trail along the Kananaskis River or another to Beaver Ponds.

Not your typical camping experience, Nimmo Bay offers modern luxuries, including massages in the forest.

TOWNSITE CAMPGROUND

94 full hookup, 46 partial hookup, 48 no hookup, 47 Windflower Avenue, Waterton Park, Alberta T0K 2M0, Canada
Open: May to September • Rates: RV/tent full hookup C$39.04, partial hookup C$33.01, no hookup C$28, tent only C$23 • Amenities: Dump station, showers, kitchen shelters, picnic tables, potable water, food storage containers, amphitheater, internet • ACA sites: Yes

Of all the incredible locations in Canada's national and provincial parks, this might just be the most stunning—a lakeside bivouac surrounded by Rocky Mountain peaks and forest beside the historic village in Waterton-Glacier National Park. If you're there for adventure, hike the Bertha Lake Loop (9.1 miles/14 km) to a pristine alpine lake or the Great Divide Trail along Upper Waterton Lake to Boundary Bay (16.2 miles/ 26 km return). If you're more the aquatic type, the lake offers paddling, kite surfing, fishing, and even scuba diving. If you're there to relax, stroll into the village and visit local hot spots like Welch's Chocolate Shop, Big Scoop Ice Cream, or the Thirsty Bear Bar.

HISTORIC REESOR RANCH

5 Maple Creek, Saskatchewan S0N 1N0, Canada
Open: Year-round • Rates: From C$129 • Amenities: Restaurant, bar, kitchenettes, private bathrooms, Jacuzzi tubs, bedding and towels, air-conditioning, barbecues, fire pits, potable water, firewood, horseback riding, ATV and walking tours, sports courts, internet • ACA sites: Partial

A homestead built in 1904 by the Reesor family, the ranch now sprawls across the open prairie on the edge of the Cypress Hills in western Saskatchewan. As a bona fide heritage property, the spread preserves five vintage structures built during or before World War I. Guests can overnight in three of those buildings. The Bunkhouse (built in 1906) is ideal for a couple or family, the Arts and Crafts–style Ranch House (1916) offers bed-and-breakfast rooms; and the Old Log Barn (1906) is reserved for larger groups. While equine activities like trail rides, breakfast or supper rides, and cattle driving are the ranch's main allure, Reesor also offers guided ATV tours through the Cypress Hills.

WASAGAMING CAMPGROUND

85 full hookup, 278 partial hookup, 20 no hookup, 29, 1, 1 micro-cube
Buffalo Drive, Riding Mountain National Park, Manitoba R0J 2H0, Canada
Open: May to October • Rates: RV/ tent full hookup C$39.04, partial hookup from C$33.01, no hookup C$28, glamping tents/yurts from C$102.20, micro-cubes from C$91.98 • Amenities: Restaurants, bar, dump station, showers, laundry, kitchen shelters, picnic tables, fire pits with grills, firewood, potable water, playground, tennis courts, bowling green, beach, marina, boat rental, scenic cruises, golf course • ACA sites: Yes

One of Canada's best-kept (outdoor) secrets, Riding Mountain National Park protects a large expanse of forest, prairie, and wetlands in southern Manitoba. Managed by a unique partnership between Parks Canada and local First Nations peoples, the park is also a UNESCO Biosphere Reserve. Wasagaming offers more than 300 tree-shaded sites near Clear Lake on the park's south side. Visitors can also overnight in glamping tents or futuristic micro-cube cabins. The beach, marina, and a grassy lakeside picnic area are just a 10- to 15-minute walk depending on where you're camped. Wasagaming village sports bars, restaurants, shops, and the park's visitors center, as well as plenty of recreation including tennis courts, a lawn bowling green, and golf courses. It also plays host to an independent film festival each summer. ∎

SOMETHING SPECIAL

Riding Mountain National Park

Set in Manitoba, Canada, Riding Mountain National Park protects windswept grasslands, silent forests, secretive wolf packs, lakes, and wetlands. Teeming with life, the park functions in coordination with the Anishinabe First Nations people to honor and protect the Indigenous heritage of the land.

If you're visiting in the summer, the park offers more than 250 miles (402 km) of hiking trails to explore, including routes that are friendly for horseback riders and cyclists. There's also plenty of swimming to be had while the weather is warm, including in Lake Katherine, Lake Audy, and Moon Lake. Sandy beaches offer the perfect picnic area after a day on the water. Come colder months, visitors can ice fish on Clear Lake or tackle one of many cross-country ski trails.

Puerto Rico & U.S. Virgin Islands

If you're looking for an easy way to enjoy an island oasis, free of the all-inclusive resort scene, look no further than a camping retreat on one of these tropical locales.

Puerto Rico

PITAHAYA GLAMPING
▲ 5

Highway 303, Cabo Rojo 00623, Puerto Rico

Open: Year-round ▪ Rates: From $125 ▪ Amenities: En suite bathrooms, mini-kitchens, grills, outdoor tables, swimming pool, communal fire pit, garden ▪ ADA sites: No

The brains behind Puerto Rico's first glamping resort couldn't have picked a better location—a secluded farm near Cabo Rojo along the island's stunning southwest coast. The safari tents are well spaced, ensuring maximum privacy, all of them equipped with a private bathroom, outlets to recharge electric devices, and a mini-kitchen on the front deck that includes a sink and fridge. When they're not out exploring the Cabo Rojo region, guests gather around the pool during daylight hours and the fire pit at night. Playa La Pitahaya is a 10-minute walk down the road. Among other local

A leader in ecotourism, Concordia Eco-Resort is located on the shore of Virgin Islands National Park.

attractions are night sky shows at the Sociedad de Astronomía del Caribe observatory and historic San Germán (founded in 1511 and one of the oldest European cities in the Americas), as well as the beaches, towering sea cliffs, and Instagram-worthy lighthouse at Cabo Rojo.

ISLA DE MONA
Sandy beach camping

Isla de Mona, Puerto Rico

Open: Year-round ▪ Rate: Acampa package $649 per person (three nights) ▪ Amenities: Restrooms, picnic shelters, boat docks, nature trails ▪ ADA sites: No

The "Galápagos of the Caribbean" lies about 40 miles (64 km) west of Mayagüez in the Mono Strait between Puerto Rico and the Dominican Republic. The entire island is a nature reserve, uninhabited except for rangers and researchers. With a permit from the Department of Natural and Environmental Resources (DRNA), primitive camping is allowed on two beaches, Playa Sardinera and Playa de Pájaros, for a maximum stay of three nights. Campfires are not permitted, and visitors must depart with all of their trash.

Despite its name, there are no monkeys on the island but plenty of other creatures, including endemic birds and the oddball Mono land iguana. The offshore reefs are great for scuba and snorkeling, but campers need to bring all of their own equipment. The easiest way to overnight on Mona is an organized tour through Acampa Nature Adventures in San Juan.

PARADOR VILLAS SOTOMAYOR
🏠 34

Highway 123, Km. 36.6, Adjuntas 00601, Puerto Rico

Open: Year-round ▪ Rate: $126 ▪ Amenities: Restaurant, bar, swimming pool, gardens, playground, basketball, volleyball, billiards, gym, horseback riding ▪ ADA sites: Yes

One of Puerto Rico's oldest mountain retreats has been around since

1970, a villa complex tucked way up in the highlands about 30 minutes north of Ponce. Equipped with full kitchens, private bathrooms, air-conditioning, and colorful one-off decor, they are scattered along broad lawns and leafy lanes with jungle-covered mountains as a backdrop. There's a great little cantina with cocktails, cold beer, and live music, as well as Restaurant Las Garzas with Puerto Rican specialties. Trail rides are a big part of the Sotomayor experience, but it's also easy to pop into Ponce, the island's second largest city, renowned for its exquisite colonial-era architecture and one of the best art museums in the Caribbean.

FINCA ORO ROJO
🏕️4

Calle Gregorio, Barrio Damian Arriba, Orocovis 00720, Puerto Rico
Open: Year-round ▪ Rate: $150 ▪ Amenities: Cooking facilities, barbecue grill, kitchen utensils, dinnerware, fire pit, private bathrooms, showers, yard games, hammocks ▪ ADA sites: Yes

Located almost directly on Puerto Rico's geographical center, Red Gold

Farm bills itself as an agro-ecological experience in the rugged highlands around 90 minutes from San Juan. The glamping tents are decorated with queen bed, carpets, nature books, flowers, and fine bedding, and the decor can be customized for birthdays, honeymoons, or other special occasions. Complimentary breakfast comes with fresh eggs, plantains, green tomatoes, and other ingredients straight from the farm. Glampers can harvest from the Oro Rojo gardens and cook their own lunch or dinner in the shared kitchen. The farm strives for zero waste, and guests are encouraged not to bring any plastics. Chill out with a forest therapy session or work up a sweat at nearby Toro Negro State Forest or Toro Verde Adventure Park and its Monster zip line (longest in the Western Hemisphere).

TORO NEGRO STATE FOREST
Lawn area for tents
Ruta Panorámica (Highway 143), Orocovis 00766, Puerto Rico
Open: Year-round ▪ Rate: $4 per person ▪ Amenities: Restroom, showers, picnic area, fire pits, grills, potable water ▪ ADA sites: No

Set in the lush highlands near the island's east end, El Yunque is the only tropical rainforest in the U.S. National Forest system. The hiking is awesome, but there are no campgrounds or other ways to spend the night inside the park. However, Puerto Rico's 20 state forests *(bosques estatal)* offer plenty of scope for overnights amid the exotic smells and sounds of the Caribbean jungle. Positioned near the park headquarters, Toro Negro's Área de Acampar provides a lawn area for pitching tents beside wooden rain/sun picnic shelters and a brick platform to stoke a campfire. Nearby are a restroom and showers.

A short trail links the campground with Charco La Confesora, a small waterfall and swimming hole. Toro Negro is about a two-hour drive from central San Juan but less than an hour from the fascinating city of Ponce on the island's south coast. The Puerto Rico Department of Natural and Environmental Resources (DRNA) requires that visitors obtain a permit before camping at Toro Negro, but it appears that most campers simply pay the overnight fee to a ranger on arrival.

PLAYA FLAMENCO CAMPGROUND
Sandy spots amid the trees
Playa Flamenco, Isla Culebra 00775, Puerto Rico
Open: Year-round ▪ Rate: $20 ▪ Amenities: Snack bars, restroom, outdoor showers, picnic tables, fire pits ▪ ADA sites: No

Ranked as one of the world's best beaches in several surveys, Playa Flamenco on Culebra Island offers the whole tropical paradise package: talcum-powder-fine sand curving

Disconnect and relax on sandy shores at Pitahaya Glamping in Puerto Rico.

Isla de Mona is Puerto Rico's third largest island, with coastal hiking and sandy shores on Playa Cocos.

1 mile (1.6 km) around a turquoise bay flush with coral and colorful fish. It also flaunts an awesome campground, set amid shade trees along the western edge of the bay. Flamenco is tent-only camping—or hammocks for those who take their tropical nights with a dose of fresh air. The beach and warm tropical water are just footsteps away. If there's a downside, it's a lack of amenities other than picnic tables and a comfort station with cold showers.

But not to fret. Just down the strand are a couple of snack bar kiosks with local delicacies like stuffed *empanadillas* (turnovers), *carne frita* (fried pork), *pechuga* (garlic chicken), *ensalada de carrucho* (conch salad), and piña coladas that you can down on the spot or take away to your campsite. The

campground is also close to the "painted tanks" of Playa Flamenco—a pair of rusting, graffiti-covered Sherman tanks left over from the days when Isla Culebra was a military training ground rather than a holiday destination.

U.S. Virgin Islands

MOUNT VICTORY CAMP

4, lawn space for tents
Creque Dam Road, Frederiksted, St. Croix 00840, U.S. Virgin Islands
Open: Year-round ▪ Rates: Cabins from $70, tents $30 ▪ Amenities: Hot showers, cooking pavilion, shared campfire area and picnic tables, internet ▪ ADA sites: No

The four "landship" cabins at Mount Victory were crafted by a master shipwright from timber salvaged from tropical hardwood trees felled by hurricanes, old age, and other natural factors. Sleeping four to five people each, the cabins are arrayed around a base camp with shared showers, cooking, and dining facilities about 20 minutes from the St. Croix airport. Tent camping is also available on the grounds, but you need to bring all of your own equipment.

The husband-and-wife owners offer guided hikes on various island trails, as well as workshops in Indigenous ancestral skills like basketry, pottery, edible plants, and making bows, arrows, and fishing spears. They also teach tropical wilderness survival skills including a week-long

Find resort-like amenities at Virgin Island Campgrounds, set on 500-acre (202.3 ha) Water Island in the U.S. Virgin Islands.

Calabash Survival Quest with overnights in the bush. Mount Victory nurtures a colony of South American red-footed tortoises *(Geocolonius denticultata),* and the camp is close to other island landmarks like the historic Mount Washington Estate, Mahogany Road Chocolate Factory, and Rainbow Beach.

VIRGIN ISLANDS CAMPGROUND

🏠 8

64 Water Island, St. Thomas 00802, U.S. Virgin Islands

Open: Year-round ▪ Rates: From $149 (two- to three-night minimum stay) ▪ Amenities: Bathhouse, cooking pavilion, shared picnic table, snorkel gear, hot tub, media room, internet ▪ ADA sites: No

Water Island—fourth largest of the U.S. Virgin Isles—offers a secluded tropical location for this Caribbean-style glamping resort. The canvas-and-wood tent cottages feature queen or twin beds, plus towels and bedding, as well as double futons that fold out into additional beds. They're also equipped with coolers for drinks and snacks, open-air decks with chairs and ocean views, and electrical outlets fueled by wind power. The busy St. Thomas waterfront is just a seven-minute cruise from Water Island ferry pier, about a 10-minute walk from the resort. The glampground is also within easy walking distance of Honeymoon Beach, Rachel's golf cart rentals, Dinghy's Beach Bar, and the island's only convenience store.

CINNAMON BAY BEACH & CAMPGROUND

🏠 50, ▲ 55, ⛰ 30

North Shore Road, St. John 00830, U.S. Virgin Islands

Open: Year-round ▪ Rates: Cabins/glamping tents from $87, tent only from $37 ▪ Amenities: Restaurant, shop, showers, picnic tables, water sports rentals and lessons ▪ ADA sites: Yes

One of the world's original glamping spots, Cinnamon Bay offers cottages, safari tents, and bare sites for tents beside a coral-flush bay in Virgin Islands National Park along the north shore of St. John. The resort was severely damaged in 2017 by Hurricanes Irma and Maria, which hit the island two weeks apart. The privately run resort reopened in late 2021 with totally new indoor and outdoor overnight digs, as well as rebuilt restaurant, shop, and other facilities. Cinnamon Bay is the most obvious attraction with its snorkeling, scuba, swimming, sailing, and paddling. But there are also trails into the interior, the ruins of an 18th-century Dutch sugar plantation, and archaeological digs that have uncovered ancient Taino Indian sites.

CONCORDIA ECO-RESORT

🏠 8, ▲ 30

St. John 00830, U.S. Virgin Islands

Open: Year-round ▪ Rates: Cabins from $229, glamping tents from $169 (three-night minimum stay) ▪ Amenities: Restaurant, gift shop, swimming pool, water sports equipment, internet, private bathrooms with showers, kitchens ▪ ADA sites: Yes

A dramatic bluff-top location overlooking St. John's southeast shore—with the deep blue Caribbean Sea spreading to the horizon—makes it feel like you've arrived at the end of the earth. Aiding and abetting the resort's romantic ambience are spiffy eco-studio cottages and glamping tents that flow down a cactus-studded slope above Drunk Bay, Salt Pond, and Ram Head. Perched on wooden stilts and platforms, the tents feel more like tree houses than ground-level glamping abodes. Concordia is perfectly placed for exploring the secluded beaches and trails that suffuse the east end of Virgin Islands National Park. Given that it's situated a good 40-minute drive from Cruz Bay village and the interisland ferry pier, the resort owners strongly suggest that guests rent a car or 4x4 for the duration of their stay. ▪

SOMETHING SPECIAL

Virgin Islands National Park

The elements of a dream tropical vacation can be found on St. John, one of the U.S. Virgin Islands, located east of Puerto Rico in the Caribbean Sea. Some of the world's most beautiful beaches invite sunbathing and swimming, and the coral reefs and sea-grass beds located just offshore offer the beauty of diverse marine life to snorkelers and divers. Hiking trails wind through moist and dry tropical forests and cactus scrubland, allowing visitors to enjoy an array of hundreds of species of birds.

Virgin Islands National Park covers most of St. John, and 40 percent of the park is underwater. The park houses more than 500 species of fish, including barracuda, nurse sharks, stingrays, yellow snappers, and kingfish. See as many of the species as you can, and the protected colorful reefs, at Trunk Bay, the park's most popular snorkeling spot.

CAMPSITE DIRECTORY

ALABAMA

DeSoto State Park
7104 DeSoto Parkway NE, Fort
  Payne, AL 35967
alapark.com/parks/desoto-state
  -park

Bear Creek Log Cabins
923 County Road 252, Fort Payne,
  AL 35967
bearcreeklogcabins.com

Noccalula Falls Park Campground
1500 Noccalula Road, Gadsden, AL
  35904
noccalulafallspark.com/

Cheaha State Park
19644 State Highway 281, Delta, AL
  36258
alapark.com/parks/cheaha-state
  -park

University Station RV Resort
3076 State Highway 14 West,
  Auburn, Alabama 36832
universitystationrvpark.com/

Eagle Cottages at Gulf State Park
Bald Eagle Circle, Gulf State Park,
  Gulf Shores, AL 36542
eaglecottagesatgsp.com/

Dauphin Island Park Campground
109 Bienville Boulevard, Dauphin
  Island, AL 36528
dauphinisland.org/camping/

**Wales West RV Park & Light
  Railway**
13670 Smiley Street, Silverhill, AL
  36576
waleswest.com/

Millers Ferry Campground
111 East Bank Park Road,
  Camden, AL 36726
sam.usace.army.mil/Missions/Civil
  -Works/Recreation/Alabama-River
  -Lakes/

Clear Creek Recreation Area
8079 Fall City Road, Jasper, AL
  35503
fs.usda.gov/recarea/alabama/
  recreation/camping-cabins/

ALASKA

Between Beaches Alaska
64605 MacDonald Spit,
  Seldovia, AK 99663
beachesalaska.com/luxurycabins

Alaska Adventure Cabins
2525 Sterling Highway, Homer, AK
  99603
alaskaadventurecabins.com/

Orca Island Cabins
Humpy Cove & Resurrection Bay,
  Seward, AK 99664
orcaislandcabins.com

Eklutna Lake Campground
Mile 10, 39370 Eklutna Lake Rd,
  Chugiak, AK 99567
dnr.alaska.gov/parks/aspunits/
  chugach/eklutnalkcamp.htm

Riley Campground
Denali Park Road, Denali National
  Park and Preserve, AK 99755
nps.gov/dena/planyourvisit/
  campground-riley.htm

Alpenglow Luxury Camping
31090 West Glenn Highway,

Chickaloon, AK 99674
alpenglowluxurycamping.com/

Ultima Thule Lodge
Wrangel–St. Elias National Park, AL
ultimathulelodge.com/

Brooks Lodge
Brooks River, King Salmon, AK
  99613
katmailand.com/the-lodge/

Silver Salmon Creek Lodge
Lake Clark National Park,
  Soldotna, AK 99669
silversalmoncreek.com/index.php

Bartlett Cove Campground
Park Road, Gustavus, AK 99826
nps.gov/glba/planyourvisit/
  campground.htm

ARIZONA

Bonita Canyon Campground
Bonita Canyon Drive, Chiricahua
  National Monument, AZ 85643
nps.gov/chir/planyourvisit/bonita
  -canyon-campground.htm

The Shady Dell
1 Old Douglas Road, Bisbee, AZ
  85603
theshadydell.com/

Tanque Verde Ranch
14301 East Speedway Boulevard,
  Tucson, AZ 85748
tanqueverderanch.com/lodging/
  lodging-gallery/

Antler Ridge Cabins
103 Main Street, Greer, AZ 85927
antlerridge.com

**Canyon de Chelly
  National Monument**
South Rim Drive (Highway 7),
  Chinle, AZ 86503
nps.gov/cach/planyourvisit/
  outdooractivities.htm

Shash Diné EcoRetreat
U.S. Highway 89, Navajo Route
  6211, Page, AZ 86040
shashdine.com/accomodations

Manzanita Campground
5900 North State Route 89A,
  Sedona, AZ 86336
fs.usda.gov/recarea/coconino/
  recreation/camping-cabins/

Arizona Nordic Village
16848 U.S. Highway 180,
  Flagstaff, AZ 86001
arizonanordicvillage.com

Under Canvas Grand Canyon
979 Airpark Lane, Valle, AZ 86046
undercanvas.com/camps/grand
  -canyon/

Havasupai Campground
Havasu Creek, Havasupai Indian
  Reservation, Supai, AZ 86435
havasupaireservations.com/

ARKANSAS

Mississippi River State Park
2955 State Highway 44,
  Marianna, AR 72360
arkansasstateparks.com/parks/
  mississippi-river-state-park

**The Cabins at Dry Creek at the
  Ozark Folk Center**
1030 Park Avenue, Mountain View,
  AR 72560
arkansasstateparks.com/parks/
  ozark-folk-center-state-park/
  lodging-food/cabins

Buffalo Outdoor Center
4699 State Highway 43, Ponca, AR
  72670
buffaloriver.com/pages/cabins
  -lodge/cabin-list/

Treehouse Cottages
165 West Van Buren (U.S. Highway
  62), Eureka Springs, AR 72632
treehousecottages.com

StoneWind Retreat
15840 Wilson Branch Drive, Chester,
  AR 72934
stonewindretreat.com

Cove Lake Recreation Area
19 Cove Lake Loop, Paris, AR
  72855
fs.usda.gov/recarea/osfnf/
  recreation/camping-cabins/

Lake Ouachita State Park
5451 Mountain Pine Road, Mountain
  Pine, AR 71956
arkansasstateparks.com/parks/lake
  -ouachita-state-park

Gulpha Gorge Campground
305 Gorge Road, Hot Springs
  National Park, AR 71901
nps.gov/hosp/planyourvisit/
  campground.htm

Catherine's Landing
1700 Shady Grove Road,
  Hot Springs, AR 71901
catherineslanding.com/

Crater of Diamonds State Park
209 State Park Road, Murfreesboro,
  AR 71958
arkansasstateparks.com/parks/
  crater-diamonds-state-park

CALIFORNIA

Elk Prairie Campground
127011 Newton B. Drury Scenic

Parkway, Orick, CA 95555
nps.gov/redw/planyourvisit/
  developedcampgrounds.htm

Wildhaven Sonoma
2411 Alexander Valley Road,
  Healdsburg, CA 95448
wildhavensonoma.com

Lago Lomita Vineyard Treehouse
25200 Loma Prieta Avenue,
  Los Gatos, CA 95033
lagolomita.com/Airbnb

Ventana Big Sur Glamping
48123 Highway 1, Big Sur, CA
  93920
ventanabigsur.com/glamping/
  overview

Orangeland RV Park
1600 West Struck Avenue,
  Orange, CA 92867
orangeland.com

Crystal Cove Beach Cottages
35 Crystal Cove (off Pacific Coast
  Highway), Newport Beach, CA
  92657
crystalcove.org/beach-cottages/

Kate's Lazy Desert
58380 Botkin Road, Landers, CA
  92285
lazymeadow.com/lazy-desert-ca

Grant Grove Village
Generals Highway (State Route
  180), Grant Grove Village, CA
  93628
nps.gov/seki/planyourvisit/azalea
  .htm

Yosemite High Sierra Camps
Tioga Road (State Highway 120),
  Tuolumne Meadows, CA 95389
travelyosemite.com/lodging/high
  -sierra-camps/

Emerald Bay State Park
89 South Shore Lake Tahoe,
  Tahoma, CA 96142
parks.ca.gov/

COLORADO

State Forest State Park
State Highway 14, Walden, CO
  80480
cpw.state.co.us/placestogo/parks/
  StateForest/Pages/Camping.aspx

Moraine Park Campground
Morane Park Road, Rocky Mountain
  National Park, Estes Park, CO
  80517
nps.gov/romo/planyourvisit/mpcg
  .htm

Reverend's Ridge Campground
313 Reverends Ridge Road, Golden
  Gate State Park, Black Hawk, CO
  80422
cpw.state.co.us/placestogo/Parks/
  goldengateCanyon

Mountaindale Cabins & RV Resort
2000 Barrett Road, Colorado
  Springs, CO 80926
mountaindalecampground.com

Royal Gorge Cabins
45054 West U.S. Highway 50,
  Cañon City, CO 81212
royalgorgecabins.com

Piñon Flats Campground
State Highway 150, Great Sand
  Dunes National Park & Preserve,
  Mosca, CO 81146
nps.gov/grsa/planyourvisit/
  pinonflatscampground.htm

Morefield Campground
Mile Marker 4, Mesa Top ruins
  Road, Mesa Verde National Park,
  CO 81330
nps.gov/meve/planyourvisit/
  camping2.htm

Dunton Hot Springs
52068 Road 38, Dolores, CO 81323
duntondestinations.com/hot
  -springs/lodging-rates/

South Rim Campground
South Rim Road, Black Canyon
  of the Gunnison National Park,
  Montrose, CO 81401
nps.gov/blca/planyourvisit/camp
  _southrim.htm

Collective Vail
4098 State Highway 131, Wolcott,
  CO 81655
collectiveretreats.com/retreat/
  collective-vail/

CONNECTICUT

Housatonic Meadows State Park
90 U.S. Highway 7, Sharon, CT
  06069
portal.ct.gov/DEEP/State-Parks/
  Parks/Housatonic-Meadows
  -State-Park

Club Getaway
59 South Kent Road, Kent, CT 06757
clubgetaway.com

Winvian Farm
155 Alain White Road, Morris, CT
  06763
winvian.com

Bear Creek Campground
Bear Creek Highway, Bristol, CT
  06010
lakecompounce.com/bearcreek

Charlie Brown Campground
98 Chaplin Road, Eastford, CT
  06242
charliebrowncampground.com/

Green Falls Area Campground
Green Fall Pond Road, Voluntown,
  CT 06384

portal.ct.gov/DEEP/State-Parks/
  Forests/Pachaug-State-Forest

Strawberry Park Campground
42 Pierce Road, Preston, CT 06365
strawberrypark.net/

Odetah Camping Resort
38 Bozrah Street Extension #1300,
  Bozrah, CT 06334
odetah.com

Hawk's Nest Beach Cottages
West End Drive, Old Lyme, CT
  06371
hawksnestbeach.com/cottages

Hammonasset Beach State Park
1288 Boston Post Road (Highway
  1), Madison, CT 06443
portal.ct.gov/DEEP/State-Parks/
  Parks/Hammonasset-Beach-State
  -Parkow

DELAWARE

Lums Pond State Park
1068 Howell School Road, Bear, DE
  19701
destateparks.com/PondsRivers/
  LumsPond

Blackbird State Forest
502 Blackbird Forest Road, Smyrna,
  DE 19977
agriculture.delaware.gov/forest
  -service/state-forests

Yogi Bear's Delaware Beaches
Jellystone Park Camp Resort
8295 Brick Granary Road, Lincoln,
  DE 19960
delawarejellystone.com/index.html

Tall Pines Campground Resort
29551 Persimmon Road, Lewes, DE
  19958
tallpines-del.com/camping

Cape Henlopen State Park
15099 Cape Henlopen Drive, Lewes, DE 19958
destateparks.com/Beaches/ CapeHenlopen

Big Oaks Camping
35567 Big Oaks Lane, Rehoboth Beach, DE 19971
bigoakscamping.com/rentals.html

Delaware Seashore State Park
39415 Inlet Road, Rehoboth Beach, DE 19971
destateparks.com/Beaches/ DelawareSeashore

Holly Lake Campsites
32087 Holly Lake Road, Millsboro, Delaware 19966
hollylakecampsites.com/amenities/ cabins.html

Massey's Landing
20628 Long Beach Drive, Millsboro, DE 19966
masseyslanding.com/activities/blog/ glamping-101

Trap Pond State Park
33587 Baldcypress Lane, Laurel, DE 19956
destateparks.com/PondsRivers/ TrapPond

FLORIDA

Coldwater Gardens
7009 Creek Stone Road, Milton, FL 32570
coldwatergardens.com

Fancy Camps at Topsail Hill
7525 West County Highway 30A, Santa Rosa Beach, FL 32459
fancycamps.com

Pellicer Creek Campground, St. Augustine
10255 US Highway 1, St. Augustine, FL 32086
pellicercreekcampground.com

Jetty Park Campground, Port Canaveral
9035 Campground Circle, Cape Canaveral, FL 32920
portcanaveral.com/Recreation/ Jetty-Park-Campground

Lake Louisa State Park
7305 U.S. Highway 27, Clermont, FL 34714
lakelouisastatepark.com/

Disney's Fort Wilderness Retreat
4510 North Fort Wilderness Trail, Lake Buena Vista, Florida 32830
disneyworld.disney.go.com/resorts/ campsites-at-fort-wilderness -resort/

Periwinkle Park & Campground
1119 Periwinkle Way, Sanibel, FL 33957
sanibelcamping.com

Ten Thousand Islands Wilderness Waterway
Everglades National Park, FL
nps.gov/ever/planyourvisit/ wilderness-trip-planner.htm

John Pennekamp Coral Reef State Park
Mile Marker 102.5 Overseas Highway, Key Largo FL 33037
floridastateparks.org/parks-and -trails/john-pennekamp-coral-reef -state-park

Garden Key Campground
Dry Tortugas National Park
nps.gov/drto/planyourvisit/ camping.htm

GEORGIA

Sea Camp Campground
Cumberland Island National Seashore, Cumberland Island, GA 31558
nps.gov/cuis/planyourvisit/seacamp .htm

Stephen C. Foster State Park
17515 State Highway 177, Fargo, GA 31631
gastateparks.org/StephenCFoster

Kolomoki Mounds State Park
205 Indian Mounds Road, Blakely, GA 39823
gastateparks.org/KolomokiMounds

Historic Banning Mills
205 Horseshoe Dam Road, Whitesburg, GA 30185
historicbanningmills.com/lodging/ rooms-rates-packages/

Cloudland Canyon State Park
122 Cloudland Canyon Park Road, Rising Fawn, GA 30738
gastateparks.org/CloudlandCanyon

Lake Winfield Scott Campground
439 Lake Winfield Scott Road, Suches, GA 30572
fs.usda.gov/recarea/conf/recreation/ camping-cabins/

Black Rock Mountain State Park
3085 Black Rock Mountain Parkway, Mountain City, GA 30562
gastateparks.org/BlackRockMountain

Margaritaville at Lanier Islands
7650 Lanier Islands Parkway, Buford, GA 30518
margaritavillervresorts.com/ lakelanier/rv-sites

Glamping at Clarks Hill Lake
Wildwood Park, 3780 Dogwood Lane, Appling, GA 30802

georgiaglamping.com/glamping
-clarks-hill-lake

River's End Campground & RV Park
5 Fort Avenue, Tybee Island, GA 31328
riversendcampground.com/

HAWAII

Hawaii Volcanoes National Park
Hawaii Volcanoes National Park, HI 96718
nps.gov/havo/planyourvisit/camp .htm

Punalu'u Black Sand Beach Park
Ninole Loop Road, Pahala, HI 96777
hawaiicounty.ehawaii.gov/camping/

Haleakala National Park
30000 Haleakala Highway, Kula, HI 96790
nps.gov/hale/planyourvisit/drive-up -camping.htm

Camp Olowalu
800 Olowalu Village Road, Lahaina, HI 96761
campolowalu.com/cabins/

Wai'anapanapa State Park
Honokalani Road, Waianapanapa, Hana, HI 96713
dlnr.hawaii.gov/dsp/parks/maui/ waianapanapa-state-park

Kōke'e State Park
3600 Kokee Road, Hanapepe, HI 96716
kokee.org/index.php?ccc-camp -staying-at

Kalalau Trail Camping
Kuhio Highway, Hanalei, HI 96714
kalalautrail.com

Pālā'au State Park
Kalae Highway, Kualapuu, HI 96757
dlnr.hawaii.gov/dsp/parks/molokai/ palaau-state-park

Malaekahana Beach Campground
56-335 Kamehameha Highway, Kahuku, HI 96731
malaekahana.net

Hulopoe Beach Park
Manele Road, Lanai City, HI 96763
lanai96763.com/wp-content/ uploads/2019/12/Hulopoe-Beach -Camping_2020.pdf

IDAHO

Huckleberry Tent & Breakfast
180 Thunderbolt Drive, Clark Fork, ID 83811
huckleberrytentandbreakfast.com

Camp Coeur d'Alene
10588 East Wolf Lodge Bay Road, Coeur d'Alene, ID 83814
campcoeurdalene.com

MaryJanesFarm
1000 Wild Iris Lane, Moscow, ID 83843
shop.maryjanesfarm.org/our-bnb

River Dance Lodge
7743 U.S. Highway 12, Kooskia, ID 83539
riverdancelodge.com/

Ponderosa State Park
1920 Davis Avenue, McCall, ID 83638
parksandrecreation.idaho.gov/ parks/ponderosa

Glacier View Campground
Redfish Lake Road, Stanley, ID 83278
fs.usda.gov/recarea/sawtooth/ recreation/camping-cabins/

Eagle Cove Campground
27608 Bruneau Sand Dunes Road, Bruneau, ID 83604
parksandrecreation.idaho.gov/ parks/bruneau-dunes

Lava Flow Campground
1266 Craters Loop Road, Arco, ID 83213
nps.gov/crmo/planyourvisit/ camping.htm

Silver Spur Ranch
2385 Medicine Lodge Road, Dubois, ID 83423
silverspurranchidaho.com/ horsedrive

Moose Creek Ranch
2733 East 10800 South, Victor, ID 83455
moosecreekranch.com/

ILLINOIS

Mississippi Palisades State Park
16327A State Route 84, Savanna, IL 61074
illinois.gov/dnr/Parks/Pages/ MississippiPalisades.aspx

Camp Sullivan
14630 Oak Park Avenue, Oak Forest, IL 60452
fpdcc.com/places/locations/camp -sullivan/#camping

Starved Rock State Park
State Highway 178, Oglesby, IL 61348
illinois.gov/dnr/Parks/Pages/ StarvedRock.aspx

Camp Aramoni Glamping
809 North 2199th Road, Tonica, IL 61370
camparamoni.com

Lincoln's New Salem
15588 History Lane, Petersburg, IL
62675
lincolnsnewsalem.com

Cabins & Cottages at Shale Lake Winery
1499 Washington Avenue, Staunton,
IL 62088
shalewine.com/The_Cabins_and
_Cottages.html

Eldon Hazlet State Recreation Area
20100 Hazlet Park Road, Carlyle, IL
62231
illinois.gov/dnr/Parks/Pages/
EldonHazlet.aspx

Giant City Lodge
460 Giant City Lodge Road,
Makanda, IL 62958
giantcitylodge.com/cabins/

Timber Ridge Outpost
546 North Iron Furnace Road,
Elizabethtown, IL 62931
timberridgeoutpost.com/cabins

Fort Massac State Park
1308 East 5th Street, Metropolis, IL
62960
illinois.gov/dnr/Parks/Pages/
FortMassac.aspx

INDIANA

Indiana Dunes State Park
County Road 100 East, Chesterton,
IN 46304
in.gov/dnr/parklake/2980.htm

Shipshewana North Park Campground
5970 State Highway 5,
Shipshewana, IN 46565
shipshewanacampgroundnorth
.com/

Lost Bridge West Campground
9214 Lost Bridge Road West,
Andrews, IN 46702
in.gov/dnr/parklake/2952.htm

Prophetstown State Park
State Highway 225, West Lafayette,
IN 47906
in.gov/dnr/parklake/2971.htm

White River Campground
11299 East 234th Street, Cicero, IN
46034
hamiltoncounty.in.gov/Facilities/
Facility/Details/White-River
-Campground-1

Glamptown at Indianapolis Motor Speedway
4790 West 16th Street, Indianapolis,
IN 46222
indianapolismotorspeedway.com/
events/indy500/fan-info/glamping

Abe Martin Lodge & Cabins
1405 State Road 46 West, Nashville,
IN 47448
in.gov/dnr/parklake/inns/abe-martin
-lodge-at-brown-county-state-park/

Hardin Ridge Recreation Area
6464 Hardin Ridge Road,
Heltonville, IN 47436
fs.usda.gov/recarea/hoosier/
recarea/?recid=41468

Lincoln State Park
15476 County Road 300 East,
Lincoln City, IN 47552
in.gov/dnr/parklake/2979.htm

Colucci River Cabins
17735 Magnet Valley Road,
Cannelton, IN 47520
coluccirivercabins.com

IOWA

Sugar Bottom Campground
2192 Mehaffey Bridge Road

Northeast, Solon, IA 52333
mvr.usace.army.mil/Missions/
Recreation/Coralville-Lake/
Recreation/Camping/Sugar
-Bottom/

Honey Creek State Park
12194 Honey Creek Place, Moravia,
IA 52571
iowadnr.gov/Places-to-Go/
State-Parks/Iowa-State-Parks/
ParkDetails/ParkID/610104

Lewis & Clark State Park
21914 Park Loop, Onawa, IA 51046
iowadnr.gov/Places-to-Go/
State-Parks/Iowa-State-Parks/
ParkDetails/ParkID/610142

Fillenwarth Beach Cottage Colony
87 Lakeshore Drive, Arnolds Park,
IA 51331
fillenwarthbeach.com/

Red Cedar Lodge
1880 Gilbert Street, Charles City,
IA 50616
theredcedarlodge.com/cabins

Harvest Farm Campground Resort
3690 318th Avenue, Cresco, IA,
52136
wecamp.com

Pikes Peak State Park
32264 Pikes Peak Road, McGregor,
IA 52157
iowadnr.gov/Places-to-Go/
State-Parks/Iowa-State-Parks/
ParkDetails/ParkID/610141

Maquoketa Caves State Park
9688 Caves Road, Maquoketa, IA
52060
iowadnr.gov/Places-to-Go/
State-Parks/Iowa-State-Parks/
Maquoketa-Caves-State-Park

Moon River Cabins
905 South Riverview Drive (U.S.
 Highway 52), Bellevue, IA 52031
moonrivercabins.com/cabins

**Pine Grove Campgrounds &
Cabins**
18850 270th Street, Eldridge, Iowa
 52748
scottcountyiowa.gov/conservation/
 scott-county-park/cabins/pine
 -grove-cabins

KANSAS

Deer Creek Valley RV Park
3140 Southeast 21st Street,
 Topeka, KS 66607
deercreekvalleyrvpark.com/

Acorns Resort
3710 Farnum Creek Road, Milford,
 KS 66514
acornsresortkansas.com

Shady Grove Cabins
1319 Kansas Street, Downs, KS
 67437
shadygrovecabins.com/our-cabins
 .html

Prairie Dog State Park
13037 State Highway 261, Norton,
 KS 67654
ksoutdoors.com/State-Parks/
 Locations/Prairie-Dog

Historic Lake Scott State Park
101 West Scott Lake Drive, Scott
 City, KS 67871
ksoutdoors.com/State-Parks/
 Locations/Historic-Lake-Scott

Cimarron Campground
Forest Route 700, Elkhart, KS 67950
fs.usda.gov/recarea/psicc/
 recreation/camping-cabins/

Gunsmoke RV Park
11070 108th Road @ Wyatt Earp
 Boulevard, Dodge City, KS 67801
gunsmokervpark.com

**Lighthouse Landing RV Park &
Cabins**
9 Heartland Drive, South
 Hutchinson, KS 67505
lighthouselandingrvpark.com/

Bluestem Point Camping Area
618 Northeast Bluestem Road,
 El Dorado, KS 67042
ksoutdoors.com/State-Parks/
 Locations/El-Dorado

Elk City State Park
4825 Squaw Creek Road,
 Independence, KS 67301
ksoutdoors.com/State-Parks/
 Locations/Elk-City

KENTUCKY

Columbus-Belmont State Park
350 Park Road, Columbus, KY 42032
parks.ky.gov/columbus/parks/
 historic/columbus-belmont-state
 -park

Lake Barkley Canal Campground
1010 Canal Campground Road,
 Grand Rivers, KY 42045
lrn.usace.army.mil/Locations/Lakes/
 Lake-Barkley/Campgrounds/
 Canal/

John James Audubon State Park
3100 U.S. Highway 41, Henderson,
 KY 42420
parks.ky.gov/henderson/parks/
 historic/john-james-audubon
 -state-park

**Mammoth Cave Campgrounds &
Cottages**
1 Mammoth Cave Parkway,
 Mammoth Cave, KY 42259

nps.gov/maca/planyourvisit/
 camping.htm

Blue Heron Campground
Camp Ground Road, Strunk, KY
 42649
nps.gov/biso/planyourvisit/
 blueheroncampground.htm

**Levi Jackson Wilderness Road
Park**
998 Levi Jackson Road, London, KY
 40744
levijacksonpark.com

HomeGrown HideAways
500 Floyd Branch Road, Berea, KY
 40403
homegrownhideaways.org/stay.html

Zilpo Campground
Zilpo Road, Salt Lick, KY 40371
fs.usda.gov/recarea/dbnf/recreation/
 camping-cabins/

Kentucky Horse Park Campground
Campground Road, Lexington, KY
 40511
kyhorsepark.com/visit-khp/park
 -info-resources/khp-campground/

Camp Bespoke
500 Mercedes Drive, Williamstown,
 KY 41097
campbespoke.com

LOUISIANA

Poverty Point
1500 Poverty Point Parkway,
 Delhi, LA 71232
lastateparks.com/parks-preserves/
 poverty-point-reservoir-state-park

Darbonne Pointe
147 Old Highway 15, Farmerville,
 LA 71241
darbonnepointe.com

Cloud Crossing Campground
Cloud Crossing Road, Goldonna,
LA 71031
fs.usda.gov/recarea/kisatchie/
recreation/camping-cabins/

Sam Houston Jones State Park
107 Sutherland Road, Lake Charles,
LA 70611
stateparks.com/sam_houston
_jones_state_park_in_louisiana.html

Kincaid Lake Recreation Area
214 Kisatchie Lane, Boyce, LA 71409
fs.usda.gov/recarea/kisatchie/
recreation/camping-cabins/

Chicot State Park
3469 Chicot Park Road, Ville Platte,
LA 70586
lastateparks.com/parks-preserves/
chicot-state-park

Lake Fausse Pointe State Park
5400 Levee Road, St. Martinville, LA
70582
lastateparks.com/parks-preserves/
lake-fausse-pointe-state-park

Grand Isle State Park
108 Admiral Craik Drive, Grand Isle,
LA 70358
lastateparks.com/parks-preserves/
grand-isle-state-park

Bayou Log Cabin
200 West Kass Lane, Port Sulphur,
LA 70083
bayoulogcabins.com

Pontchartrain Landing
6001 France Road, New Orleans,
LA 70126
pontchartrainlanding.com

MAINE

Huttopia Southern Maine
149 Sand Pond Road, Sanford,
ME 04073
canada-usa.huttopia.com/en/site
/southern-maine

Seguin Tree Dwellings
5 Islands Road, Georgetown, ME
04548
seguinmaine.com/home

Tops'l Farm
365 Bremen Road, Waldoboro, ME
04572
topslfarm.com

Under Canvas Acadia
702 Surry Road, Surry, ME 04684
undercanvas.com/camps/acadia

Blackwoods Campground
155 Blackwoods Drive, Otter Creek,
ME 04660
nps.gov/acad/planyourvisit/
camping.htm

Cobscook Bay State Park
40 South Edmunds Road,
Dennysville, ME 04628
maine.gov/cgi-bin/online/doc/
parksearch/details.pl?park
_id=15

Aroostook State Park
87 State Park Road, Presque Isle,
ME 04769
maine.gov/cgi-bin/online/doc/
parksearch/details.pl?park_id=7

Wilderness Edge Campground
71 Millinocket Lake Road,
Millinocket, ME 04462
wildernessedgecampground.com/

Daicey Pond Cabins
Daicey Pond Road, Baxter State
Park, Millinocket, ME 04462
baxterstatepark.org/camp-summer/

AMC Gorman Chairback Lodge
Gorman Chairback Camp Road,
Greenville, ME 04441
outdoors.org/lodging-camping/
lodges/gorman/

MARYLAND

Hollofield Campground
8020 Baltimore National Pike,
Ellicott City, MD 21043
dnr.maryland.gov/publiclands/
Pages/central/patapsco.aspx

Elk River Camping Area
4395 Turkey Point Road, North
East, MD 21901
dnr.maryland.gov/publiclands/
Pages/central/ElkNeck/River
-Camping-Area.aspx

Oceanside Campground
Bayberry Drive, Berlin, MD 21811
nps.gov/asis/planyourvisit/
marylandcamping.htm

Janes Island State Park
26280 Alfred J. Lawson Drive,
Crisfield, MD 21817
dnr.maryland.gov/publiclands/
Pages/eastern/janesisland.aspx

Greenbelt Park Campground
6565 Greenbelt Road, Greenbelt,
MD 20770
nps.gov/gree/planyourvisit/
campground.htm

Cherry Hill Park
9800 Cherry Hill Road, College
Park, MD 20740
cherryhillpark.com/

Owens Creek Campground
15882 Foxville-Deerfield Road,
Sabillasville, MD 21780
nps.gov/cato/planyourvisit/
campgrounds.htm

Antietam Creek Campground
Canal Road, Sharpsburg, MD
21782
nps.gov/choh/planyourvisit/
camping.htm

Savage River Lodge
1600 Mount Aetna Road, Frostburg, MD 21532
savageriverlodge.com

Wild Yough Glamping Huts
1976 Herrington Manor Road, Oakland, MD 21550
mdglamping.com

MASSACHUSETTS

Lee Campground, October Mountain State Forest
256 Woodland Road, Lee, MA 01238
mass.gov/locations/october -mountain-state-forest

Mohawk Trail State Forest
Cold River Road, Charlemont, MA 01339
mass.gov/locations/mohawk-trail -state-forest

Tully Lake Campground
Doane Hill Road, Royalston, MA 01368
thetrustees.org/place/tully-lake -campground/

Boston Minuteman Campground
264 Ayer Road, Littleton, MA 01460
minutemancampground.com

Boston Harbor Islands
Long Wharf North, Boston, MA 02110 or Hingham Shipyard, 28 Shipyard Drive, Hingham, MA 02043 (ferry terminals)
bostonharborislands.org/camping/

Waquoit Bay National Estuarine Research Reserve
131 Waquoit Highway, East Falmouth, MA 02536
mass.gov/locations/waquoit-bay -national-estuarine-research -reserve

Autocamp Cape Cod/Falmouth
836 Palmer Avenue, Falmouth, MA 02540
autocamp.com/cape-cod/

Martha's Vineyard Family Campground
569 Edgartown Road, Vineyard Haven, MA 02568
campmv.com

Nickerson State Park, Cape Cod
3488 Main Street, Brewster, MA 02631
mass.gov/locations/nickerson -state-park

Dunes Edge Campground, Cape Cod
386 U.S. Highway 6, Provincetown, MA 02657
thetrustees.org/place/dunes-edge -campground

MICHIGAN

Wild Cherry RV Resort
8563 East Horn Road, Lake Leelanau, MI 49653
wildcherryresort.com

Platte River Campground
5685 Lake Michigan Road, Honor, MI 49640
nps.gov/slbe/planyourvisit/ platterivercamp.htm

The Fields of Michigan
154 68th Street, South Haven, MI 49090
thefieldsofmichigan.com

Port Crescent State Park
1775 Port Austin Road, Port Austin MI, 48467
dnr.state.mi.us/parksandtrails/ Details.aspx?id=486&type=SPRK

Au Sable Loop Campground
Federal Trail 4366, Cadillac, MI 49601
fs.usda.gov/recarea/hmnf/ recreation/camping-cabins/

Mackinaw Mill Creek Camping
9730 U.S. Highway 23, Mackinaw City, MI 49701
campmackinaw.com

Lime Island
De Tour Village, MI 49725
michigan.org/property/lime-island -recreation-area

Twelvemile Beach Campground
Twelvemile Beach Road, Grand Marais, MI 49839

Union Bay Modern Campground
107th Engineers Memorial Highway, Ontonagon, MI 49953
dnr.state.mi.us/parksandtrails/ Details.aspx?id=74&type=SPCG

Rock Harbor Lodge
Rock Harbor, Isle Royale National Park, MI 49931
rockharborlodge.com/lodging-and -cabin-rentals

MINNESOTA

Blue Mounds State Park
1410 161st Street, Luverne, MN 56156
dnr.state.mn.us/state_parks/park .html?id=spk00121

Prairie View RV Park & Campground
5590 Prairies Edge Lane, Granite Falls, MN 56241
prairiesedgecasino.com/lodging/ rv-park

Itasca State Park
36750 Main Park Drive,

Park Rapids, MN 56470
dnr.state.mn.us/state_parks/park
.html?id=spk00181

Norway Beach Recreation Area
Norway Beach Road Northwest,
Cass Lake, MN 56633
fs.usda.gov/recarea/chippewa/
recreation/camping-cabins/

Pines of Kabetogama
12443 Burma Road, Kabetogama,
MN 56669
thepineskab.com/

Voyageur Canoe Outfitters
189 Sag Lake Trail, Grand Marais,
MN 55604
voyageuroutfitters.com/
accommodations/

Breezy Point Cabins
540 Old North Shore Road, Two
Harbors, MN 55616
odysseyresorts.com/breezy-point
-cabins/breezy-point-lodging

**Pete's Retreat Family
Campground & RV Park**
22337 State Highway 47, Aitkin, MN
56431
petesretreat.com

Kamp Dels
14842 Sakatah Lake Road,
Waterville, MN 56096
kampdels.com

Great River Bluffs State Park
43605 Kipp Drive, Winona, MN
55987
dnr.state.mn.us/state_parks/park
.html?id=spk00244

MISSISSIPPI

Davis Bayou Campground
3500 Park Road, Ocean Springs,
MS 39564

nps.gov/guis/planyourvisit/db
-campground.htm

Big Biloxi Recreation Area
19551 Desoto Park Road, Saucier,
MS 39574
fs.usda.gov/recarea/mississippi/
recreation/camping-cabins/

Turkey Fork Recreation Area
746 Turkey Fork Lake Road, 968
Highway 15 South, Laurel, MS
39443
fs.usda.gov/recarea/mississippi/
recreation/camping-cabins/

Campground at Barnes Crossing
125 Campground Road, Tupelo, MS
38804
cgbarnescrossing.com

Tishomingo State Park
105 County Road 90, Tishomingo,
MS 38873 (Milepost 304 on the
Natchez Trace Parkway)
mdwfp.com/parks-destinations/
state-parks/Tishomingo

USACE Piney Grove Campground
County Road 3550, New Site, MS
38859
sam.usace.army.mil/Portals/46/
docs/recreation/OP-CO/tenntom/
pdfs/rec/isheet/campgrounds/
pgcg.pdf

EZ Daze RV Park
536 W. E. Ross Parkway,
Southaven, MS 38671
ezdazervpark.com/

Jeff Busby Campground
Milepost 193.1 Natchez Trace
Parkway, Ackerman, MS 39735
nps.gov/natr/planyourvisit/camping
.htm

Rocky Springs Campground
Milepost 54.8, Natchez Trace
Parkway, Hermanville, MS 39086

nps.gov/natr/planyourvisit/camping
.htm

Natchez State Park
230B Wickcliff Road, Natchez, MS
39120
mdwfp.com/parks-destinations/
state-parks/natchez/

MISSOURI

Worlds of Fun Village
8000 Northeast Parvin Road,
Kansas City, MO 64161
worldsoffun.com/stay/village

Hawley Farm Glamping
3406 Northeast Hardy Drive,
Hamilton, MO 64650
hawleyfarmglamping.com

Lake of the Ozarks State Park
257 Public Beach Road, Brumley,
MO 65017
mostateparks.com/park/lake
-ozarks-state-park

**Cooper Creek Resort &
Campground**
471 Cooper Creek Road, Branson,
MO 65616
coopercreekresort.com/wp/

River of Life Farm
1746 River of Life Drive, Dora, MO
65637
riveroflifefarm.com

Alley Spring Campground
State Highway 106, Eminence, MO
65466
nps.gov/ozar/planyourvisit/camping
-information.htm

Meramec State Park
115 Meramec Park Drive, Sullivan,
MO 63080
mostateparks.com/park/meramec
-state-park

KOA Route 66 St. Louis West
18475 Old Highway 66, Eureka, MO
63069
koa.com/campgrounds/st-louis
-west/site-type/lodging/

Glamping St. Louis
800 Wilson Road, St. Charles, MO
63301
glampingstl.com

Mark Twain Cave Campground
300 Cave Hollow Road, Hannibal,
MO 63401
marktwaincave.com/campground/

MONTANA

St. Mary Campground
Going-to-the-Sun Road, St. Mary,
MT 59417
nps.gov/applications/glac/cgstatus/
camping_detail.cfm?cg=St.%20
Mary

Holland Lake Campground
Holland Lake Lodge Road, Condon,
MT 59826
fs.usda.gov/recarea/flathead/
recreation/camping-cabins/

The Resort at Paws Up
40060 Paws Up Road, Greenough,
MT 59823
pawsup.com/glamping

Downstream Campground
Yellowstone Road, Nashua, MT
59248
corpslakes.erdc.dren.mil/visitors/
projects.cfm?Id=G606230

7th Ranch RV Park
514 Reno Creek Road, Garryowen,
MT 59031
historicwest.com

Tiny Town Campground
9 Counts Lane, Emigrant, MT 59027
airbnb.com/rooms/41557084

Dreamcatcher Tipi Hotel
20 Maiden Basin Drive, Gardiner, MT
59030
dreamcatchertipihotel.com/

Grizzly RV Park & Cabins
210 South Electric Street, West
Yellowstone, MT 59758
grizzlyrv.com

Bar W Guest Ranch
2875 U.S. Highway 93, Whitefish,
MT 59937
thebarw.com/montana-guest-ranch
-lodging/montana-glamping

Bannack State Park
Bannack Road, Dillon, MT 59725
stateparks.mt.gov/bannack/

NEBRASKA

Niobrara State Park
89261 522 Avenue, Niobrara, NE
68760
outdoornebraska.gov/niobrara

Ponca State Park
88090 Spur 26 East, Ponca, NE
68770
outdoornebraska.gov/ponca

Two Rivers State Recreation Area
27702 F Street, Waterloo, NE 68069
outdoornebraska.gov/tworivers/

Kimberley Creek Retreat
30010 Kimberly Drive, Ashland, NE
68003
kimberlycreekretreat.com/

**Prairie Oasis Campground &
Cabins**
913 Road B, Henderson, NE 68371
prairieoasiscampground.com/

Fort Kearny State Recreation Area
Fort Kearny State Recreation Area
Road, Gibbon, NE 68840
outdoornebraska.gov/fortkearnysra/

**Bessey Recreation Complex &
Campground**
40637 River Loop, Halsey, NE
69142
recreation.gov/camping/
campgrounds/234120

**Chimney Rock Pioneer Crossing
Campground**
10012 Road 75, Bayard, NE 69334
chimneyrockpioneercrossing.com

Robidoux RV Park
585 Five Rocks Road, Gering, NE
69341
gering.org/robidoux-rv-park

**Toadstool Geological Park &
Campground**
FS Road 902, Harrison, NE 69346
fs.usda.gov/recarea/nebraska/
recarea/?recid=10616

NEVADA

Boulder Beach Campground
268 Lakeshore Road, Boulder City,
NV 89005
nps.gov/lake/planyourvisit/
campgrounds.htm

Oasis Las Vegas RV Resort
2711 West Windmill Lane,
Las Vegas, NV 89123
oasislasvegasrvresort.com/

Valley of Fire State Park
Valley of Fire Highway, Moapa
Valley, NV 89040
parks.nv.gov/parks/valley-of
-fire

Wheeler Peak Campground
Wheeler Peak Scenic Drive, Great
Basin National Park, Baker, NV
89311
nps.gov/grba/planyourvisit/
campgrounds.htm

Mustang Monument Eco-Resort & Preserve
Great Basin Highway (U.S. 93),
  Wells, NV 89835
mustangmonument.com/
  accommodations

South Ruby Campground
Ruby Valley, NV 89833
fs.usda.gov/recarea/htnf/recreation/
  camping-cabins/

Berlin-Ichthyosaur State Park
State Route 844, Austin, NV 89310
parks.nv.gov/parks/berlin-ichthyosaur

Walker River Resort
700 Hudson Way, Smith, NV 89430
wrresort.com

Nevada Beach Campground
Bittlers Road, Zephyr Cove, NV
  89448
tahoesouth.com/hotels/nevada
  -beach

Zephyr Cove Resort
760 U.S. Highway 50, Zephyr Cove,
  NV 89448
zephyrcove.com

NEW HAMPSHIRE

Hampton Beach State Park
160 Ocean Boulevard, Hampton, NH
  03842
nhstateparks.org/Visit/State-Parks/
  Hampton-Beach-State-Park

Getaway Blake Brooke
76 Mountain Road, Epsom, NH
  03234
getaway.house/boston

Savoie's Lodging & Camping
396 Daniel Webster Highway (Route
  3), Center Harbor, NH 03226
lodgingnh.com

Lafayette Place Campground
Styles Bridge Highway (I-93),
  Franconia Notch State Park,
  Franconia, NH 03580
nhstateparks.org/Visit/State-Parks/
  Franconia-Notch-state-park

Partridge Cabins
3 Partridge Road (off U.S. Route 3),
  Pittsburg, NH 03592
partridgecabins.com

Dolly Copp Campground
Dolly Copp Campground Road
  (off Route 16), Gorham, NH 03581
forestcamping.com/dow/eastern/
  wmcmp.htm#dolly%20copp

Dry River Campground
1464 U.S. Route 302, Crawford
  Notch State Park, Harts Location,
  NH 03812
nhstateparks.org/Visit/State-Parks/
  Crawford-Notch-State-Park

Saco River Camping Area
1550 White Mountain Highway,
  North Conway, NH 03860
sacorivercampingarea.com

Huttopia White Mountains
57 Pine Knoll Road, Albany, NH
  03818
canada-usa.huttopia.com/en/site/
  white-mountains/

Beaver Pond Campground
600 Lower Road, Deerfield, NH
  03037
nhstateparks.org/visit/state-parks/
  bear-brook-state-park

NEW JERSEY

Sawmill Lake Camping Area
1480 State Route 23, High Point
  State Park, Sussex, NJ 07461
state.nj.us/dep/parksandforests/
  parks/highpoint.html

AMC Mohican Outdoor Center
50 Camp Mohican Road,
  Blairstown, NJ 07825
outdoors.org/lodging-camping/
  lodges/mohican/

The Great Divide Campground
68 Phillips Road, Newton, NJ 07860
campthegreatdivide.com

Camp Gateway
Hartshorne Drive, Gateway NRA,
  Highlands, NJ 07732
nps.gov/gate/planyourvisit/camp
  -sandy-hook.htm

Allaire State Park
Atlantic Avenue (Route 524),
  Howell Township, NJ 07731
state.nj.us/dep/parksandforests/
  parks/allaire.html

Atsion Campground
Atsion Road, Wharton State Forest,
  Shamong, NJ 08088
state.nj.us/dep/parksandforests/
  parks/wharton.html

Baker's Acres Campground
230 Willets Avenue, Little Egg
  Harbor Township, NJ 08087
bakersacres.com

Bass River State Forest
Stage Road, Tuckerton, NJ 08087
state.nj.us/dep/parksandforests/
  parks/bass.html

Belleplain State Forest
Champion Road, Woodbine, NJ
  08270
state.nj.us/dep/parksandforests/
  parks/belle.html

Holly Shores Camping Resort
491 U.S. Highway 9, Cape May, NJ
  08204
hollyshores.com/safari-glamping
  -tents

NEW MEXICO

Chaco Canyon Glamping
Chaco Culture NHP, Nageezi, NM 87037
heritageinspirations.com/chaco
-tours/chaco-canyon-glamping
-overnight/

Stone House Lodge
1409 State Highway 95, Los Ojos, NM 87551
stonehouselodge.com/
accommodations

Luna Mystica
25 ABC Mesa Road, El Prado, NM 87529
hotellunamystica.com

Cliff River Springs
283 State Highway 111, La Madera, NM 87539
cliffriversprings.com

Juniper Campground
15 Entrance Road, Bandelier National Monument, Los Alamos, NM 87544
nps.gov/band/planyourvisit/juniper
-family-campground.htm

Rancho Gallina, Santa Fe
31 Bonanza Creek Road, Santa Fe, NM 87508
glamping.com/destination/north
-america/new-mexico/santa-fe/
rancho-gallina

Enchanted Trails RV Park & Trading Post
14305 Central Avenue Northwest, Albuquerque, NM 87121
enchantedtrails.com

White Sands National Park
Dunes Drive, White Sands National Park, Alamogordo, NM 88310
nps.gov/whsa/planyourvisit/permits
-for-backcountry-camping.htm

Aguirre Springs Campground
Aguirre Springs Road, Las Cruces, NM 88011
blm.gov/visit/aguirre-spring
-campground

Faywood Hot Springs
165 State Highway 61, Faywood, NM 88034
faywoodhotsprings.com/lodging

NEW YORK

Hither Hills State Park
164 Old Montauk Highway, Montauk, NY 11954
parks.ny.gov/parks/122/details
.aspx

Camp Rockaway
Fort Tilden, Davis Road, Breezy Point, NY 11697
camprockaway.com

Collective Governors Island
Governors Island National Monument, New York, NY 10004
collectiveretreats.com/retreat/
collective-governors-island-5/

North-South Lake Campground
County Route 18, Haines Falls, NY 12436
dec.ny.gov/outdoor/24487.html

White Pine Camp
White Pine Road, Paul Smiths, NY 12970
whitepinecamp.com

Wellesley Island State Park
Lake of the Island Road, Wellesley Island, NY 13640
parks.ny.gov/parks/52/details
.aspx

Ithaca by Firelight
1150 Danby Road, Ithaca, NY 14850
firelightcamps.com/

Highbanks Campground
Park Road, Mount Morris, NY 14510
parks.ny.gov/parks/79/details.aspx

Branches of Niagara Campground Resort
2659 Whitehaven Road, Grand Island, NY 14072
branchesofniagara.com

Allegany State Park Cabin Trail
Allegany State Park Route 1, Salamanca, NY 14779
parks.ny.gov/parks/1/details.aspx

NORTH CAROLINA

Carolina Beach State Park
State Park Road, Carolina Beach, NC 28428
ncparks.gov/carolina-beach-state
-park/camping

Great Island Cabins
South Core Banks, Cape Lookout National Seashore, Davis, NC 28531
nps.gov/calo/planyourvisit/lodging
.htm

Oregon Inlet Campground
12001 State Highway 12, Nags Head, NC 27959
nps.gov/caha/planyourvisit/
campgrounds.htm

Hanging Rock State Park
1790 Hanging Rock Park Road, Danbury, NC 27016
ncparks.gov/hanging-rock-state
-park/camping

Carowinds Camp Wilderness Resort
14609 Carowinds Boulevard, Charlotte NC 28273
carowinds.com/stay/camp
-wilderness

Pilot Cove Forest Lodging
319 Gateway Junction Drive,
  Pisgah Forest, NC 28768
pilotcove.com/lodging/

Pisgah Glamping
375 Wesley Branch Road, Asheville,
  NC 28806
pisgahglamping.com

Paint Rock Farm
1295 Paint Rock Road, Hot Springs,
  NC 28743
paintrockfarm.com

Cataloochee Campground
Cataloochee Entrance Road,
  Waynesville, NC 28785
nps.gov/grsm/planyourvisit/
  cataloochee-campground.htm

River's Edge Treehouse Resort
Old U.S. Highway 129, Robbinsville,
  NC 28771
riversedgetreehouses.com

NORTH DAKOTA

Woodland Resort
1012 Woodland Drive, Devils Lake,
  ND 58301
woodlandresort.com

Lindenwood Campground
1955 Roger Maris Drive, Fargo, ND
  58103
fargoparks.com/facilities-recreation/
  lindenwood-campground.html

KOA Bismarck Journey
3720 Centennial Road, Bismarck,
  ND 58503
koa.com/campgrounds/bismarck/

Fort Abraham Lincoln State Park
4480 Fort Lincoln Road, Mandan,
  ND 58554
parkrec.nd.gov/fort-abraham
  -lincoln-state-park

Cross Ranch State Park
1403 River Road, Center, ND 58530
parkrec.nd.gov/cross-ranch-state
  -park

Cottonwood Campground
East River Road, Theodore
  Roosevelt National Park, Medora,
  ND 58645
nps.gov/thro/planyourvisit/camping
  .htm

Wannagan Creek Cabins
2440 East River Road, Medora, ND
  58645
wannagancreekcabins.com

Sather Lake Campground
State Highway 16, Alexander, ND
  58831
fs.usda.gov/recarea/dpg/recreation/
  camping-cabins/

Lake Metigoshe State Park
East Shore Park Road, Roland, ND
  58318
parkrec.nd.gov/lake-metigoshe
  -state-park

International Peace Garden
10939 U.S. Highway 281, Dunseith,
  ND 58329
peacegarden.com/camping

OHIO

South Bass Island State Park
1523 Catawba Avenue, South Bass
  Island, OH 43456
ohiodnr.gov/wps/portal/gov/odnr/
  go-and-do/plan-a-visit/find-a
  -property/south-bass-island-state
  -park

Lighthouse Point at Cedar Point
1 Cedar Point Road, Sandusky, OH
  44870
cedarpoint.com/stay/lighthouse
  -point

Columbia Woodlands
6608 Rieger Drive Northwest,
  Dover, OH 44622
columbiawoodlands.com/rentals.php

Berlin RV Park & Campground
5898 Amish County Byway (State
  Route 39), Millersburg, OH 44654
berlinrvpark.com/

The Mohicans Treehouse Resort
23164 Vess Road, Glenmont, OH
  44628
themohicans.net/treehouses.html

The Wilds at Columbus Zoo
14000 International Road,
  Cumberland, OH 43732
thewilds.columbuszoo.org

Old Man's Cave Campground
19852 State Route 664, Logan, OH
  43138
ohiodnr.gov/wps/portal/gov/odnr/
  go-and-do/plan-a-visit/find-a
  -property/hocking-hills-state-park

Lake Vesuvius Recreation Area
6518 Ellisonville-Paddle Creek Road
  (State Route 93), Pedro, OH 45659
fs.usda.gov/recarea/wayne/
  recreation/camping-cabins/

Shawnee State Park
4404 State Route 125,
  West Portsmouth, OH 45663
ohiodnr.gov/wps/portal/gov/odnr/
  go-and-do/plan-a-visit/find-a
  -property/shawnee-state-park

Hueston Woods State Park
6301 Park Office Road, College
  Corner, OH 45003
ohiodnr.gov/wps/portal/gov/odnr/
  go-and-do/plan-a-visit/find-a
  -property/hueston-woods-state
  -park

OKLAHOMA

Twin Fountains RV Resort
2727 Northeast 63rd Street,
  Oklahoma City, OK 73111
twinfountainsrvresort.com

Roman Nose State Park
3236 State Highway 8A,
  Watonga, OK 73772
travelok.com/state-parks/roman
  -nose-state-park

Bobcat Creek RV Park
2005 Northeast Highway 66,
  Sayre, OK 73662
bobcatcreekrvpark.com

Doris Campground
State Highway 49, Wichita
  Mountains National Wildlife Refuge,
  OK 73552
fws.gov/refuge/Wichita_Mountains/
  activities/camp/doris.html

Buckhorn Campground
Buckhorn Road, Chickasaw National
  Recreation Area, OK 73086
nps.gov/chic/planyourvisit/
  campgrounds.htm

Lake Murray Floating Cabins
3323 Lodge Road, Ardmore, OK
  73401
lake-murray.org/floating-cabins

Rebel Hill Guest Ranch
420175 East 1930 Road,
  Antlers, OK 74523
rebelhillguestranch.com/cabins.html

Beavers Bend Log Cabins
576 Split Shot Circle, Broken Bow,
  OK 74728
beaversbendlogcabins.com/cabins
  .htm

Robbers Cave State Park
State Highway 2, Wilburton, OK
  74578

travelok.com/state-parks/robbers
  -cave-state-park

Riverside Resort
5116 State Highway 10,
  Tahlequah, OK 74464
riversideresortokla.com

OREGON

Fort Stevens State Park
1675 Peter Iredale Road,
  Hammond, OR 97121
stateparks.oregon.gov/index
  .cfm?do=park.profile&parkId=129

Sutton Campground
4840 Vista Road, Florence, OR
  97439
fs.usda.gov/recarea/siuslaw/
  recreation/camping-cabins/

**Honey Bear by the Sea RV Resort
& Campground**
34161 Ophir Road, Gold Beach, OR
honeybearbythesea.com

Cave Creek Campground
15500 Caves Highway (State Route
  46), Cave Junction, OR 97523
nps.gov/orca/planyourvisit/
  campgrounds.htm

Mazama Campgrounds & Cabins
569 Mazama Village Drive, Crater
  Lake National Park, OR 97604
nps.gov/crla/planyourvisit/mazama
  _campground.htm

**Elk Lake Resort & Marina
Campground**
60000 Southwest Century Drive,
  Bend, OR 97701
elklakeresort.net/resort

Lost Lake Resort & Campground
9000 Lost Lake Road, Hood River,
  OR 97031
lostlakeresort.org

The Vintages Trailer Resort
16205 Southeast Kreder Road,
  Dayton, OR 97114
the-vintages.com

Caravan: The Tiny House Hotel
5009 Northeast 11th Avenue,
  Portland, OR, 97211
tinyhousehotel.com/book-a-tiny
  -house

Wallowa Alpine Huts
500 North River Street,
  Enterprise, OR 97828
wallowahuts.com

PENNSYLVANIA

Kentuck Campground
400 Kentuck Road, Dunbar, PA
  15431
dcnr.pa.gov/StateParks/FindAPark/
  OhiopyleStatePark/Pages/Stay
  .aspx

Sara's Campground on the Beach
50 Peninsula Drive, Erie, PA 16505
sarascampground.com

Cook Forest State Park
State Highway 36, Cooksburg,
  PA 16217
dcnr.pa.gov/StateParks/FindAPark/
  CookForestStatePark/Pages/Stay
  .aspx

Cherry Springs State Park
4639 Cherry Springs Road,
  Coudersport, PA 16915
dcnr.pa.gov/StateParks/FindAPark/
  CherrySpringsStatePark/Pages/
  default.aspx

**Pine Cradle Lake
Family Campground**
220 Shoemaker Road,
  Rome Township, PA 18850
pclake.com/index.html

Keen Lake Camping & Cottage Resort
155 Keen Lake Road, Waymart, PA 18472
poconomountainsglamping.com

Pickerel Point Campground
Pickerel Point Road, Greene Township, PA 18426
dcnr.pa.gov/StateParks/FindAPark/PromisedLandStatePark/Pages/Stay.aspx

Lake in Wood Campground & Cabins
576 Yellow Hill Road, Narvon, PA 17555
lakeinwoodcampground.com

Hersheypark Camping Resort
1200 Sweet Street, Hummelstown, PA 17036
hersheyparkcampingresort.com

Artillery Ridge Campground & Horse Park
610 Taneytown Road, Gettysburg, PA 17325
artilleryridge.com

RHODE ISLAND

East Beach
East Beach Road, Charlestown, RI 02813
riparks.com/Locations/LocationEastBeach.html

Burlingame State Campground
75 Burlingame State Park Road, Charlestown, RI 02813
riparks.com/Locations/LocationBurlingameCampground.html

Ashaway RV Resort
235 Ashaway Road, Bradford, RI 02808
zemanrv.com/resorts/ashaway-pines-rv-resort

Whispering Pines Campground
41 Saw Mill Road, Hope Valley, RI 02832
whisperingpinescamping.com

George Washington State Campground
2185 Putnam Pike, Glocester, RI 02814
riparks.com/Locations/LocationGeorgeWashington.html

Melville Ponds Campground
181 Bradford Avenue, Portsmouth, RI 02871
melvillepondscampground.com

Fort Getty Park & Campground
1050 Fort Getty Road, Jamestown, RI 02835
jamestownri.gov/town-departments/parks-rec/fort-getty

Fishermen's Memorial State Park & Campground
1011 Point Judith Road, Narragansett, RI 02882
iparks.com/Locations/LocationFishermens.html

Hathaway's Guest Cottages
4470 Old Post Road, Charlestown, RI 02813
hathawayscottages.com/cottages

Charlestown Breachway
Charlestown Beach Road, Charlestown, RI 02813
riparks.com/Locations/LocationCharlestownBreachway.html

SOUTH CAROLINA

Hilton Head Island Motor Coach Resort
133 Arrow Road, Hilton Head Island, SC 29928
hhimotorcoachresort.com/

Hunting Island State Park
2555 Sea Island Parkway, St. Helena Island, SC 29920
southcarolinaparks.com/hunting-island

Carolina Heritage Outfitters
1 Livery Lane, St. George, SC 29477
canoesc.com

Edisto Beach State Park
8377 State Cabin Road, Edisto Island, SC 29438
southcarolinaparks.com/edisto-beach

The Campground at James Island County Park
871 Riverland Drive, Charleston, SC 29412
ccprc.com/1434/Campground

Myrtle Beach Travel Park
10108 Kings Road, Myrtle Beach, SC 29572
myrtlebeachtravelpark.com

River Island Adventures
1249 Vera Road, Longs, SC 29568
rivr.info

Congaree National Park
100 National Park Road, Hopkins, SC 29061
nps.gov/cong/planyourvisit/camping.htm

Mountain Bridge Wilderness Area
Geer Highway (U.S. 276), Cleveland, SC 29635
southcarolinaparks.com/caesars-head

Oconee State Park
624 State Park Road, Mountain Rest, SC 29664
southcarolinaparks.com/oconee

SOUTH DAKOTA

Elkhorn Ridge RV Resort & Campground
20189 U.S. Highway 85, Spearfish, SD 57783
elkhornridgeresort.com

Yak Ridge Cabins & Farmstead
24041 Cosmos Road, Rapid City, SD 57702
yak-ridge.com/cabins/

Under Canvas Mount Rushmore
24342 Presidio Ranch Road, Keystone, SD 57751
undercanvas.com/camps/mount -rushmore/

Game Lodge Campground
U.S. Highway 16A, Custer State Park, East Custer, SD 57730
gfp.sd.gov/csp-campgrounds

Elk Mountain Campground
26611 U.S. Highway 385, Hot Springs, SD 57747
nps.gov/wica/planyourvisit/ campgrounds.htm

French Creek Camping Area
East French Creek Road, Fairburn, SD 57738
fs.usda.gov/recarea/nebraska/ recreation/camping-cabins/

Cedar Pass Lodge & Campground
20681 State Highway 240, Interior, SD 57750
cedarpasslodge.com

Fort Sisseton Historic State Park
11907 434th Avenue, Lake City, SD 57247
gfp.sd.gov/parks/detail/fort -sisseton-historic-state-park

Newton Hills State Park
28767 482nd Avenue, Canton, SD 57013
gfp.sd.gov/parks/detail/newton -hills-state-park

Lewis & Clark Recreation Area
43349 SD-52, Yankton, SD 57078
midwaygulch.com/rental-cabins

TENNESSEE

Roan Mountain State Park
527 State Highway 143, Roan Mountain, TN 37687
tnstateparks.com/parks/roan -mountain

Cosby Campground
127 Cosby Entrance Road, Cosby, TN 37722
nps.gov/grsm/planyourvisit/cosby -campground-information.htm

Little Arrow Outdoor Resort
118 Stables Drive (off State Highway 73), Townsend, TN 37882
camplittlearrow.com

Charit Creek Lodge
Fork Ridge Road, Jamestown, TN 37862
ccl-bsf.com/rates

Fall Creek Falls State Park
2009 Village Camp Road, Spencer, TN 38585
tnstateparks.com/parks/fall-creek -falls

Nashville KOA
2626 Music Valley Drive, Nashville, TN 37214
koa.com/campgrounds/Nashville

Forest Gully Farms
6016 Fly Hollow Road, Santa Fe, TN 38482
forestgullyfarms.com/facilities

Meriwether Lewis Campground
191 Meriwether Lewis Park Road (Milepost 386 Natchez Trace Parkway), Hohenwald, TN
nps.gov/natr/learn/historyculture/ exploring-the-meriwether-lewis -site.htm

Paris Landing State Park
16055 U.S. Highway 79N, Buchanan, TN 38222
tnstateparks.com/parks/paris -landing

Reelfoot Lake State Park
2595 State Highway 21, Tiptonville, TN 38079
tnstateparks.com/parks/reelfoot -lake

TEXAS

Caddo Lake State Park
245 Park Road 2, Karnack, TX 75661
tpwd.texas.gov/state-parks/ caddo-lake

Country Woods Inn
420 Grand Avenue, Glen Rose, TX 75043
countrywoodsinn.com/adventure -lodging.htm

Palo Duro Canyon Glamping
11450 Park Road 5, Canyon, TX 79015
paloduroglamping.com

Davis Mountains State Park
State Highway 118, Fort Davis, TX 79734
tpwd.texas.gov/state-parks/davis -mountains

Terlingua Ghost Town Casitas
100 Ivey Road, Terlingua, TX 79852
bigbendholidayhotel.com/casitas .html

Rio Grande Canoe Camping
Rio Grande River, Big Bend
  National Park, TX 79852
bigbendfarflung.com

Roosevelt Stone Cottages
Basin Junction Road, Big Bend
  National Park, TX 79834
chisosmountainslodge.com/
  roosevelt-stone-cottages

Collective Hill Country
7431 Fulton Ranch Road,
  Wimberley, TX 78676
collectiveretreats.com/retreat/
  collective-hill-country-3/

Malaquite Campground
20420 Park Road 22, Padre Island
  National Seashore, Corpus
  Christi, TX 78418
nps.gov/pais/planyourvisit/
  camping.htm

Stella Mare RV Resort
3418 Stella Mare Lane,
  Galveston, TX 77554
stellamarervresort.com

UTAH

Conestoga Ranch
427 North Paradise Parkway,
  Garden City, UT 84028
conestogaranch.com

Bridger Bay Campground
4528 West 1700 South, Syracuse,
  UT 84075
stateparks.utah.gov/parks/
  antelope-island/camping
  -opportunities/

Mirror Lake Campground
State Highway 150, Kamas, UT
  84032
fs.usda.gov/recarea/uwcnf/
  recarea/?recid=9510

Devils Garden Campground
Campground Road, Arches National
  Park, Moab, UT 84532
nps.gov/arch/planyourvisit/camping
  .htm

Wingate Campground
State Highway 313, Moab, UT
  84532
stateparks.utah.gov/parks/dead
  -horse/

Under Canvas Moab
13784 U.S. Highway 191, Moab, UT
  84532
undercanvas.com/camps/moab

Fruita Campground
Camp Ground Road, Capitol Reef
  National Park, Torrey, UT 84775
nps.gov/care/planyourvisit/
  fruitacampground.htm

Basin Campground
Cottonwood Canyon Road,
  Cannonville, UT 84718
stateparks.utah.gov/parks/
  kodachrome-basin

**Bryce Canyon Lodge Western
  Cabins**
State Highway 63, Bryce Canyon
  National Park, UT 84764
brycecanyonforever.com/lodging
  -and-cabin-rentals

Zion Ponderosa Ranch Resort
Twin Knolls Road, Orderville, UT
  84758
zionponderosa.com/
  accommodations/

VERMONT

Limehurst Lake Campground
4104 State Route 14,
  Williamstown, VT 05679
limehurstlake.com

Sterling Ridge Resort
155 Sterling Ridge Drive,
  Jeffersonville, VT 05464
sterlingridgeresort.com/cabins

Crofter's Green
2956 Mountain Road,
  Montgomery Center, VT 05471
croftersgreen.com

Tyler Place Family Resort
175 Tyler Place, Swanton, VT 05488
tylerplace.com/cottages-and-suites/

Grand Isle State Park
36 East Shore South, Grand Isle, VT
  05458
vtstateparks.com/grandisle.html

Button Bay State Park
5 Button Bay State Park Road,
  Ferrisburgh, VT 05491
vtstateparks.com/buttonbay.html

Robert Frost Mountain Cabins
2430 North Branch Road,
  Ripton, VT 05766
robertfrostmountaincabins.com/
  guest-cabins-view-all

Moosalamoo Campground
Forest Road 24, off the Goshen-
  Ripton Road, Salisbury, VT 05769
moosalamoo.org/camping

Half Moon Pond State Park
1621 Black Pond Road,
  Hubbardton, VT 05743
vtstateparks.com/halfmoon.html

Greenwood Lodge & Campsites
311 Greenwood Drive,
  Woodford, VT 05201
campvermont.com/greenwood

VIRGINIA

First Landing State Park
2500 Shore Drive, Virginia Beach,
  VA 23451

dcr.virginia.gov/state-parks/first
-landing

Chippokes Plantation
695 Chippokes Park Road,
Surry, VA 23883
dcr.virginia.gov/state-parks/
chippokes-plantation#cabins
_camping

Williamsburg/Busch Gardens Area KOA
4000 Newman Road,
Williamsburg, VA 23188
koa.com/campgrounds/
williamsburg/

Oak Ridge Campground
6975 Oak Ridge Road, Triangle, VA 22172
nps.gov/prwi/planyourvisit/camping
.htm

#1 Rock Tavern River Kamp
1420 South Page Valley Road,
Luray, VA 22835
massanuttensprings.com/rock
-tavern-river-kamp.html

Skyland Cabins
Mile 41.7 Skyline Drive, Shenandoah
National Park, Luray, VA 22835
goshenandoah.com/lodging/skyland

Douthat State Park
14239 Douthat State Park Road,
Millboro, VA 24460
dcr.virginia.gov/state-parks/
douthat#cabins_camping

Primland Cottages & Treehouses
2000 Busted Rock Road,
Meadows of Dan, VA 24120
primland.com/stay

Grayson Highlands State Park
829 Grayson Highland Lane,
Mouth of Wilson, VA 24363
dcr.virginia.gov/state-parks/grayson
-highlands#cabins_camping

Wilderness Road Campground
854 National Park Road, Ewing,
VA 24248
nps.gov/cuga/planyourvisit/
camping.htm

WASHINGTON

Expedition Old Growth
Gifford Pinchot National Forest,
Carson, WA 98648
expeditionoldgrowth.com/

Cape Disappointment State Park
244 Robert Gray Drive, Ilwaco, WA
98624
parks.state.wa.us/486/Cape
-Disappointment

Log Cabin Resort & Campground
3183 East Beach Road,
Port Angeles, WA 98363
olympicnationalparks.com/lodging/
log-cabin-resort/

The Inn at Saltwater Farm
176 Sea Breeze Lane, Friday Harbor,
WA 98250
saltwaterfarmsji.com/inn-at
-saltwater-farm

Cranberry Lake Campground
41229 State Route 20, Oak Harbor,
WA 98277
parks.state.wa.us/497/Deception
-Pass

TreeHouse Point
6922 Preston-Fall City Road SE,
Issaquah, WA 98027
treehousepoint.com/lodging.phtml

Cougar Rock Campground
Paradise Valley Road, Mount Rainier
National Park, Longmire, WA
98304
nps.gov/mora/planyourvisit/
campgrounds.htm

North Cascades Lodge at Stehekin
#1 Stehekin Landing, North
Cascades National Park,
Stehekin, WA 98852
lodgeatstehekin.com/
accommodations

Rolling Huts
18381 State Highway 20,
Winthrop, WA 98862
rollinghuts.com

Premier RV Resort Granite Lake
306 Granite Lake Drive, Clarkston,
WA 99403
premierrvresorts.com/granite-lake
-wa.html

WEST VIRGINIA

Battle Run Campground
2981 Summersville Lake Road,
Summersville, WV 26651
lrh.usace.army.mil/Missions/Civil
-Works/Recreation/West-Virginia/
Summersville-Lake/

Country Road Cabins
1508 Sunday Road, Hico, WV 25854
wvcabins.com/cabins/

Adventures on the Gorge
219 Chestnutburg Road,
Lansing, WV 25862
adventuresonthegorge.com/

Beckley Exhibition Coal Mine Campground
513 Ewart Avenue, Beckley, WV
25801
beckley.org/underground-tour/
campground

Buffalo Trail Cabins
190 Buffalo Trail, Bluefield, WV
24701
buffalotrailcabins.com

Pipestem Resort State Park
3405 Pipestem Drive, Pipestem, WV
25979
wvstateparks.com/park/pipestem
-resort-state-park/

Watoga State Park
4800 Watoga Park Road, Marlinton,
WV 24954
wvstateparks.com/park/watoga
-state-park/

Seneca Shadows Campground
State Highway 28, Seneca Rocks,
WV 26884
fs.usda.gov/recarea/mnf/recreation/
camping-cabins/

Canaan Valley Resort State Park
230 Main Lodge Road, Davis, WV
26260
wvstateparks.com/park/canaan
-valley-resort-state-park/

**Harper's Ferry/Civil War
Battlefields KOA**
343 Campground Road,
Harpers Ferry, WV 25425
koa.com/campgrounds/harpers
-ferry

WISCONSIN

Interstate State Park
1275 State Highway 35,
St. Croix Falls, WI 54024
dnr.wisconsin.gov/topic/parks/
interstate/recreation/camping

Natura Treescape Resort
400 County Road A,
Wisconsin Dells, WI 53965
staynatura.com

Quartzite Campground
S5975 Park Road, Baraboo, WI
53913
devilslakewisconsin.com/camping/
quartzite-campground-images

Mauthe Lake Campground
N1490 County Road GGG,
Campbellsport, WI 53010
dnr.wisconsin.gov/topic/parks/
kmn/recreation/camping

Candlewood Cabins
29493 State Road 80,
Richland Center, WI 53581
candlewoodcabins.com

**Nicolet Bay Campgrounds—
Peninsula State Park**
Shore Road, Fish Creek, WI 54212
dnr.wisconsin.gov/topic/parks/
peninsula/recreation/camping

Peshtigo River Outpost
N12080 Allison Lane,
Athelstane, WI 54104
wildmanranch.com/outdoor
-adventures-in-wisconsin/
peshtigo-river-outpost

Lost Lake Recreation Area
Lost Lake/Chipmunk Rapids Road,
Tipler, WI 54121
fs.usda.gov/recarea/cnnf/
recreation/camping-cabins/

Coadys' Point of View
3932 North Primich Way,
Phelps, WI 54554
povresort.com

**Apostle Islands National
Lakeshore**
415 Washington Avenue,
Bayfield, WI 54814
nps.gov/apis/planyourvisit/
camping.htm

WYOMING

Belle Fourche River Campground
Devils Tower National Monument
Road, Devils Tower, WY 82714
nps.gov/deto/planyourvisit/
campgrounds.htm

**The Hideout Lodge &
Guest Ranch**
3170 County Road 40 1/2,
Shell, WY 82441
thehideout.com

Horseshoe Bend Campground
Horseshoe Bend Road (off
Highway 37), Lovell, WY 82431
nps.gov/bica/planyourvisit/
horseshoe-bend-campground
.htm

Buffalo Bill State Park
4192 North Fork Highway,
Cody, WY 82414
wyoparks.wyo.gov/index.php/
places-to-go/buffalo-bill

Mammoth Campground
North Entrance Road, Yellowstone
National Park, WY 82190
nps.gov/yell/planyourvisit/
mammothhscg.htm

Colter Bay
100 Colter Bay Campground
Road, Colter Bay RV Park,
Moran, WY 83013
nps.gov/grte/planyourvisit/
colterbayrv.htm

Fireside Resort Cabins
2780 North State Highway 390,
Wilson, WY 83014
firesidejacksonhole.com

Eagle RV Park & Campground
204 U.S. Highway 20 South,
Thermopolis, WY 82443
eaglervpark.com

Brush Creek Ranch
66 Brush Creek Ranch Road,
Saratoga, WY 82331
brushcreekranch.com

Guernsey State Park
2187 Lake Side Drive,
Guernsey, WY 82214

wyoparks.wyo.gov/index.php/
places-to-go/guernsey

EASTERN CANADA

Berry Hill Campground
Route 430, Rocky Harbour,
Newfoundland A0K 4N0 Canada
pc.gc.ca/en/pn-np/nl/grosmorne/
activ/camping

Murphy's Camping on the Ocean
308 Murphys Road, Murphy Cove,
Nova Scotia B0J 3H0, Canada
murphyscamping.ca/

Headquarters Campground
11 Headquarters Campground
Road, Fundy National Park, New
Brunswick E4H 4S7 Canada
pc.gc.ca/en/pn-np/nb/fundy/activ/
camping

Parc Aventures Cap Jaseux
250 Chemin de la Pointe aux Pins,
Saint-Fulgence, Quebec G0V
1S0, Canada
capjaseux.com/en/hebergement

Entre Cîmes et Racines Forest Lodges
80 Chemin Simard, Bolton-Est,
Quebec J0E 1G0, Canada
entrecimesetracines.com/en/
forest-ecolodges/

Bel Air Tremblant
80 Rue des Sept Sommets, Mont-
Tremblant, Quebec J0T 1M0,
Canada
belairtremblant.com/resort
-concept/

Long Point Eco-Adventures
1730 Front Road, St. Williams,
Ontario N0E 1P0, Canada
lpfun.ca/

Cyprus Lake Campground
Cyprus Lake Road, Tobermory,
Ontario N0H 2R0, Canada
pc.gc.ca/en/pn-np/on/bruce/activ/
camping/cyprus

Mew Lake Campground
Frank MacDougall Parkway (Route
60), Algonquin Provincial Park,
Ontario, Canada
algonquinpark.on.ca/visit/
camping/mew-lake-campground
.php

Marie Louise Lake Campground
Route 587, Sleeping Giant
Provincial Park, Silver Islet,
Ontario, P0T 2M0 Canada
ontarioparks.com/park/
sleepinggiant/camping

WESTERN CANADA

Kathleen Lake Campground
Kathleen Lake Road (off Haines
Highway), Kluane National Park,
Destruction Bay, Yukon Y0B 1H0,
Canada
pc.gc.ca/en/pn-np/yt/kluane/visit/
services/Kathleen

REO Rafting Resort
61755 Nahatlatch Forest Service
Road, Boston Bar, British
Columbia V0K 1C0, Canada
reorafting.com/site/glamping.html

Nimmo Bay Wilderness Resort
100 Little Nimmo Bay, Mackenzie
Sound, Mount Waddington
A, British Columbia V0N 2R0,
Canada
nimmobay.com/

Clayoquot Wilderness Retreat
Bedwell River Valley, Alberni-
Clayoquot C, British Columbia
V0R 2Z0, Canada
wildretreat.com

Whistlers Campground
Icefields Highway, Jasper, Alberta
T0E 1E0, Canada
pc.gc.ca/en/pn-np/ab/jasper/activ/
passez-stay/camping

Tunnel Mountain Village
Tunnel Mountain Road, Banff,
Alberta T1L 1B3, Canada
pc.gc.ca/en/pn-np/ab/banff/activ/
camping

Sundance Lodges
2 Sundance Road (off Highway
40), Kananaskis, AB T0L 2H0,
Canada
sundancelodges.com/

Townsite Campground
Windflower Avenue, Waterton
Park, Alberta T0K 2M0, Canada
pc.gc.ca/en/pn-np/ab/waterton/
activ/camping

Historic Reesor Ranch
Maple Creek, Saskatchewan, S0N
1N0, Canada
reesorranch.com/lodging

Wasagaming Campground
Buffalo Drive, Riding Mountain
National Park, Manitoba R0J
2H0, Canada
pc.gc.ca/en/pn-np/mb/riding/visit/
wts/activ2/activ2_i

PUERTO RICO

Pitahaya Glamping
Highway 303, Cabo Rojo 00623,
Puerto Rico
pitahayaglamping.com

Isla de Mona
Isla de Mona, Puerto Rico
islandsofpuertorico.com/isla-de
-mona

Parador Villas Sotomayor
Highway 123, Km. 36.6, Adjuntas
  00601, Puerto Rico
paradorvillassotomayor.com

Finca Oro Rojo
Calle Gregorio, Barrio Damian
  Arriba, Orocovis 00720 Puerto
  Rico
fincaororojo.com/

Toro Negro State Forest
Ruta Panorámica (Highway 143),
  Orocovis 00766, Puerto Rico
drna.pr.gov/wp-content/
  uploads/2015/04/El-Bosque
  -Estatal-de-Toro-Negro.pdf

Playa Flamenco Campground
Playa Flamenco, Isla Culebra 00775,
  Puerto Rico
islaculebra.com/puerto-rico/
  camping.html

U.S. VIRGIN ISLANDS

Mount Victory Camp
Creque Dam Road, Frederiksted, St.
  Croix 00840, U.S. Virgin Islands
mtvictorycamp.com

Virgin Islands Campground
64 Water Island, St. Thomas 00802,
  U.S. Virgin Islands
virginislandscampground.com

**Cinnamon Bay Beach &
  Campground**
North Shore Road, St. John 00830,
  U.S. Virgin Islands
cinnamonbayresort.com

Concordia Eco-Resort
St. John 00830, U.S. Virgin Islands
concordiaecoresort.com

ACKNOWLEDGMENTS

50 States, 500 Campgrounds was very much a team effort that involved Allyson Johnson (editor), Kay Hankins (designer), Jill Foley (photo editor), Sanaa Akkach (art director), Susan Blair (director of photography), and Judith Klein (senior production editor) at National Geographic headquarters in Washington, D.C. Like myself, a lot of their labor was accomplished working from home during the COVID-19 lockdown. I'm sure we all felt a bit of cabin fever (pun intended).

Huge thanks to Julia Clerk, who proofread all 530 campsite write-ups without complaint, as well as undertaking a lot of the research for this book and acting as my sounding board. Along with our daughters, Chelsea and Shannon, Julia also accompanied me on many of the journeys to discover camping, glamping, and cabin spots across North America. Kudos also to the hundreds of folks—national and state park rangers, campground managers and staff, public relations executives, state and local tourism representatives—who assisted in my explorations and information gathering.

Cranking back the clock, it was my parents (Marjorie and Henry Yogerst) who introduced me to camping when I was still a toddler. My passion for sleeping beneath the stars was further stoked by the Boy Scouts of America and much later by the YMCA Adventure Guides & Princesses program and Mount Mingus Camp in northern Arizona when I started camping with my own kids. Last but not least, a nod to Russ Stringham and his son, Austin, in Utah, who introduced me to RV camping.

ABOUT THE AUTHOR

During three decades as an editor, writer, and photographer, Joe Yogerst has lived and worked in Asia, Africa, Europe, and North America. His writing has appeared in *Condé Nast Traveler, CNN Travel, Islands* magazine, the *International New York Times* (Paris), *Washington Post, Los Angeles Times,* and *National Geographic Traveler.* He has written for 34 National Geographic books, including the best-selling *50 States, 5,000 Ideas* and the sequel, *100 Parks, 5,000 Ideas.* His first U.S. novel, a murder-mystery titled *Nemesis,* was published in 2018. Yogerst is the host of a National Geographic/Great Courses video series on America's state parks.

INDEX

ILLUSTRATIONS CREDITS

Front cover: (MAIN) Melissa Goodwin, (UP) Matt Kisiday/Auto-Camp, (LO LE) Scott Dickerson/Design Pics, (LO RT) Jonathan Irish; spine, Kevin Boutwell/Getty Images; back cover, Stella Levi/Getty Images.

2-3, Arkansas Department of Parks, Heritage and Tourism; 4, Ken Gillespie/All Canada Photos/Alamy Stock Photo; 6, Odyssey Resorts/Aaron Bosanko; 8, Jonathan Irish; 10, Pat & Chuck Blackley/Alamy Stock Photo; 12, Jeffrey Isaac Greenberg 11+/Alamy Stock Photo; 13, The best photo is earned/Getty Images; 14, George Dodd/Alamy Stock Photo; 16, Arturo Polo Ena; 18, HagePhoto/robertharding; 19, NPS/Kent Miller; 20, James + Courtney Forte/Getty Images; 22, John Burcham; 24, @baileymade; 25, Phil Degginger/Alamy Stock Photo; 26, Graddy Photography; 28, GracedByTheLight/Getty Images; 30, Keith Sutton; 31, Arkansas Department of Parks, Heritage and Tourism; 32, Arkansas Department of Parks, Heritage and Tourism; 34, Larry Gerbrandt/Getty Images; 36, Ventana Big Sur; 37, Evergreen Lodge at Yosemite/Kim Carroll; 38, Mahallia Budds; 40, Juergen Ritterbach/Alamy Stock Photo; 42, Helen H. Richardson/MediaNews Group/The Denver Post via Getty Images; 43, © Colorado Parks and Wildlife — Vic Schendel; 44, Dunton Hot Springs; 46, Courtesy of Winvian Farm; 48, Lake Compounce; 49,

Jerry and Marcy Monkman/Danita Delimont/Alamy Stock Photo; 50, J. G. Coleman/Alamy Stock Photo; 52, Delaware State Parks; 54, Blue Water Development; 55, Delaware State Parks; 56, Delaware State Parks; 58, Lee Rentz/Alamy Stock Photo; 60, Nick Phoenix; 61, Disney Enterprises, Inc./Matt Stroshane; 62, Stephen Frink/Alamy Stock Photo; 64, Pat & Chuck Blackley/Alamy Stock Photo; 66, Margaritaville at Lanier Islands; 67, Chattahoochee-Oconee National Forests; 68, Andy Brophy/One Nine Images, courtesy of Georgia Glamping Company; 70, Jim Sugar/Getty Images; 72, Kevin Boutwell/Getty Images; 73, Rosanna U/Getty Images; 74, VisualCommunications/Getty Images; 76, Silver Spur Ranch Idaho; 78, © Chad Case; 79, Tuck Fauntleroy, courtesy of Moose Creek Ranch; 80, Vincent Anzalone/Getty Images; 82, YuziS/Alamy Stock Photo; 84, Seth Perlman/AP/Shutterstock; 85, Brandon Huttenlocher/Cavan Images/Alamy Stock Photo; 86, Jason Lindsey/Alamy Stock Photo; 88, Jon Lauriat/Getty Images; 90, Dirk Garriott; 91, Don Smetzer/Alamy Stock Photo; 92, John Maxwell/Indiana Department of Natural Resources; 94, Prisma/Christian Heeb/Alamy Stock Photo; 96, Stephen Schiller; 97, Northeast Iowa RC&D; 98, Greg Vaughn/Alamy Stock Photo; 100, Charlie Riedel/AP/Shutterstock; 102, Gerrit Vyn/NPL/Minden Pictures; 103, Jim Talbert; 104,

Mathias Kuhl; 106, Alexey Stiop/Alamy Stock Photo; 108, Jonathan Irish; 109, Jessa Turner/HomeGrown HideAways; 110, Gary W. Carter/Alamy Stock Photo; 112, Christian Heeb; 114, Tim Mueller Photography; 115, Randall Sigler/Alamy Stock Photo; 116, Stephen Saks Photography/Alamy Stock Photo; 118, Ida Lennestål; 120, Courtesy of Maine Bureau of Parks and Lands; 121, Deb Snelson/Getty Images; 122, Corey Fitzgerald, courtesy of the Appalachian Mountain Club; 124, Jeff Mauritzen; 126, © Cherry Hill Park; 127, NPS Photo; 128, Jon Bilous/Alamy Stock Photo; 130, Frits Meyst/MeystPhoto; 132, NPS Photo; 133, Howard Grill/Getty Images; 134, Matt Kisiday/AutoCamp; 136, The Fields; 138, Michigan Department of Natural Resources; 139, NPS Photo; 140, Stephen Saks Photography/Alamy Stock Photo; 142, Odyssey Resorts/Dan Jandl; 144, Scottie Tuska; 145, Jenn Ackerman and Tim Gruber; 146, PVstock/Alamy Stock Photo; 148, Marc Muench/TandemStock; 150, NPS/Peyton Breault; 151, traveler jordan/Shutterstock; 152, Clint Farlinger/Alamy Stock Photo; 154, clearviewstock/Shutterstock; 156, Missouri Department of Natural Resources; 157, Kampgrounds of America, Inc.; 158, Missouri Department of Natural Resources; 160, Hollice Looney/DanitaDelimont/Alamy Stock Photo; 162, NPS/Jacob W. Frank; 163, @baileymade; 164, David R. Frazier

Photolibrary, Inc./Alamy Stock Photo; 166, Michelle Arnold/EyeEm/Getty Images; 168, Nebraskaland Magazine/Nebraska Game and Parks Commission; 169, Kimberly Creek Retreat/Chris Petersen; 170, Nebraskaland Magazine/Nebraska Game and Parks Commission; 172, James Hager/robert harding; 174, Michael Partenio; 175, Courtesy of Aramark; 176, Cavan Images/Alamy Stock Photo; 178, Nikki Cox; 180, Enrico Della Pietra/Alamy Stock Photo; 181, Getaway; 182, Huttopia; 184, Steve Greer; 186, Paula Champagne, courtesy of the Appalachian Mountain Club; 187, New Jersey Department of Environmental Protection; 188, Frank DeBonis/Getty Images; 190, Amanda Powell (@adrift_adream); 192, NPS/Sally King; 193, Ryan Alonzo; 194, Tim Fitzharris/Minden Pictures; 196, Camp Rockaway at Jacob Riis Bathhouse; 198, Audrey Spears; 199, Sara Fox Photography; 200, Melissa Goodwin; 202, Clarence Holmes Photography/Alamy Stock Photo; 204, Single Point Media; 205, D Guest Smith/Alamy Stock Photo; 206, LL28/Getty Images; 208, NPS/Jeff Van Hooser; 210, Chuck Haney; 211, © International Peace Garden; 212, Jason Lindsey/Alamy Stock Photo; 214, Chris McLelland—Compelling Photo; 216, Courtesy of Cedar Point; 217, Grahm S. Jones, Columbus Zoo and Aquarium; 218, Zachary Justus/Getty Images; 220, GracedByTheLight/Getty

Images; 222, Richard Smith/Alamy Stock Photo; 223, Lori Duckworth/Oklahoma Tourism; 224, Megan Rossman/Oklahoma Tourism; 226, Jeff Freeman; 228, Shayan Bastani, courtesy of Vintages Trailer Resort; 229, Daniel Mulcahy; 230, wonrin/Shutterstock; 232, Michael Ver Sprill/Getty Images; 234, Hershey Entertainment & Resorts Company; 235, Keen Lake Camping and Cottage Resort/Campground Studios; 236, Peter Pellend/Pellend Advertising; 238, lucky-photographer/Alamy Stock Photo; 240, Hathaways Guest Cottages; 241, Rhode Island DEM—Division of Parks and Rec.; 242, Rhode Island DEM—Division of Parks and Rec.; 244, Peter Frank Edwards/Redux; 246, Courtesy of Charleston County Parks; 247, Myrtle Beach Travel Park; 248, Mac Stone/TandemStock; 250, NPS Photo; 252, Lisa Duncan Photography; 253, Dominique Braud/Dembinsky Photo Associates/Alamy Stock Photo; 254, @baileymade; 256, Malcolm MacGregor/Getty Images; 258, Little Arrow Outdoor Resort; 259, Jon Giffin; 260, Kennan Harvey/Cavan Images; 262, Earl Nottingham, TPWD; 264, IrinaK/Shutterstock; 265, Country Woods Inn; 266, Chase Fountain, TPWD; 268, @baileymade; 270, Briana Scroggins; 271, Dirk Collins, courtesy of Conestoga Ranch; 272, J./imageBROKER/Alamy Stock Photo; 274, Kristin Khan; 276, Nate

McKeen, Vermont State Parks; 277, Ski the East; 278, Caleb Kenna; 280, Primland; 282, Courtesy of the Virginia Department of Conservation and Recreation; 283, Kampgrounds of America, Inc.; 284, Bram Reusen for Delaware North; 286, TMI/Alamy Stock Photo; 288, Guest Services, Inc.; 289, Courtesy of Washington State Parks; 290, Brad Mitchell/Alamy Stock Photo; 292, Courtesy of Adventures on The Gorge; 294, Jay Young; 295, Kampgrounds of America, Inc.; 296, Amanda Joy Mason; 298, Alex Messenger/TandemStock; 300, Anton Sorokin/Alamy Stock Photo; 301, Courtesy of Coadys' Point of View Lake Resort & Campground; 302, John D. Ivanko/Alamy Stock Photo; 304, Whitney Tressel; 306, Courtesy of Brush Creek Luxury Ranch Collection; 307, NPS/Jacob W. Frank; 308, Courtesy of Fireside Resort; 310, Bel Air Tremblant Resort/Olivier Langevin; 312, © 2019 Marco Bergeron; 313, Ken Gillespie Photography/Alamy Stock Photo; 314, Parks Canada/D. Wilson; 316, Sierra Fogelman; 318, Karl Lee Photography; 319, Jenn Ackerman and Tim Gruber; 320, Jeremy Koreski; 322, Jonathan A. Mauer/Shutterstock; 324, Manolo Ramos Lugo; 325, BebiChurch; 326, Virgin Islands Campground.

Since 1888, the National Geographic Society has funded more than 14,000 research, conservation, education, and storytelling projects around the world. National Geographic Partners distributes a portion of the funds it receives from your purchase to National Geographic Society to support programs including the conservation of animals and their habitats.

Get closer to National Geographic Explorers and photographers, and connect with our global community. Join us today at nationalgeographic.org/joinus

For rights or permissions inquiries, please contact National Geographic Books Subsidiary Rights: bookrights@natgeo.com

ISBN: 978-1-4262-2217-7

Printed in the United States of America

21/WOR/1

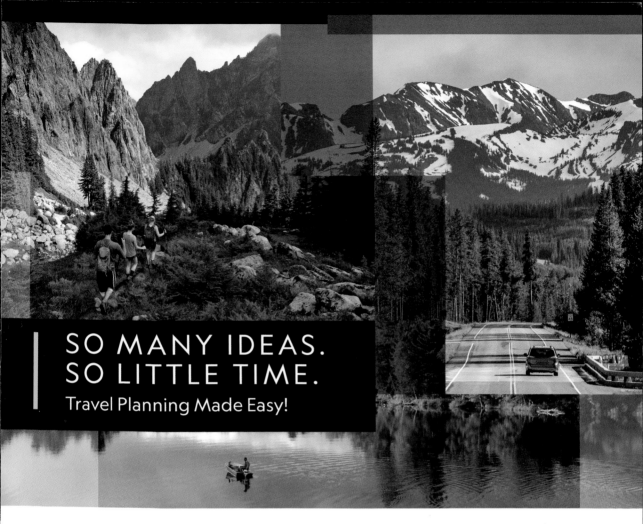

SO MANY IDEAS.
SO LITTLE TIME.
Travel Planning Made Easy!

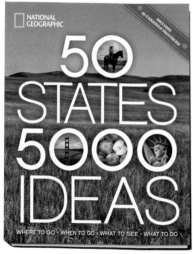

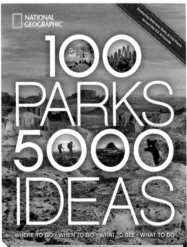